# Leadership and Workplace Culture in the Digital Era

Ebtihaj Al-A'ali
*University of Bahrain, Bahrain*

Meryem Masmoudi
*University of Bahrain, Bahrain*

IGI Global
PUBLISHER of TIMELY KNOWLEDGE

A volume in the Advances in Logistics, Operations, and Management Science (ALOMS) Book Series

Published in the United States of America by
IGI Global
Business Science Reference (an imprint of IGI Global)
701 E. Chocolate Avenue
Hershey PA, USA 17033
Tel: 717-533-8845
Fax: 717-533-8661
E-mail: cust@igi-global.com
Web site: http://www.igi-global.com



Library of Congress Cataloging-in-Publication Data

Names: Al-A'Ali, Ebtihaj Ahmad, 1957- editor. | Masmoudi, Meryem, 1979- editor.
Title: Leadership and workplace culture in the digital era / Ebtihaj Al A'ali, and Meryem Masmoudi, editor.
Description: Hershey, PA : Business Science Reference, [2023] | Includes bibliographical references and index. | Summary: "The book attempts to explore leadership changes in the current digital era with the digital transformation prevailing leading leaders, employees and their organizations to reshape business strategies"-- Provided by publisher.
Identifiers: LCCN 2022023477 (print) | LCCN 2022023478 (ebook) | ISBN 9781668458648 (hardcover) | ISBN 9781668458655 (paperback) | ISBN 9781668458662 (ebook)
Subjects: LCSH: Leadership. | Educational leadership. | Organizational behavior.
Classification: LCC HD57.7 .L43157 2023 (print) | LCC HD57.7 (ebook) | DDC 658.4/092--dc23/eng/20220518
LC record available at https://lccn.loc.gov/2022023477
LC ebook record available at https://lccn.loc.gov/2022023478

This book is published in the IGI Global book series Advances in Logistics, Operations, and Management Science (ALOMS) (ISSN: 2327-350X; eISSN: 2327-3518)

British Cataloguing in Publication Data
A Cataloguing in Publication record for this book is available from the British Library.

All work contributed to this book is new, previously-unpublished material. The views expressed in this book are those of the authors, but not necessarily of the publisher.

For electronic access to this publication, please contact: eresources@igi-global.com.

# Advances in Logistics, Operations, and Management Science (ALOMS) Book Series

John Wang
Montclair State University, USA

ISSN:2327-350X
EISSN:2327-3518

## Mission

Operations research and management science continue to influence business processes, administration, and management information systems, particularly in covering the application methods for decision-making processes. New case studies and applications on management science, operations management, social sciences, and other behavioral sciences have been incorporated into business and organizations real-world objectives.

The **Advances in Logistics, Operations, and Management Science** (ALOMS) Book Series provides a collection of reference publications on the current trends, applications, theories, and practices in the management science field. Providing relevant and current research, this series and its individual publications would be useful for academics, researchers, scholars, and practitioners interested in improving decision making models and business functions.

## Coverage

- Production Management
- Marketing engineering
- Computing and information technologies
- Political Science
- Services management
- Finance
- Organizational Behavior
- Operations Management
- Information Management
- Networks

IGI Global is currently accepting manuscripts for publication within this series. To submit a proposal for a volume in this series, please contact our Acquisition Editors at Acquisitions@igi-global.com or visit: http://www.igi-global.com/publish/.

The Advances in Logistics, Operations, and Management Science (ALOMS) Book Series (ISSN 2327-350X) is published by IGI Global, 701 E. Chocolate Avenue, Hershey, PA 17033-1240, USA, www.igi-global.com. This series is composed of titles available for purchase individually; each title is edited to be contextually exclusive from any other title within the series. For pricing and ordering information please visit http://www.igi-global.com/book-series/advances-logistics-operations-management-science/37170. Postmaster: Send all address changes to above address. 

## Titles in this Series

*For a list of additional titles in this series, please visit: www.igi-global.com/book-series*

*Examining the Vital Financial Role of SMEs in Achieving the Sustainable Development Goals*
Dalila Taleb (A. Belkaid University, Algeria) Mohammed El Amine Abdelli (University Of Brest, France) Afef Khalil (University Of Tunis Carthage, Tunisia) and Asma Sghaier (University Of Sousse, Tunisia)
Business Science Reference • copyright 2023 • 325pp • H/C (ISBN: 9781668448342) • US $250.00 (our price)

*Advanced Research and Real-World Applications of Industry 5.0*
Mahmoud Numan Bakkar (Abu Dhabi Vocational Education and Training Institute (ADVETI), Institute of Applied Technology (IAT), UAE) and Elspeth McKay (Cogniware.com.au, Australia)
Business Science Reference • copyright 2023 • 315pp • H/C (ISBN: 9781799888055) • US $250.00 (our price)

*Cases on Servant Leadership and Equity*
Ursula Thomas (Georgia State University, USA)
Business Science Reference • copyright 2023 • 335pp • H/C (ISBN: 9781668458129) • US $240.00 (our price)

*Managing Inflation and Supply Chain Disruptions in the Global Economy*
Ulas Akkucuk (Uşak University, Turkey)
Business Science Reference • copyright 2023 • 358pp • H/C (ISBN: 9781668458761) • US $250.00 (our price)

*Handbook of Research on Entrepreneurship and Organizational Resilience During Unprecedented Times*
Wassim J. Aloulou (Imam Mohammad Ibn Saud Islamic University, Saudi Arabia & University of Sfax, Tunisia)
Business Science Reference • copyright 2023 • 736pp • H/C (ISBN: 9781668446058) • US $325.00 (our price)

*Considerations and Characteristics of the Millennial Leader in Today's Global Society*
Tymon M. Graham (TMGraham Consulting, LLC, USA)
Business Science Reference • copyright 2023 • 300pp • H/C (ISBN: 9781668447116) • US $240.00 (our price)

*Handbook of Research on Digital Transformation Management and Tools*
Richard Pettinger (University College London, UK) Brij B. Gupta (Asia University, Taiwan) Alexandru Roja (Babeş-Bolyai University, Cluj-Napoca, Romania) and Diana Cozmiuc (Ioan Slavici University, Timisoara, Romania)
Business Science Reference • copyright 2022 • 732pp • H/C (ISBN: 9781799897644) • US $325.00 (our price)

*Advancing Interpersonal Emotion Regulation and Social Regulation*
Donta S. Harper (Argosy University, USA)
Information Science Reference • copyright 2022 • 384pp • H/C (ISBN: 9781668424780) • US $215.00 (our price)

IGI Global
PUBLISHER of TIMELY KNOWLEDGE

701 East Chocolate Avenue, Hershey, PA 17033, USA
Tel: 717-533-8845 x100 • Fax: 717-533-8661
E-Mail: cust@igi-global.com • www.igi-global.com

# Editorial Advisory Board

# Table of Contents

# Detailed Table of Contents

explain why prevalence of technology-based interaction in organization makes it difficult for leader to develop close interpersonal relationship with their followers, which is followed by the suggestions on how to overcome these barriers.



In today's business world, digital leadership is needed to keep up with the speed of change. The digital workplace is centered on collaboration, communication, and human interaction. Corporate employees nowadays are looking for more than autonomy and productivity. Power and responsibility are both affected by technology, and this fact cannot be ignored. Leaders are required by everyone who is impacted by digital technology. In transitions, digital leadership is prevalent since neither technology nor process has a monopoly on the situation. The hybrid work model has become the most popular way for people to return to work. Every industry will need to develop its own methodology and determine its productivity. Using the findings of this study, leaders may better understand how technology is changing their workforces, markets, and whole industries. Leadership in the digital age should be based on a new set of values and rules. Future research must focus on digital leadership styles and traits. In this regard, a new empirical study should measure digital leadership's effectiveness.



The organization's culture is a key part of its successful move into the digital age. Industrial organisations are implementing company-wide digital transformation programmes in response to new risks and opportunities provided by fast emerging digital technologies. There is a serious shortage of adaptable project and organisational teams with a well-defined implementation approach. Companies must assess their current competencies, organisational structure, and corporate culture to identify which technologies are crucial and how they will be implemented. This chapter focuses on technology-based attributes like strategy, leadership, and culture. Researchers, practitioners, and industrial organisations will benefit from the findings of this study because it provides a digital strategy for commercial organisations. It is imperative to review the relationship between a company and its partners and customers in light of digital technology's impact on business operations and market offerings. This chapter makes it possible for future research, which helps this field and theories move forward.



The chapter reveals the problem of health in the context of digitalization and building an organizational culture based on hybrid communication, workplace practices, and burnout prevention. Health is the main human resource, which is becoming a predictor of organization success in the 21st century; and it is the responsibility of business to create conditions conducive to the health of employees. The problem of technological stress and understanding of health based on medical and psychological approaches are considered. It is concluded that the psychological approach allows a broader consideration of health

participants were analyzed. The results showed a positive relationship between perceived HR digitalization and positive employee outcomes such as AC. This relationship was moderated by resilience such that satisfaction with HR digitalization predicted AC in employees with low resilience. A positive correlation was found between perceived digitalization and resilience. No strong relationship was found between perceived digitalization and WE. Perceived digitalization of HR tools that enabled communication and training opportunities positively impacted outcomes such as commitment and motivation. Employees with experience working digitally and with a higher perceived digitalization reported the most favorable WFH experience. These employees had a more positive view of HR digitalization.



Motivated by the significant role and importance of big data analytics in health care sector and the critical influence of innovation leadership, the authors study the impact of innovation leadership on adoption of big data analytics in Indian health care sector. Besides, the authors study the mediating effect of organization readiness on the relationship of innovation leadership and big data analytics adoption. The conceptual framework is built keeping in view the organization information processing theory as the theoretical lens. To conduct the study, the authors adopted survey method that was administered to the sample of general managers, senior and junior managers and other healthcare professionals acting as decision authorities for adopting new technologies within organization.



From business boardrooms to senate chambers, universities to the courts, philanthropic groups to religious institutes, men are far more likely than women to be leaders. Society has determined that only men make good leaders, and this notion has denied easy access for women seeking leadership roles as they do not fit in the norm. Women with leadership aspirations continue to struggle for leadership positions in all spheres of governance in both the public and private sector however, the journey is never easy. Such bias against women is detrimental to the survival of all kinds of organisations in the growing digital era. For this reason, the chapter will specifically focus on women leadership and the challenges they face due to masculine workplace culture. It will also highlight the necessity of hiring women as leaders in the growing digital world. Recommendations will be stated that can assist the organisations in redesigning their workplace culture to support the initiative of providing opportunities to women and take up leadership positions for the future survival of organisations.

# Preface

This book examines the leadership and workplace culture in the digital era. Digital technologies, since the former two decades of the last century, have transformed all aspects in relation to organizations. Digitalization instigates changes concerning leadership, financial, human resources, organizational structures and processes and all other stakeholders. Digitalization is seen to sweep all aspects of personal lives as well. COVID-19 has accelerated the process of digitalisation. This transforms the roles of both leaders and employees in organisations. Organizational cultures are remoulded then. New values are inculcated in digital era.

The books revolves around the following themes:

- Digital transformation
- Digital leadership styles
- Digital transformation and stakeholders
- Humble leadership
- Workplace culture and leadership development
- Organizational change
- Employee commitment and satisfaction
- People management
- Innovation
- Technological stress and employees health
- Sustainability
- School leadership and
- Gender and digitalisation

Chapter 1 examines literature concerning leadership in digital era, changes resulting from digitalisation and future research in relation to digital technologies to expand knowledge.

Chapter 2 elaborates on the issue of leadership styles followed during digital era. The impacts of digitalisation on emerging new styles of leadership and evolving of new cultural values are explored.

The authors in Chapter 3 investigate the impacts of digitalisation on stakeholders. The relationships between leaders and stakeholders during before and after digital transformation are scrutinized. Leaders, shareholders and board of directors, employees, customers and regulators are the major stakeholders are the focus of this chapter.

Chapter 4 postulates that humble leaders and humility lead to virtuous environment. This environment ushers to promote radical innovation and success of innovation.

The author in chapter 5 claims that accountability, managing diversity, delegation and decision making are the most traditional competencies related to classics leadership. Leadership in digital transformation era requires to adopt different business models based on open communication, innovation and changes.

The author in chapter 6 probes the models of power in conjunction to the models of employees commitment. It is argued that referent power leads to the greatest level of volition while the coercive power instigates the least.

Chapter 7 Illustrates that the new styles of employment resulting from digital era lead to the development of values reflecting requirements of digitalisation. Digital workplace according to this chapter is based on collaboration. Communication and human interactions.

The author in Chapter 8 focuses on studying the changes in organisations required to implement digital transformation. Leadership, structure and culture are the main aspects to analysed.

Chapter 9 contemplates on the issue of employees health in organisations as being affected by digitalisation. It is stated that employees health reflects the relationships between education, gender, values of culture and stress. Leadership roles are to promote healthy behaviour.

This Chapter 10 shows that digital technologies and school improvement inseparable. COVID-19 leads the educational systems to encounter serious challenges. It is argued by the author of the chapter that leaders of educational systems have to adopt to changes caused by digitalisation to maintain sustainability.

The authors of Chapter 11 discuss the work constructs enhancing satisfaction of young technology natives. The authors state that job security, automated workplace, recognition, information security, quality and work-life balance are the work constructs.

Chapter 12 affirms that there is a relationship between HR digitalisation and employees and positive employees outcomes such as affective commitment and efforts. This is due to the moderating role of employees resilience.

The authors of Chapter 13 argue that there is a relationship between innovative leadership and the adoption of big data analytics in health sector. This relationship, according to authors of the chapter, is strengthened by organizational readiness.

The last chapter reviews literature concerning men and women in leadership during digital era. The authors assert that women and men are both competent to manage organizational changes and to direct employees.

*Ebtihaj Al A'ali*
*University of Bahrain, Bahrain*

*Meryem Masmoudi*
*University of Bahrain, Bahrain*

# Chapter 1
# Review of Leadership in the Digitalized World

**Asma Ayari**
https://orcid.org/0000-0002-2134-0624
*University of Bahrain, Bahrain*

## ABSTRACT

*The influence of technology on business cannot be reversed. As the moveable type of printing altered the course of history, digitalization is transforming organizations, work environments, and processes, requiring leaders to address new challenges. Experts in the social sciences have attempted to comprehend this complex phenomenon, but their findings have been dispersed across various disciplines and do not appear to form a unified picture. In order to correct this flaw in the literature and improve the clarity and coherence of scholarly discourse, this chapter's specific purpose is to evaluate how the debate on digital transformation and leadership has evolved over the previous few years, to highlight significant theories and discoveries, and to recommend potential future study routes. The chapter looks at all of the research that has been done on leadership and digitalization, looking for patterns of thought and findings across different social science fields, like management and psychology.*

## INTRODUCTION

Today companies face much strain in an internationalized and competitive environment because of the increased demands on their products and processes (Roman et al., 2018). As a result of the pressure, firms have begun adopting new organizational and managerial forms and methods, in addition to introducing innovative technology, to boost their flexibility, employees' performance, and ability to compete (Ekechukwu & Lammers, 2019). In fact, new technology in the business may impose fresh and more rigorous requirements on staff members in terms of their level of expertise, degree of autonomy, and degree of adaptability (Avolio et al., 2000, 2014; Horner-Long and Schoenberg, 2002; Hambley et al., 2007; Butcher et al., 2021). It has also been demonstrated that expanded opportunities for involvement and increased needs can lead to a rise in an effort, amount of pressure that is placed on staff, job intensity, responsibility, and options, which in turn leads to stress and a poor working environment (Kodama, 2007).

DOI: 10.4018/978-1-6684-5864-8.ch001

The technological transition that the world is currently undergoing is at least as significant as the industrial revolution. The digital age requires businesses to re-evaluate their management and organizational structures to develop and transfer value. (Lee, 2009). In the near future, the majority of companies will be involved in one way or another in the digitization process. Even traditional sectors such as agriculture will not be spared. The question of leadership is once again front and center in corporations' HR policies and strategies. Today, organizations need leaders who are comfortable in their job as entrepreneurs, in their role as managers, with charisma but also, and above all, a good command of digital tools. In his time, the leader took also, his/her company to conquer the markets. The e-leader does the same but using the multiplier effect of digital tools. He/she has changed his traditional posture by developing managerial and leadership roles that leverage social media and allow him to reach many more people in a shorter time (Avolio et al., 2000, 2014; Horner-Long and Schoenberg, 2002; Hambley et al., 2007; Salvetti & Bertagni, 2020; Butcher et al., 2021).

So what is the impact of this digital transformation on leadership? Which leadership style should be favoured for a successful digital transformation, and which attributes are essential for a leader to have in the 21st century?

As a first step, it is essential to introduce and define the concept of the digital transition.

### The Concept of Digital Transformation or Transition

"Digital transformation" or "digital transition" refers to integrating digital technologies into a company's value chain to improve organization and production. The digital transition is a lengthy process that impacts all core businesses and requires specialized management (Barley, 2015; Cortellazzo et al., 2019). The digital transition is a process that compels businesses to reevaluate their economic model and organizational model and to assist in this transformation by shifting from directive management to collaborative management. A digitalized company's objective is to boost productivity and profits. However, if not properly managed, the digital transformation can have the opposite effect (Bolden & O'Regan, 2016; Salvetti & Bertagni, 2020; Butcher et al., 2021).

## THE DIGITAL TRANSFORMATION: ASSET AND PERFORMANCE DRIVER

Digitalization is now present in almost all companies and constitutes a crucial step in their development. Companies see it as an opportunity to facilitate innovation, reinvent consumption patterns, be as close as possible to their target, and, above all, gain productivity through the virtues it is supposed to bring to the employees and the organization (Carte et al., 2006). Among the advantages that can offer the digital transition to the employees of companies, we can cite some examples such as continuous access to information, the dematerialization of information flows, the instantaneity of exchanges between employees, or automation of most time-consuming tasks, which must intrinsically contribute to the improvement of the quality of life at work. Interorganizational cooperation has developed as a result of an increase in the use of technology within organizations, as well as enhanced coordination and communication across numerous channels, levels, and hierarchies (such as social media). According to the research, organizational communication can take many forms, but leadership is essential in making decisions and establishing ground rules for the group (Roman et al., 2018). Leadership is essential in managing resources, efforts, recruitment, and hiring new staff members. These specialized and established roles determine the boundaries of public and private communication in a social space, build formal alliances, and strengthen institutional commitments (Avolio et al., 2000, 2014; Horner-Long and Schoenberg, 2002; Hambley et al., 2007; Butcher et al., 2021).

## KEY ELEMENTS OF DIGITAL TRANSFORMATION

The keystone of this digital transformation process can be summed up in four elements: awareness, adaptability, expertise and leadership.

**Raising awareness of digitization**: it's a no-brainer! basic knowledge and skills must be made available to everyone within the company. The aim here is to enable employees to meet new needs and requirements for technology and innovation under the best auspices (Boyatzis et al., 2006).

**Adaptability**: this high quality allows employees to get involved in digital projects with boldness and serenity, while gradually learning the new practices they need to excel. To do this, employees must devote part of their time to initiatives that offer them the opportunity to increase their innovation capabilities (Heinz et al., 2006). Continuing education is an excellent solution!

**Digital expertise:** ultimately, profiles who master key concepts (data collection, organization and classification of information, algorithmic processing) will be able to identify areas for creating digital initiatives that produce long-term outcomes. Developing digital competence also encourages collaboration between firms to design and test alternative forms of value generation.

**Digitalization leadership**: Last but not least, leadership is essential for change management. Leaders must receive training and certification for end-to-end digital commerce across the entire value chain. These leaders will operate as change agents to accelerate the company's adoption of new technologies. Senior management should view personnel and skills change management as a strategic goal (Kirkland et al., 2009; Butcher et al., 2021).

## THE DIGITAL TRANSFORMATION: A NECESSARY CHALLENGE TO DEVELOPMENT

The shift to digital has been able to meet expectations. However, it is also a risk factor that may cause unexpected results. Businesses are expected to benefit from the digital shift in terms of efficiency and accessibility; what is the current situation? How can an idea intend to simplify and automate work become a source of stress and psychologically harm the affected employees?

The major areas for improvement are, therefore, the following:

**Time-saving by automation**: Indeed, the automation of chores like tracking, for instance, provides for improved time management. Proofreading, research, correction of abnormalities, and data retention are all facilitated by digitalization, which also allows for the reduction of human error in routine tasks (Henttonen et al., 2012; Salvetti & Bertagni, 2020).

**An enhancement in presentation and communication**: A company's introduction into the digitization era enables it to be a part of its time and demonstrate its modernity to its clients. Digitalization is currently one of our foundations, and adhering to this progression helps reassure stakeholders regarding the company's ability to adapt and innovate (Huber, 1990). In addition to the image, communication is organically altered and enhanced by the new methods and marketing opportunities made possible by digitalization. Today, a company using digital correctly can do without service providers and manage its communication and advertising campaigns through software, social networks, data analysis, and audience (Kahai et al., 2006; Butcher et al., 2021).

**Connection to an industry without boundaries:** The growth of the digital age has been a true revolution on a worldwide scale; today, anyone with internet access may speak with anyone on the planet, regardless of location. Digital knowledge is not limited by space or time (Hughes, 2004). This can represent a substantial audience and scope advantage as part of the digital business. A magazine can now reach thousands of readers instantly. This is a tremendous chance to expand its network and market beyond its specific service region (Lisk et al., 2012; Butcher et al., 2021).

**Instant Exchanges and Interactions:** This notion of instantaneity is also found in everyday exchanges and interactions. We have seen above that the notion of distance no longer interferes in digital exchanges, making it possible to keep in touch continuously with a large number of people in the context of the service customer since the company can now be more responsive and process the request quickly for the consumer or customer. In a more internal context, employees within the company can now communicate or collaborate in real-time via instant digital platforms, thus avoiding physical travel.

**Continuous and on-demand access to information:** Digital communication is not limited by geographical area or the notion of time; it is also the case for information, which Internet users can perceive in real-time without limit. Let us also find the notion of instantaneity, which is essential in the digital age. Thus, as part of the business. It is helpful to keep real-time information about everything happening worldwide, not only in a delimited geographical area. (Boe and Torgersen, 2018; Butcher et al., 2021).

**Better performance and sales:** Thanks to digitization, businesses have access to data and large data streams that let them analyze market trends and learn more about their customers or potential customers (Gupta and Pathak, 2018). They can also change how their sales channels work to meet customer needs better. Digital technology at the workstation can also make employees more productive, mainly because of the rise of collaboration platforms that make it easier to work on a typical project (Cascio and Montealegre, 2016). Lastly, digitization makes it possible to cut some costs. For example, digitizing accounting documents makes finding and keeping data more manageable. Since the company saves paper and storage space, it can cut its costs by a significant amount (Jawadi et al., 2013; Butcher et al., 2021).

**A new way to do business with customers:** one of the essential parts of the digital revolution in business is how it is changing customer relationships. Now, the customer is an essential part of the business. He can find out everything he needs to know about the company and talk to his contacts directly. This change makes the relationship between a company and its customers even more vital. It makes people feel like they belong and are loyal to a company, and it reassures customers that they will be able to get what they want (Coutu, 2000; Butcher et al., 2021).

Thus, the digital transition, an essential element of entrepreneurial development, has many advantages that greatly benefit today's companies. This is even more true in companies where people from different generations work together. For example, employees from Generations Y and Z, or "digital natives," have more advantages than those from the baby boomer generation or Generation X. The second is less flexible and sticks to old ways of doing things.

## Digital Transformation and Leadership

In the case of the digital transition, the leader's job will be to ensure everyone is on the same page. They must also know how to get people from different generations to work together, even if their ways of doing things seem different. (Cortellazzo et al., 2019). It would be about creating synergies by using one to train the other. Thus, we can link to our second observation, which is that the digital can call into question the skills and know-how of each organization and company and therefore be a psychosocial risk factor. Indeed, when we talk about digital transformation, we believe in using new tools that can be seen as a threat and create behaviors of resistance to change. This new way of doing things can contribute to the deterioration of working conditions (O'Boyle et al., 2017; Butcher et al., 2021).

Indeed, the most frequent observation observed by companies is that digital technology is putting people back. It forces everyone to use their skills, and the leader's job is to help the actors through this change (Toepfl, 2018). This means that working methods and organization need to be rethought. Digital transformation is a significant reason working conditions are worsening (Jawadi et al., 2013). It creates a culture of urgency and immediacy that is not in line with how work is usually done. This makes workers physically and mentally tired, and they must deal with significant changes regarding time, moving rooms, and recognition (Gupta and Pathak, 2018; Butcher et al., 2021).

**A misunderstanding of the need for change:** in many cases of resistance to change, this reluctance is because most "opponents" do not understand the need for change. Some employees, such as those who have worked the longest at the company, do not. I do not think changing the work habits that have been effective for many years is beneficial. The need for change arises from constant innovation, which is not necessarily perceived in the same way by all employees, who are not always aware of the emergency. You could potentially find a company that has not taken charge of digitalization; the will to change is, above all, a desire to align with the market (Toepfl, 2018; ; Salvetti & Bertagni, 2020).

**Apprehension related to the unknown**: is not a secret, employee evolves thanks to his perpetual will to understand everything and everything. To know the unknown often represents a danger, an obstacle. Apprehension related to the unknown is not a secret. Man evolves thanks to his perpetual will to understand everything and everything. The unknown often represents a danger, an obstacle (Cascio and Montealegre, 2016). These cases are often settled as soon as these individuals understand the facts. These cases are often settled as soon as these individuals understand that the fact of not changing can cause much more significant damage than those associated with the action of change and the unknown (Cortellazzo et al., 2019; Butcher et al., 2021).

**The questioning of know-how:** the company's transition to digitalization sometimes requires adaptations of skills and operating methods. There may indeed be a significant need for some employees to upgrade and train their skills (O'Boyle et al., 2017). This lack of digital training is often perceived as a real obstacle. This idea is also directly related to a lack of confidence, on the one hand in the entrepreneurial structure, which might not be able to manage such a change, but also in its power of adaptation. This idea is directly related to employees' fear of becoming "obsolete" within their company, seeing their skills replaced by software and digital tools (Cascio and Montealegre, 2016; ; Salvetti & Bertagni, 2020).

**Changing Habits:** Changing how a company has been used for many years is not trivial. Some habits are ingrained and, in some ways, define a comfort zone for many people in the company. Questioning the usual reassurance can lead to a natural feeling of endangerment and exposure, especially where the benefits of such a change are not perceived or perceived. Benefits favor one group at the expense of another unevenly. The perception of digitalization plays a significant role. The perception of digitalization plays a significant role (Lorenz et al., 2015; Butcher et al., 2021).

**An imposed transition**: the absence of consultation and communication with people directly concerned by the digital transition is a powerful resistance motor (Roman et al., 2018). Involving individuals in the change process will transform their status; they will thus suffer less but rather be actors in the transition. Imposing changes without employees being able to express their opinion can lead to a sense of indifference towards them on the part of the manager and create a different distance between individuals (Avolio et al., 2000, 2014; Horner-Long and Schoenberg, 2002; Hambley et al., 2007; Butcher et al., 2021).

**Poor communication:** It seems evident that communication between all group members is paramount during such a transition. However, digitizing the company leads to a noticeable reduction. human relations, relegated to data sharing platforms and messaging instant (Avolio et al., 2000, 2014). Even though some interlocutors are in the same room, communication is done through screens. Trade is shrinking. The impact of digitalization on human and social relations in companies is also a critical factor in the psychological distress that employees may experience (Lorenz et al., 2015).

**A new workload**: the digital transition has created a culture of urgency and immediacy, as we mentioned earlier. This desire for speed, a priori, facilitated by digitalization and the use of tools and software, brings employees (Cortellazzo et al., 2019). They will have to manage a workload significantly higher than what they could have had before the changes for the same allotted time. Digital tools and processing even help them. Fast and continuous computerized tasks can lead to employee exhaustion and saturation. This saturation is usually accompanied by a loss of motivation and a form of disengagement (Cascio and Montealegre, 2016). We are never totally disconnected from work because, even in a private setting, we often receive notifications or alerts related to our professional sphere (Lorenz et al., 2015). As a result, the work environment is changed as it becomes flexible; temporal boundaries and the boundaries between life and death are no longer clearly defined, profoundly affecting the balance between life and death. Employees find themselves perpetually connected in private and professional life and are likely to be solicited on professional topics. All these possible risks are potential criteria for hindering the development of digital in business (O'Boyle et al., 2017; Butcher et al., 2021).

However, if this first part of our study, based on the existing literature to date, does not claim to provide all the elements to respond exhaustively to our research problem, it does provide us with valuable information on the perception of digital across the social spectrum and from a pragmatic point of view. Indeed, this allows us to highlight the most cited characteristics not only in terms of benefits but also in terms of risks (Cortellazzo et al., 2019).

According to our definition of leadership, a leader is responsible for a group of people, an organization, or their transformational process. For the second reason, we did not include any research on companies that serve as the face of a market or industry leader. As a last consideration, we looked at research that made a strong case for digital or technical change. For the fourth time, we did not include studies in which there was no evident connection between information technology and leadership (such as municipal leaders maintaining urban economies' physical and digital infrastructure in light of climate change). Because of this, the following research questions served as the basis for our evaluation: Where do academic discussions on digital transformation and leadership typically begin? "Digital transformation and leadership" is a common theme that has emerged from the various essays on the subject. Scholars should also consider (iii) the most promising future research directions.

The following is how the chapter is organized: First, it explains the methodology utilized; second, it suggests a classification of findings based on theoretical frameworks and content classifications. Finally, it discusses our findings' research and practice implications and suggests future study areas.

## RESEARCH DESIGN

By looking at how the digital transformation and leadership debate has changed over time, we hope to find essential theories and findings and develop new research ideas. As part of a "mixed methods" approach, we use quantitative and qualitative research to answer our research questions.

### Data Collection

The Scopus database is one of the best ways to find scientific research; that is where we got the papers. We also looked through the Web of Science and Ebsco databases to ensure we had not missed any articles. We chose only to use Scopus because we could not find any critical differences between these databases on this topic. We started using the database on June 1, 2022.

Since our research questions concerned how academics talk about digital transformation and leadership, we limited our search to academic articles from peer-reviewed journals and unpublished sources like unpublished manuscripts. We did not look for books and other articles that were not meant for educational purposes because they were not part of our study. We started our search with targeted keywords like "leader" and "digital" or "e-leader." We used the keywords to figure out what the topic should be (title, keywords, or abstract). We looked for English papers that had been reviewed by experts and were published in business, management, accounting, psychology, and social science journals. Since this topic is covered by more than just business and management, we decided to look at articles from other fields. Based on these criteria, the first group of 500 articles was chosen. Figure 1 shows how the debate has grown since 2000 and how much it has grown since 2015.

To avoid a potential publishing bias (O'Boyle et al., 2017; Butcher et al., 2021) and examine recent works that may not have had time to go through the entire publication process, we searched conference proceedings published since 2015 using the same criteria. The initial collection of articles consisted of 97 pieces.

In the second round of data collection, we selected articles according to their quality. Since the number of citations is a traditional metric of scientific quality and influence in academia, we began by examining publications that were published before 2013 and had at least one citation (Garfield, 1979, 2004; Peteraf et al., 2013). Considering that citation-based approaches can be biased against recent publications (Crossan and Apaydin, 2010), we retained all papers published after 2013. We discarded studies that did not appear in the first 200 journals on the Scimago list for management and business, social science, and psychology since we believed that only the most prestigious journals would publish high-quality research. The abstracts of peer-reviewed articles and conference proceedings were then compared to the topic and the boundary conditions to see if they were relevant.

The articles were chosen based on the following criteria:

1. A leader is a person who directs the transformational processes of a group, an organization or both.
2. There was a strong connection between information technology and leadership and an apparent allusion to digital or technological transformation. We did not accept publications that discussed digital transformation or leadership alone.
3. In addition, we did not accept papers that did not meet our criteria, such as research on how industry leaders utilize digital platforms.

## Data Analysis and Qualitative Coding

To obtain a "systematic, transparent, and repeatable review process" (Zupic and Cater, 2015, p. 429) and to identify research streams and seminal works, we initially performed a bibliometric analysis of the initial dataset of 790 publications. All the publications were subjected to rigorous coding analysis to understand where the academic discussion on digital transformation and leadership originated and how it has evolved. Then, as we read and talked about the final set of articles, the following categories started to emerge that helped guide our analysis (Strauss and Corbin, 1998):

1. theoretical or empirical studies;
2. research methodology;
3. analysis level (micro and macro);
4. leadership and digitalization definitions;
5. Themes or objectives of the article;
6. Principal conceptions;
7. Academic discipline (e.g., management and planning, economics and business, psychology, and so on).

According to this coding scheme, the different researchers separately read and coded each article. Then, they discussed who was responsible for each code until everyone reached a consensus on the final code for each piece.

# FINDINGS

## Dataset Description

The complete database contains 54 articles. There are 42 peer-reviewed articles from 33 journals and 12 conference proceedings.

Most of the peer-reviewed articles in our collection (22 articles) are in the fields of economics, business and management, and information and communication sciences (10 articles). There have been only three studies undertaken in the discipline of psychology.

As for where these articles are published, "The Leadership Quarterly" and "Strategy and Leadership" are two journals that focus on leadership. The other 31 journals cover economics, business and management, information and communication sciences, psychology, educational and health sciences, and political sciences. The fact that the topic is new and written about in many different journals shows that people from many different fields are interested in digital transformation and leadership. Because the literature is so scattered and allows for different points of view, it is clear that future research needs to be more organized and focused.

Most of the articles in the conference proceedings are drawn from worldwide, peer-reviewed conferences that promote the debate on digital transformation in the corporate world. Among these are the International Conference on Electronic Business, the Scandinavian Conference on Information Systems, and the IEEE Conference on e-Learning, e-Management, and e-Services.

The human resources-specific journals "Leadership Quarterly" and "Organizational Behavior and Human Decision Processes" account for three of our sample's top five most-cited articles. These studies (Avolio et al., 2000, 2014; Horner-Long and Schoenberg, 2002; Hambley et al., 2007) focus on the roles and behaviors of digital leaders and emphasize that technology is altering how leaders view communication and interact with followers.

During the early 2000s, as depicted in Figure 1, pioneering work began to explore the shifts in leadership that digitalization entails and how leadership is influenced by these technological innovations (Avolio et al., 2000; Coutu, 2000). However, the subject has gained much attention in the previous decade. Involuntary eye movement. It is conceivable that the vast majority of technology has had a more significant effect on society. Technical advancements are expected to impact businesses in the foreseeable future positively, and evolution will be even more disruptive due to heightened interest in the subject. Sixty percent of the peer-reviewed articles in our sample were published prior to 2000 in works that were released after 2014. Conference proceedings are limited to the following:

- We considered post-2015 contributions to make a decision. be aware of the changes in the argument during the last few years. Most people prefer micro over macro analysis, and most of our sample's contributions are micro-level (30). A macro viewpoint is taken in only 24 articles (articles). It is in this latter group that.
- It is interesting to note that many papers have been written on the subject, which is unrelated to management. When it comes to the kind of vehicle you will be driving.
- A total of 37 publications in our sample make an essential contribution. Only a few pieces of research are conceptual; the vast majority are empirical. This lack of theorization reveals that there is still an imbalance in technology's influence on leadership effectiveness. Despite this, the next section will. In this chapter, we summarize the essential theoretical framework employed to talk about this subject.

## Theoretical Framework

According to our study, only a limited group of studies directly relate to existing theoretical frameworks addressing digital transformation's impact on leadership. According to Huber (1990), the application of information technology influences the organizational structure, information consumption, and decision-making procedures. Scholars concur on the significant impact of technology on leadership behavior and identify IT innovations as a catalyst for disruptive transformation in organizations and leadership positions across organizational domains. (Bartol and Liu, 2002; Geoffrion, 2002; Weiner et al., 2015; Sousa and Rocha, 2018).

Scholars have coined new terminology to describe the e-world, e-business, and e-organizations due to the magnitude of these developments (Horner-Long and Schoenberg, 2002). Recent studies (Gerth and Peppard, 2016; Schwarzmüller et al., 2018) have examined digital ubiquity, or the prevalence of technology (Roman et al., 2018). This term refers to an environment where humans and technology frequently interact.

It presents a situation in which computer sensors (RFID tags, wearable technology, smartwatches) and other equipment (tablets, mobile devices) are merged with objects, people, information, computers, and the physical environment (Cascio and Montealegre, 2016, p. 350).

Scholars have several ideas and definitions of leadership. Horner-Long and Schoenberg (2002) compare universal and contingency theories. The former suggests that leaders distinguish themselves from others due to a generic set of leadership traits and behaviors (Lord et al., 1986; Kirkpatrick and Locke, 1991). The latter contends that good leadership must match the context. The writers compare e-business and brick-and-mortar CEOs' leadership profiles. Both methods lack clear evidence. In both circumstances, most leadership traits are rewarded. E-world leaders have distinct traits from traditional industry leaders. Richardson and Sterrett (2018) use a longitudinal approach to examine how digital advancements affected the role of tech-savvy K-12 district leaders through time. Hitt and Tucker (2016) base their work on a unified model of learning-influencing leadership approaches. Although the leadership practice concept is preserved, the writers note modifications in implementation. Only Obschonka et al. (2017) take a universal, trait-approach perspective (Stogdill, 1974). By analysing Twitter discourse, the authors identify effective managers and entrepreneurs' personalities. Heinz et al. (2006) emphasize the necessity to consider context and situational factors that can influence leadership and cooperation. Most of our sample assumes that technology innovation may affect leadership.

According to Lu et al. (2014, p. 55), "offline leadership qualities cannot be directly translated to virtual leadership". Some authors assume this tacitly (e.g., Schwarzmüller et al., 2018) without addressing any corresponding theoretical framework. Bolden and O'Regan (2016) write, "There is no one approach to leadership" since it must be modified to the situation. Lu et al. (2014) argue that practical leadership actions depend on the context. Jawadi et al. (2013) utilize the framework of leadership behavioral complexity theory to address the diversity of events and environments. Jawadi et al. (2013) utilize the leadership behavioral complexity theory framework to address the diversity of events and environments (Denison et al., 1995). In a complex, unpredictable environment, leaders need a behavioral repertoire to handle situational contradictions (Denison et al., 1995). As contingencies evolve quickly, an effective leader must be able to envision and play various roles. Like Bartol and Liu (2002), the authors use a structuration framework (Adaptive Structure Theory; DeSanctis and Poole, 1994).

According to them, digital technology and leadership have a recursive relationship. In their view, technology influences leadership, but leaders also appropriate it. The effect of technology on individuals, groups, and organizations occurs through the interaction between IT and organizational structures. In this view, context is not only shaped by leaders but is also part of e-leadership itself. Avolio et al. (2000, 2014) conceptualized e-leadership, which has since been used by several authors (Avolio et al., 2000; Lynn Pulley and Sessa, 2001; Roman et al., 2018). Orlikowski (1992) developed a structural model of technology whereby technology influences actor performance but is also produced and socially constructed by its users (Van Outvorst et al., 2017).

Scholars look at the relationships between leaders and their teams through three main theories: transactional leadership theory, transformational leadership theory (Burns, 1978; Bass, 1981, 1985), and leader-member exchange theory (LMX; Graen and Scandura, 1987). Transactional and transformational leadership are popular behavioral leadership theories (DiazSaenz, 2011). Transformational leaders motivate and inspire followers to perform above expectations, while transactional leaders gain follower compliance through contingent reinforcement and rewards (Bass, 1985). Leadership styles may affect virtual team interactions and performance (Sosik et al., 1997, 1998; Kahai and Avolio, 2006). Hambley et al. (2007) compare face-to-face, desktop videoconferencing, and text-based chat to compare the effects of transactional and transformational leadership on team interactions and outcomes. Lu et al. (2014) analyze virtual and offline interactions using transactional and transformational leadership theories to see if MMOG players' leadership approaches are related to their offline leadership status. This association is meant exclusively for offline leadership jobs in nonprofits, not companies. Hambley et al. (2007) found that the relationship between leadership style, team interaction, and performance is independent of the communication medium. Transactional and transformational leadership theories focus on how the leader acts toward the follower. On the other hand, the leader-member exchange theory (LMX) looks at the relationship between the leader and follower.

Leader-member exchange theory looks at what kind of relationship leaders have with their team members and how good that relationship is. Gerstner and Day (1997) think that the quality of this relationship, which is marked by trust, respect, and a sense of mutual obligation, can predict how people, groups, and organizations will do. Jawadi et al. (2013) use the idea of leader-member exchange as a dependent variable to study how different leadership roles affect relationships of cooperation and collaboration in virtual teams. Bartol and Liu (2002) used the theory of leader-member exchange to suggest policies and practices that HRM professionals can use to share IT-related information with employees and change how they feel about it.

Distributed power dynamics got a boost from the spread of information power. Instead of making the vertical leader the most important person, team members are seen as potential sources of leadership under the shared leadership method (Pearce, 2004; Ensley et al., 2006; Pearce et al., 2009). "More than one individual can conduct "leadership behaviors that direct, structure, or facilitate the group" as a result of fully developed team empowerment, and different people may perform the same leadership behaviors at different times," which is known as "shared leadership" (Pearce, 2004, p. 48). (Carte et al., 2006, p. 325).

Even though more connectivity is essential in the digital age, some studies stress how important it is to look at things from a network perspective. Lynn Pulley and Sessa (2001) compare and contrast the industrial economy with the networked economy we have now. Bartol and Liu (2002) say that networked organizations have three main types of connections: between organizations (also called "boundaryless"; Nohria and Berkley, 1994), within organizations, and outside of organizations. Kodama (2007) says that the organization comprises different types of networked strategic communities where knowledge is shared and evaluated. By drawing a network, Sullivan et al. (2015) show how shared leadership works. Gordon (2007) looks at how the network fits into the current idea of what the web is.

## Future Research

Despite the need felt by scholars to comprehend how leaders keep up with technological progress, the literature appears to lack a unified method for analysing and conceptualizing this phenomenon. Although academics have introduced practical new concepts such as e-leader and e-organizations, the literature lacks well-established and consensus-based definitions. According to our review, scholars have utilized several leadership theories to describe the relationship between leadership and digital transformation. However, we question whether theories based on traditional views of industrial organization and business, which still predominate in the literature, are the most appropriate to comprehend the multifaceted phenomenon of digital transformation and its impact on all aspects of leadership within organizations, and communities, teams, and even the self. According to Kahai et al. (2013), experts may need to look beyond traditional leadership theories to explain the effect digitalization has on leadership and leaders. Existing social science theories may describe this disruptive phenomenon's causes, characteristics, and results; nevertheless, new theoretical lenses may be required to make sense of how leaders may adapt to this transformation.

(Un)ethical e-leadership is an important topic. The higher-risk leaders face unethical use of personal and sensitive information. Or the lack of a code of conduct for ethical leadership behavior. These are essential issues to address in any e-leadership debate (Lee, 2009). Collaboration via digital technologies raises new challenges for the role of leaders in a digital context. What role do leaders have in ensuring the ethical adoption of digital technologies? What can e-leaders do to set an example for their followers and establish an ethical culture? How can digital resources such as social media and online communities and forums affect the upkeep of ethical behavior? These are questions that future studies must answer. While some of these concerns have already been addressed by theorists, empirical research remains underdeveloped.

This review reveals a paucity of contributions addressing the role of institutions in promoting ethical leadership conduct. Specifically, it is unknown whether and how leaders will be prepared to tackle the new surge of data and policies that will affect their capacity to manage privacy and regulatory challenges. Thus, research in this field is strongly encouraged.

The leader-follower interactions mediated by ICTs may be impacted by privacy and information concerns. Social media engagements, for instance, generate digital fingerprints that leaders and organizations can monitor, which may undermine the interactions and responses of followers who believe their privacy is at stake. The same holds for digital technologies' tools for tracking individual productivity. Project management tools, for instance, track individual contributions to a specific project, but if the relationship between individual effort and contribution to the results is unclear, unbiased appraisal may be compromised, thereby eroding trust in the relationship with leaders. Future studies should explore these factors and strive toward a more comprehensive understanding of how to balance the need for greater transparency in ICT-mediated relationships and the followers' demand for greater autonomy and privacy.

We recognize that the introduction and use of digital tools are inextricably tied to organizational cultures that promote the use of technology and that this demonstrates the readiness of businesses to integrate digital tools successfully. Therefore, we advise that additional study is required to determine how organizational culture influences the selection and successful deployment of digital technology. This question also elicits essential information regarding how digital technology modifies organizational identity and establishes new organizational boundaries. Exploring this investigation line using theoretical and empirical methods may shed light on the formation of new organizational identities and their relationships with various types of organizations and institutions.

People are sharing it more and more since digitalization makes it easier to share information. As a result, the boundaries between organizations are becoming more fluid and are spreading beyond the formal ones. So, collective ways of leading are likely to become more common. Notably, distributed or shared leadership is expected to grow, especially if it is seen as a better fit for the features of virtual teams, like the informality of their communication channels, the interdependence of their tasks, and the autonomy of their members (Avolio et al., 2014; Hoch and Kozlowski, 2014). What is unclear is what leaders should do to recognize and encourage distributed leadership in their teams. Also, how much does the organization's culture affect how well shared leadership styles work? How does shared leadership change the way a virtual team works? We think these are essential questions that should be looked at in more depth in the future.

Networked enterprises and virtual teams show how digital technology has permitted endless connectivity. Empirical studies on virtual teams show that digital tools can separate individuals and destabilize power dynamics. Despite increased connectivity, few studies use a network approach to investigate how leaders and followers are related.

Literature has already noted that the absence of face-to-face interactions makes directing virtual teams more difficult (Purvanova and Bono, 2009). Indeed, the physical and cultural distance that characterizes virtual teams poses a danger to the team members' ability to establish trust, generate commitment, and strengthen cohesion (Hoch and Kozlowski, 2014). As suggested by Lee (2009), trust in virtual teams is related to ethics: how leaders and team members conduct themselves, the degree to which they demonstrate transparency when interacting with others, and the integrity and adherence to the rules and procedures of the organization and the team are crucial issues that should not be neglected. However, little is known about the approaches and behaviors that good leaders might employ to develop trust in virtual teams. Literature on this subject requires contributions that focus explicitly on the process of trust development in virtual teams, identifying its characteristics and mechanisms, and providing information on which digital tools can promote such a process. Indeed, along with the capacity to build trust among team members, virtual team leaders must be able to select and utilize the most effective communication methods (Jawadi et al., 2013; Roman et al., 2018). Future research should investigate the impact of various communication tool characteristics on team dynamics and leader-follower interactions. The lack of face-to-face interaction also presents new difficulties for applying social skills. Interpersonal comprehension processes may be hindered by distance and the use of interfaces. Compared with pure virtual teams, Balthazard et al. (2009) discovered that leader traits that are easier to perceive from nonverbal cues, such as personality traits, predicted the emergence of transformational leadership in face-to-face teams but not in computer-mediated teams. Considering the significance of social understanding and affect-based perceptions, we recommend further study examining how leaders might foster positive emotional contagion through technology. For instance, it would be intriguing to investigate whether the use of facial and emotional recognition devices (Pentland and Choudhury, 2000) and affective haptics (Arafsha et al., 2012; Salvetti & Bertagni, 2020) can contribute to interpersonal emotional understanding and sharing, as well as how this affects leader-follower relationships and team dynamics.

Balthazard et al. (2009) discovered a good correlation between the quality of written communication and the emergence of transformational leadership in virtual teams. Indeed, the increasing use of written communication-based tools such as chats, social media, and document-sharing platforms necessitates linguistic analysis of online communication to comprehend how leaders effectively instil emotions, convey their vision, and communicate urgency through text.

According to Avolio et al. (2014), gender may impact leadership in the digital world. Men and women may use distinct factors when deciding which technology to use. However, this research issue has received scant attention in the literature. We contend that additional research is required to study gender inequalities and their impact on organizational results in greater depth.

Future researchers must also investigate how leaders acquire the competencies necessary to succeed in the digital age. Some researchers believe virtual games may be useful tools for developing social and technical skills (Ducheneaut and Moore, 2005; Lu et al., 2014). However, research has not yet demonstrated whether virtual games have a demonstrable effect on developing social and computer skills. Future research might examine the types of virtual behaviors that promote team engagement and higher team performance in multiplayer virtual games and the significance of these variables in organizational contexts. Other scholars suggest that digital natives and technical experts in businesses could be involved in training people who are less familiar with technology or have a negative attitude toward its adoption, for instance, through reverse mentorship programs (Coutu, 2000).

However, it is necessary to study the variables that can facilitate the successful digital transformation of enterprises. Young generations' technological edge may disrupt old power structures. A closer examination of this phenomenon is recommended.

In a digital age where physical presence is becoming increasingly obsolete, it is not implausible that some leadership functions will eventually be done by AI-based technology.

(Avolio et al., 2014). There is a heated debate about whether robots can be trained to express emotions and how this raises the possibility that robots could be superior leaders to humans. Future research should shed light on whether and how robots, algorithms, and technological tools replace or supplement leaders, complementing the literature that has so far emphasized the importance of emotions and emotional intelligence for leaders' performance (see, for example, Boyatzis, 2006; Boyatzis et al., 2017; Salvetti & Bertagni, 2020).

Even if social science academics investigate the macro and micro levels of analysis, the management literature will lack a micro and macro-level examination of the issue of leadership and digitalization. Incorporating many levels of analysis could be an effective means of merging micro and macro levels of theory. Several of the publications in our collection move in this direction, although it is unclear how digitalization impacts the interactions between various companies.

From a methodological standpoint, our study reveals a plethora of methods used by scholars to analyze leaders' behavior (Hambley et al., 2007; Malhotra et al., 2007; Jawadi et al., 2013), leadership skills (Horner-Long and Schoenberg, 2002; Roman et al., 2018), or technology adoption (Horner-Long and Schoenberg, 2002; Roman et al., 2018) (Bartol and Liu, 2002; Weiner et al., 2015). If, on the one hand, this diversity gives a portfolio of methodologies that researchers may employ based on the subject of their analysis, on the other hand, it demonstrates that there is still confusion regarding how to monitor this contemporary phenomenon. In addition, we see that contributions are limited to their particular discipline boundaries. For example, the literature on social movements, which relies mainly on qualitative methodologies such as ethnography, case studies, and interviews, should instruct organizational researchers on examining power dynamics within corporations. Existing research on the abilities necessary for digital transformation leadership is primarily based on surveys and interviews with experts. According to the available literature, there is a dearth of empirical research examining the relationship between defined leadership skills and successful performance in highly digitalized businesses. Future research should also consider the extent to which this link may influence the leader's operating environment.

## CONCLUSION

Today, all businesses, regardless of size or industry, must undergo digital transformation. Leaders must adapt to new technologies daily and make decisions based on the available information. Therefore, we strongly urge future studies to shed more light on the impact of digital transformation on leadership, both at the organizational and individual levels. If the discussion over the link between humans and machines is not new (Turing, 1950), neither in management literature nor in the social sciences, then the relationship between digital transformation and leadership demands current lenses.

This systematic review provides a structured framework for a promising field, and we believe it will aid future research in generating coherent attempts to acquire new and pertinent knowledge in this research issue.

This review had a threefold objective. First, we reviewed how leadership in the digital era has been framed by evaluating the theoretical views employed in previous studies. Our literature study did not uncover a solid unifying theory of the relationship between leadership and digital transformation, necessitating a greater emphasis on theoretical contributions.

Second, we mapped the scholarly discourse on the relationship between digital change and leadership, organizing and structuring the most prominent emergent themes at the macro and micro levels of research. We found that both micro and macro contributions emphasize the need for improved alignment between information technology and strategic management. Long-term digital transformation success is achieved when the organizational objectives align with the need to adopt new digital tools or instruments. Individuals accept technical progress only when they consider it to apply to their work. It is the role of the leader, especially C-suite executives, to steer this strategic alignment and the spread of digital culture. In a globalized economy, digitalization has prompted enterprises to open their borders and establish connections with other industries, stakeholders, and customers to drive innovation. Leaders who must invest in networking from a micro perspective also demand this openness, which requires being "out there" (Grafstrom and Falkman, 2017), present in the network (Gordon, 2007), and willing to connect with many stakeholders using digital technologies and social media. Digital tools, especially for leaders, are no longer a small container of daily life; instead, they are instruments from which daily life emerges (Gordon, 2007).

Even though the introduction of digital tools influenced organizational and leadership boundaries, for example, by fostering the development of concepts such as shared leadership, research indicates that leaders' intervention is still necessary to establish and maintain trust among members and employees (Carte et al., 2006). Cascio and Montealegre (2016, p. 356) remind us that inspirational leaders will continue to play a crucial role in decision-making because "people will continue to have a significant comparative advantage over robots." However, the increasing usage of AI-based decision-making technologies necessitates a deeper grasp of what leadership will entail in the future. Increasing ethical problems regarding the application of artificial intelligence in management activities and the appropriation of technology and data are becoming a pressing issue. To overcome the challenges posed by the digital transformation, leaders must develop a combination of digital and human skills, particularly the ability to communicate effectively in a digitalized context, create cohesion among geographically dispersed followers, foster initiative and alter attitudes, and deal with complex and rapid problem-solving.

Thirdly, we emphasized the current gaps and unanswered problems in the literature and outlined a future research plan that focuses on the potential to expand empirical and theoretical knowledge.

While this analysis is timely and incorporates the most recent contributions, future research should acknowledge and overcome some constraints. First, while our objective was to map existing research, we have not presented explicit propositions for the recommended categories; future studies should fill this deficiency. The second issue concerns the sample. Only the Scopus database was utilized. Even though we searched different databases to exclude the possibility of bias, we may have missed some pertinent articles. Third, despite the rigorous methodology of our systematic review, the inclusion of only peer-reviewed articles and conference proceedings is considered a constraint. A future study could also incorporate industrial research reports, professional channels disseminating research-based conclusions, and other non-peer-reviewed publications to elucidate how the multidimensional phenomena of digitization influence organizations and leadership. According to our exclusion criteria, we excluded papers that regarded organizations as digital transformation leaders and studies that covered digital platforms. Future research should embrace a larger perspective of the macro-organizational and strategic effects to comprehend how digital transformation is executed throughout many businesses, communities, and teams.

## REFERENCES

Agarwal, S. D., Barthel, M. L., Rost, C., Borning, A., Bennett, W. L., and Johnson, C. N. (2014). Grassroots organizing in the digital age: considering values and technology in Tea Party and Occupy Wall Street. *Inform. Commun. Soc. 17*, 326–341. doi:. 873068 doi:10.1080/1369118X.2013

Arafsha, F., Masudul Alam, K., & El Saddik, A. (2012). EmoJacket: consumer centric wearable affective jacket to enhance emotional immersion. In *Proceedings of the 2012 International Conference on Innovations in Information Technology (IIT)*, 350–355. 10.1109/INNOVATIONS.2012.6207766

Avolio, B. J., Kahai, S., & Dodge, G. E. (2000). E-leadership: Implications for theory, research, and practice. *The Leadership Quarterly, 11*(4), 615–668. doi:10.1016/S1048-9843(00)00062-X

Avolio, B. J., Sosik, J. J., Kahai, S. S., & Baker, B. (2014). E-leadership: re-examining transformations in leadership source and transmission. Leader. Q. 25, 105–131. doi:10.1016/j.leaqua.2013.11.003

Bakardjieva, M., Felt, M., & Dumitrica, D. (2018). The mediatization of leadership: Grassroots digital facilitators as organic intellectuals, sociometric stars and caretakers*. *Information Communication and Society, 21*, 899–914. doi:10.1080/1369118X.2018.1434556

Balthazard, P. A., Waldman, D. A., and Warren, J. E. (2009). Predictors of the emergence of transformational leadership in virtual decision teams. *Leader. Q. 20*, 651–663. doi:. 06.008 doi:10.1016/j.leaqua.2009

Barley, S. R. (2015). Why the internet makes buying a car less loathsome: How technologies change role relations. *Academy of Management Discoveries, 1*(1), 5–35. doi:10.5465/amd.2013.0016

Bartol, K. M., & Liu, W. (2002). Information technology and human resources management: Harnessing the power and potential of netcentricity. *Research in Personnel and Human Resources Management, 21*, 215–242. doi:10.1016/S0742-7301(02)21005-1

Bass, B. M. (1981). *Stogdill's Handbook of Leadership: A Survey of Theory and Research. Revised and Expanded Edition* (2nd ed.). Free Press.

Bass, B. M. (1985). *Leadership and Performance Beyond Expectations* (1st ed.). Free Press.

Bass, B. M., and Avolio, B. J. (1993). Transformational leadership and organizational culture. *Public Admin. Q. 17*, 112–121.

Bekkhus, R., & Hallikainen, P. (2017). A new dualistic Cio toolbox: towards ambidexterity in the digital business transformation. In *Proceedings of the 17th Conferência da Associação Portuguesa de Sistemas de Informação, CAPSI'* (Guimarães), 23–41.

Bennett, W. L., & Segerberg, A. (2013). *The Logic of Connective Action: Digital Media and the Personalization of Contentious Politics*. Cambridge University Press. doi:10.1017/CBO9781139198752

Bergiel, J. B., Bergiel, E. B., & Balsmeier, P. W. (2008). Nature of virtual teams: A summary of their advantages and disadvantages. *Management Research News, 31*(2), 99–110. doi:10.1108/01409170810846821

Berman, S., & Korsten, P. (2014). Leading in the connected era. *Strategy and Leadership, 42*(1), 37–46. doi:10.1108/SL-10-2013-0078

Bjorn, P., & Ngwenyama, O. (2009). Virtual team collaboration: Building shared meaning, resolving breakdowns and creating translucence. *Information Systems Journal*, *19*(3), 227–253. doi:10.1111/j.1365-2575.2007.00281.x

Boe, O., & Torgersen, G. E. (2018). Norwegian "digital border defense" and competence for the unforeseen: A grounded theory approach. *Frontiers in Psychology*, *9*, 1–15. doi:10.3389/fpsyg.2018.00555 PMID:29725314

Bolden, R., & O'Regan, N. (2016). Digital disruption and the future of leadership: An interview with Rick Haythornthwaite, chairman of Centrica and MasterCard. *Journal of Management Inquiry*, *25*(4), 438–446. doi:10.1177/1056492616638173

Boyatzis, R. E. (2006). Using tipping points of emotional intelligence and cognitive competencies to predict financial performance of leaders. *Psicothema 18*, 124–131. https://www.redalyc.org/articulo.oa?id= 72709519

Boyatzis, R. E., Thiel, K., Rochford, K., & Black, A. (2017). Emotional and social intelligence competencies of incident team commanders fighting wildfires. *The Journal of Applied Behavioral Science*, *53*(4), 498–516. doi:10.1177/0021886317731575

Brown, M. E., Trevino, L. K., & Harrison, D. A. (2005). Ethical leadership: A social learning perspective for construct development and testing. *Organizational Behavior and Human Decision Processes*, *97*(2), 117–134. doi:10.1016/j.obhdp.2005.03.002

Burns, J. M. (1978). *Leadership*. Harper & Row.

Butcher, K., Power, M. J., & Orr, M. P. (2021). Museum Leadership for Engaging, Equitable Education: The Transformative Potential of Digitized Collections for Authentic Learning Experiences. *Curator (New York, N.Y.)*, *64*(2), 383–402. doi:10.1111/cura.12423

Bygstad, B., Aanby, H., & Iden, J. (2017). Leading digital transformation: the Scandinavian way. Lecture notes in Business Information Processing. In *Proceedings of the 8th Scandinavian Conference on Information Systems*, SCIS (Halden), 1–14.

Carte, T. A., Chidambaram, L., & Becker, A. (2006). Emergent leadership in self-managed virtual teams. *Group Decision and Negotiation*, *15*(4), 323–343. doi:10.100710726-006-9045-7

Cascio, W. F., & Montealegre, R. (2016). How technology is changing work and organizations. *Annual Review of Organizational Psychology and Organizational Behavior*, *3*(1), 349–375. doi:10.1146/annurev-orgpsych-041015-062352

Castells, M. (2012). *Networks of Outrage and Hope: Social Movements in the Internet Age*. Wiley-Blackwell.

Cortellazzo, L., Bruni, E., & Zampieri, R. (2019, August). The Role of Leadership in a Digitalized World: A Review. *Frontiers in Psychology*, *10*, 1–21. doi:10.3389/fpsyg.2019.01938 PMID:31507494

Coutu, D. L. (2000). Too old to learn? *Harvard Business Review*, *78*, 37–42. https://hbr.org/2000/11/too-old-to-learn PMID:11184976

Crossan, M. M., & Apaydin, M. (2010). A multi-dimensional framework of organizational innovation: A systematic review of the literature. *Journal of Management Studies*, *47*(6), 1154–1191. doi:10.1111/j.1467-6486.2009.00880.x

Davenport, T. H., & Harris, J. G. (2007). *Competing on Analytics: The New Science of Winning*. HBS Review Press.

David, Y., & Baden, C. (2018). Reframing community boundaries: The erosive power of new media spaces in authoritarian societies. *Information Communication and Society*. doi:10.1080/1369118X.2018.1486869

Denison, D. R., Hooijberg, R., & Quinn, R. E. (1995). Paradox and performance: Toward a theory of behavioral complexity in managerial leadership. *Organization Science*, *6*(5), 524–540. doi:10.1287/orsc.6.5.524

DeSanctis, G., & Poole, M. S. (1994). Capturing the complexity in advanced technology use: Adaptive structuration theory. *Organization Science*, *5*(2), 121–147. doi:10.1287/orsc.5.2.121

Diamante, T., & London, M. (2002). Expansive leadership in the age of digital technology. *Journal of Management Development*, *21*(6), 404–416. doi:10.1108/02621710210430597

Diaz-Saenz, H. R. (2011). In A. Bryman, D. Collinson, K. Grint, B. Jackson, & M. Uhl-Bien (Eds.), *"Transformational leadership," in The Sage Handbook of Leadership,* (pp. 299–310). Sage Publications Ltd.

Dimitrov, A. (2018). The digital age leadership: a transhumanistic perspective. In *Symposium: "Envisioning Future Leadership: Utopia, Dystopia, or More of the Same?"*, University of Phoenix. 10.1002/jls.21603

Ducheneaut, N., & Moore, R. J. (2005). More than just 'XP': Learning social skills in massively multiplayer online games. *Interactive Technology and Smart Education*, *2*(2), 89–100. doi:10.1108/17415650580000035

Ekechukwu, J., & Lammers, T. (2019). *Digital Technology to Enhance Project Leadership Practice: The Case of Civil Construction*. Digital Transformation in Business and Society.

Ensley, M. D., Hmieleski, K. M., & Pearce, C. L. (2006). The importance of vertical and shared leadership within new venture top management teams: implications for the performance of startups. *Leader. Q. 17*, 217–231. doi:10.1016/j.leaqua.2006.02.002

European Commission (2017). Attitudes Towards the Impact of Digitisation and Automation on Daily Life. 1–171.

Eyal, H. (2016). Digital fit as a leg-up for Nongovernmental Organizations' media and political success. *Political Communication*, *33*(1), 118–135. doi:10.1080/10584609.2015.1011294

Foerster, C., & Duchek, S. (2018). Leaders' resilience – A systematic literature review and future research agenda. In *Proceedings of the 78th Annual Meeting of the Academy of Management, AOM 2018*, Chicago, IL. 10.5465/AMBPP.2018.212

Gardner, W. L., Lowe, K. B., Moss, T. W., Mahoney, K. T., & Cogliser, C. C. (2010). Scholarly leadership of the study of leadership: A review of The leadership quarterly's second decade, 2000–2009. *The Leadership Quarterly*, *21*(6), 922–958. doi:10.1016/j.leaqua.2010.10.003

Garfield, E. (1979). In E. Garfield (Ed.), *"Citation indexing: its theory and application in science, technology, and humanities," in Mapping the Structure of Science,* (pp. 98–147). Wiley.

Garfield, E. (2004). Historiographic mapping of knowledge domains literature. *Journal of Information Science, 30*(2), 119–145. doi:10.1177/0165551504042802

Geoffrion, A. M. (2002). Progress in operations management. *Production and Operations Management, 11*(1), 92–100. doi:10.1111/j.1937-5956.2002.tb00186.x

Gerbaudo, P. (2017). Social media teams as digital vanguards: The question of leadership in the management of key Facebook and Twitter accounts of Occupy Wall Street, Indignados and UK Uncut. *Information Communication and Society, 20*(2), 185–202. doi:10.1080/1369118X.2016.1161817

Gerstner, C. R., & Day, D. V. (1997). Meta-analytic review of leader-member exchange theory: Correlates and construct issues. *The Journal of Applied Psychology, 82*(6), 827–844. doi:10.1037/0021-9010.82.6.827

Gerth, A. B., & Peppard, J. (2016). The dynamics of CIO derailment: How CIOs come undone and how to avoid it. *Business Horizons, 59*(1), 61–70. doi:10.1016/j.bushor.2015.09.001

Gheni, A. Y., Jusoh, Y. Y., Jabar, M. A., Ali, N. M., Abdullah, R. H., & Abdullah, S., (2016). The virtual teams: E-leaders challenges. In *Proceedings of the IEEE Conference on E-Learning, e-Management and e-Services*, Melaka, 38–42.

Goleman, D. (2000). Leadership that gets results. *Harvard Business Review, 78*, 78–90. https://hbr.org/2000/03/leadership-that-gets-results

Gordon, E. (2007). Mapping digital networks from cyberspace to Google. *Information Communication and Society, 10*, 885–901. doi:10.1080/13691180701751080

Graen, G. B., & Scandura, T. A. (1987). Toward a psychology of dyadic organizing. *Research in Organizational Behavior, 9*, 175–208.

Grafström, M., & Falkman, L. L. (2017). Everyday narratives: CEO rhetoric on Twitter. *Journal of Organizational Change Management, 30*(3), 312–322. doi:10.1108/JOCM-10-2016-0197

Grisoni, L., & Beeby, M. (2007). Leadership, gender and sense-making. *Gender, Work and Organization, 14*(3), 191–209. doi:10.1111/j.1468-0432.2007.00339.x

Gupta, S., & Pathak, G. S. (2018). Virtual team experiences in an emerging economy: A qualitative study. *Journal of Organizational Change Management, 31*(4), 778–794. doi:10.1108/JOCM-04-2017-0108

Haddud, A., & McAllen, D. (2018). Digital workplace management: exploring aspects related to culture, innovation, and leadership. In *Proceedings of the Portland International Conference on Management of Engineering and Technology, PICMET 2018*, Honolulu: HI, 1–6. 10.23919/PICMET.2018.8481807

Hambley, L. A., O'Neill, T. A., & Kline, T. J. B. (2007). Virtual team leadership: The effects of leadership style and communication medium on team interaction styles and outcomes. *Organizational Behavior and Human Decision Processes, 103*(1), 1–20. doi:10.1016/j.obhdp.2006.09.004

Harris, J. G., & Mehrotra, V. (2014). Getting value from your data scientists. *MIT Sloan Manage. Rev. 56*, 15–18. https://sloanreview.mit.edu/ article/getting-value-from-your-data-scientists/

Harvard Business Review Analytic Services. (2017). Operationalizing Digital Transformation: New Insights Into Making Digital Work. 1–12. https://hbr.org/sponsored/2017/05/operationalizing-digital-transformation-new-insights-into-making-digital-transformation-work

Heinz, U., Baga, T., Gebert, D., & Kearney, E. (2006). Leadership and cooperation as success factors in innovative R&D projects on electronic platforms. *Team Perform. Manage. Int. J.*, *12*(3/4), 66–76. doi:10.1108/13527590610674077

Henttonen, K., Pussinen, P., & Koivumäki, T. (2012). Managerial perspective on open source collaboration and networked innovation. *Journal of Technology Management & Innovation*, *7*(3), 135–147. doi:10.4067/S0718-27242012000300012

Hitt, D., & Tucker, P. D. (2016). Systematic review of key leader practices found to influence student achievement: A unified framework. *Review of Educational Research*, *86*(2), 531–569. doi:10.3102/0034654315614911

Hoch, J. E., & Kozlowski, S. W. J. (2014). Leading virtual teams: Hierarchical leadership, structural supports, and shared team leadership. *The Journal of Applied Psychology*, *99*(3), 390–403. doi:10.1037/a0030264 PMID:23205494

Hoegl, M., & Muethel, M. (2016). Enabling shared leadership in virtual project teams: A practitioners' guide. *Project Management Journal*, *47*(1), 7–12. doi:10.1002/pmj.21564

Horner-Long, P., & Schoenberg, R. (2002). Does e-business require different leadership characteristics? An empirical investigation. *European Management Journal*, *20*(6), 611–619. doi:10.1016/S0263-2373(02)00112-3

Huber, G. P. (1990). A theory of the effects of Advanced Information Technologies on organizational design, intelligence, and decision making. *Academy of Management Review*, *15*(1), 47–71. doi:10.2307/258105

Hughes, T. (2004). *Human-Built World: How to Think About Technology and Culture*. Chicago University Press. doi:10.7208/chicago/9780226120669.001.0001

Jawadi, N., Daassi, M., Favier, M., & Kalika, M. (2013). Relationship building in virtual teams: A leadership behavioral complexity perspective. *Human Systems Management*, *32*(3), 199–211. doi:10.3233/HSM-130791

Jones, M. (2017). E-leadership case study and the impact of (un)faithful appropriation of technology. In *Proceedings of the 5th International Conference on Management Leadership and Governance, ICMLG 2017,* Johannesburg, 191–199.

Kahai, S. S., & Avolio, B. J. (2006). Leadership style, anonymity, and the discussion of an ethical issue in an electronic context. *International Journal of e-Collaboration*, *2*(2), 1–26. doi:10.4018/jec.2006040101

Kahai, S. S., Sosik, J. J., & Avolio, B. J. (2013). Effects of transformational leadership and media on collaboration and performance in virtual teams. In *Leadership in Virtual Groups: Looking Back and Charting Paths Forward. Symposium Conducted at the Meetings of the Academy of Management*, N. S. Hill and N. M. Lorinkova, Eds, Orlando, FL.

Kidwell, R. E., & Sprague, R. (2009). Electronic surveillance in the global workplace: Laws, ethics, research, and practice. *New Technology, Work and Employment*, *24*(2), 194–208. doi:10.1111/j.1468-005X.2009.00228.x

Kirkland, R. (2014). Artificial Intelligence Meets the C-suite. McKinsey Quarterly. https://www.mckinsey.com/insights/strategy/artificial_ intelligence_meets_the_c-suite.

Kirkpatrick, S., & Locke, E. (1991). Leadership: Do traits matter? *The Academy of Management Perspectives*, *5*, 48–60. doi:10.5465/ame.1991.4274679

Kodama, M. (2007). Innovation through boundary management - A case study in reforms at Matsushita electric. *Technovation*, *27*, 15–29. doi:10.1016/j.technovation.2005.09.006

Kolb, A. Y., & Kolb, D. A. (2005). Learning styles and learning spaces: Enhancing experiential learning in higher education. *Academy of Management Learning & Education*, *4*(2), 193–212. doi:10.5465/amle.2005.17268566

Lee, F. L. F., & Man Chan, J. (2016). Digital media activities and mode of participation in a protest campaign: A study of the Umbrella Movement. *Information Communication and Society*, *19*(1), 4–22. doi:10.1080/1369118X.2015.1093530

Lee, M. R. (2009). E-ethical leadership for virtual project teams. *International Journal of Project Management*, *27*(5), 456–463. doi:10.1016/j.ijproman.2008.05.012

Lisk, T. C., Kaplancali, U. T., & Riggio, R. E. (2012). Leadership in multiplayer online gaming environments. *Simulation & Gaming*, *43*(1), 133–149. doi:10.1177/1046878110391975

Lopes, M. C., Fialho, F. A., Cunha, C. J., & Niveiros, S. I. (2013). Business games for leadership development: A systematic review. *Simulation & Gaming*, *44*(4), 523–543. doi:10.1177/1046878112471509

Lord, R., De Varder, C., & Alliger, G. (1986). A meta-analysis of the relation between personality traits and leadership perceptions: An application of validity generalization procedures. *The Journal of Applied Psychology*, *71*(3), 402–410. doi:10.1037/0021-9010.71.3.402

Lorenz, M., Rüßmann, M., Strack, R., Lueth, K. L., & Bolle, M. (2015). *Man and Machine in Industry 4.0. How Will Technology Transform the Industrial Workforce Through 2025?* The Boston Consulting Group.

Lu, L., Shen, C., and Williams, D. (2014). Friending your way up the ladder: connecting massive multiplayer online game behaviors with offline leadership. *Comput. Hum. Behav. 35*, 54–60. doi:.02.013 doi:10.1016/j.chb.2014

Lynn Pulley, M., & Sessa, V. I. (2001). E-leadership: Tackling complex challenges. *Industrial and Commercial Training*, *33*(6), 225–230. doi:10.1108/00197850110405379

Malhotra, A., Majchrzak, A., & Rosen, B. (2007). Leading virtual teams. *The Academy of Management Perspectives*, *21*(1), 60–70. doi:10.5465/amp.2007.24286164

Manz, C. C., & Sims, H. P. Jr. (1987). Leading workers to lead themselves: The external leadership of self-managing work teams. *Administrative Science Quarterly*, *32*(1), 106–129. doi:10.2307/2392745

McAfee, A., & Brynjolfsson, E. (2008). Investing in the IT that makes a competitive difference. *Harvard Business Rev. 86*, 98–107. https://hbr.org/2008/07/investing-in-the-it-that-makes-a-competitive difference

Morgareidge, D., Cai, H., & Jia, J. (2014). Performance-driven design with the support of digital tools: Applying discrete event simulation and space syntax on the design of the emergency department. *Frontiers of Architectural Research*, *3*(3), 250–264. doi:10.1016/j.foar.2014.04.006

Morris, A., & Staggenborg, S. (2004). In D. A. Snow, S. A. Soule, & H. Kriesi (Eds.), *"Leadership in social movements," in The Blackwell Companion to Social Movements,* (pp. 171–196). John Wiley & Sons.

Nohria, N., & Berkley, J. D. (1994). In C. Heckscher & A. Donnellon (Eds.), *"The virtual organization: bureaucracy, technology, and the implosion of control," in The Post-Bureaucratic Organization: New Perspectives on Organizational Change,* (pp. 108–128). Sage Publications Ltd.

O'Boyle, E. H. Jr, Banks, G. C., & Gonzalez-Mule, E. (2017). The Chrysalis effect: How ugly initial results metamorphosize into beautiful articles. *Journal of Management*, *43*(2), 376–399. doi:10.1177/0149206314527133

Obschonka, M., Fisch, C., & Boyd, R. (2017). Using digital footprints in entrepreneurship research: A Twitter-based personality analysis of superstar entrepreneurs and managers. *J. Business Venturing Insights*, *8*, 13–23. doi:10.1016/j.jbvi.2017.05.005

Orlikowski, W. J. (1992). The duality of technology: Rethinking the concept of technology in organizations. *Organization Science*, *34*(3), 398–427. doi:10.1287/orsc.3.3.398

Pearce, C. L. (2004). The future of leadership: Combining vertical and shared leadership to transform knowledge work. *The Academy of Management Executive*, *18*(1), 47–57. doi:10.5465/ame.2004.12690298

Pearce, C. L., Manz, C. C., & Sims, H. P. Jr. (2009). Where do we go from here? Is shared leadership the key to team success? *Organizational Dynamics*, *38*(3), 234–238. doi:10.1016/j.orgdyn.2009.04.008

Penney, J. (2017). Social media and citizen participation in "official" and "unofficial" electoral promotion: a structural analysis of the 2016 Bernie Sanders digital campaign. *J. Commun. 67,* 402–423. doi:. 12300 doi:10.1111/jcom

Pentland, A., & Choudhury, T. (2000). Face recognition for smart environments. *Computer*, *33*(2), 50–55. doi:10.1109/2.820039

Peteraf, M. A., Di Stefano, G., & Verona, G. (2013). The elephant in the room of dynamic capabilities: Bringing two diverging conversations together. *Strategic Management Journal*, *34*(12), 1389–1410. doi:10.1002mj.2078

Petrucci, T., & Rivera, M. (2018). Leading Growth through the Digital Leader. In *Symposium: "Envisioning Future Leadership: Utopia, Dystopia, or More of the Same?"*, Phoenix, AZ. 10.1002/jls.21595

Phoenix, A. Z., Druskat, V. U., & Wheeler, J. V. (2003). Managing from the boundary: The effective leadership of self-managing work teams. *Academy of Management Journal*, *46*(4), 435–457. doi:10.2307/30040637

Plowman, D. A., Solansky, S., Beck, T. E., Baker, L. K., Kulkarni, M., & Travis, D. V. (2007). The role of leadership in emergent, self-organization. *The Leadership Quarterly*, *18*(4), 341–356. doi:10.1016/j.leaqua.2007.04.004

Prince, K. A. (2017). Industrie 4.0 and Leadership. In *Proceedings of the 17th International Conference on Electronic Business, ICEB 2017,* Dubai, 132–139.

Purvanova, R. K., & Bono, J. E. (2009). Transformational leadership in context: Face-to-face and virtual teams. *The Leadership Quarterly*, *20*(3), 343–357. doi:10.1016/j.leaqua.2009.03.004

Rafaeli, A., Ravid, S., & Cheshin, A. (2009). Sensemaking in virtual teams: The impact of emotions and support tools on team mental models and team performance. *International Review of Industrial and Organizational Psychology*, *24*, 151–182. doi:10.1002/9780470745267.ch5

Richardson, J. W., & Sterrett, W. L. (2018). District technology leadership then and now: A comparative study of district technology leadership from 2001 to 2014. *Educational Administration Quarterly*, *54*(4), 589–616. doi:10.1177/0013161X18769046

Robin, B. R., McNeil, S. G., Cook, D. A., Agarwal, K. L., & Singhal, G. R. (2011). Preparing for the changing role of instructional technologies in medical education. *Academic Medicine*, *86*(4), 435–439. doi:10.1097/ACM.0b013e31820dbee4 PMID:21346506

Roman, A. V., Van Wart, M., Wang, X., Liu, C., Kim, S., & McCarthy, A. (2018). *Defining e-leadership as competence in ICT-mediated communications: An exploratory assessment.* Public Admin. Rev. doi:10.1111/puar.12980

Rosenbloom, R. S. (2000). Leadership, capabilities, and technological change: The transformation of NCR in the electronic era. *Strategic Management Journal*, *21*(10-11), 1083–1103. doi:10.1002/1097-0266(200010/11)21:10/11<1083::AID-SMJ127>3.0.CO;2-4

Salvetti, F., & Bertagni, B. (2020). Leadership 5.0: An Agile Mindset for a Digital Future. *International Journal of Advanced Corporate Learning*, *13*(2), 57–66. doi:10.3991/ijac.v13i2.17033

Schwarzmüller, T., Brosi, P., Duman, D., & Welpe, I. M. (2018). How does the digital transformation affect organizations? Key themes of change in work design and leadership. *Management Review*, *29*(2), 114–138. doi:10.5771/0935-9915-2018-2-114

Shachaf, P., & Hara, N. (2007). Behavioral complexity theory of media selection: A proposed theory for global virtual teams. *Journal of Information Science*, *33*(1), 63–75. doi:10.1177/0165551506068145

Sitrin, M. (2006). *Horizontalism: Voices of popular politics*. Cambridge University Press.

Sosik, J. J., Avolio, B. J., & Kahai, S. S. (1997). Effects of leadership style and anonymity on group potency and effectiveness in a group decision support system environment. *The Journal of Applied Psychology*, *82*(1), 89–103. doi:10.1037/0021-9010.82.1.89

Sosik, J. J., Kahai, S. S., & Avolio, B. J. (1998). Transformational leadership and dimensions of creativity: Motivating idea generation in computer-mediated groups. *Creativity Research Journal*, *11*(2), 111–121. doi:10.120715326934crj1102_3

Sousa, M. J., & Rocha, Á. (2018). Skills for disruptive digital business. *Journal of Business Research, 94*, 257–263. doi:10.1016/j.jbusres.2017.12.051

Stephens, K. K., & Rains, S. A. (2011). Information and Communication Technology sequences and message repetition in interpersonal interaction. *Communication Research, 38*(1), 101–122. doi:10.1177/0093650210362679

Stogdill, R. (1974). *Handbook of Leadership*. Free Press.

Stolze, A., Sailer, K., & Gillig, H. (2018). Entrepreneurial mindset as a driver for digital transformation - A novel educational approach form university-industry interactions. In *Proceedings of the 13th European Conference on Innovation & Entrepreneurship, ECIE 2018*, Aveiro, 806–813.

Strauss, A., & Corbin, J. (1998). *Basics of Qualitative Research.* Sage Publications Ltd.

Sullivan, S. D., Lungeanu, A., Dechurch, L. A., & Contractor, N. S. (2015). Space, time, and the development of shared leadership networks in multiteam systems. *Network Science, 3*(1), 124–155. doi:10.1017/nws.2015.7

Tannenbaum, R., & Schmidt, W. (1973). How to choose a leadership pattern. *Harvard Business Review, 51*, 162–180.

Toepfl, F. (2018). From connective to collective action: Internet elections as a digital tool to centralize and formalize protest in Russia. *Information Communication and Society, 21*(4), 531–547. doi:10.1080/1369118X.2017.1290127

Tsai, W. H. S., & Men, L. R. (2017). Social CEOs: The effects of CEOs' communication styles and parasocial interaction on social networking sites. *New Media & Society, 19*(11), 1848–1867. doi:10.1177/1461444816643922

Turing, A. M. (1950). Computing Machinery and Intelligence. *Mind, 49*(236), 433–460. doi:10.1093/mind/LIX.236.433

Van Outvorst, F., Visker, C., & De Waal, B. (2017). Digital leadership: the consequences of organizing and working in a digital society. In *Proceedings of the 5th International Conference On Management, Leadership & Governance, ICMLG 2017,* Johannesburg, 43–471.

Van Wart, M., Roman, A., Wang, X. H., & Liu, C. (2017). Integrating ICT adoption issues into (e-) leadership theory. *Telematics and Informatics, 34*(5), 527–537. doi:10.1016/j.tele.2016.11.003

Vidgen, R., Shaw, S., & Grant, D. B. (2017). Management challenges in creating value from business analytics. *European Journal of Operational Research, 261*(2), 626–639. doi:10.1016/j.ejor.2017.02.023

Wang, C. H., Liu, G. H. W., Lee, N. C. A., & Chen, K. J. (2018). On online engagement: Does the leadership style matter? In *Proceedings of the 18th International Conference on Electronic Business, ICEB*, Guilin, 430–438.

Weiner, J., Balijepally, V., & Tanniru, M. (2015). Integrating strategic and operational decision making using data-driven dashboards: The case of St. Joseph mercy Oakland hospital. *Journal of Healthcare Management, 60*, 319–330. doi:10.1097/00115514-201509000-00005

World Economic Forum. (in collaboration with Accenture) (2018). Digital Transformation Initiative - Unlocking $100 Trillion for Business and Society from Digital Transformation (Executive Summary), 1–71. https://reports.weforum.org/digital-transformation/wp-content/blogs. dir/94/mp/files/pages/files/dti-executive-summary-20180510.pdf

Zupic, I., & Cater, T. (2015). Bibliometric methods in management and organization. *Organizational Research Methods*, *18*, 429–447. doi:10.1177/1094428114562629

# Chapter 2
# Leadership Styles During the Digital Transformation Era

**Mohammed Al-Mannaei**
*Arabian Gulf University, Bahrain*

**Gardenia AlSaffar**
*Royal Bahrain Hospital, Bahrain*

**Ebtihaj Ahmed Al A'ali**
*University of Bahrain, Bahrain*

## ABSTRACT

*This chapter examines leadership styles during digital transformation and digital technologies in organizations. Such transformation and technologies have transfigured leadership and organizations. The various digital tools and applications have modified different aspects related to organisational functions and processes, leadership traits, actions, behaviours, and styles. Hence, cultures are to reform illustrating new values of openness and creativity. The research is based on qualitative methodology. In-depth interview is the method used to collect information from participants to this research. The conclusions of this research uphold the literature review in relation to the impacts of digital transformation and technologies on leadership styles, and on the cultural values.*

## INTRODUCTION

Digital transformation has spread across businesses. Digital technologies and transformation have initiated changes in Organizations. Such changes are related to leadership, employees, customers and all other stakeholders. This instigates changes in organizational culture. The cultural changes are assumed to enhance productivity, effectiveness and efficiency. This chapter consists of seven sections. The first section discusses the definition of leadership based on the literature of organizational behaviour. The second section then elaborates on theories related to organizational leadership. The definitions of digital transformation and technologies, are explored in section three. Definitions of leadership and theories

DOI: 10.4018/978-1-6684-5864-8.ch002

concerning leadership in digital era are investigated in section four. Section five presents the methodology employed in this research and analysis of collected information . Section six addresses the findings and conclusions of this chapter. Finally, section seven explores subjects for future researches.

## DEFINITION OF LEADERSHIP IN ORGANIZATIONS:

Leadership as a term was highlighted in 1700s (King, 1990). He adds that researches on leadership were started In the 20th century, He also expound that the definition of leadership varies. The variations reflect the perspectives through which the phenomenon of leadership is examined. This justifies the claim of Tosi and Jackson (1999) that there are more than 350 definitions of organizational leadership. Creto and Creto (2019) state the leadership aims to achieve influence. The influence is to motivate employees to accomplish visions, strategies and targets developed by leaders. Henderikx & Stoffers (2022) examine leadership and management in the organisations . They state that management is required to perform functions related to planning, decision making, organising and controlling. They also elaborate that leadership is needed to relate organizations to future. Their definition of leadership is argued to be in congruent to that of Creto and Creto (2019) stating that leadership is about creating influence .

The earlier definitions refer to the phenomenon of leadership in Organizations. Digital leadership refers to leaders working in the segment of digitalisation (Goethals et al., 2002). This research however investigates the impacts of digital transformation and technologies on leadership in Organizations rather than digital leadership.

## LEADERSHIP THEORIES

### Literature Review

Ebert & Griffin (2019) and Kinicki & Williams (2020) classify leadership theories based on their focus. Their classifications may insignificantly vary. This research however adopts Ebert and Griffin (2019) ‘ categorization as it is compatible to the classifications of leadership theories explored by Griffin & Moorhead, (2014); Creto & Creto (2019) ; and Kinicki & Williams (2020). Ebert & Griffin (2019) discuss three major perspectives of leadership theories based on their focuses.

The first is named universal Leadership theories. It consists of two sub types. The first type is the trait approach for leadership. The trait approach assumes that leaders possess physical, psychological and mental traits that non leaders do not have .

The second sub type is behavioural approach. This approach postulates that leaders exhibit two kinds of behaviours. The first is task-oriented behaviour. The task-oriented behaviour indicates that leaders focus on employees ‘ performance to achieve organizational targets. The second kind is employees-focus. The employee-focus implies that leaders motivate, attain well being and maintain satisfaction for employees.

The second perspective of leadership is called situational approach. Ebert & Griffin (2019) examine three kinds of theories in relation to the situational approach. The first kind is Path-Goals theory. The path-Goal theory states that a leader’ job is to make rewards desired by employees available in the organizations. A leader as well clarifies the paths for employees to achieve organizational goals. The second kind is Decision Tree Approach. The decision-tree approach assumes that specific characteristics of the situation decides the degree of employees' participation into the decision making. The degree of participation allowed determines the style of leadership followed. The third approach is Leader-Member Exchange Model. The model supposes that leaders develop different relationships with subordinates. Subordinates are grouped into two categories. The first is in- group. Members of in-group are close to the leadership. The second is out-group which members are not parts of the inner circle of the leaders. The third perspective discussed by Ebert & Griffin (2019) is viewing leadership through the eyes of followers. This perspective refers to transformational and charismatic leadership styles. Transformational leadership style is about dealing with changes. Leaders set the visions, develop the strategies to execute in order to accomplish the changes. Transactional leadership is about managing employees through providing desirable rewards . The effective leader is argued to follow both of these styles based on the requirements of the situations. The second perspective of examining leadership through the eyes of followers is charismatic leadership. Charisma of the leaders is the essence of this style. Leaders set high expectations for themselves and for their followers. They have confidence in their visions. Leaders as well inspire and emphasise their employees.

Ebert & Griffin (2019) mention another two styles of leadership. These are strategic and virtual leadership. Strategic leadership explains that a leader examines, understands and analyse the internal and external environments to develop the desirable strategies to achieve organizational vision. The virtual leadership is employed in Organizations using digital technologies. Leaders have to put efforts to develop relationships with subordinates. Words of appreciation and positive feedbacks in emails can partially assist in promoting effective leadership with employees.

The following section three elaborates on the definitions of digital transformation and technologies.

## Definition of Digital Transformation and Technology

Digital technology has prevailed in use since 1990. Digital transformation is not only concerned with the present organizational processes, it extends to all future practices as well. It is related to all internal and external organizational processes concerning employees, suppliers and customers. Digital transformation strategies aims to instigate changes in order to add values, to improve efficiency and to enhance innovation. Such transformation entails socio-technical programs (Larjovuori, Bordi & Heikkila-Tammi ;2018) . Digital transformation employs the use of computers, laptops, smartphones, social media, ICT information and communication technology. ICT connects audiovisual, telephone networks and computer networks. ICT users have access to information to store, transmit, comprehend, control and utilize information. (en.m. Wikipedia.org.). Larjovuori, Bordi and Heikkila-Tammi (2018) state that digitalisation is to employ digital technologies to transform business models to enhance effectiveness, efficiency and revenue. This to them (2018) leads to organizational changes assisting to achieve digital transformation.

There is no single acceptable definition for the digital workplace term. It varies based on the size of the organizations, business challenge and business requirements. The underlying assumptions for the definitions of digital workplace is that different stakeholders access to different digital tools in order to achieve organizational efficiency and effectiveness (khan; 2021). He states that organizations utilise different technologies to establish various platforms to enhance experiences of employees, customers and other stakeholders

## Definition of Leadership in Digital Era

This section presents the definition and theories of leadership in digital era. The presentation attempts to exhibit the remoulding of leadership styles in the digital transformation era. Leaders have to cope up with the large scale changes encountered due to the digitalisation. Sow & Aborbie (2018) explicate that leaders have to develop business strategies accommodating to technological, financial and human requirements. Leaders, according to them, have to espouse changes, to inspire and empower employees and to enhance creativity to implement successful digital transformation processes. This is compatible to the arguments of Larjovuri, Bordi & Heikkila-Tammi (2018) illustrating that recently a complexity leadership model has emerged based on modern leadership theories. The model is based on leaders' learning, adaptability and innovation to cope up with the requirements of digital transformation era.

In conclusion leaders, according to the earlier literature, are said to deal with changes confronted during digital transformation era.

## LEADERSHIP THEORIES CONCERNING DIGITAL TRANSFORMATION ERA

Cortellazzo, Bruni & Zampieri (2019) mention that studies concerning digital transformation and leadership are fragmented. This is due to the different disciplines contributing to such studies. They explain that the majority of the studies are based on empirical researches rather than theoretical . Digital transformation, according to them, lead to changing communication channels, speeding up decisions making processes, leading to structural modification, promoting networking with stakeholders, and improving competitiveness and team work .

Shafiq & Mujawar (2021) examine the leadership theories pertinent to the era of digital transformation. Their examination is compatible to the findings of Cortellazzo, Bruni and Zampieri (2019) stating that most of studies concerning digital transformation and leadership are empirical in nature. Shafiq & Mujawar (2021) discuss three major perspectives in relation to leadership during the digital transformation era. The first perspective is named value-based leadership. The value-based perspective is said to bring justice and integrity. This perspective reflects four styles of leaders. The first style is coherence leaders who develop coherent groups to achieve values and visions. The second style is based on trust through which the leaders acting as servants for the groups who accordingly unite themselves. The third style is the listening leaders who listen to views of groups members. Leaders then embrace what is good for their organisations and what is suitable for themselves. The last style is based on the respect through consulting rather than controlling the groups .

The second major perspective discussed by Shafiq and Mujawar (2021) is described as transformational. There are two sub styles in relation to this perspective. The first is transformational leadership which develops a vision and set strategies based on understandings of organizational situations. The visions and strategies developed are to accomplish changes needed. This sub type is examined by literature of organizational leadership discussed above. The transformational style according to Shafiq & Mujawar (2021), is based on four components. These components are influence, inspiration, intellectual intensive and consideration for individuals. The second style is transactional leadership which sets and operationalizes the achievement of organizational goals and targets. This is accomplished through motivating employees by making rewards desirable available. Leaders also state punishments for not achieving the targets. The transformational and transactional leadership are discussed above by Ebert and Griffin (2019) and Kinicki & Williams (2020).

The last perspective presented by Shafiq and Mujawar (2021) is Authentic leadership which is based on four qualities. Self awareness is the first quality. Leaders to connect with employees have to be self-aware to make the right decisions. The second quality is "relational transparency ". This quality means that leaders share their visions, affection and information with employees in order to build trust. The leaders who analyse information to make decisions are reflecting the third quality . This third quality is named balanced processing. The fourth quality assumes that leaders internalise their moral perspectives to underline values reflected in actions and goals.

Shafiq and Mujawar (2021) examine another three kinds of leadership. The first is described as being destructive leaders who through their actions jeopardise the existence of Organizations and promote negative effects on employees. The second is the charismatic leadership that develops visions and has high expectations in themselves and their employees. The charismatic style is discussed above in the literature review concerning organisational leadership. The last kind is democratic leadership that has positive impacts on the organizations due to the sharing decision processes with their employees.

Shafiq & Mujawar 's argument (2021) is compatible to Sow & Aborbie (2018) stating that no single leadership style is optimal for the digital transformation era. Leaders have to develop strategies based on collaboration. The leaders collaborate with employees in using resources. However it is argued that transformative leader can have positive impacts on employees ' motivation and creativity (Shafiq & Mujawar, 2021, and Sow Aborbie, 2018). Leaders, according to Sow & Aborbie (2018), have to create strong organisational culture which is based on change. They conclude their research by stating that leaders have to possess variety of characteristics to deal with digital transformation era such as emotion intelligence empowerment and motivation. Henderikx & Stoffers (2022) mention that most of literature concerning digital transformation and leadership focus on top managers. They argue that such literature call for top managers to follow strategic leadership approach. However their study (2022) examines middle managers ' roles during the digital transformation era. This explains that middle managers have to be digitally intelligent, to improve their soft skills and to enhance creativity.

Larjovuori, Bordi & Heikkila-Tammi (2018) scrutinise the focal points of leadership styles during digital transformation era. They mention that leadership is continuously interacting with business strategies, cultures, structures and organizational processes. They conclude their research by presenting elaboration on the focal points of leadership during digital transformation era. The first focal point is about developing strong vision related to the commitment to digitalisation. Goals based on such visions are specified and are communicated to employees. Commitment to digitalisation requires allocating financial resources for investment in digital technologies and human resources. The second focal point then focuses on cultural changes. The cultural changes instigate modifications of mind-set of leaders and employees in relation to organisational processes. The cultures during digital transformation have to be based on innovation, experimentation and risk taking, learning from failure and agile attitudes and actions. The third focal point is concerned with enabling. This leads to remould the relationships between leaders and employees. The traditional leadership styles, according to Larjovuori, Bordi & Heikkila-Tammi (2018), based on hierarchical organizations do not accommodate to the requirements of digital transformation era. Employees especially the young digital technologies natives have more expertise than their leaders. This entails leaders to change their roles and skills. They explicate that enablers are the new role for leaders during the digital transformation era. The enablers role includes the tasks of coaching and participation . The coaching task requires leaders to be supportive to their employees. Leaders as well have to motivate and empower their employees. This is to encourage the later to be autonomous and active. The task of participation however means that leaders utilize employees ' expertise. Leaders inspire employees to engage in the process of changes and to share responsibility. This creates the participation opportunities for employees especially the young digital technologies natives. The last focal point is leading networks. This point refers to two aspects of leadership functions. These two functions are customers orientation and partnership and collaboration. The digital technologies can assist leaders and organizations to identify needs and desires of customers. Developing friendly users digital systems allow customers to participate to improving products and services of the organizations. The digital systems as well enable business organizations to be customers oriented. The second function is partnerships and collaboration. Organizations to maintain their competitive edge have to seek partnerships with digital-focused businesses. Besides organizations collaborate with smaller businesses to provide them with some of the needed services and expertise. The collaboration necessitates leaders to acquire new thoughts and attitudes based on trust and openness.

The above literature illustrates that the styles of leadership change during the digital transformation era. Most of the literature reviewed argue that leaders follow strategic styles of leading ( Henderikx & Stoffers 2022; Larjovuori, Bordi & Heikkila-Tammi, 2018). Shafiq & Mujawar (2021) and Sow and Aborbie (2018) postulate though that transformational leadership can assist to motivate, inspire and encourage creativity by employees. Shafiq and Mujawar (2021) however elaborate that leadership styles are complex and there is no optimal leadership styles to be followed during the digital transformation era.

The following section presents the definition of organizational culture. The impacts of leadership in digital transformation era on culture then is addressed

## ORGANIZATIONAL CULTURE IN DIGITAL ERA

The earlier literature reviewed concerning leadership during the digital transformation era exhibits that organizational changes are becoming inevitable. Such changes lead to reform aspects related to leaders, employees' behaviours and organizational contexts as well. The changes then initiate modifications to organizational culture.

### Definition of Organizational Culture

Sow and Aborbie (2018) state that digital transformation can not be successfully accomplished without making drastic changes in organizational processes and culture. They add that the culture can be viewed as mechanisms to achieve organizational goals through enhancing organizational commitments. Ebert and Griffin (2019) and Knicks and Williams (2020) elaborate on the definition of organizational culture. The culture reflects norms, values, beliefs and experiences which differentiate organizations from each others (Ebert & Griffin, 2019; Kinicki & Williams, 2020).

### Impacts of Digital Transformation on Organizational Culture

The components of cultural changes during digital transformation era are mind-set of leaders and employees, emphasis on innovation, encouraging experimentation and risk taking, agile actions and processes (Larjovuori, Bordi & Heikkila-Tammi , 2018).

Khan (2021) illustrates that organizations to adapt to future workplace have to consider the continuous changes in technologies and employees' competency and new ways for employments. He contends that workplace of Organizations has changed and never be the same due to Covid-19. Employment will take different forms leading to transformation. There will be full time on site and full time remote employees. Human resources will follow hybrid strategies in relation to recruitment. He elaborates on methods to enable organizations to adapt to future. Such methods are as Investing in technologies, digital tools and human resources. Digital technologies facilitate employees' communication and collaboration. Different information and communication platforms can enhance experiences of employees

Moore 's (2020) analysis is compatible to khan (2021)' claim that the post Covid-19 period has accelerated the era of work place digitalisation. Moore (2020) states that organizations have to consider three intertwined future aspects resulting from employing digital technologies. The first aspect is concerned with automation of many of organizational processes including some of those of managers. He illustrates that managers in post COVID-19 era will focus on two functions. These functions are related to developing creative strategies and adopting people–centred approach of leadership. This is in congruent to the findings of Larjovuori, Bordi & Heikkila-Tammi (2018) claiming that leaders-employees relationships have changed as a result of relinquishing the traditional leadership styles based on organizational hierarchy. The second aspect is referring to digital dexterity. This implies that organizations have to continuously train employees to use new technologies. The third and last aspect states that hybrid workforce has become the norm. Organizations will rely on full time on job and full time remote employees.

Tech (2021) analysis is compatible as well to the discussions of Moore (2020) and Khan (2021) . Tech (2021) explains that there are three future trends for digital workplace. Two trends are similar to the discussions of Moore (2020) and Khan (2021) in relation to employment; hybrid working model and on demand employees collaborating virtually. The reliance on virtual collaboration allow for faster communication and making some jobs less needed in Organizations such as IT personnel as the later do not work on each computer individually. The third trend is referring to organizations moving to decentralisation. The third trend is in harmony with the Larjovuori, Bordi & Heikkila-Tammi (2018) affirming that traditional leadership styles based on organizational hierarchy have changed .

Institute for Management Development (2022) discusses 21 strategies to successfully accomplish digital transformation processes. The strategies are based on research conducted on chief executives' experiences in different organisations . Such strategies reflect the same cultural values stated above. The common themes underlying the strategies expressed by executives are focusing on the following:

The first focus is related to the roles of leadership in adopting, implementing and developing digital transformation and technologies. Leaders have major roles to develop and implement digital transformation processes. To do so, leaders have to diagnose the situations, to develop cohesive business strategies and action plans and to enact policies and procedures. The emphasis on the roles of leaders to developing business strategies are examined above by Henderikx & Stoffers (2022) and Moore (2021).

The second focus is concerned with leadership roles to internalize digital transformation through conducting more researches and experimentations. This requires establishing research and development teams. Khan (2021) urges organizations to continuously invest in new digital technologies to maintain their competitiveness.

The third focus is concerned with promoting and developing cultures which enhance innovation and creativity . Policies and procedures are set to initiate and to continue improving the cultural changes. Innovation and creativity requirements are findings stated earlier by Larjovuori Bordi & Heikkila-Tammi (2018); Sow & Aborbie (2018) and Moore (2020).

The fourth is focusing on the roles of employees to accept and to commit to the digital transformation processes. This is achieved by allowing employees to participate in the process of changes related to digital transformation. Open communication can enhance employees acceptance and commitment to digital transformation. Training is utmost important strategy for employees to benefit from digital transformation processes. The changing roles of employees are mentioned above by Shafiq & Mujawar (2021) and Sow & Aborbie (2018).

The fifth focus is to involve customers and clients in the processes of digital transformation. Friendly users technologies and digital systems can improve loyalty of customers and clients. Customers expressing their opinions on digital systems assist organizations to improving and to introducing new services and products. The roles of customers in digital transformation processes are highlighted earlier by Larjovuori, Bordi & Heikkila-Tammi (2018).

The sixth focus is for organizations to improve their cybersecurity of their businesses digital systems by frequently changing their passwords, fixing VPN to all organizational connections, and instituting Ad blockers to their networks.

Finally firms and businesses have to establish networks with digital-based organizations. Such networks facilitate exchanging knowledge and expertise to foster the processes of digital transformation. This is similar to the arguments of Larjovuori, Bordi & Heikkila-Tammi (2018) and Cortellazzo, Bruni & Zampieri (2019) in relation to the need for business organizations to develop collaboration and networks with digital-based firms.

In conclusion, leaders during digital transformation era have inculcated new values to succeed in the era of digitalisation. The new values are to Institute new talents, skills, attitudes and behaviours for leadership. Values aim to improve communication, motivating and inspiring employees, allowing to participation, encouraging experimentation and creativity and enhancing collaboration. These values foster leaders ' decision making processes as a consequence of changing organizational structure to be more decentralised. The same values reflect the changes related to leaders-employees relationships. The relationships during digital transformation era are based on trust that leaders assume and invest in their subordinates. The leadership becomes people- oriented (Sow & Aborbie, 2018; Larjovuori, Bordi & Heikkila-Tammi, 2018; Cortellazzo, Bruni & Zamieri, 2019; Shafiq & Mujawar, 2021; Henderikx & Stoffers, 2022; and IMD, 2022)

## METHODOLOGY

The chapter on hand utilizes qualitative methodology. This is due to the fact that the digital transformation and technologies issue is not fully investigated as mentioned above by the literature. Besides there is no research on leadership and digital transformation and technologies conducted in Bahrain. Qualitative methodology, according to Al A'Ali and Al-Sarraf (2016), is appropriate to employ for examining contemporary issues. Such methodology enables to seize, comprehend and shed light on meanings and perceptions of participants to research (Patton, 2002). Four chief executives were interviewed based on snowballing technique. No additional interviews were conducted once no new information was gathered. This chapter intends to develop understandings of leadership styles and models before and after implementation of digital transformation and technologies. It also examines the general impacts of leadership on organizational cultures during digital transformation era.

The research investigates the following issues:

1. The definition of leadership
2. Comparing leadership styles during before and after digital transformation era.
3. Impacts of leadership on organizational culture before and after the digital transformation eras.

The following is the analysis of the above questions:

## Analysis of the First Question Concerning the Definition of Leadership

Charisma according to the first Interviewee differentiates between a leader and a non leader. He adds that a leader is to have long term view about his/her organization. He/she has the abilities to design actions and strategies to reach that long term view. The leaders inspires and motivate employees to accomplish the strategies developed. The definition of leadership for this first interviewee is compatible to the charismatic leadership style discussed above be Ebert & Griffin (2019).

The second interviewee states that leadership is about time management . The leader before digital era focuses on planning, delegating work and enhancing employees' commitment. This is to enable leaders to develop visions and to implement organizational strategies for the different situations. The definition of the second interviewee is congruent to the definition of Henderikx & Stoffers (2022) stating that management and leadership are needed to accomplish organizational visions and strategies. Leaders however do not assume to know everything. They are life-time learners. The leaders according to the second interviewee, are still concerned with time management during digital transformation era. However some of their functions are performed better due to the availability of information at any time and at any place. Leaders also become free from routine tasks delegated virtually to employees or performed by technologies. Leadership style during digital transformation era is the same to the era before the digitalisation. Leaders still focus on the visions developing and related strategies to achieve organizational targets. The definition of this second interviewee revolves around the strategic leadership discussed earlier by Ebert & Griffin (2019) ; Creto & Creto (2019) and kinicki & Williams (2020).

The third interviewee explains that leadership is about making ordinary individuals to achieve extraordinary targets. This is done through setting visions and developing strategies, communicating targets based on visions and inspiring employees to implement. The leaders also are to communicate with all stakeholders. This is to improve commitment to the visions achievement. The definition of the third interviewee is congruent to strategic leadership style discussed by Shafiq and Mujawar (2021) and to the findings of research conducted by International Institute of Management (2022). The third interviewee states that leadership style is strategic but focusing on employees' participation during digital transformation era.

The fourth interviewee works for an international bank. He defines leadership in term of trust that should spread across the chain of command. This definition is examining leadership in the light of value-based perspective as explained above by Shafiq & Mujawar (2o21). The leaders are argued to have and to express trust in their followers. The later based on trust invested in them commit themselves to the achievement of organizational visions. The visions and strategies for the international bank, according to the fourth interviewee, are developed in the bank home land. This exhibits the variations between the earlier three definitions and the definition of the fourth interviewee in relation to leadership.

In conclusion leaders are defined in term of charismatic, strategic and value-based perspectives during before and after digital transformation era. The following question compare leadership styles for before and after the digital transformation era.

## Analysis of Collected Information for Question Two: Comparison of Leadership Styles During Before and After Digital Transformation Era

The first interviewee defines digital transformation as the contemporary tools helping organisations to render services and products (Khan, 2021). Such technologies can facilitate and can improve the services and products provided locally, regionally and internationally. The interviewee adds that the essence of leadership remains the same for before and after the digital transformation. Charisma and visions are the required essences for effective leadership. However the interviewee elaborates that digital transformation and technologies can enable the leaders to lead better. The leading better is due to two factors. The first factor is attributed to time safe. Meeting can be conducted on different organizational platforms. The virtual meetings can reduce travel cost and physical commuting. The second factor is related to the availability of information at any point of time and at any place. This can foster and improve decision making processes. Leaders according to this interviewee, can have more time to focus on innovations as a result of reducing time on physical interactions with employees. The later are delegated assignments through different organizational platforms . This is compatible to Moore 's (2020) and Larjovuori, Bordi & Heikkila-Tammi (2018) arguments that digital technologies and transformation lead to social and technical changes. Digital transformation according to the first interviewee, free managers from some routine works and hence allowing them to focus more on strategies. The leadership style however, according to the interviewee, is the same during the eras before and after digital transformation. It is as mentioned above that leaders follow the charismatic leadership style focusing on developing visions and strategies to achieve digital transformation. The first interviewee defines leadership in term of charismatic leadership styles as explained by Shafiq & Mujawar (2021) and Ebert and Griffin (2019).

The second interviewee contends that time management, the essence of leadership, has been transformed with the introduction of digital technologies. The availability of information at any time and at any place due to digital technologies has improved the performance of leadership. Meetings of leaders can be done virtually with out the need to commute and to collect and carry information. This enhances leadership efficiency through cost reduction as a result of eliminating cost of commuting (Khan, 2021). This as well improves productivity as a consequence of reinforcing decision making processes. Leaders in digital era have more time to strategize their work due to virtually delegating work and communication . Strategic management style, according to the second interviewee, is followed by leadership during before and after the digital era. This is congruent to the findings of Henderikx &Stoffers (2022), Larjovuori, Bordi & Heikkila-Tammi (2018) and the IMD research (2022).

The third interviewee explains that digital technologies and digital transformation have changed leadership. He adds that the major traits of leadership are humbleness and credibility remain the same and valid for the before and after digital transformation eras. However the introduction of digital technologies alters the relationships between leaders and employees. Tasks of employees are assigned virtually. Leaders delegate tasks on different organizational platforms. Leaders during digital transformation era become people oriented to make sure that employees understand and commit themselves to the visions and strategies developed . This is in harmony with Moore 's (2020) arguments stating that leaders-members relationships have changed as a result of digitalisation. This is unlike the product-oriented actions and behaviours of leaders exhibited during the before digital transformation era (Larjovuori, Bordi & Heikkila-Tammi ; 2018). The digital era through availability of information at any time makes leaders have more holistic and comprehensive view of the different situations. Leaders therefore travel between the holistic and detailed perspectives in relation to organizational activities. To the interviewee however the leadership style before and after digital transformation and technologies is the same. Leaders follow strategic style but emphasising democratic attitude relying on the decentralised attributes of situations (IMD, 2022, and Shafiq & Mujawar (2021) . Leaders are more agile in the era of digital technologies. They also allow reversed mentorship to follow. Young technology natives act as mentors for older employees. The reversed mentorship claim of the third interviewee is compatible to the findings of Larjovuori, Bordi & Heikkila-Tammi (2018) mentioning that young technology natives should participate to spread knowledge and expertise.

The fourth interviewee who works for an international bank defines leadership in term of trust. Such trust is a major trait for before and after digital transformation era. The interviewee expounds that decision making processes are slower for leaders before the era of digital technologies. This is due to the time required to collect and to analyse information. Digital technologies and transformation however, foster decision making processes due to the availability of information at any time and at any place. The digital transformation and technologies, according to the fourth interviewee, transform leadership behaviour. He claims that the boss-centre approach followed by leaders before digital era has changed. This is in harmony with findings of Moore (2020) and Larjovuori, Bordi & Heikkila-Tammi (2018) explaining that leaders- members relationships are becoming more people-oriented in the digital era. The introduction of digital technologies instigates participation of employees through digital mechanisms. Leadership in the digital transformation era therefore, is argued to reflect participative attitude based on trust invested in the employees as stated above . This is in agreement with the value-based style of leadership that attempts to unite the organizations as discussed above by Shafiq and Mujawar (2021).

The first interviewee claims that charismatic leadership style is followed by leaders during the before and after digital transformation eras. However this interviewee highlights the importance of visions and strategies development. The second and third interviewees argue that leaders follow strategic leadership styles during before and after digital transformation era. This finding is compatible to the conclusions of Henderikx & Stoffers(2022) ; Larjovuori, Bordi & Heikkila-Tammi (2018) and IMD research (2022) stating that leaders during digital transformation era follow strategic style of leadership. The third interviewee however accentuates the democratic attitude of strategic leadership. This allows employees to participate in the decision making processes. The fourth interviewee then contends that the leadership style followed in digital transformation era is found on value-based perspective. The value-based perspective reflects trust invested in the employees.

## Analysis of Collected Information for Question Three: Impacts of Leadership on Organizational Culture During Before and After The Digital Era

The first interviewee states that culture refers to values underpinning employees' behaviours and shaping organizational structure. This is in harmony with the definition of culture stated by Kinicki and Williams (2020) . The interviewee adds that the digital transformation and technologies have impacts on organisational culture . He explains that the digital transformation and technologies help to develop a holistic culture . Such transformation and technologies bring values, experiences, structure and organizational laws together. This is in congruent with the arguments of Larjovuori, Bordi & Heikkila-Tammi (2018) claiming that digitalisation lead to changes related to all organisational aspects. Organizational culture, according to the first interviewee, was based on elementalistic perspective for the era before digital transformation. This is to say that different professionals representing different working groups in the same organisation developed partial views in relation the definition of culture. The partial views reflect different assumptions of organizations held by those professionals. The first interviewee explains that the holistic view of culture promoted during digital transformation era can improve communication and can enhance quality of interactions between employees in the bank. It also assists to boost innovation. The bank hierarchy , according the first interviewee, will be less tightened however it will not change to be decentralized. This first interviewee defines leadership in term of charismatic theory as explained by Shafiq & Mujawar (2021). The interviewee elaborates on advantages of employing digital technologies. The advantages of digital transformation and technologies, according to the first interviewee, are availability of information at any time and at any place, virtual meetings, speeding up decisions making and freeing top management from daily routines through virtual delegations. The virtual delegation hence can enhance creativity of leaders. The discussion of the first interviewee is consistent with the findings of Larjovuori, Bordi, Heikkila-Tammi (2018) and IMD (2022) in relation to organizational culture during digital transformation as mentioned above.

The second interviewee defines organizational culture in term of behaviours exhibited by members of a given organizations. This definition is consistent with the definition of culture stated by Ebert &Griffin (2019). The second interviewee states that behaviour in organizations is classified as two types. The first type refers to the behaviour acquired from an individual 'personal life. It is described as artistic by the first interviewee. The second type can be classified as scientific behaviour. This behaviour can be learned by individuals through working in organizations. The interviewee elaborates that artistic type may change to be scientific behaviour after acquiring more experiences in the organizations. Organizational culture is not static. It changes as result of external and internal factors. Digital technologies lead to change behaviour due to the development of virtual relationships among individuals in organizations (kinicki & William, 2020). Digital transformation according to the second interviewee, speeds up decisions making processes, improves communication and enhance productivity, efficiency and effectiveness. This is in congruent with Khan 'analysis (2021) concerning perspectives of future workplace.

The third and the fourth interviewees seem to agree that culture represents values of Organizations. Values refer to identity of the organizations and also shape human behaviour. Culture according to these two interviewees, is about how things are done in the organizations before the digital era. Their definition is compatible to the definitions of culture stated by Larjovuori, Bordi & Heikkila-Tammi (2018); Ebert & Griffin (2019); and Kinicki & Williams (2020). The third interviewee adds however that digital era has instigated the evolution of paradigm shift in relation to the meaning of culture. Culture in digital era is about innovation and simplification of organizational processes. Leaders are more agile in the era of digital technologies. They also allow reversed mentorship to follow. Young technology natives act as mentors for older employees. This is highlighted by the arguments Larjovuori, Bordi & Heikkila-Tammi (2018) . They (2018) expands that young technology natives have expertise that older generation lack.

The fourth interviewee differs than the third one in relation to the impacts of digital transformation on organizational culture. He explicates such impacts by stating that the bank followed a centralized approach of management before the digital transformation era. Leaders followed top-down communication. This made organizations to be centralized based on formal hierarchy. The digital technologies and transformation spread information all through the bank encouraging employees to participate in decision-making processes. The fourth interviewee expounds that the digital era changes the bank to be decentralized-like in term of culture and not changing the structure itself. The attributes of decentralized-like culture of digital era enhances communication, fosters decisions making, boosts innovation, improves collaboration and exchanging knowledge and expertise and leaders become people-oriented (Larjovuori, Bordi & Heikkila-Tammi, 2018; and Tech, 2021).

The above analysis exhibits that the definitions of culture according to interviewees are consistent with definitions of culture stated by the literature review. Besides interviewees' elaborations on the impacts of digital technologies and transformation on organizational culture seem to be in harmony with the literature reviewed stated above. However, the issue of changing the structure to be decentralized, mentioned by the literature, is not acknowledged by the interviewees. The attributes of decentralized culture is only mentioned by the Chief Executive of international Bank.

## CONCLUSION

This chapter investigates the issues of digital transformation and technologies and their impacts on leadership styles. The impacts of leadership during digital transformation and technologies on organisational culture are examined as well . Researches and studies on the issues of digital transformation and leadership are fragmented . This is due to the various disciplines such researches and studies are based on as stated above. The majority of researches and studies are empirical in nature based on organizational leadership theories. A few studies and researches conclude that there is no optimal leadership style for the digital transformation era. However, some of researches and studies argue that transformation leadership can facilitate the successful implementation of digital transformation processes. Strategic leadership are mentioned by many studies and researches as the required style to accomplish the processes of changes resulting from digital transformation era. Strategic leadership can set the new visions, develop the strategies. enact technological and human resources 's procedures and policies. These, according to literature reviewed, can motivate and enhance commitments of employees, improve efficiency and effectiveness, and encourage participation and collaboration among all members of the organizations. The first interviewee states that charismatic leadership style focusing on strategic orientation is suitable for the before and after digital transformation era. The second and third interviewees argue that strategic leadership is the desirable style to follow during digital transformation era. The fourth interviewee claims that digital transformation requires the value-based style of leadership. This is based on trait of trust which the fourth interviewee Invests in employees. This interviewee develops values of decentralised culture. Finally interviewees express cultural values related to digital transformation era. The cultural values expressed by interviewees are related to improving communication, fostering decision-making processes, motivating employees, encouraging participation, nurturing collaboration and espousing innovation. The values expressed are compatible to those examined by literature discussed earlier.

### Suggested Future Research

This chapter is an exploratory in nature. There is a need to examine the issues of leadership and its Impacts on organizational culture during digital transformation era from different angles. The suggested future researches are as follows:

- This chapter is based on studying opinions of Chief executives in services sector; i.e banking. Applying similar research on different types of industries may shed more light on the issues related to the leadership styles during digital transformation era.
- The chapter on hand is empirical in nature. There may be a need to investigate the issue of leadership during digital transformation era in depth. The in depth investigation can lead to develop

different theory or modify the existing perspectives in relation to leadership during digital transformation era.

- The work on hand is based on qualitative methodology. Replicating similar research employing quantitative methodology might lead to different findings and conclusions.
- The literature concerning leadership during the digital transformation era highlights the importance of networked organizations. This has to be scrutinized and to be probed in order to promote holistic understandings of the issue of leadership during the digital transformation era.
- The literature reviewed above illustrates the significant roles of employees in the implementation of digital transformation processes. This calls for conducting research on such roles to grasp their contribution.
- Finally the impacts of leadership styles during digital era on organizational culture have to be thoroughly investigated to develop better understandings of actions, behaviours and attitudes of all organizational members.

## REFERENCES


Al A'Ali, E. (2020). The Role of Auditing Firms in Promoting Ethical Consumerism. In *Ethical Consumerism and Comparative Studies Across Different Cultures,* (pp. 39–52). IGI GLOBAL. doi:10.4018/978-1-7998-0272-3.ch004

Al A'ali, E., & Al-Sarraf, A. R. (2016). Ethical Consumerism: Contextual Issues Of Ethical Decision-making Processes: An Exploratory Study. In Ethical and Social Perspectives on Global Business interaction in Emerging Markets, (pp.133-149). IGI Global

Broadbelt, G. (2016) *Leadership in the Digital Age.* Impact. https://www.impactinternational.com/blog/2016/02/leadership-digital-age

Cooper, D. R., & Schindler, P. S. (2008). *Business Research Methods,* (10th ed.). McGraw Hill.

Cortellazzo, L. Bruni, E. & Zampieri, R. (2019). The Role of Leadership in a Digitalized world: A Review. *Frontiers in psychology, 10,* 1938. doi:10.3389/fpsyg.2019.1938

Creto, S. C., & Creto, S. T. (2019) Modern Management; concepts and skills (global edition). UK. Pearson Education limited.

Ebert, R. J., & Griffin, R. W. (2019) Business essential. New York, NY. Pearson.

Goethals, G. R., Sorenson, G., & MacGreger Burns, J. (2002). Leadership in the Digital Ag. Wilson III, Ernest J. " Scholarship and 17 Practice in the Transactions to Knowledge Society. *Items, 2002*(Spring/Summer), 1–44.

Griffin, R. W. & Moorhead, G. (2014) *Organizational Behavior.* Boston, MA, Cengage learning

Henderikx, M., & Stoffers, J. (2022). An Exploratory Literature Study into Digital Transformation and Leadership: Tiward Future-Proof Middle Managers. *Sustainability, 14*(2), 687. https://DOI.org/10.3390/su14020687. doi:10.3390u14020687

IMD. (2022, September 27). *Top 21 Digital Transformation Strategies (part 1)*. IMD business school for management and leadership courses. https://www.imd.org/imd-reflections/digital-programs-reflections/digital-transformation-strategies/

King, A. S. (1990). *Evolution of Leadership Theory*. http.//journals.sagepub.com/doi/pdf/10.1177/0256090919900205

Kinicki, A., & Williams, B. K. (2020). *Management* (9th ed.). McGraw-Hill Education.

Larjovuori, R.-L., Bordi, L., & Heikkila-Tammi, K. (2018). in *Proceeding of the 22nd International Academic Mindtrek*. 10.1145/3275116.3275122

Mouhamadou Sow & Solomon Aborbie. (2018) Impact of Leadership on Digital Transformation. In Macrothink Institute, Business and Economic Research, 8(3), (pp.139-148).

Patton, M. Q. (2002). *Qualitative Research & Evaluation Methods*. California, USA. Sage publication

Shafiq, M., & Mujawar, S. B. S. (2021). Influence Of Digitalization On Leadership: The Case Of Sandvik In Sweden [Thesis]. University of Gavle.

Sow, M., & Aborbie, S. (2018). Impact of Leadership on Digital Transformation, Macrothink Institute. *Business and Economic Review*, *8*(3), 138–148.

Tosi, D., & Jackson, S. F. (1999). Influencing Others yo Act in Harold D. Stolovitech and Erica, J.Keeps (eds) Handbook of Human Performance and Technology.San Francisco: International Society fir performance improvement

Wikimedia Foundation. (2022, October 7). *Information and Communications Technology*. Wikipedia. https://en.wikipedia.org/wiki/Information_and_communications_technology https://en.wikipedia.org/wiki/Digital_transformation

# Chapter 3
# The Impact of Digital Transformation on Relationships Between Leadership and Stakeholders

**Ebtihaj Al A'ali**
*University of Bahrain, Bahrain*

**Ralla Alazali**
*University of Bahrain, Bahrain*

**Mohammed Al-Mannaei**
*Arabian Gulf University, Bahrain*

## ABSTRACT

*The chapter attempts to investigate the impacts of leadership styles during digital transformation era on stakeholders. The styles employed by leaders affect stakeholders. It focuses on examining leaders' perceptions of digitalization and its impacts on stakeholders. Leaders, boards of directors and shareholders, employees, customers, and regulators are the major subjects for investigation. Qualitative research is employed for the contemporary nature of the topic being studied. Open-ended interviews are the research method. Chief executives of banks representing services sector are the participants to this research.*

## INTRODUCTION

The chapter elaborates on the impact of digital transformation and technologies on organizations. Two main aspects are examined; the leadership roles and stakeholders. The second section of the chapter define digital transformation, its tools, and impact. That is followed by leadership definition and styles. The fourth section discusses stakeholder definition and ranks. The fifth section highlights the impact of

DOI: 10.4018/978-1-6684-5864-8.ch003

digital transformation on leadership and stakeholders. The methodology, analysis, and interpretation of the study collected information are discussed in the following sections. Finally, the chapter conclusion and future suggested researches are stated.

## DIGITAL TRANSFORMATION DEFINITION AND TOOLS

Technology is one of the significant factors that influences changes in the business world. Companies are transformed because of the new technologies. Organizations from different industries and various sizes need digital transformation (Mahraz, Benabbou, & Berrado, 2019). This section presents the meaning of digital transformation. In their study of the literature, Morakanyane, Grace, and O'Reilly (2017) claim that there is no agreement on the definition of technology. They contend that researchers define technology (digital) transformation as a strategy, process, business model, or paradigm shift. Thus, digital transformation is not only concerned with the present organizational processes, but it also extends to all future practices. It is related to all internal and external organizational processes of employees, suppliers, and customers.

Digital transformation strategies aim to instigate changes to add values, to improve efficiency and to enhance innovation. Consequently, technology has significant impact on various aspects in organizations (Morakanyane, Grace, & O'Reilly, 2017). The underlying assumptions for the definitions of digital workplace is that employee's access to different digital tools to accomplish their work in a virtual manner (Sambandam, 2021). Khan (2021) states that organizations utilize different technologies to establish various platforms to enhance experiences of employees.

Herman (2022) claims that organizations need to employ different tools for digital transformation to be successful. He adds that the tools facilitate companies' goals by achieving various advantages that improve company's management, communication, and collaboration with different stakeholders. There are many tools that are available in the market, however the tools used by the company depend on organizational needs and goals. The four main trends in digital transformation are big data, cloud computing, the internet of things, and blockchain (Mahraz, Benabbou, & Berrado, 2019).

### Positive and Negative Impacts of Digital Transformation

Rogers (2016) highlights five main domains of companies' strategies that are changed by technology, they are:

1. Customers: connection and interaction with customers become easier and more frequent.
2. Competition: increase competition between businesses (even from different industries) and motivate cooperation between rivals.
3. Data: easy and open access to data with better tools for analysis.
4. Innovation: create different approaches to innovation that is based on learning through fast experimentation.
5. Value: technology encourages companies to constantly evolve by extending or improving their products and services for their customers.

Dahlström, Desmet, and Singer (2017) argue that there are three major decisions to make to accomplish digital transformation. Decisions are related to developing future vision, leaders committed to digitalization and understanding stakeholders needs. They also add that companies must invest in human, financial, and technological capital to deal with digital transformation.

Digital transformation affects life in various ways. Cortellazzo, Bruni, and Zampieri (2019) state that organizations in different sectors and sizes are becoming digital workplaces. A survey conducted in Europe illustrated that respondents' belief in digitization positive impact on economy (European Commission, 2017). Therefore, it can be predicted that digital transformation has a positive impact on organizations that leads to improve economy. Mahraz, Benabbou, and Berrado (2019) expound that digital transformation open new opportunities for companies. They argue that it adds to company's growth, develop competitive advantages, simplifying operations, and eventually increasing their profitability. However, despite the positive impact of digital transformation, there are negative consequences. For example, increasing costs for developing employee's technological skills, changing the organization structure, and applying new methods for employee's recruitment process (Cortellazzo, Bruni, & Zampieri, 2019).

## LEADERSHIP DEFINITIONS AND STYLES

This section discusses the definitions of leadership and the leadership styles related to digital transformation era.

### Leadership Definition

Leadership is one of the important cornerstones for organizations' success. Organizations can achieve their goals by selecting the most effective leadership styles at different situations (Al-Aali & Alazali, 2022). It is claimed that there is no single definition of leadership (Gill, 2011; Klingborg, Moore, & Varea-Hammond, 2006; Silva, 2016). Klingborg, Moore, and Varea-Hammond, (2006) notice a reusing of ''Great Man''. Silva (2016; p. 3) defines leadership as "the process of interactive influence that occurs when, in a given context, some people accept someone as their leader to achieve common goals". It can be argued that the role of leaders is not only to achieve organizational goals, but also to enable their organizations to deal with present challenges (Jones & George, 2022).

Today, one of the many challenges that leaders are facing is related to the existence of technology. Cortellazzo, Bruni, and Zampieri (2019) explicate that leaders deal with changes in work enivronment and processes as a result of digitazliation. Therefore, it is vital for leaders to create a leadership strategy that helps to deal with changes successfully and over a long period of time (Sow & Aborbie, 2018). Jones and George (2022) illustrate that despite of technology challenge, leaders need to utilize it to improve their organization's performance.

### Leadership Styles

Many leadership styles have been discussed in the literature. However, this chapter focuses on contemporary leadership styles as it is more related to technology. This section briefly highlights transactional, transformational, charismatic, participative and strategic leadership styles. Transactional leadership is a leader-follower exchange relationship in which followers are rewarded when they meet leaders' goals. In contrast, the transformational leaders create a shared vision, inspire their followers, motivate them, believe in their abilities, and understand their unique needs (Bass, 1999). Charismatic leaders transform followers' self-interests "needs, values, preferences, desires and aspirations" to collective interests (House & Howell, 1992, p. 82). The similar is stated by Kinicki & Williams (2020). Participative leadership style, according to Ebert and Griffin (2019), is based on empowering employees to contribute to decision making processes. The empowerment reflects trust of leaders invest in their employees. The trust invested boosts employees' commitment, engagement and satisfaction. Finally, strategic leaders set directions, apply the company strategy, align people with the company strategy, encourage employees' involvement, and enhance their capabilities (Ebert & Griffin, 2019; Davis, 2004).

## STAKEHOLDERS' DEFINITION AND RANKS

This section examines the definitions of stakeholders. Literature related to ranks of stakeholders based on importance is reviewed.

### Definition of Stakeholders

Stakeholders are "individuals, groups, and other entities that affect, or are affected by, the organization's objectives and actions" (McShane & Glinow, 2021, p. 9). Benn, Abratt, and O'Leary (2016) claim that there is an agreement on stakeholders' identification. The stakeholder theory was introduced in the 1980s (Mainardes, Alves, & Raposo, 2012), however, the development of the theory and its spreading across different disciplines lead to change in the definition (Miles, 2017). Stakeholders are defined as people and groups inside and outside the organization who are affecting and/or effected by the organization actions. Miles (2017) declares that stakeholders have both positive and negative impacts on the organization. Some of these stakeholders may have a clear and direct relationship with the company, while the others are not.

### Stakeholders' Ranks

Filho, Penha, and Silva, (2021) classify stakeholders as internal and external. Alternatively, stakeholders can be divided into two groups primary and secondary (Benn, Abratt, & O'Leary, 2016). This supports Mainardes, Alves, and Raposo (2012) claim that there is a diverse group of stakeholders that interact with the organization. They provide a broader classification of stakeholders' groups. The stakeholders' groups are regulatory, dependent, controller, passive, partner, and non-stakeholder. Furthermore, McShane and Glinow (2021) assert that organizations' effectiveness is related to stakeholders' satisfaction. Thus, regardless of stakeholders' classification, definition, or identification they are always related to the organization. Employees, customers, partners, providers of technologies, networks of organizations using similar technologies, and first movers setting the benchmarks related to technology are all stakeholders. Shareholders, employees, customers, suppliers, and government entities are known as primary stakeholders (Benn, Abratt, & O'Leary, 2016). There is no one valid ranking of stakeholders, as it differs from one company to the other. The importance of stakeholders depends on power, legitimacy, and urgency to the organization concerned (Mainardes, Alves, & Raposo, 2012).

This chapter examines the effects of the digital technologies on leadership and stakeholders in organizations. Leaders, shareholders and Board of Directors, employees, customers, and regulators are investigated.

## Impacts of Digital Transformation on Leadership and Stakeholders

Technology is one of the important external factors that affects organizations. Companies and organizations must deal with technological changes introduced in their industry to survive and to thrive. This leads to changes in these organizations to accommodating to the requirements of new technologies. As discussed above, digital transformation has both positive and negative impacts on organizations. Stakeholders are influenced by this transformation. This section highlights the impacts of digital technologies on different on stakeholders being studied

### Leaders

Employing new technologies in the organization is not easy. Leaders need to study this option carefully. The cost of technology change is enormous, that include money, time, and effort. Chief Executive Officers are facing a hard decision from choosing to introduce the new technology to how to implement it successfully (Dahlström, Desmet, & Singer, 2017). The authors propose four phases to ensure digital transformation success: (1) the value of transformation, (2) the targeted customers, (3) the ecosystem changes, and (4) the transformation de-risking. Additionally, Albukhitan (2020) suggests a guideline for leaders to adopt digital transformation development strategy that includes the following steps:

(a) the creation of digital transformation vision and objectives;
(b) assess the organization' s capabilities for the adoption;
(c) design end user experience;
(d) review and select the suitable solution and vendor;
(e) establish the roadmap for implementation; and
(f) make any necessary adjustments to organization culture and infrastructure.

There is another important point to be considered by leaders during digital transformation that is attracting and employing the right human capital to effectively handle the transformation. Gilch and Sieweke (2020) argue that dexterity in digital technologies is a requirement for successful implementation of transformation. The authors add that recruiters (leaders) need to change the organization recruitment measures and processes reflecting changes in their mindset.

Ivancic, Vuksic, and Spremic (2019) state that every organization has its unique strategy and vision and need to develop a knowledge-sharing culture. There is an agreement that changes are prerequisite for digital transformation in organizations. Leaders are the main engine for change is organization. Therefore, it is vital for organizations to apply an appropriate leadership style that facilitates implementation of digital transformation (Sow & Aborbie, 2018). The effective leadership style depends on time, place, need, and circumstances of a given organization (Klingborg, Moore, & Varea-Hammond, 2006). Khan, Nawaz, and Khan (2016) assert that there are two main styles of leadership transactional and transformational. They state that creating a vision, long-term goals, system alignment and change, and followers training and development are the emphasis of transformational leaders. Holten and Brenner (2015) find that transformational leaders provide positive impact on followers' acceptance to change. They argue that transformational leader set a good example for employees by inspiring them, developing shared vision, and empowering their creativity. However, Sow and Aborbie (2018) conclude that there is no specific leadership style that impact the implementation of digital transformation. They realize that limited technical knowledge, partial scope of change, and poor alignment between change strategy and organizational culture are the factors that influence digital transformation. Brunetti, et al. (2020) recommend leaders to create a "digital" culture and invest in improving employees' technical skills. They explain that the success factor for digital transformation is to educate and cooperate with stakeholders. The impacts of leadership and digital transformation on stakeholders are presented below

## SHAREHOLDERS AND BOARD OF DIRECTORS

Shareholders have their influence on the digital transformation process, Ntim (2017) states that they have an important role in corporate governance. This means that their input in the digital transformation decision making process is vital. Shareholders can control the organization as they have the power to choose the board of directors and can reject their decisions (Ntim, 2017). The board of directors – like the shareholders – are responsible for decision making in the organization. The board of directors are elected members who are having the authority to rule the company during a specific period (Varoglu, Gokten, & Ozdogan, 2021). Srinivas, Lamm, and Ramsay (2019) declare that the board of directors' main tasks are to create organization strategies and find ways to implement it and to predict future risks. They recommend that the board of directors to think outside the box to discover new technological opportunities. Both the shareholders and the board of directors are influencing the decision of digital transformation. Furthermore, they are both going to be benefited from the digital transformation various tools. Digital transformation represented by big data tools allow shareholders and board of directors to have a holistic overview of the company financial and non-financial operations that increase their trust (Varoglu, Gokten, & Ozdogan, 2021).

Therefore, it is important for shareholders and board of directors to recognise the benefits of digital transformation for the company and at the same time the accompanied challenges. The problem here is that the benefits are not clear as the costs of implementing digital transformation. In a study of the Chinese manufacturing sector, the researchers find that digital transformation has a clear positive impact on operating performance than in financial performance (Guo & Xu, 2021). Varoglu, Gokten, and Ozdogan (2021) notice that the literature gave no clear explanation of the role of board of directors toward digital transformation. They add that digital transformation empowers other stakeholders. This may work against the boards benefit. There are other challenges that board of directors will face because of technology transformation such as lack of technological skills, information overload, and security issues (Srinivas, Lamm, & Ramsay, 2019). Digital transformation makes it easier, accurate, and quicker for stakeholders to get information about the company. Nevertheless, the board of directors never study the influence of digital transformation on themselves rather they focus on its impact on the organization (Srinivas, Lamm, & Ramsay, 2019). The authors state that the board members contend the positive impacts of digitalisation on communication and document management.

### Employees

Digital transformation and technologies impact employees. Technologies are directly related to employees' processes and work procedures. Employees' skills, knowledge, attitudes, and competencies are positively affected by technology (Bikse, Lusena-Ezera, Rivza, & Rivza, 2021). In an innovative workplace – in which employees use technology – innovation and engagement increase (Oeij, Dhondt,

Rus, & Hootegem, 2019). Technology introduces change in organizations as it helps employees to perform their job in a better and faster way (Cascio & Montealegre, 2016). DeSanctis and Poole (1994) claim that changes occur in the organization due to employees' interaction with new technology. The interactions lead to generating ideas, dealing with conflict, and making decisions. However, these changes create new challenges for employees. Bikse, et al. (2021) find that employees who lack technological skills need to enroll in training programs. Cascio and Montealegre (2016) highlight another challenge. The challenge is that employees in the "middle-skill jobs" have been replaced by high tech jobs. They add that employees' motivation to use technology is a vital condition in digital transformation. The motivation depends on employees' perception of how technology is easy, useful, affordable, and popular (Cascio & Montealegre, 2016).

The relationship between employees and their managers has been also affected by technology. Employees are becoming "self-manager" as they independently working and learning remotely especially during the last few years during the COVID-19 pandemic (Bikse, Lusena-Ezera, Rivza, & Rivza, 2021). Brunetti, et al. (2020) go beyond this and describe the relationship between young employees and their managers as mentorship. They explain that during digital transformation managers who lack digital skills can be mentored by young employees. This is titled 'reversed mentorship. Furthermore, the utilization of technology in organizations change the way employees communicate with their managers. The virtual communication makes it more efficient for leaders to contact their subordinates in a direct way that increase their responsibility and productivity (Zilkiqi & Tsolias, 2020).

## Customers

Stakeholders are influenced by technology transformation in organizations. Sow and Aborbie (2018) mention that stakeholders' benefit should be considered before the implementation of digital transformation. One of these benefits is highlighted by Gouveia, Perun, and Daradkeh (2020). The benefit is concerned with providing better customer services. They affirm that customers' satisfaction is enhanced. The enhancement is due to communication improvement and services customization based on customers' preferences. Digital transformation has changed the way businesses are dealing with customers. This transformation shifts the role of customers from being passive – receiver of products/services – to being active groups that influence brand and market (Rogers, 2016). Besides, digital transformation affects the customer experience in three major ways: customer understanding, top-line growth, and customer touch points (Westerman, Bonnet, & McAfee, 2014). The authors explain that social media help companies and organizations to understand customer preferences, improve their sales experience, and foster two-way communication. Schwertner (2017) agrees that customers' behavior, loyalty, and interaction are positively transformed in the digital era. Digital transformation decisions should positively improve the way organizations are satisfying customers' needs. Several organizations, based on the use of digital technologies, have redesigned their products and services, have provided better customer services and have supported for their customers (Ivancic, Vuksic, & Spremic, 2019).

## Regulators

The publication s of open Government License in UK (2022) state that the regulatory bodies aim to provide stability to businesses and customers. The regulatory bodies are to clarify rules and procedures to enhance confidence. Innovation is the cornerstone of regulatory bodies during digital transformation era. Therefore, the target of digital regulation is to protect customers. There is hence a need to develop national strategy to counteract cyber acts.

There is a lack of study on examining the impacts of digitalization on regulatory bodies in Bahrain. Regulators play a vital role in the technology transformation, as they are the main source for rules and regulations. This chapter focuses only on the role of the Central Bank of Bahrain (CBB). The CBB is a governmental body that was established in 2006 to set financial laws in the Kingdom of Bahrain in order to maintain stability in the economy (CBB, 2022). The CBB believes in the importance of digital transformation for the Kingdom and established a unit responsible for Fintech and innovation. The unit provides services to individuals and organizations to guarantee Fintech and innovation development in the financial sector through the introduction of Regulatory Sandbox.

## THE METHODOLOGY

Due to the contemporary nature of the issue of digital technology at one hand and the rare of studies on such issue in Bahrain at the other, this chapter employs qualitative methodology. Besides, studies related to the impacts of digital technologies on stakeholders are a few. The chapter then attempts to grasp participants' views and perspectives in relation to the impacts of digital transformation and technologies on stakeholders in the context of banks in the kingdom of Bahrain. The chapter at hand is being exploratory in nature. Cooper and Schindler (2008) state that qualitative methodology captures the individuals' meanings held concerning a given phenomenon. Al-A'Ali (2020) and Al A'ali & Alazali (2018) explain that qualitative methodology seeks themes underlying views and understandings of participants. Snowballing technique is used to select interviewees. No more interviews are conducted once no new information is generated. Four Chief Executives of banks have participated. Three of banks are regional and one is international. This can help to triangulate perspectives of interviewees. The interviews have lasted between one hour and thirty minutes to two hours. Questions examined are as follows:

1. Definition of leadership
2. Definition of stakeholders
3. Ranks of stakeholders based on importance
4. Relationships between leadership and stakeholders before and after digital technologies and digital transformation

The following is the analysis of collected information:

### Analysis of Question Number One: Definition of Leadership

The first interviewee states that a leader has a vision. He/ she can accomplish the vision through inspiring and motivating employees. In conclusion this interviewee claims that charisma is the core of leadership. However, the leading processes and functions are improved due to digital transformation. Digital transformation can spread information leading to foster decision-making processes. Digitalization also improves, leaders-employees relationship; motivates and inspires employees, encourages innovation and instigates collaboration. This is congruent to the definition of charismatic leadership style explained by Kinicki & Williams (2020).

The second interviewee explains that the leader is a person who plans, delegates, makes decisions and controls others' work. Time management is crucial in relation to all such activities of management. Leadership roles however focuses on setting visions and developing strategies and enacting procedures. Management activities and leadership roles have been enhance during digital transformation era. The digitalization improves communication, spreads information, instigates collaboration and fostering decision making processes and instigating innovation and creativity. The definition of the second interviewee is compatible to strategic leadership elaborated on by Ebert & Griffin (2019).

The third interviewee mentions that leadership is about achieving desirable targets by individuals in the organization. This interviewee expounds that the leader has to set future visions and develop strategies to achieve. He adds that leadership before and after digital transformation is about strategy. He elaborates stating that visions development becomes more effective due to the availability of information at any time and at any place. This enhances efficiency of leaders and employees, improves communication, motivates employees and encourages to participate in the decision-making processes. Leaders due to delegating tasks through digital systems have more time to innovations and creativity. The third interviewee contends that leadership style is compatible to strategic leadership style examined by Davis (2004).

The fourth defines leadership in term of mutual trust between employees and leaders. Empowerment is the method resulting from trust. This is an attribute of participative leadership styles. Employees due to trust invested in them and participation allowed, according to the fourth interviewee, commit themselves to organizational visions and strategies. He elucidates those employees as results of availability of information through digital systems are motivated to participate to decisions making. Leaders encourage employees to be creative as well. The leadership definition of this interviewee is in harmony with the trust invested in employees as an attribute of participative theory leading to empowerment as describe by Ebert & Griffin (2019) and Kinicki & Williams (2020).

All interviewees assert that the essence of leadership styles remain the same for the periods before and after digital transformation. In conclusion, the first three interviewees highlight the important roles of leaders in setting visions and developing strategies and enacting actions plans and procedures. However, they differ in term of specifying the leadership styles employed. The first interviewee claims that leadership is viewed through charismatic style. However, the second and the third interviewees argue that leaders follow strategic leadership style. The fourth then defines leadership in term of participation and trust invested in their employees.

## Analysis of Question Number Two: Definition of Stakeholders

All interviewees affirm that the definition of stakeholders has transformed over time. Shareholders were the only stakeholders that the organizations had to accommodate their concerns in the past. At the present there are different types of stakeholders. There are internal and external stakeholders (Filho, Penha and Silva, 2021). The stakeholders are shareholders, employees, customers, Boards of Directors, Regulators as elaborated by Benn, Abratt & O'Leary (2016). The literature as mentioned above states that there is no single ranking of stakeholders based on importance. The importance of stakeholders varies based on situational differences. However. Interviewees as presented below illustrate stakeholders' importance from their own personal perspectives.

## Analysis of Questions Three and Four: Stakeholders Rank Based on Importance and Impacts of Digital Technologies on Stakeholders and Relationships With Leadership

This section discusses the analysis of collected information for questions three and four. Question three seeks to study the rank of stakeholders based on importance as viewed by participants concerned. The survey and analysis of collected information related to question four then is scrutinized. Question four probes on impacts of digital technologies on stakeholders and leadership.

## RANK OF STAKEHOLDERS

The first two interviewees agree that shareholders are ranked as number one in term of importance. However, the same interviewees differ in relation to the ranking of other stakeholders. Customers are second for the first interviewee and employees are second for the third interviewee. Employees are the third in ranking for the first interviewee and regulators are the third for the second interviewee. Customers rank as number four for the second interviewee. The third interviewee ranks stakeholders differently than the first and the second interviewees. To the third interviewee customers and employees are ranked as number one. They are equally important. Shareholders are number two in ranking. Board of directors and regulators are then followed. The fourth interviewee's response to ranking question is compatible to the literature stating that there is no single well recognized ranking for stakeholders' importance. This is in agreement with discussion of Mainardes, Albers & Raposo (2012) confirming that there is ranking for stakeholders based on importance.

## IMPACTS OF DIGITAL TECHNOLOGIES ON STAKEHOLDERS AND LEADERS

The examination of impacts of digital technologies on stakeholders studied is presented below. The stakeholders being scanned are leaders, shareholders and board of directors, employees, customers and regulators.

### Leaders

All interviewees affirm that digital technologies and digital transformation have affected their styles of leading. Interviewees illustrate that their leadership styles are becoming more people oriented. Leaders value continuous changes reflected on visions, strategies and procedures. This is compatible to the arguments of Albukhiran (2020) in relation to the suggested guidelines to develop and to promote digital transformation strategies. This is illustrated in the arguments of the first, the second and the third interviewees accentuating the importance of setting visions, developing strategies, enacting implementation procedures and recruiting the qualified individuals. All interviewees focus on planning and offering continuous training programs for their employees to cope with the requirements of digital transformation era. The focus on training as mentioned by interviewees agrees with the Gilch & Sieweke (2020) discussion about dexterity prerequisites in digital technologies era. However, the impacts of changes related to leadership due to digital technologies on other stakeholders are explored below.

## Shareholders and Board of Directors

The first interviewee elaborates stating that organizations are aimed to serve shareholders' interests. Shareholders can be seen as customers as well. They use bank services to pay salaries of their employees. This increases the number of customers. Profit generated then is increased as results of rendering such services by the bank. Digital technologies foster communication between shareholders and the bank. The technologies also produce different types of information enabling shareholders and the bank to make better decisions.

The second interviewee elucidates those digital technologies empower shareholders. They can sell and can buy shares on the internet. Digital technologies provide shareholders with the latest disclosure on timely basis; how many shares are traded and their prices. Shareholders through using digital technologies have access to information assisting them to make decisions.

The Shareholders are ranked after employees and customers in term of importance, according to the third interviewee. Values and ethics according to the third interviewee are the concern of shareholders. Communication and annual meetings with shareholders were slower before digital technologies. The digital technologies foster the communication between organizations and their shareholders. However, executives have to illustrate to shareholders the return for investing in such technologies which facilitates shares trading. Attention should be paid toward active shareholders who are involve in watching activities of their organizations. This is due to the availability of information resulting from the use of digital technologies.

Board of Directors are the fourth stakeholder according to this third interviewee. Board of Directors have to embrace and approve the visions, strategies and budgets of the organizations concerned. The Board of Directors have to authorize the cost of the digital technologies adoption by their organization or the bank. This entails to justify to shareholders the cost for human resources new recruitment and training. Cyber concerns are other issues to be examined and to be approved by the Board of Directors.

Interestingly the fourth interviewee has not mentioned shareholders as internal stakeholders. This is due to the fact that the bank is a branch of international nature. Visions, strategies and procedures are set at home land of the bank. Besides the bank is not focusing on commercial businesses with individuals.

The internal type of stakeholders, according to the fourth interviewee, consists of the leaders, the Board of Directors, CEO, and employees. He elaborates that there is no Board of Directors and hence there is no CEO in Bahrain. The bank is a branch to implement the vision, the strategies and procedures that are enacted at home country. The leader of the bank in Bahrain is the first internal stakeholder. Leaders according to this interviewee are obliged to modify their relationships and leading styles during digital transformation era. This is due to the virtual nature of communication in digital organizations. The top-down relationships based on hierarchy change to be more horizontal and loops like. This affects the second type of internal stakeholders i.e., employees.

The first and the second have not refer to board of directors as stakeholder. The fourth mentions board of directors as stakeholder but it is not related to operations in Bahrain. He expounds that the bank in Bahrain is a branch that does not developing visions, strategies, and procedures. The literature above states that shareholders elect board of directors (Varoglu, Gokten & Ozdogan, 2021). Only the third interviewee asserts that board of directors represents internal stakeholder. He contends that shareholders' roles are to approve and to disapprove decisions made the board of directors. The roles mentioned are compatible to the explanations of Ntim (2017 concerning the effects of shareholders on board of directors. The third interviewee adds that the board of directors and chief executives have to make the decisions concerning the use of technologies that shareholders have to approve. This is in agreement with explanation of Srinivas, Lamm & Ramsay (2019) mentioning that shareholders have to approve decisions made by chief executive. This also justifies the urge expressed by the third interviewee to pay attention to active shareholders. However, the first, the second and third interviewees state that shareholders gain from digital technologies. This is in harmony with the arguments of Srinivas, Lamm and Ramsay (2019) noting that shareholders and board of directors benefit from digital technologies. The same interviewees explain that digital technologies provide holistic views of the operations of the banks. This leads to enhance mutual trust between shareholders and board of directors. Communication then is improved. This is consistent with Varoglu, Gokten and Ozdogan (2021) claiming that digital technologies furnish shareholders and board of directors with financial and non financial information. The holistic information enables banks and organizations to develop better understandings of their businesses.

## Employees

The first interviewee asserts that employees represent the heart of the bank. Introducing digital banking requires to train present employees. Training becomes life time issue for the bank. Continuous training can promote different talents, skills and competencies. The young technology natives are knowledgeable however according to the interviewee are less committed. Young technology natives are ambitious and consider organizations as passages to better future posts. Organizations have roles to enhance commitment by providing certain motives. The interviewee adds that interactions between leaders-employees based on virtual platforms improve relationships.

Employees are the second in ranking according to the second interviewee. They work on full time basis due to the confidentiality of bank services. Digital technologies change the landscape of work for employees. Training is a life time issue for the banks. Banks also recruit young technology natives. Old generation employees have to seek training to improve their talents, skills and competencies. Employees who adapt to change will remain in the bank and will survive. Virtual communication leads leaders-employees' relationships to be less hierarchical. Virtual platforms enhance the relationships due to the direct contacts between leadership and employees at all levels in the bank.

The third interviewee states that services are rendered through employees. Employees before digital technologies should know and accept their assignments. Employees should receive constant personal feedback for their work based on social interactions with their leaders before digital transformation. Leaders communicate directly with their employees based on virtual platforms during digital transformation. Visions and organizational targets are virtually communicated to employees. Virtual platforms, according to this interviewee, improve leaders-employees' relationships. Employees' involvement is encouraged. Involvement enhances performance and boosts innovation. Training is a life time commitment for the banks and employees. Organizations recruit technology native individuals. The technology native employees can assist old employees to acquire new talents. However, the interviewee adds that the reversed mentorship phenomenon does not exist in banks.

Employees, according to the fourth interviewee, are encouraged to participate in decision making processes during the digital transformation era. Digital technologies link all organizational levels together. Such linkages change relationships between leaders and employees. People-oriented leadership followed, during digital transformation era, allow employees to participate in the decision-making. participation made by employees was limited before digitalization due to the hierarchical nature of the bank. Digital technologies also foster communication leading employees to have access to information. Accessing information instigates participation, enhances innovation and commitment. The interviewee explicates that employees' participation is based on empowerment reflecting trust invested in employees. This, according to the third interviewee, boosts employees' efficiency and effectiveness. Continuous training programs intensify participation of employees as well. Training programs equip employees with new skills, talents and competencies that improve the quality of participation.

The interviewees express that digital transformation and digital technologies require employees to acquire different skills, talents and competencies. Therefore, continuous training programs are becoming mandatory. Training programs according to interviewees can achieve two targets. The first is to upgrade competencies of existing employees. The second target is to re qualify old employees. This is compatible to the argument of Bike, Lusena-Ezera, Rivza & Rivza (2021) stating that the digital technologies assist employees to acquire new skills, talents and competencies. The interviewees claim as well that leaders-employees' relationships during digital transformation era have changed. The majority of the interviewees expound those virtual platforms improve relationships between leaders and employees. The fourth interviewee however elaborates stating that the leaders-members relationships convert to be people-oriented rather than being based on hierarchy. This is in harmony with the explanation of Bikse, Lysenko-Ezera, Rivza & Rivza (2021) regarding the impact of technologies on managers-employees leadership as discussed above. Interviewees explicate as well that the changing relationships are reflected positively on employees' motivation, involvement, communication and innovation. This upholds the findings of Cascio & Montealegre (2026); Odin, Dhondt, Rus & Hootegem (2019) affirming that technologies strengthen communication, motivation, engagement and innovation. The third interviewee highlights the importance of recruiting young technology natives. He clarifies that technology natives can spread knowledge. However, he states the issue of reversed mentorship is not followed in his organization. This disapproves the findings of Brunetti, et al. (2020) about the existing of reversed mentorship during digital transformation era.

## Customers

The first interviewee ranks customers as the second in term of importance to the organization. Communication with customers is improved due to the friendly users' virtual systems. Besides customers in the digital era are provided by the services at their own places and at the time convenient to them. This safe customers' time and efforts. Therefore, customers' satisfaction is enhanced. Digital technology used in dealing with customers can reduce the load of employees at banks' branches. This can increase employees' productivity. The interviewee adds that the continuous survey of customers' opinions, desires and suggestions are examined. The findings of survey ushers banks to modify and introduce new products and services leading to improve the bank- customers relationships.

The second interviewee mentions that the business with customers have been drastically affected by digital technologies. Customers used to come to banks to get services desired. Banks now render services to customers at their own place and at their convenience. Friendly users' technologies are used by banks to facilitate work with customers. The open banking system is in implementation to provide customers with more access to their accounts in different banks. Customers' survey is conducted as well to have better understandings of customers' complaints if any, requests and ideas. In general communication with customers is enhanced due to digital transformation and technologies. Relationships with customers hence are upgraded.

Customers, according to the third interviewee, pay salaries for all employees of the bank. Customers used to commute to the different locations of the bank to get services desired before the introduction of digital technologies. The interviewee states that customers' concerns and problems would take so much paper work and longer time to attend by the bank before digitalization. This required more efforts and more costs. Digital technologies and mobile banking reduce such efforts and costs for attending such concerns. Cost reduction of handling customers' concerns leads to increase revenue which serves shareholders' interest and customers' satisfaction. Banks through mobile banking can survey customers' views, ideas and suggestions. The customers' survey enables the banks to accommodate to the needs and the concerns of their customers leading to innovation. This makes customers to be more content. Simplifying mobile banking systems, according to this interviewee, can qualify the bank to attract and then to acquire more customers.

The second external stakeholder, according to the fourth interviewee, is organizations utilizing services of corporate banking. Services of lending money to manufacturing firms, foreign exchange and treasury management are rendered. Due to the international nature, many international corporations prefer to deal with the bank. This, according to the fourth interviewee, is the source of competitive edge for the bank. Digital technologies assist in providing services to international corporations effectively and efficiently. The fourth interviewee explains that ordinary individuals are not any more customers for the bank. This is, according to the interviewee, due to the limited abilities of his bank to compete with national and regional banks focusing on serving individuals as customers.

All of the interviewees state the digital technologies and transformation enhance customers' satisfaction. This is in harmony with Sow and Aborbie (2018) explaining that customers are more satisfied with services provided by digital technologies. Interviewees illustrate that banks utilize the findings of customers' survey conducted regularly to renew and to introduce new services and products. This is compatible to Gouveia, Perun and Daradkeh (2020) affirming that digital technologies and digital transformation benefit the customers. The benefits of digital technologies have reformed the relationships between banks with customers. Interviewees, similar to the argument of Rogers (2016), explain that roles of customers have changed from being passive- receiver to being active participators.

## Regulators

The first interviewee has not mentioned the regulators as stakeholders.

Regulators, according to the second interviewee, are the last but not the least important stakeholder to have impacts on work environment of banks. Regulators are Central Bank of Bahrain, Ministry of Industry and Commerce, Ministry of Labor and other ministries. Central Bank of Bahrain enacts rules and procedures to support stability in the financial system. The interviewee states that the Central Bank in Bahrain encourages banks and financial institutions to utilize digital technologies. There are positive and negative impacts for the use of digital technologies. The Interviewee explains that the technologies simplify and cut time requires to finish transactions between banks. He adds that Cheques clearance has become easier and faster. Exchange of Information between the Central Bank and banks are facilitated. This fosters the decision-making processes. Digital technologies however make the bank systems open on air. This, according to the interviewee, leads the virtual systems to expose to cyber attacks. Banks therefore have to change their passwords regularly.

The third interviewee states that the Regulators are the fifth stakeholders. He states that his bank maintains ongoing relationship with Central Bank of Bahrain. This is to establish credibility and to build trust which is accentuated during the digital era. Digital acts have to be approved by the Central Bank. The later aims to keep stable financial systems.

The fourth interviewee then states that the first external stakeholder is regulators. Central Bank of Bahrain represents the first and the main external stakeholder. The bank has to comply to regulations of the Central Bank. The banks have to adopt forward vision in term of digitalization. The digital technologies assist the local leadership to learn faster about the latest regulations enacted by the central Bank of Bahrain to uphold stability. The leader of the bank in Bahrain has to learn about regulations and rules of the country.

Though regulators are important external stakeholder affecting businesses and their processes; banks specifically, there is a lack of literature examining such effects. Interviewees illustrate that there are many types of regulators. Governmental ministries and bodies represent regulators. The major regulator, according to the interviewees, is the Central Bank of Bahrain. All interviewees expound that the Central Bank of Bahrain approves and encourages to utilize digital technologies. This is mentioned above stating that Fintech and innovation unit is responsible in introducing digital regulations (CBB, 2022). Interviewees explicate that their organizations have to develop forward visions. Digital technologies strengthen the relationships between banks and Central Bank of Bahrain. The later enact rules and procedures to maintain confidence in the financial systems. This is consistent with CBB publication (2022) and the publication of Open Government License in UK (2022) contending that the role of regulators to set processes and procedures to maintain stability. The second interviewee accentuates the issue of cyber problems. This is in harmony with the call of open Government License in UK (2022) in relation to the developing of cyber national strategies.

## CONCLUSION

The chapter attempts to examine the impacts of digital technologies on leadership styles and on stakeholders. Examination of influences of leadership on stakeholders are also explored. The chapter presents transformational, transactional, charismatic, strategic and participative theories as framework for leadership styles. Due to the lack of research concerning impacts of digital technologies and leadership on stakeholders in Bahrain at one hand and the a few research on the same subject in general at the other hand, qualitative methodology is employed. Open ended interview is the research method to collect information. The chapter scrutinizes selected internal and external stakeholders. The selection is based on two factors. The first factor is the value of importance of a given stakeholder to the organization investigated. The second factor is the availability of research related to stakeholders selected. The internal stakeholders are leaders, shareholders and Board of Directors and employees. The external stakeholders are customers and regulators represented by The Central Bank of Bahrain. The majority of leaders follow strategic leadership. The charismatic style is the leadership of the first interviewee. The fourth interviewee believes in participative leadership based on trust. The definitions of stakeholders indicated by interviewees are compatible to those of literature. There are two types of stakeholders. These are the internal and external ones.

The analysis of collected information illustrates that leadership styles remain the same before and after digital transformation era. The leadership styles however reshape leaders-employees' relationships during digitalization era. The relationships are becoming less hierarchical.

The chapter affirms that digital technologies and digital transformation affect the work of shareholders and then the board of directors positively. Digitalization provides holistic financial and non financial perspectives which enable both shareholders and the board of directors to make better decisions. Employees become more committed, engage and innovative. This is because of virtual communication platforms followed and the people- oriented relationships based on trust invested in employees. Training is a life time strategy to cope with the requirements of changing technologies. Though young technology natives spread knowledge in organizations the issue of reversed mentorship does not exist in Bahrain according to interviewees. Interviewees state that the products and services of their banks revolve around the preferences of customers. The friendly users' virtual platforms empower customers to express their opinions in relation to services and products received. Finally, regulators as stakeholder enact rules and regulations to follow by the banks and financial institutions. The issue of cyber National strategy is a focal point for regulators.

## FUTURE RESEARCH

Due to the contemporary nature of the subject being studied in this chapter, this work is exploratory in nature. There is a few research on examining impacts of leadership styles on stakeholders during digital transformation era. The suggested future research hence are as follows:

- Qualitative methodology is used to collect information from participants to the study of this chapter. Employing quantitative methodology to explore the impacts of leadership styles on stakeholders may reveal different findings.
- Though a few literatures are found, Interviewees highlight the importance of regulators as stakeholder. There is a need to conduct research to comprehend the relationships between leadership and regulators during digital transformation era.
- There is a necessity to conduct extensive research to exploring the roles of leadership during digital transformation era. The exploration should be extended to explicate the impacts of leadership roles on stakeholders,

## REFERENCES

A'Ali, E. & Alzzali, R. (2018). Gender Differences in Relation to Organizational Sources of Power. In Arab Women an Their Evolving Roles in The Global Business Landscape, (pp.1-25). IGI Global.

A'Ali, E., & Alazali, R. M. (2022). Leadership Styles: The Case of Islamic Banks. In E. Al-Aali, M. Masmoudi, & G. J. AlSaffar, Religion and Its Impact on Organizational Behavior, (p. 326). IGI Global.

Al-A'ali, E. A. (2020). The Role of Auditing Firms in Promoting Ethical Consumerism: Ethical Programs for Business Companies. In E. Al-A'ali, & M. Masmoudi (Eds.), Ethical Consumerism and Comparative Studies Across Different Cultures: Emerging Research and Opportunities, (pp. 39-52). IGI Global. https://doi.org/10.4018/978-1-7998-0272-3.ch004 doi:10.4018/978-1-7998-0272-3.ch004

Albukhitan, S. (2020). Developing Digital Transformation Strategy for Manufacturing. *The 3rd International Conference on Emerging Data and Industry 4.0 (EDI40)* (pp. 664–671). Warsaw: Procedia Computer Science.

Bass, B. M. (1999). Two decades of research and development in transformational leadership. *European Journal of Work and Organizational Psychology*, *8*(1), 9–32. doi:10.1080/135943299398410

Benn, S., Abratt, R., & O'Leary, B. (2016). Defining and identifying stakeholders: Views from management and stakeholders. *South African Journal of Business Management*, *47*(2), 1–11. doi:10.4102ajbm.v47i2.55

Bikse, V., Lusena-Ezera, I., Rivza, P., & Rivza, B. (2021). The Development of Digital Transformation and Relevant Competencies for Employees in the Context of the Impact of the COVID-19 Pandemic in Latvia. *Sustainability*, *13*(16), 1–17. doi:10.3390u13169233

Brunetti, F., Matt, D. T., Bonfanti, A., Longhi, A. D., Pedrini, G., & Orzes, G. (2020). Digital transformation challenges: Strategies emerging from a multi-stakeholder approach. *The TQM Journal*, *32*(4), 697–724. doi:10.1108/TQM-12-2019-0309

Cascio, W. F., & Montealegre, R. (2016). How Technology Is Changing Work and Organizations. *Annual Review of Organizational Psychology and Organizational Behavior*, *3*(1), 349–375. doi:10.1146/annurev-orgpsych-041015-062352

CBB. (2022, July 21). *Central Bank of Bahrain*. https://www.cbb.gov.bh/about-cbb/

Commission, E. (2017). *Attitudes Towards the Impact of Digitization and Automation on Daily Life*. 1-171.

Cortellazzo, L., Bruni, E., & Zampien, R. (2019). The Role of Leadership in a Digitized World: A Review. *Frontiers in Psychology*, *10*, 1938. doi:10.3389/fpsyg.2019.01938 PMID:31507494

Creto, S. C., & Creto, S. T. (2019) Modern Management; concepts and skills (global edition). UK. Pearson Education limited.

Dahlström, P., Desmet, D., & Singer, M. (2017). *The seven decisions that matter in a digital transformation: A CEO's guide to reinvention*. Digital McKinsey.

Davies, B. D. (2004). Strategic leadership. *School Leadership & Management*, 13–36.

DeSanctis, G., & Poole, M. S. (1994). Capturing the Complexity in Advanced Technology Use: Adaptive Structuration Theory. *Organization Science*, *5*(2), 121–147. doi:10.1287/orsc.5.2.121

Ebert, R. J., & Griffin, R. W. (2019) Business essential (12 ed.). New York, NY. Pearson.

Filho, J. R., Penha, R., & Silva, L. F. (2021). Stakeholders And The Impact That Exercise On Digital Transformation Projects. *Journal on Innovation and Sustainability*, *12*(3), 98–108. doi:10.23925/2179-3565.2021v12i3p98-108

Gilch, P. M., & Sieweke, J. (2020). Recruiting Digital Talent: The Strategic Role of Recruitment in Organisations' Digital Transformation. *German Journal of Human Resource Management*, 2-47.

Gill, R. (2011). *Theory and Practice of Leadership*. SAGE.

Gouveia, L. B., Perun, M., & Daradkeh, Y. I. (2020). Digital Transformation and Customers Sevices: The Banking Revolution. *International Journal of Open Information Technologies*, *8*(7), 124–128.

Guo, L., & Xu, L. (2021). The Effects of Digital Transformation on Firm Performance: Evidence from China's Manufacturing Sector. *Sustainability*, *13*(22), 1–18. doi:10.3390u132212844

Herman, M. (2022, June 14). *10 Essential Tools to Support Your Digital Transformation*. LumApps. https://www.lumapps.com/digital-workplace/digital-transformation-tools/

Holten, A.-L., & Brenner, S. O. (2015). Leadership style and the process of organizational change. *Leadership and Organization Development Journal*, *36*(1), 2–16. doi:10.1108/LODJ-11-2012-0155

House, R. J., & Howell, J. M. (1992). Personality And Charismatic Leadership. *The Leadership Quarterly*, *3*(2), 81–108. doi:10.1016/1048-9843(92)90028-E

Ivancic, L., Vuksic, V. B., & Spremic, M. (2019). Mastering the Digital Transformation Process: Business Practices and Lessons Learned. *Technology Innovation Management Review*, *9*(2), 36–50. doi:10.22215/timreview/1217

Jones, G. R., & George, J. M. (2022). *Contemporary Management*. McGraw Hill.

Khan, Z. A., Nawaz, A., & Khan, I. (2016). Leadership Theories and Styles: A Literature Review. *Journal of Resources Development and Management*, *16*, 1–7.

Kinicki, A., & Williams, B. K. (2020). management (ninth edition). New York, NY. McGraw-Hill Education.

Klingborg, D. J., Moore, D. A., & Varea-Hammond, S. (2006). What Is Leadership? *Journal of Veterinary Medical Education*, *33*(2), 280–283. doi:10.3138/jvme.33.2.280 PMID:16849311

Mahraz, M.-I., Benabbou, L., & Berrado, A. (2019). A Systematic literature review of Digital Transformation. *International Conference on Industrial Engineering and Operations Management,* (pp. 917-931), Toronto. IEOM Society International.

Mainardes, E. W., Alves, H., & Raposo, M. (2012). A model for stakeholder classification and stakeholder relationships. *Management Decision*, *50*(10), 1861–1879. doi:10.1108/00251741211279648

McShane, S. L., & Glinow, M. A. (2021). *Organizational Behavior: Emerging Knowledge. Global Reality*. McGraw Hill.

Miles, S. (2017). Stakeholder theory classification, definitions and essential contestability. *Stakeholder management.*

Morakanyane, R., Grace, A. A., & O'Reilly, P. (2017). Conceptualizing Digital Transformation in Business Organizations: A Systematic Review of Literature. 30th Bled Econference: Digital Transformation, Slovenia, (pp. 427-444). AIS eLibrary.

Ntim, C. G. (2017). Defining Corporate Governance: Shareholder Versus Stakeholder Models. In Global Encyclopedia of Public Administration, Public Policy, and Governance, (pp. 1-15).

Oeij, P. R., Dhondt, S., Rus, D., & Hootegem, G. V. (2019). The digital transformation requires workplace innovation: An introduction. *International Journal of Technology Transfer and Commercialisation, 16*(3), 199–207.

Rogers, D. L. (2016). *Digital Transformation Playbook: Rethink your business for the digital age*. Columbia University Press. doi:10.7312/roge17544

Schwertner, K. (2017). Digital Transformation Of Business. *Trakia Journal of Sciences, 15*(1, Suppl.1), 388–393. doi:10.15547/tjs.2017.s.01.065

Silva, A. (2016). What is Leadership? *Journal of Business Studies Quarterly, 8*(1), 1–5. PMID:29355200

Sow, M., & Aborbie, S. (2018). Impact of Leadership on Digital Transformation. *Business and Economic Research*, 139-148.

Sow, M. & Aborbie, S. (2018). Impact of Leadership on Digital Transformation. In *Macrothink Institute, Business and Economic Research, 8*(3), (pp.139-148)

Srinivas, V., Lamm, R., & Ramsay, T. (2019). The impact of digital transformantion on companies' boards. *Deloitte Insights*, 1-11.

Varoglu, A., Gokten, S., & Ozdogan, B. (2021). Digital Corporate Governance: Inevitable Transformation. In U. Hacioglu & T. Aksoy (Eds.), *Financial Ecosystem and Strategy in the Digital Era: Global Approaches and New Opportunities,* (pp. 219–236). Springer. doi:10.1007/978-3-030-72624-9_10

Westerman, G., Bonnet, D., & McAfee, A. (2014). The Nine Elements of Digital Transformation. *MIT Sloan Management Review*.

Zilkiqi, A., & Tsolias, P. (2020). Leaders Perception of Virtual Communication - leadership and communication mediated through technology.

# Chapter 4
# Humble Leadership:
## Effects on Innovation

**Emilio Domínguez-Escrig**
https://orcid.org/0000-0002-5380-2774
*Universitat Jaume I, Spain*

**Francisco Fermín Mallén Broch**
*Universitat Jaume I, Spain*

## ABSTRACT

*Following a stream of research that analyzes the effect of humble leaders on innovation, the central value of this study is to expand the current knowledge of this relationship by elucidating the impact of this type of leadership on radical innovation and innovation success (considering both financial and non-financial performance). The study was conducted in Spain. 263 different organizations participated in the research. The authors tested and confirmed the hypotheses using structural equations. Humble leadership promotes radical innovation and, in turn, innovation success.*

## INTRODUCTION

Many studies and streams of research have emphasized the usefulness of innovation for companies to survive in the current competitive context. The development of technologies, the appearance of new products and services, changes in consumer behaviors or the entry of new competitors, force companies to change. As a result, innovation is one of the most relevant strategies to increase their competitiveness. Consequently, it is essential to study the circumstances that encourage organizations to innovate, enhance their creativity and generate new ideas.

On the other hand, literature has pointed out that there are different types of innovation. Each of them has specific characteristics, affecting differently on the results of companies (OECD, 2018). In addition, the factors that promote their development are also different. Therefore, it is useful to discriminate between types of innovation when studying their antecedents. One of the most widely used classifications in academia differentiates between incremental and radical innovation. These innovations are character-

DOI: 10.4018/978-1-6684-5864-8.ch004

ized by the degree of change they produce in companies and markets. Among these innovations, radical innovation stands out for its potential to improve firm performance (Al-Khatib & Al-Ghanem, 2021).

However, despite the capacity of innovation to improve firm performance, it is a tortuous and unpredictable process that involves many risks and possibilities of failure. In this sense, it is likely that many innovations will not achieve the expected success, especially in the case of radical innovation, due to its higher degree of novelty. In this sense, radical innovations may not be understood by the market. In other cases, consumers may be reluctant to change behaviors when adopting a new product or service (Slater et al. 2014). Therefore, when analyzing the conditions that favor innovation, it is necessary to study the factors that promote its development, but also its success.

One of the factors that has been positively related to innovation is leadership. Recently, different studies evaluated how different types of leadership promote innovation at the organizational, team or individual level. Leaders create the conditions within companies for employees to work with trust, respect, or autonomy, generating new ideas that can be translated into innovations. For example, a growing number of studies highlighted the positive effect of styles such as servant, ethical, authentic or transformational to promote creativity and innovation (e.g. Mallén et al., 2020). These studies, in turn, demonstrated the importance of new leadership styles and the need to lead companies in a more humane and respectful way.

This study focuses on the humility of leaders. News about financial scandals, unethical behavior of managers and toxic work environments, attributable to the uncontrolled ego, arrogance, and sense of self-importance of organizational executives (Boje et al., 2004), have driven a change in the way companies are managed. This new paradigm includes changes in leadership styles. In this context, the study of humble leadership is increasingly important (e.g., Ou et al., 2014). Authors such as Argandona (2015) highlighted the importance of humility of leaders to fight against these problems. Other authors have stressed out the relevance of humble leaders to generate more virtuous work contexts. Owens and Heckman (2012, p.788) affirmed that humility comes from the Latin word "virtutem" that connotes moral strength, valor, excellence and worth. In the organizational context, they considered that virtues such as humility "have been generally viewed as that which is good, human, and produces social bet". Humble leadership may be defined as "a leadership style in which a leader evaluates him/herself and subordinates through a multifaceted and objective lens, appreciating subordinates' positive worth, strengths, and contributions" (Zhu et al., 2019, p.2).

For all these reasons, this chapter presents a study that analyzes the effect of humble leadership on innovation success. Regarding the type of innovations studied, this research focuses on radical innovation. Although leaders' humility favors innovation and creativity (e.g. Lei et al., 2021; Chen et al., 2021), there are no studies that analyzed their influence on radical innovation. Nor have any studies analyzed the effect of humble leadership on the results of the innovations developed by companies. This study attempts to shed light on this field by analyzing the effect of these leaders on the financial and non-financial results of the new products and services developed by companies.

Previous research examined the consequences of humble leadership, studying its effects at different levels of analysis (individual, team, and organizations). Most of these studies focused on the positive consequences of this type of leadership. Although previous studies have also analyzed behavioral outcomes or attitudinal outcomes, this study relates to a stream of research that investigates performance outcomes of humble leadership (Kelemen et al., 2022). The central objective of this chapter is to expand the knowledge about the consequences of this type of leadership, analyzing the capability of these leaders to promote radical innovations and studying the financial and non-financial performance of such innovations.

*Figure 1. Conceptual Model*

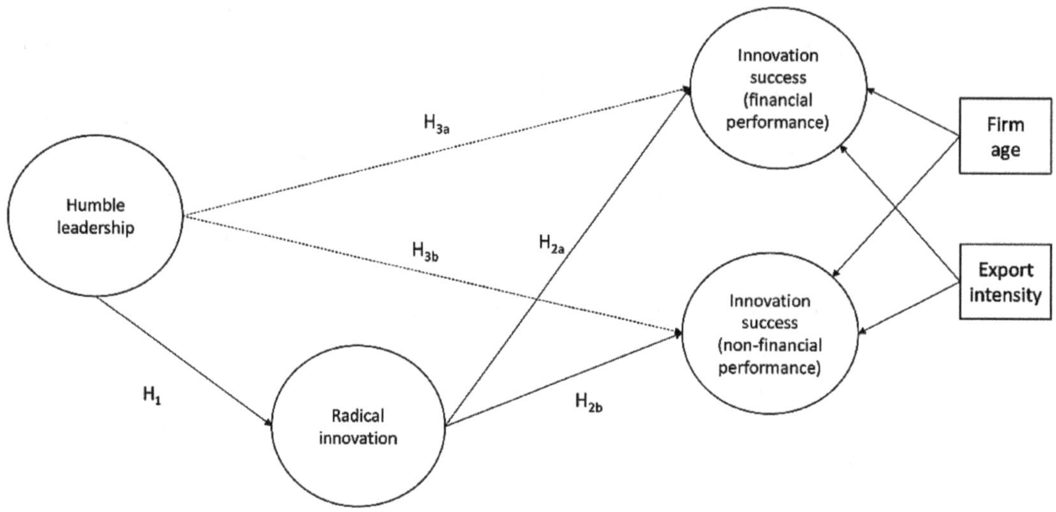


The chapter begins with a literature review of humble leadership, radical innovation and innovation success. Then, the hypotheses are proposed (Figure 1): Does humble leadership positively affect radical innovation? Is the effect of radical innovation on firms' financial and non-financial performance positive? Can radical innovation mediate the positive effect of humble leadership on innovation success? To answer these questions, a sample of Spanish companies has been obtained. Data was analyzed through structural equation modeling. Results, conclusions and suggestions for future studies are proposed at the end of the chapter.

## BACKGROUND

### Humble Leadership

According to Owens and Heckman (2012), humility is one of the main organizational virtues to foster positive and moral behavior in the workplace. Owens et al. (2013, p.1518) defined humility as "an interpersonal characteristic that emerges in social contexts that connotes (a) a manifested willingness to view oneself accurately, (b) a displayed appreciation of others ' strengths and contributions, and (c) teachability". Humble people are seen as understanding, willing to admit their own mistakes and learn from them.

From a leadership approach, Van Dierendonck and Nuijten (2011) stated that humility involves putting one's own achievements in perspective. People have both strong and weak points. Everyone, including leaders, may make mistakes and it is important to learn from them. The first step to improve is to acknowledge our limitations. Humble leaders learn from criticism, admit mistakes, and try to understand other points of view and opinions. Similarly, Rego et al. (2017, p. 641) highlighted that being humble means having a conscious view of oneself and others, which means acknowledging one's own "personal strengths and weaknesses (as well as those of others) without fostering feelings of superiority or inferiority".

Ali et al. (2020) stressed out that humility is considered an interpersonal trait, reflected in the conduct of the leaders, and that is recognized by followers during social interactions. Zhou and Wu (2018, p. 376) considered humble leadership as a "bottom-up leadership approach that involves listening, observing others and learning by doing". After conducting a literature review, Kelemen et al. (2022) concluded that the three main dimensions of humble leadership are an accurate self-view/self-awareness, teachability/openness to feedback, and appreciation for others, which form the core of this leadership style.

On the other hand, different authors have included humility in their definitions of diverse leadership styles, such as servant leadership or spiritual leadership (e.g. Van Dierendonck & Nuijten, 2011), highlighting the importance of this behavior in the new trends of leadership and the current competitive context.

A large number of research has underlined the relevance of humility and humble leadership for organizations and companies. Different empirical studies have presented evidence of their positive effect at the individual, team and organizational levels. For example, it facilitates altruistic behaviors in the workplace (Mallén et al., 2019), team creativity (Hu et al., 2018), firm innovativeness (Mallén et al., 2019), team performance (Owens & Heckman, 2016), knowledge sharing (Anand et al., 2019), follower voice behaviors (Zhou et al., 2021), employee resilience (Zhu et al., 2019), relational energy (Wang et al., 2018), follower's engagement (Ou et al., 2014), etc. Finally, humility should not be confused with other concepts, such as modesty, which have been defined differently and are proposed to be studied separately.

## Radical Innovation

Radical innovation is a prominent field of study and finding out its antecedents and consequences for organizations is a compulsory task (Story et al., 2014). There are different classifications of innovation but one of the most common typologies differentiates between incremental and radical innovation (García-Villaverde et al., 2017). However, the distinction between the two categories is not always obvious (Domínguez-Escrig et al., 2016). Some authors consider that we cannot refer to these types of innovation in absolute terms and state that there is a continuum from incremental to radical innovation. However, the conditions to boost radical innovations differ from those required to promote incremental ones (Story et al., 2014). As a result, it is helpful to discern between types of innovation when analyzing their facilitators and effects in the organizational context.

Incremental innovation consists of doing things better, satisfying existing needs and enhancing the ongoing offer. It focuses on achieving immediate objectives. On the contrary, radical innovation requires entirely new ideas and superior levels of creativity. It is related to the satisfaction of latent needs, and has a long-term horizon (e.g. Marvel & Lumpkin, 2007). According to OECD (2018), radical innovations transform the status quo.

However, radical innovations are hard to achieve and do not seem to be affordable by all organizations (Sorescu et al., 2003). These innovations are associated with risky, complex and uncertain projects (Büschgens et al., 2013). Generally, organizations need a long time and many investments to develop radical innovations, without any assurance of their future success (Sorescu et al., 2003). Furthermore, it is commonly difficult in organizations to find support to develop these innovations, so the incremental type is prioritized because it is less risky, less troublesome, and facilitates benefits (Baker & Sinkula, 2007). Thus, organizations often seek a balance between incremental and radical innovations.

Due to its importance, several authors have proposed different theories about the antecedents of radical innovations, considering both external and internal organizational factors, such as organizational culture, risk taking, experimentation or informal networks (e.g. Marvel & Lumpkin, 2007).

## Innovation Success

In a context of uncertainty and instability, innovation is one of the factors that make it easier for organizations to be competitive and ensure their continuity in the long term. However, innovation per se is not a guarantee of success. Launching a new product or service, changing the production process, developing new distribution channels, etc. might fail, having unexpected consequences. Organizations should anticipate what results they might obtain with their innovations, so it is important to have adequate means to do so, including the organizational factors that may facilitate their success. Several authors have tried to figure out what factors promote success or failure in the development of new products and services (e.g. Nijssen & Ordanini, 2020). Nonetheless, Cozijnsen et al. (2000) pointed out that the factors that have a positive effect on innovation success are not always clear

Innovation success may be considered a guideline to evaluate the outcomes derived from innovation (Cabello-Medina et al., 2011). Nonetheless, there is not a single definition for innovation success. For instance, The Oslo Manual (OECD, 2018, p.253) states that "success of innovations refers to economic returns generated by the commercialization or the internal use of innovations. The definition of business innovation does not require an innovation to be a commercial, financial or strategic success at the time of measurement. A product innovation can fail commercially or a business process innovation may require more time to meet its objectives".

On the other hand, other authors have a wider point of view. Cabello-Medina et al. (2011) also include, along with the monetary benefits, the consequences on non-financial areas. For example, they measure the capacity of innovation to ameliorate the image of the organization, the positive effect on other products and services that are currently offered by the company, etc. The present study adopts the proposal of these authors, using both financial and non-financial indicators to estimate innovation success.

Factors that determine the success of innovation are diverse. They may be related to the market, technology, or the productive capacity of the organization. In the academic field, there is a great interest in understanding why some companies achieve more successful innovations than others. Finding out which factors help an innovation to be successful is crucial for both scholars and practitioners.

## Humble Leadership and Radical Innovation

There are studies that have empirically analyzed how humble leadership or humility facilitate innovation in the organizational context. For instance, at the organizational level, Mallén et al. (2019) studied a sample of Spanish companies and concluded that humble behaviors of the leaders facilitated firm innovativeness through altruism. In these organizations, employees voluntarily help each other, develop extra role behaviors and are more prone to propose new ideas.

Other studies have analyzed the positive effects of humility on innovation and creativity at the individual or team level. For example, Lei et al. (2021) concluded that humble leaders promote the creativity of their followers by becoming role models. Zhou and Wu (2018) demonstrated that humility of leaders facilitated innovative work behavior of their followers through core self-evaluation. On the other hand, at the team level, humble leaders promote team creativity and team innovation as they facilitate learning behaviors, psychological capital, job crafting or team voice climate (e.g. Chen et al., 2021; Liu et al., 2017).

Notwithstanding, no previous research analyzed the effects of this type of leadership on radical innovation. However, literature provides some theoretical support to the hypothesis that humble leadership may promote radical innovation. For example, these leaders are open to other points of view, facilitating dialogue and communication, which have been elements positively associated to the development of radical innovations (Domínguez-Escrig et al., 2018). They also consider criticism as an opportunity to learn, which may help to rethink current formulas and working methods, being the first step that might lead to radical and completely new ideas.

Besides, different studies have provided evidence that humility increases trust in the supervisors, psychological safety, learning orientation, information sharing, knowledge exchange, empowering behaviors, engagement, organizational identification, etc. (for a review, see Kelemen et al., 2022). These variables have been positively related to radical innovation by previous researchers. Consequently, it may be assumed that there may be a relationship with humility, in which humble leaders facilitate the conditions that help radical innovations to flourish.

Therefore, the first hypothesis of the study is:

*Hypothesis 1:* The effect of humble leadership on radical innovation is positive.

## Radical Innovation and Innovation Success

The advantages of radical innovation are noteworthy. For example, it is decisive for companies' future progress (Nabi et al., 2022), improves firm performance, profits and results (Domínguez-Escrig et al. 2021), sets the bases for future services and products (Domínguez-Escrig et al., 2018) or helps companies to improve and maintain their competitive position (Slater et al., 2014).

Radical innovation also provides non-financial benefits. For instance, it allows companies to differentiate from competitors, improves their image and boost consumer satisfaction (e.g. Al-Khatib & Al-Ghanem, 2021). This type of innovation also helps companies to react to changes in the environment (Slater et al., 2014). In addition, it may also facilitate temporary advantages, since competitors need time to learn and catch up with new innovations. During this period, companies may ameliorate their results and strengthen their competitive position (Chang et al., 2014).

Consequently, the second hypothesis has two sections:

*Hypothesis 2a*: The relationship between radical innovation and innovation success (financial performance) is positive.

*Hypothesis 2b*: The relationship between radical innovation and innovation success (non-financial performance) is positive.

## Humble Leadership and Innovation Success: The Mediating Role of Radical Innovation

Different studies have demonstrated the capability of humble leaders to positively influence performance (Kelemen et al., 2022). These leaders facilitate the conditions that boost the potential of their followers to work more efficiently and effectively, which may lead to better financial results, higher profits, or more consumer satisfaction. Humble leaders foster environments in which workers are empowered, enhance subordinates' self-esteem or encourage learning behaviors, facilitating the development of new ideas, creativity and innovation. All these variables act as potential mechanisms that improve company results.

For example, Mao et al. (2019) concluded that leader humility improves task performance by triggering followers' self-expansion and followers' self-efficacy. In this context, employees enhance both the quantity and the quality of their work, which may lead to the development of new ideas and better results. Moreover, Owens and Heckman (2016) tested a theoretical model in different contexts and concluded that humble leaders boost the potential of their followers and enhance team performance, by becoming role models that subordinates try to emulate.

There are other studies that demonstrated the capability of humble leadership to achieve success, by timely accomplishing the projects and satisfying the needs of consumers. For example, Ali et al. (2020) showed that humble leaders promote project success by facilitating innovative work behaviors and psychological empowerment. These leaders support their followers to work autonomously and create new ideas, which may lead to results with which stakeholders and clients are satisfied.

Overall, considering the potential of leader's humility to ameliorate performance and achieve success, and the capability of this leadership behavior to foster organizational environments that boost radical innovation, the last hypotheses are:

*Hypothesis 3a:* Radical innovation mediates the relationship between humble leadership and innovation success (financial performance).

*Hypothesis 3b:* Radical innovation mediates the relationship between humble leadership and innovation success (non-financial performance).

## METHODOLOGY

### Data Collection

This study took into account a sample frame of 11,594 Spanish companies that were included in databases published by the Spanish Ministry of Economy and Competitiveness. 900 companies were randomly selected and invited to participate in the study. These companies were different in terms of export intensity or firm age. Finally, 263 different companies participated in the research and 526 valid questionnaires were gathered, which implied a response rate of 29.2%.

We collected and analyzed data from two different sources. This method is known as dyadic data analysis and refers to the study of data from pairs of people (Frey, 2018). It allows evaluating the influence of an individual's opinion on the opinion of another individual. Therefore, two different questionnaires were sent to each company. 263 human resources managers gave their point of view about humble leadership, while 263 general managers provided their opinion about radical innovation and innovation success. This method was followed to avoid common method bias. Besides, there are examples of previous studies that used these professional profiles to gather similar information. To promote participation and honesty in the responses, the anonymity of all the participants was ensured, enhancing the reliability of the results. Respondents were interviewed by telephone and a 7-point Likert scale was used to measure the different scales.

Finally, as the study was conducted in Spain, the questionnaire was administered in Spanish. Given that the original scales used in the study to measure radical innovation and innovation success were created in English, a double-back translation was utilized.

### Measurement Instruments

Humble leadership was measured using the scale developed by Rodríguez-Carvajal et al. (2006), who developed and validated a scale to measure this behavior in Spain. Cronbach's alpha value of this construct was 0.92.

Studies by Gatignon et al. (2002), and Marvel and Lumpkin (2007) were considered to measure radical innovation. This construct obtained a Cronbach's alpha of 0.96.

Finally, innovation success was measured with the scale validated by Cabello-Medina et al. (2011), who differentiated between financial and non-financial performance of the innovations developed by organizations. This construct obtained a Cronbach's alpha of 0.94 in the case of the financial results and 0.90 in non-financial results. (Table 2).

### Control Variables

Firm age and export intensity were used as control variables. Previous research pointed out that these variables may influence the results achieved by companies and organizations. For instance, higher export intensity may boost incremental and radical innovation by increasing firm's knowledge, learning breadth or technological skills, which lately affect firm performance (Freixanet & Rialp, 2022). On the other hand, there are evidences of how firm age affects innovation performance, financial performance, or exports (Coad et al., 2017). These authors considered that firm age is a significant variable that deserves consideration in theoretical and empirical studies that analyze the determinants of firms' performance. Consequently, the present research controlled their influence on the financial and non-financial success of the companies under study.

### Analyses

The maximum likelihood estimate method was used to empirically validate the hypotheses of the conceptual model, using structural equation modeling and the statistical program SPSS AMOS-26. The SPSS-26 statistical program was used to calculate other metrics. Structural equation modeling (SEM) is one of the dominant methods for the analysis of dyadic data (Ledermann & Kenny, 2017).

## RESULTS

### Descriptive Statistics and Psychometric Properties of the Measurement Scales

Table 1 provides data on means, standard deviations, and correlations for all of the constructs examined in the study. To assess the psychometric features of the measuring scales, accepted procedures in the literature (Anderson & Gerbing, 1988) were used. Their dimensionality, reliability, and content, as well as their convergent and discriminant validity, were all investigated.

The reliability analysis results were satisfactory, according to Nunnally's (1978) recommendations. Cronbach's alpha values and composite reliability values both exceeded the allowed minimum of 0.7. Furthermore, in each construct, the average variance extracted exceeded the minimum limit of 0.5 (Table 2). Moreover, content validity was ensured by employing measuring scales that have previously been validated in other studies.

Convergent validity of the constructs was also supported. For each construct, the average variance was greater than 0.5, and the magnitude of factorial loadings was greater than 0.4, which is the minimum accepted value (Hair et al., 2006).

*Table 1. Factor correlations, means and standard deviations*

| | Mean | s.d. | HL | RI | FP | NFP |
|---|---|---|---|---|---|---|
| Humble leadership | 5.06 | 1.00 | 1 | | | |
| Radical innovation | 4.76 | 1.59 | 0.13* | 1 | | |
| Innovation success (financial performance) | 5.01 | 1.30 | 0.13* | 0.72** | 1 | |
| Innovation success (non-financial performance) | 5.17 | 1.20 | 0.16* | 0.70** | 0.86** | 1 |

Notes: For the standard deviations and factor correlations, we used the mean of the items making up each dimension. * Significant correlation at $p < 0.05$. ** Significant correlation at $p < 0.01$. HL=Humble leadership; RI=Radical innovation; FP=Innovation success (financial performance); NFP=Innovation success (non-financial performance)

*Table 2. Reliability of the measurement scales*

| Construct | Composite reliability | Average Variance extracted | Cronbach's alpha |
|---|---|---|---|
| Humble leadership | 0.92 | 0.69 | 0.92 |
| Radical innovation | 0.97 | 0.80 | 0.96 |
| Innovation success (financial performance) | 0.95 | 0.73 | 0.94 |
| Innovation success (non-financial performance) | 0.90 | 0.65 | 0.90 |

Finally, we also conducted a test of discriminant validity, which determines whether the correlations between factors are significantly different from +1 or -1 (Bagozzi et al., 1991). The resulting 95% confidence intervals are computed as parameter estimate ±1.96 * (SE) and unity was not present in any of the intervals (showing discriminant validity).

## Testing the Research Hypotheses

Firstly, a total effect model was tested. Results showed that the effect of humble leadership on innovation success was statistically different from zero, both for the financial performance ($f = 0.17$, $t = 2.62$, $p < 0.01$) and non-financial performance ($g = 0.19$, $t = 2.86$, $p < 0.01$). Control variables were non-significant, both in the case of financial results (firm age: $h1 = 0.12$, $t = 1.83$, $p > 0.05$; export intensity: $h2 = 0.06$, $t = 1.01$, $p > 0.05$) and non-financial results (firm age: $i1 = 0.06$, $t = 1.02$, $p > 0.05$; export intensity: $i2 = 0.02$, $t = 0.28$, $p > 0.05$).

To support the mediation, the significant relationship between humble leadership and innovation success must decrease or become non-significant in the mediation model. The mediation model explains more variance in innovation success than the total model effect. Moreover, the relationships between humble leadership and radical innovation, and radical innovation and innovation success must be significant.

Given that the former conditions were met (Figure 2), the mediating role of radical innovation was confirmed (Hypotheses 3a and 3b). Firstly, the significant relationship between humble leadership and innovation success decreased when the mediating effect of radical innovation was included, both in the case of the financial performance ($c1 = 0.06$, $t = 1.27$, $p > 0.05$) and non-financial performance ($c2 =$

*Figure 2. Mediating Effect Model*

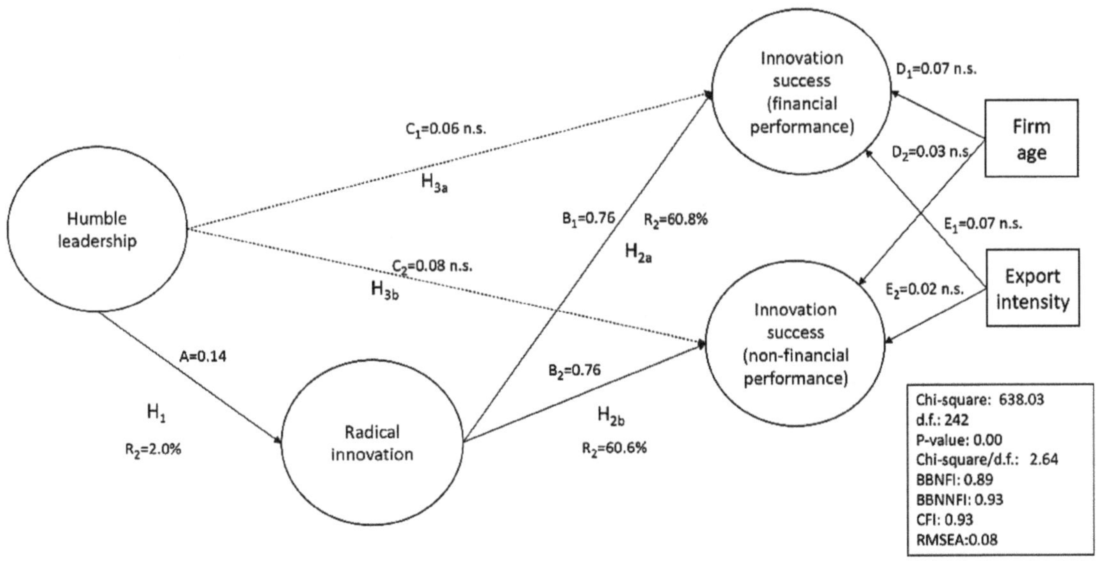


0.08, $t = 1.68$, $p > 0.05$), becoming non-significant. The mediated model explained more variance than the direct effect model: financial performance (4.5% vs. 60.6%) and non-financial performance (4.1% vs 60.8%). The relationship between humble leadership and radical innovation was significant ($a = 0.14$, $t = 2.12$, $p < 0.05$), confirming Hypothesis 1. Besides, the relationship between radical innovation and innovation success (financial performance) was significant ($b1 = 0.76$, $t = 12.61$, $p < 0.01$), which confirmed Hypothesis 2a. There was also a significant effect of radical innovation on innovation success (non-financial results), confirming hypothesis 2b ($d = 0.76$, $t = 11.82$, $p < 0.01$).

The overall fit statistics of the mediation model were, in general, good: chi-square (d.f.) =638.03 (242); $p = 0.00$; chi-square/d.f. = 2.63; NFI = 0.89; NNFI = 0.93; CFI = 0.93; RMSEA = 0.08. The only value that did not achieve the minimum accepted threshold was NFI, which was below 0.9. However, given that this indicator is sensitive to sample size, some authors suggested the importance of relying on other indicators that are not affected by this issue, recommending indicators such as NNFI and CFI (Kline 2005). As both indicators were above 0.9, they showed an acceptable level fit (Marsh et al., 2004).

Regarding the control variables, none of them had a significant effect on innovation success: financial performance (firm age: $d1 = 0.07$, $t = 1.70$, $p > 0.05$; export intensity: $d2 = 0.07$, $t = 1.62$, $p > 0.05$) and non-financial performance (firm age: $e1 = 0.03$, $t = 0.55$, $p > 0.05$; export intensity: $e2 = 0.02$, $t = 0.45$, $p > 0.05$).

## CONCLUSION

All the hypotheses put forward in the study have been validated. Therefore, the present study expands the knowledge of the factors that favor radical innovation in companies. This type of innovation may be problematic and is associated with high failure rates. In this sense, it is important to know what organizational variables promote their success. The role played by the humility of the leaders is one of the central elements of the conclusions obtained in this study. These leaders generate the conditions that favor companies to develop radical innovations and, in turn, to succeed. It is likely that in this space, which facilitates criticism, communication and debate, new ideas can be put forward which, in turn, are subjected to the critical analysis of all members of the organization, thus favoring their improvement and enhancing their success.

Furthermore, the results obtained in the study are significant for the literature on humble leadership or humility of leaders. There are previous studies that have analyzed the effects of these leaders on innovation, creativity or performance, but this is the first study that analyzes and demonstrates its positive effects on radical innovation and innovation success, both on financial and non-financial performance.

The study also has implications for the literature on the antecedents of radical innovation, positioning humble leadership as a new variable to consider as an enabler of this type of innovation. Therefore, these results join other factors such as absorptive capacity, corporate culture or human resource practices (e.g. Barba-Aragón & Jiménez-Jiménez, 2020). Especially important is the linkage with the stream of research that relates different leadership styles to radical innovation. Humble leadership can be added as a promoter of radical innovation to forgiveness, empowerment, authenticity or altruistic behavior (e.g. Mallén & Domínguez-Escrig., 2021).

Also noteworthy is the contribution to the literature on innovation success. The results corroborate the importance of radical innovation in improving firm performance. As seen in the results, there is no difference between financial and non-financial performance, so the positive impact occurs in both areas. In work environments empowered by humble leaders, companies can develop innovations that improve their performance, increasing profits and sales, exceeding the objectives, enhancing the company's image, boosting consumer loyalty or positively influencing the current product and service offer.

This study has implications for companies and organizations that want to improve their innovative performance. The results highlight the importance of changing traditional leadership styles for others that humanize organizations and work environments. It seems clear that those leaders who listen to their followers and care about their well-being are not compromising the viability of their companies. This way of leading can yield significant benefits. Radical innovations can put companies at an advantage over competitors, change the rules in markets and compromise the leadership of large corporations.

Given that this is not the only study that has obtained similar conclusions, it seems that companies could bet on humble leaders in their organizational charts. Through the different human resources policies, people with these characteristics could be recruited and selected for management positions. Interviews and different personality or behavioral tests should measure the humility of candidates as a behavior that can bring positive results to the organization. The same could be applicable for promotions within companies, which could bet on those people who accept criticism and are open to consider suggestions and other points of view.

## FUTURE RESEARCH DIRECTIONS

Some limitations must be remarked. On the one hand, the study was focused on Spain. Therefore, the conclusions of this study should be limited to companies from this country. Future studies should extend the samples to other contexts and countries. For example, comparisons could be made between countries with different innovative performance. Studies could also focus on companies in specific sectors or compare between companies with different export intensity.

Other studies could introduce new methodologies for data collection and analysis. It would be interesting to use multilevel methodologies and to ask employees about their perception of the humility of their leaders. The present study has used the point of view of human resources managers, which could be a limitation when interpreting the reality of companies.

Finally, other studies could incorporate new types of innovation that have not yet been studied in relation to leaders' humility. For example, it would be interesting to know whether these leaders favor green innovation or social innovation, concepts that are very relevant in the current conditions of climate change and commitment to sustainability. Besides, the present study has analyzed the effects of humble leadership on radical innovation and innovation performance, but does not provide details on how these leaders can create the work context that leads to such performance.

Besides, future research should place more emphasis on the changing working conditions. Many companies, belonging to different sectors, are in transition phases, transforming their organizational structures and cultures. The current era is knowledge-centric and marked by digitalization and technology. In these contexts, virtual working relationships and teleworking are gaining much prominence, especially after the Covid-19 crisis. New leadership styles are required and renewed study approaches must be adopted. Recent studies stressed the importance of humble leadership to compete in this context. Maldonado et al. (2021) stated that humble leader behaviors support the implementation of technology and the development of complex innovations. Cho et al. (2021a) concluded that humble leaders fit better in a globalized world that demand more innovation and creativity, and rely on heavy use of technology. On the other hand, Cho et al. (2021b) found that humility is relevant to promote the conditions that foster performance under conditions of virtuality.

Finally, future studies should incorporate mediating variables to explain how these leaders enhance the development of these innovations. To begin with, some of the variables for which there is already evidence of a positive relationship with humble leadership, such as psychological capital, engagement or learning behaviors, could be included. The inclusion of moderating variables such as gender, organizational identification or the perception of the leaders' motives should also be considered, along with the effects of organizational variables such as type of industry, firm size and the differences between public and private companies.

## REFERENCES

Al-Khatib, A. W., & Al-ghanem, E. M. (2021). Radical innovation, incremental innovation, and competitive advantage, the moderating role of technological intensity: Evidence from the manufacturing sector in Jordan. *European Business Review*, *34*(3), 344–369. doi:10.1108/EBR-02-2021-0041

Ali, M., Zhang, L., Shah, S. J., Khan, S., & Shah, A. M. (2020). Impact of humble leadership on project success: The mediating role of psychological empowerment and innovative work behavior. *Leadership and Organization Development Journal*, *41*(3), 349–367. doi:10.1108/LODJ-05-2019-0230

Anand, A., Walsh, I., & Moffett, S. (2019). Does humility facilitate knowledge sharing? Investigating the role of humble knowledge inquiry and response. *Journal of Knowledge Management*, *23*(6), 1218–1244. doi:10.1108/JKM-06-2018-0353

Anderson, J. C., & Gerbing, D. W. (1988). Structural equation modeling in practice: A review and recommended two-step approach. *Psychological Bulletin*, *103*(3), 411–423. doi:10.1037/0033-2909.103.3.411

Argandona, A. (2015). Humility in management. *Journal of Business Ethics*, *132*(1), 63–71. doi:10.100710551-014-2311-8

Bagozzi, R. P., Yi, Y., & Phillips, L. W. (1991). Assessing construct validity in organizational research. *Administrative Science Quarterly*, *36*(3), 421–458. doi:10.2307/2393203

Baker, W. E., & Sinkula, J. M. (2007). Does market orientation facilitate balanced innovation programs? An organizational learning perspective. *Journal of Product Innovation Management*, *24*(4), 316–334. doi:10.1111/j.1540-5885.2007.00254.x

Barba-Aragón, M. I., & Jiménez-Jiménez, D. (2020). HRM and radical innovation: A dual approach with exploration as a mediator. *European Management Journal*, *38*(5), 791–803. doi:10.1016/j.emj.2020.03.007

Boje, D. M., Rosile, G. A., Durant, R. A., & Luhman, J. T. (2004). Enron spectacles: A critical dramaturgical analysis. *Organization Studies*, *25*(5), 751–774. doi:10.1177/0170840604042413

Büschgens, T., Bausch, A., & Balkin, D. B. (2013). Organizing for radical innovation—A multilevel behavioral approach. *The Journal of High Technology Management Research*, *24*(2), 138–152. doi:10.1016/j.hitech.2013.09.004

Cabello-Medina, C., Carmona-Lavado, A., Pérez-Luño, A., & Cuevas-Rodríguez, G. (2011). Do best and worst innovation performance companies differ in terms of intellectual capital, knowledge and radicalness. *African Journal of Business Management*, *5*(28), 11450–11466. doi:10.5897/AJBM11.600

Chang, W., Franke, G. R., Butler, T. D., Musgrove, C. F., & Ellinger, A. E. (2014). Differential mediating effects of radical and incremental innovation on market orientation-performance relationship: A meta-analysis. *Journal of Marketing Theory and Practice*, *22*(3), 235–250. doi:10.2753/MTP1069-6679220301

Chen, L., Liu, S., Wang, Y., & Hu, X. (2021). Humble leader behavior and team creativity: The team learning perspective. *Journal of Managerial Psychology*, *36*(3), 272–284. doi:10.1108/JMP-09-2019-0536

Cho, J., Schilpzand, P., Huang, L., & Paterson, T. (2021a). How and when humble leadership facilitates employee job performance: The roles of feeling trusted and job autonomy. *Journal of Leadership & Organizational Studies*, *28*(2), 169–184. doi:10.1177/1548051820979634

Cho, V., Roll, L. C., Wu, C. H., & Tang, V. (2021b). Changing Digital Age in the Wake of COVID-19: How Does Humility Impact on Virtual Leaderless Teams? [JGIM]. *Journal of Global Information Management*, *30*(4), 1–23. doi:10.4018/JGIM.290831

Coad, A., Holm, J. R., Krafft, J., & Quatraro, F. (2018). Firm age and performance. *Journal of Evolutionary Economics*, *28*(1), 1–11. doi:10.100700191-017-0532-6

Cozijnsen, A. J., Vrakking, W. J., & van IJzerloo, M. (2000). Success and failure of 50 innovation projects in Dutch companies. *European Journal of Innovation Management*, *3*(3), 150–159. doi:10.1108/14601060010322301

Domínguez-Escrig, E., Broch, F. F. M., Alcamí, R. L., & Gómez, R. C. (2021). Leaders who empower: A gateway to radical innovation. *Journal of Management & Organization*, *27*(5), 930–947. doi:10.1017/jmo.2019.73

Domínguez-Escrig, E., Broch, F. F. M., Gómez, R. C., & Alcamí, R. L. (2016). How does altruistic leader behavior foster radical innovation? The mediating effect of organizational learning capability. *Leadership and Organization Development Journal*, *37*(8), 1056–1082. doi:10.1108/LODJ-03-2015-0050

Domínguez-Escrig, E., Broch, F. F. M., Lapiedra, R., & Chiva, R. (2018). Promoting radical innovation through end-user computing satisfaction. *Industrial Management & Data Systems*, *118*(8), 1629–1646. doi:10.1108/IMDS-06-2017-0256

Fornell, C., & Larcker, D. F. (1981). Evaluating structural equation models with unobservable variables and measurement error. *JMR, Journal of Marketing Research*, *18*(1), 39–50. doi:10.1177/002224378101800104

Freixanet, J., & Rialp, J. (2022). Disentangling the relationship between internationalization, incremental and radical innovation, and firm performance. *Global Strategy Journal*, *12*(1), 57–81. doi:10.1002/gsj.1412

Frey, B. B. (Ed.). (2018). *The SAGE encyclopedia of educational research, measurement, and evaluation*. Sage Publications. doi:10.4135/9781506326139

García-Villaverde, P. M., Elche, D., Martinez-Perez, A., & Ruiz-Ortega, M. J. (2017). Determinants of radical innovation in clustered firms of the hospitality and tourism industry. *International Journal of Hospitality Management*, *61*, 45–58. doi:10.1016/j.ijhm.2016.11.002

Gatignon, H., Tushman, M. L., Smith, W., & Anderson, P. (2002). A structural approach to assessing innovation: Construct development of innovation locus, type, and characteristics. *Management Science*, *48*(9), 1103–1122. doi:10.1287/mnsc.48.9.1103.174

Hair, J. F., Black, W. C., Babin, B. J., Anderson, R. E., & Tatham, R. (2006). *Multivariate data analysis,* (6th ed.). Prentice Hall.

Hu, J., Erdogan, B., Jiang, K., Bauer, T. N., & Liu, S. (2018). Leader humility and team creativity: The role of team information sharing, psychological safety, and power distance. *The Journal of Applied Psychology*, *103*(3), 313–323. doi:10.1037/apl0000277 PMID:29094959

Kelemen, T. K., Matthews, S. H., Matthews, M. J., & Henry, S. E. (2022). Humble leadership: A review and synthesis of leader expressed humility. *Journal of Organizational Behavior*. doi:10.1002/job.2608

Kline, R. B. (2005). *Principles and Practice of Structural Equation Modeling*. The Guilford Press.

Ledermann, T., & Kenny, D. A. (2017). Analyzing dyadic data with multilevel modeling versus structural equation modeling: A tale of two methods. *Journal of Family Psychology*, *31*(4), 442–452. doi:10.1037/fam0000290 PMID:28165269

Lei, S., Peng, L., & Guo, Y. (2021). Investigating the effect of leader humility on subordinates' service creativity: A moderated dual path model. *Current Psychology (New Brunswick, N.J.)*, 1–13. doi:10.100712144-021-01887-1

Liu, W., Mao, J., & Chen, X. (2017). Leader humility and team innovation: Investigating the substituting role of task interdependence and the mediating role of team voice climate. *Frontiers in Psychology*, *8*, 1115. doi:10.3389/fpsyg.2017.01115 PMID:28713316

Maldonado, T., Carden, L., Brace, C., & Myers, M. (2021). Fostering Innovation Through Humble Leadership and Humble Organizational Culture. *The Journal of Business Strategy*, *38*(2), 73–94. doi:10.54155/jbs.38.2.73-94

Mallén, F., Domínguez-Escrig, E., Lapiedra, R., & Chiva, R. (2019). Does leader humility matter? Effects on altruism and innovation. *Management Decision*, *58*(5), 967–981. doi:10.1108/MD-11-2018-1180

Mallén, F. F., & Domínguez-Escrig, E. (2021). When leaders forgive: Encouraging radical innovation in more altruistic organizations. *Baltic Journal of Management*, *16*(5), 712–728. doi:10.1108/BJM-02-2021-0068

Mao, J., Chiu, C. Y., Owens, B. P., Brown, J. A., & Liao, J. (2019). Growing followers: Exploring the effects of leader humility on follower self-expansion, self-efficacy, and performance. *Journal of Management Studies*, *56*(2), 343–371. doi:10.1111/joms.12395

Marvel, M. R., & Lumpkin, G. T. (2007). Technology entrepreneurs' human capital and its effects on innovation radicalness. *Entrepreneurship Theory and Practice*, *31*(6), 807–828. doi:10.1111/j.1540-6520.2007.00209.x

McDermott, C. M., & O'Connor, G. C. (2002). Managing radical innovation: An overview of emergent strategy issues. *Journal of Product Innovation Management*, *19*(6), 424–438. doi:10.1111/1540-5885.1960424

Nabi, M. N., Liu, Z., & Hasan, N. (2022). Investigating the effects of leaders' stewardship behavior on radical innovation: a mediating role of knowledge management dynamic capability and moderating role of environmental uncertainty. Management Research Review.

Nijssen, E. J., & Ordanini, A. (2020). How important is alignment of social media use and R&D–Marketing cooperation for innovation success*? Journal of Business Research*, *116*, 1–12. doi:10.1016/j.jbusres.2020.04.056

Nunnally, J. C. (1978). *Psychometric Theory*. McGraw-Hill.

OECD/Eurostat. (2018). Oslo manual 2018: Guidelines for collecting, reporting and using data on innovation. The measurement of scientific, technological and innovation activities. 4th ed. Paris/Eurostat, Luxembourg. OECD Publishing.

Ou, A. Y., Tsui, A. S., Kinicki, A. J., Waldman, D. A., Xiao, Z., & Song, L. J. (2014). Humble chief executive officers' connections to top management team integration and middle managers' responses. *Administrative Science Quarterly*, *59*(1), 34–72. doi:10.1177/0001839213520131

Owens, B. P., & Hekman, D. R. (2012). Modeling how to grow: An inductive examination of humble leader behaviors, contingencies, and outcomes. *Academy of Management Journal*, *55*(4), 787–818. doi:10.5465/amj.2010.0441

Owens, B. P., Johnson, M. D., & Mitchell, T. R. (2013). Expressed humility in organizations: Implications for performance, teams, and leadership. *Organization Science*, *24*(5), 1517–1538. doi:10.1287/orsc.1120.0795

Rego, A., Owens, B., Leal, S., Melo, A. I., Cunha, M. P., Gonçalves, L., & Ribeiro, P. (2017). How leader humility helps teams to be humbler, psychologically stronger, and more effective: A moderated mediation model. *The Leadership Quarterly*, *28*(5), 639–658. doi:10.1016/j.leaqua.2017.02.002

Rodríguez-Carvajal, R., de Rivas, S., Herrero, M., Moreno-Jiménez, B., & Van Dierendonck, D. (2014). Leading people positively: Cross-cultural validation of the Servant Leadership Survey (SLS). *The Spanish Journal of Psychology*, *17*, 17. doi:10.1017jp.2014.73 PMID:26055345

Slater, S. F., Mohr, J. J., & Sengupta, S. (2014). Radical product innovation capability: Literature review, synthesis, and illustrative research propositions. *Journal of Product Innovation Management*, *31*(3), 552–566. doi:10.1111/jpim.12113

Sorescu, A. B., Chandy, R. K., & Prabhu, J. C. (2003). Sources and financial consequences of radical innovation: Insights from pharmaceuticals. *Journal of Marketing*, *67*(4), 82–102. doi:10.1509/jmkg.67.4.82.18687

Story, V. M., Daniels, K., Zolkiewski, J., & Dainty, A. R. (2014). The barriers and consequences of radical innovations: Introduction to the issue. *Industrial Marketing Management*, *43*(8), 1271–1277. doi:10.1016/j.indmarman.2014.09.001

Van Dierendonck, D., & Nuijten, I. (2011). The servant leadership survey: Development and validation of a multidimensional measure. *Journal of Business and Psychology*, *26*(3), 249–267. doi:10.100710869-010-9194-1 PMID:21949466

Wang, L., Owens, B. P., Li, J. J., & Shi, L. (2018). Exploring the affective impact, boundary conditions, and antecedents of leader humility. *The Journal of Applied Psychology*, *103*(9), 1019–1038. doi:10.1037/apl0000314 PMID:29781636

Zhou, F., & Wu, Y. J. (2018). How humble leadership fosters employee innovation behavior: A two-way perspective on the leader-employee interaction. *Leadership and Organization Development Journal*, *39*(3), 375–387. doi:10.1108/LODJ-07-2017-0181

Zhou, X., Wu, Z., Liang, D., Jia, R., Wang, M., Chen, C., & Lu, G. (2021). Nurses' voice behaviour: The influence of humble leadership, affective commitment and job embeddedness in China. *Journal of Nursing Management*, *29*(6), 1603–1612. doi:10.1111/jonm.13306 PMID:33706409

Zhu, Y., Zhang, S., & Shen, Y. (2019). Humble leadership and employee resilience: Exploring the mediating mechanism of work-related promotion focus and perceived insider identity. *Frontiers in Psychology*, *10*, 673. doi:10.3389/fpsyg.2019.00673 PMID:31001166

## ADDITIONAL READING

Ahn, M. J., Ettner, L. W., & Loupin, A. (2011). From classical to contemporary leadership challenges: A values-based leadership view. *The Journal of Leadership Studies*, *5*(1), 6–22. doi:10.1002/jls.20201

Carnevale, J. B., Huang, L., & Paterson, T. (2019). LMX-differentiation strengthens the prosocial consequences of leader humility: An identification and social exchange perspective. *Journal of Business Research*, *96*, 287–296. doi:10.1016/j.jbusres.2018.11.048

Morris, J. A., Brotheridge, C. M., & Urbanski, J. C. (2005). Bringing humility to leadership: Antecedents and consequences of leader humility. *Human Relations*, *58*(10), 1323–1350. doi:10.1177/0018726705059929

Owens, B. P. (2009). *Humility in organizational leadership*. University of Washington.

Qin, X., Chen, C., Yam, K. C., Huang, M., & Ju, D. (2020). The double-edged sword of leader humility: Investigating when and why leader humility promotes versus inhibits subordinate deviance. *The Journal of Applied Psychology*, *105*(7), 693–712. doi:10.1037/apl0000456 PMID:31670527

Walters, K. N., & Diab, D. L. (2016). Humble leadership: Implications for psychological safety and follower engagement. *The Journal of Leadership Studies*, *10*(2), 7–18. doi:10.1002/jls.21434

Wang, J., Zhang, Z., & Jia, M. (2017). Understanding how leader humility enhances employee creativity: The roles of perspective taking and cognitive reappraisal. *The Journal of Applied Behavioral Science*, *53*(1), 5–31. doi:10.1177/0021886316678907

Yuan, L., Zhang, L., & Tu, Y. (2018). When a leader is seen as too humble: A curvilinear mediation model linking leader humility to employee creative process engagement. *Leadership and Organization Development Journal*, *39*(4), 468–481. doi:10.1108/LODJ-03-2017-0056

## KEY TERMS AND DEFINITIONS

**Creativity:** Production of new and useful ideas.

**Financial Performance:** Capability of innovations to increase in profits, sales or market share.

**Humility:** The ability of individuals to value their own achievements and talents in an appropriate perspective.

**Humble Leadership:** Leadership style characterized by humility behavior. These leaders learn from criticism, admit mistakes, and try to understand other points of view.

**Incremental Innovation:** Minor improvements of existing processes, products or services.

**Innovation success:** Positive impact of new processes, products and services on the results of a company.

**Non-Financial Performance:** Capability of innovations to improve the loyalty of costumers or enhance the image of the company.

**Radical Innovation:** New processes, products or services that represent revolutionary changes. They may transform markets and sectors.

# Chapter 5
# Leadership Competencies for Digital Transformation

**Nada Megahed**
*University of Bahrain, Bahrain*

## ABSTRACT

*Leadership competencies are the knowledge, skills, and abilities that leaders must possess to perform their jobs proficiently. The current existing literature on leadership competencies is mainly focusing on "generic" competencies, such as: accountability, managing diversity, delegation, and decision making. Such competencies are no doubt important, yet, in the era of the digital transformation (DT), organizations require revolutionary changes to sustain themselves and remain competitive. The key drivers behind those changes might be surging customer expectations, engaging people with digital transformation, facing unprecedented competition, or even coping with exponential technological development. Those changes call for strong leadership at the helm to lead this digital transformation impactfully, however, leadership competencies required to lead DT are still unclear. Does classical leadership competencies holds true for those leaders who are leading digital transformation? Are those competencies enough to lead DT initiatives in organizations? This chapter seeks to answer those questions.*

## INTRODUCTION

Being provoked by Industrial $4^{th}$ revolution, "Digital Transformation" (DT) should not be perceived only as technological change, since it causes also fundamental changes in organizations, thus disrupting organizational processes. Such changes call for strong leadership to drive this transformation, and will have implications on current and future leadership practices. However, leadership Competences that are required to lead digital transformation impactfully are still unclear (Imran et al., 2020). The so-called "digital leaders" are expected to act flexibly and rapidly in organization structures, and to be able to manage DT of the organization. Since many countries and organizations are still in the beginning of their digital transformation, there is a lack of a common understanding of digital leadership (Klein, 2020).

The digital revolution has changed the work environment because it has made information more available, and less costly (Jakubik & Berazhny, 2017). An organization embrace digital transformation

DOI: 10.4018/978-1-6684-5864-8.ch005

for many reasons; such as developing and sustaining competitive advantages in a globalized world, or dealing with technological changes in a highly competitive market (Frankenberger et al., 2020). Such changes bring forward the need for a different kind of leadership. Digital transformation (including Big Data, Social Platforms, Artificial intelligence, Blockchain, etc.) is today's business trend (Bharadwaj et al., 2013).

Digital transformation is about gaining innovation and absorbing digital knowledge to improve value creation and organizational capabilities (Schiuma et al., 2022). For this reason, analyzing successful DT initiatives is essential provided considering people's and organization's competences. Particularly relevant are the leadership competences, which impact organizational and individual behavior. In the digital age, companies require leaders who are capable of fostering transformation towards digital era (Schiuma et al., 2022). Existing literature on leadership competences needed for digital transformation has mostly focused on technical jobs such as chief digital officers or chief technical officers, who mainly initiate and lead digital transformation programs in their organizations.

Leadership literature, however, have neglected the context of leadership practices. For example, Bolden and O'Regan (2016, 438) wrote that "digital technology has significant implications for leadership theory, practice, and development that, as yet, remain largely unexplored in mainstream of academic literature". Another deficiency is the lack of empirical studies that explores the key Competences of functional-level leaders, who actually implement DT in practice. Therefore, the main objective of this chapter is to address those research deficiencies by focusing on implications of the digital transformation on recent and future leadership practices. The chapter will also explore the key Competences required for functional-level leaders to lead DT impactfully in organizations.

## BACKGROUND

The terms digitization, digitalization, and digital transformation are often used as synonyms when referring to an organization's evolution into the digital era. Digitization, is the act of changing a process from analogue to digital while maintaining the process itself. In comparison, digitalization is the process of moving to a digital business model and generating new revenue streams by leveraging digital technologies. Digital transformation refers generally to any change related to transformation to the digital age, and thus broadly represent both digitization and digitalization.

Digital transformation (DT) can be defined as "the reinvention of a company's vision, organizational structure, strategy, processes, capabilities, and culture to match the evolving digital business context" (Dunkle & Gurbaxani, 2019). It is also defined by Vial as "a process that aims to improve an entity by triggering significant changes to its properties through combinations of information, computing, communication, and connectivity technologies" (2019, 3).

Digital transformation is becoming a hot topic for companies worldwide (Mazurchenko et al., 2019). Fenech et al. (2019) claim that digital transformation results in changes of business structures and operations by utilizing the benefits of new technologies. It is a process that aims to improve organizations by triggering significant changes to their properties through combinations of information, computing, communication, and connectivity technologies (Vial, 2019). Moreover, digital transformation enables organizations to develop collaboration, innovation, enhanced customer experience, and new streamlining business operations. Yet, it require organizations to take company-wide changes to transform culture, structure, strategy, and business processes (Sainger, 2018). Hence, digital transformation is not just about the introduction of new technologies; rather, it is about taking holistic steps to transform overall organizational properties to achieve desired benefits.

Organizational leadership act as a catalyst to ensure optimization between these new technical and social systems. Yet, empirical studies show that organizations are still to-date struggling to embrace the opportunities through digital transformation, especially when it comes to leadership competences. Understanding and analyzing the potential impact of DT, and persuading the entire organization in fostering innovating solutions has to become a shared mindset and cultural attitude in an organization. This provides further support for the fact that digital transformation is not only about technology innovation. It is more about the creation of innovation, knowledge, culture, and many other factors (Tabrizi et al., 2019).

Today, digital innovative solutions rapidly and easily becomes common. Companies need to pursue continuously those innovative solution towards digital transformation, which require the adoption of active and lean approaches. Companies also need to make necessary decisions to improve internal processes and to invest in research and development (R&D). Leadership represents one of the important catalyzers of an organizational culture-oriented digital transformation (Schiuma et al., 2022). For this reason, in today's digital age, leaders are in charge of promoting an organizational cultural attitude aimed at fostering and encouraging DT. As such, leaders who are keen to facilitate their organization's DT should be characterized by specific competences motivating and facilitating the initiation, utilization and management of digital knowledge for sustainable innovation and organizational value creation. Such leadership competences singularize a digital transformative leader, i.e. a leader capable of shaping a sustainable value-oriented organization through a business mindset approach focused on digital knowledge creation, attainment and application (Schiuma et al., 2022).

But before identifying the leadership competences required for implementing digital transformation, there is a need to reach a consensus regarding the definition of "digital transformation". Reis et al. (2018) indicated that there is no formal categorization or definition of digital transformation in academic literature. This study defined digital transformation as various initiatives necessitating technological, organizational and social elements. Moreover, there is also no commonly agreed-upon meaning for the term "digital", therefore organizations looking for developing digital leaders need to define what the term means for their particular business, so that the leaders can be effective (Hearsum, 2015).

## LEADERSHIP COMPETENCES FOR DIGITAL TRANSFORMATION

### The Competency Concept Revealed

The competency concept is not new (Draganidis & Mentzas, 2006). It was first introduced by the distinguished Harvard's psychologist, David McClelland (1973) who proposed to test for competences rather than for intelligence. Competency models are used today in many human resources functions, including hiring, performance measurement, training and development, and career planning (Spencer & Spencer, 1993). Throughout the past 27 years, the competency literature has presented competency models for a wide variety of job positions and for many purposes (see for instance Spencer and Spencer, 1993; Dubois, 1993; and Jackson; 2009). Dubois (1993, p.9) defines a competency model as "those competences required for satisfactory or exemplary job performance within the context of a person's job roles, responsibilities and relationships in an organization and its internal and external environments".

In 2009, the International Board of Standards for Training and Performance Instruction (IBSTPI) defines a competency as "a knowledge, skill, or attitude that enables one to effectively perform the activities of a given occupation or function to the standards expected in employment". The National Center for Education Statistics (NCES) of the US Department of Education defines a competency as "the combination of skills, abilities, and knowledge needed to perform a specific task" (Youn, Stepich, and Cox, 2006, p. 307). Both definitions suggest that a competency is not only an end, but a mean as well. The end refers to effective application of tasks and activities of a given job role or function up to expected standards, while the mean refers to the knowledge, skills, abilities, and behaviors needed to enable effective performance of the tasks.

Still, however, a confusion and debate exist concerning the triangulation between "competence" and "competency" to the extent that most scholars could not arrive at a definition capable of accommodating all the different ways in which both terms are used (Le Deist and Winterton, 2005). Basically, competence is a "work-related concept defining the tasks in which a person must be competent", while competency is a "person-related concept defining the behaviors underlying competent performance". Yet, many empirical studies still treat both concepts as synonymous (Brown, 1993).

While competences have become a leading concept in management practices, still, however, empirical research on competences is lagging behind, thus resulting in a gap between practice and science (Megahed, 2015). Competency models seem interesting to study in more detail using different research methods and different data sources for developing competency models, and thereby making an attempt to fill the existing gap between practice and science (Megahed, et al., 2012). In 1993, however, Spencer and Spencer introduced several reasons for opposing the extensive usage of generic competency models by many HR practitioners. On the top of those cautions is the fact that competences in generic models might be irrelevant to a particular given job profile, since they are developed to suit many generic jobs.

Secondly, generic competency models present mostly the most common behavioral scales. Meanwhile, most jobs require distinctive scales that are poorly captured or not captured at all in the generic models. For instance, organization executive managers exhibit behavioral scales of self-control or analytical thinking that are much sophisticated than those behavioral scales (of the same competences) being exhibited by junior employees. Thirdly, higher levels of the competency scale are not necessarily better. This is because an employee performing at a higher-level on a scale will also be capable of performing at the lower-levels, yet, the opposite is not true. Therefore, organizations have to determine the optimal scale level for each job level in the hierarchy.

Further critics claim that generic competency dimensions create oversimplified descriptions of competences that are required for most jobs roles, which fail adequately to reflect the density of competence in action. Leadership Competences is not an exception of this gap being more volatile and unpredictable. Knowledge about professional competences is currently one of the interesting research domains. However, despite the extensive empirical studies, there are many research deficiencies when it comes to the applicability of competency models (Megahed, 2018).

On the top of those deficiencies is the fact that the majority of competency modelling studies are US-based, which makes the majority of the current literature on competency reflecting the US culture, and this certainly restrict its applicability to other areas of the globe. This is further supported by the fact that only very few studies exist to-date in non-western countries (such as the Middle East, and Africa). Secondly, most of the empirical studies in the current literature are mainly concerned with exploring competency modelling approaches with little attention devoted to contextual factors, (such as kind of the business, size of the organization, nature of the job/career, or organizational culture). Thirdly, most of the developed competency models have mostly focused on generic managerial/leadership competences, with very little attention given to functional/job-specific competences.

## Leadership Competences: An Emerging Paradigm

The acceleration of globalization, IT innovations and new international challenges, have all changed the prerequisites for leadership and indeed also many of its tools. Classical leadership is defined by Prentice (2004) as "the accomplishment of a goal through the direction of human assistants. The man who successfully marshals his human collaborators to achieve particular ends is a leader" (p.102). Leadership Competences include skills, knowledge, abilities, and attributes that leaders must possess to perform their jobs proficiently (Imran et al., 2020). A new leadership paradigm is emerging, because new business trends running globally require a new paradigm for future leadership (Jakubik & Berazhny, 2017). Literature suggests that there is a move from the Ego-centric (i.e., Leader-focused) leadership toward the Altro-centric leadership as shown in Figure 1.

The ego-centric (or leader-focused) leadership models are not suitable for the knowledge economy or the creative economy. As such, there is a need for a new leadership model where the leader is not in the center, and whereas leadership is distributed and shared with others. Altro-centric leaders rely on cooperation, teamwork, they create and enable high-performing teams, and they are in constant connection with stakeholders. Altro-centric leaders delegate power, act with high maturity, reliability, and empathy (Salicru, 2015). The figure also indicate that the actual practices of leadership have also changed in

*Figure 1. Leadership Paradigm Shift*
*(Source: Jakubik & Berazhny, 2017)*

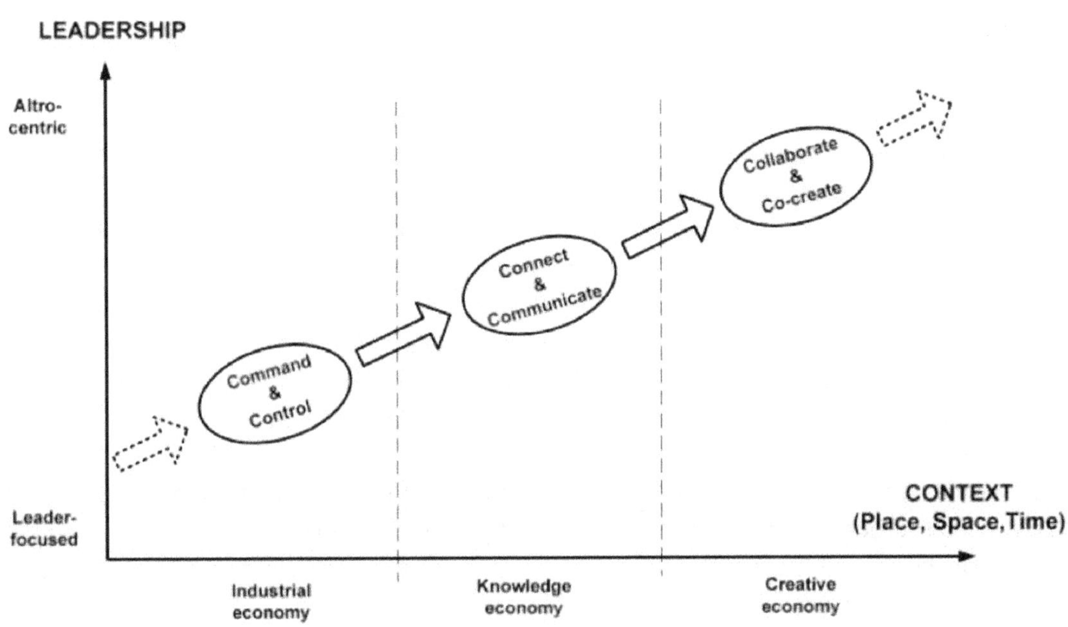

different contexts (place and time). In the knowledge and creative economy, the leader's main practices become collaborating and co-creating together, thus the focus is on communications.

To be able to make an organizational transformation, a leader surely has to possess several basic competences. These competences were grouped into three clusters as proposed by Goleman and Senge (2014), namely: 1) inner, 2) others, and 3) outer clusters, and as such were known as the triple focus. These three transformational leadership competency clusters were then developed into nine competences, which must be possessed by a transformational leader, namely; (i) visionary, (ii) breakthrough, (iii) responsiveness, (iv) emotional intelligence, (v) social intelligence, (vi) ability to influence others, (vii) ability to communicate, (viii) ability to resolve a problem, and (ix) ability to make a decision (Juhro & Aulia, 2019). Transformational leadership is a kind of leadership that stimulates and encourages the followers as well as members of the society to define a great goal and to achieve it together (Juhro, et al., 2020). It is a type of leadership which enable making changes by employing innovations in order to create impacts and sustainable outcomes (Juhro & Aulia, 2019). Due to future uncertainties, however, a transformative leader must also possess competences to confront future uncertainties.

Recent perspectives on leadership are still very controversial and paradoxical, since leadership is still a relatively recent domain of study. Accordingly, there are several questions waiting for answers: 1) Is leadership an individual competence or is it a group competence? 2) Will digitalization strengthen de-humanization in leadership practices? 3) Will the virtual communication of leaders be as effective as the physical communication? 4) Which leadership practices could be digitalized without losing the human factor? And 5) Will leadership practices face challenges in the future, when geographical and physical presence become less important due to digitalization?

## The Role of Leadership in Digital Transformation

According to Libert et al. (2016) digital transformation is not about technology (such as cloud computing or big data), but about the change in the organization based on new technology in business models and processes. Furthermore, digital transformation is not limited to an organization but can also be viewed from the perspective of societies, industries, economies and individuals. As such, digital transformation is about technology and people (Schiuma et al., 2022). For this reason, analyzing successful DT initiatives is essential to consider people's and organization's competences. Particularly relevant are the top management competences that affect organizational and individual behavior. The question that arise now is: How does digital transformation change leadership?

In order to use and integrate digital innovations, business models need to be adapted. Such an adaptation is believed to be a top priority for business leaders, since it is one of the largest challenges of digital transformation. Kane, Palmer, Phillips, and Kiron (2015) highlight that it is not about technical skills, but rather business knowledge and the ability of digital technology impact business processes that are the most essential skills required for success in the digital age. As such, lack of alertness to adapt the business's core strategy and functions can result in failure of digital transformation implementation.

Yet, in the absence of the ability to formulate a digital transformation strategy, a better understanding of the role that leadership would probably play in digital transformation is required, along with an identification of the expected gaps. For digital transformation to be successful, leadership identification is very important because strategic decisions need to find their counterpart at the operational level (Gudergan et al., 2021). This requires not only the integration and orchestration of employees in these organizations, but also the consistent involvement of leaders at all levels as well as. In addition to top-down commitment, digital transformation also requires employee commitment on the to successfully shape and implement the change, which requires employees to be encouraged to take responsibility for appointing themselves as leaders in the digital transformation process. The digital leader should show a true willingness to place a high level of trust in their employees by consistently involving them as leaders at all organizational levels.

What sets digital leaders apart from traditional leaders is that they aim for a digital strategy and a culture that enables the organization to digitally transform (Kane et al., 2015). As such, strategic mindset is needed combined with the right technologies to leverage organizational resources and culture, and to be able to turn investments in technologies and digital transformation into a competitive advantage. Therefore, digital leader (or e-leader) is perceived to be the key person responsible for the implementation of the digital transformation strategy of an organization (Brunner et al., 2021). The term "e-Leadership" is now used interchangeably with "digital leadership".

The conception of the digital transformative leader is suggested to point out leadership's role in driving organizations' digital transformation. The competences of a digital transformative leader remains to-date one of the debates in the literature. Some academics have pointed out that digital transformation leadership competences should be distinguished from those required for leading traditional organization's (Schiuma et al., 2022). A critical review of relevant academic literature focusing on the emerging leadership styles driving digital transformation has revealed the following three critical styles:

- **Wise leadership:** In 2011, Nonaka and Takeuchi underlined the need for a different style of leadership that is capable of extending the knowledge creation (both explicit and tacit) to drive organizational transformation. Nowadays, leaders are questioned to reinvent their organizations rapidly enough to cope not only with new technologies, but also with economic challenges and other priorities. For this reason, organizations need "wise leaders" who can shape a wise organization capable of surviving and succeeding. A wise leader should act as a think tank with own specific intellectual capabilities and characteristics.
- **Transformative leadership:** Another style of leadership has been addressed by many researchers in several empirical and theoretical studies (such as; Berson and Avolio, 2004; Jones et al., 2008; and Shields, 2020). Transformative leadership is a more ethically-based leadership model combining a commitment to values as well as outcomes by optimizing stakeholder and society's long-term interests and honoring the ethical duties owed by organizations to their stakeholders (Berson and Avolio, 2004). Various competences distinguish transformative leaders. They use intellectual inspiration and challenge the status quo by encouraging employees to accept innovative solutions to problems. Transformative leaders also support organizations in decision-making by encouraging the development of possible alternative solutions/opportunities and fostering a problem-solving oriented approach.
- **Digital leadership:** With the rise of digital transformation, the concept of digital leadership has been presented to tackle the competence that leaders have to develop in today's digital age. Yet, Competences distinguishing a digital leader who is capable of driving digital transformation are still unclear, and deserve further empirical studies. Imran et al., (2020) describe digital leadership as the capability of making the right decisions for the strategic success of digitalization for the organization and its business ecosystem.

The above styles of leadership highlight the role of leadership in driving an organization's digital transformation, even though they are adopting different perspectives. In conclusion, leaders have to be wise and transformative to enable an organization to achieve digital transformation. Leaders also have to embrace digital knowledge. To imply these two competences, the concept of a "digital transformative leader" is proposed as a leadership profile for distinguishing those leaders who embrace digital knowledge creation and application for supporting organizational digital transformation, as well as moving towards development of the sustainable value-oriented organizational capacity.

## Digital Leadership Competencies

True leaders recognize attentively when the change is required, provide vision for the change, understand its requirements, and foster the environment that supports such a change. Moreover, they assess the change resilience, prepare for resistance, gain backing for change, involve people in decision-making, create opportunities to apply new skills, and use the feedback loops to monitor implementation (Gebelein, 2001). Those competences holds true for those leaders who are leading and managing the change for digital transformation. Digital transformation leaders, however, need additional specific competences to be able to adequately prepare the organization for transformation. They work in a digital environment, where communication, critical thinking and reasoning, problem solving, and discipline are important (Mack, 2015).

Jakubik and Berazhny (2017) referred to digital leaders as 'the new breed of leaders'. In addition, a digital leader would be able to act as a 'quiet leader', who gets the job done, postulates the big picture, facilitates the activities of co-workers, inspires, and motivates others. The following skills for the so-called "Digileaders" were concluded (Jakubik & Berazhny, 2017):

1. Passion, social intelligence, and empathy.
2. Creativity, open mindedness, and critical thinking.
3. Co-creation, virtual teamwork, and collaboration.
4. Sharing, interpersonal communication, and collaborative learning.
5. Empowering others, and delegating tasks.
6. Provide vision, goals, while anticipating the future.

Competences required in digital leadership also differ from those required for traditional leadership in that leaders need to do business at an accelerated pace, provide more flexible workplace, and set expectations for higher levels of productivity. In addition to core traditional leadership skills, digital leaders need to continuously improve themselves through learning and re-learning. They need to have organizational transformative vision and strategy, build teams which show exceptional performance, and prepare for future. A good digital leader also requires the ability to make proper investment decisions given available time and resources, maintain adaptability for the digital transformation, and empower employees to succeed. A study done by Hearsum (2015) concluded ten capabilities to be perceived as key competences for digital leaders:

1. Adaptability to implement change appropriately many times.
2. Ability to collaborate with and challenge colleagues at all levels.
3. Ability to take risks, fail, and learn innovative lessons.

4. Ability to put customers and clients first (i.e. supports user-centricity).
5. Self, general and organizational awareness.
6. Understanding of the organizational systems.
7. Ability to listen to everybody at all levels.
8. Distinguishing between digital innovation/technology and digital culture.
9. Understanding the influence of technology on the business ecosystem.
10. Ability to decide on the appropriate pace which is not always fast.

Giving the fact that leadership before the digitalization was classical leadership. In contrary, another work defines the function of "digital leaders" by their contribution to the conversion toward a digital organization (Wilson et.al., 2004). As such, a digital leader is not only leading the digital transformation process itself, as the resulting digital organization has also to be led. The more digital transformation is completed the more a digital organization has to be led (Klein, 2020). Giving the fact that leadership before the digitalization was classical leadership, while after digitalization has changed a lot, a conceptual framework of leadership theories can be introduced, including classical leadership and combining new leadership requirements for digital transformation. The framework divid leadership competences into three groups as indicated in Figure 2.

The leadership before the digitalization is the classical leadership. With the emergence of digitalization, digital leadership became concerned with both: 1) the digital transformation process, and 2) leading the organization in a digital environment (see Figure 2). When digital transformation would come to final phases, the organization would be totally digital, then leadership would then have the mission to lead a digital organization.

In a recent study by Imran et al. (2020), five main leadership competences have emerged that are critical for digital transformation in organizations. These five competences are: 1) Digital Vision: which require leaders to look beyond previous strategies and/or procedures in order to envision the digital future of their organizations. Moreover, it requires leaders to align their actions with their vision and make it comprehensible for their subordinates; 2) Digital Knowledge: which require having the knowledge of

*Figure 2. Conceptual Framework of Leadership Theories*
*(Source: Author, 2022)*

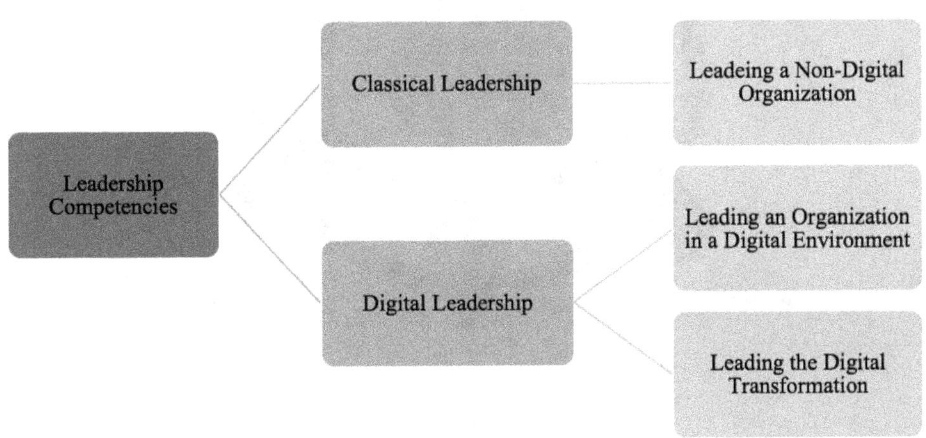

emerging digital technologies to lead digital transformation, 3) Failing Fast: that is the capability to fail and learn from that failure as fast as possible to save time and resources for the organization. Such a competency enable organizations to cease work on specific task/project rather than investing more time and resources on it; 4) Empowerment: which require delegating decision making to employees lower down the hierarchy to help in enhancing the meaningfulness of work, encouraging participation in decision making, and communicating confidence in high performance; and 5) Managing Diverse Teams: which require leaders to develop cross-functional teams (e.g. business, information technology), and manage diverse teams through different mediums, including virtual one.

In a more recent study published in 2022 by Schiuma et al., an inclusive view of the digital transformative leader's competences was presented. The main research question was: What are the competences characterizing a "Digital Transformative Leader" capable of promoting and encouraging digital transformation? In answering this research question, six specific competences were proposed throughout a transformative leadership compass. The compass of transformative leadership integrates and introduces six essential leadership competences as shown in Figure 3. Following is a more elaboration on each of the six dimensions of the compass:

**Adopting the essence of the digital transformation:** The first dimension of a digital transformative leader reflects the capacity of linking digital knowledge with business challenges to resolve problems and dilemmas, and finding innovative solutions. This competency comes on the top of the list since it

*Figure 3. The Digital Transformative Leadership Compass*
*(Source: Schiuma et al., 2022)*

highlights how organizations recognize the importance of digital transformation. According to Nonaka and Takeuchi (2011), this competency reveals what really the digital transformation is for, because wise leaders do not merely focus on what they do but on the ultimate value of what they do. Five main abilities are linked to this competency: (1) The ability to practice critical thinking through understanding the idea behind the digital transformation; (2) The ability to observe and pinpoint both the details and the big picture, which is crucial for leaders who want to be fully aware of a problem or situation; (3) The ability to raise and test hypotheses following a scientific research method; (4) The ability to clarify the organizational strategic objectives, and advise the proper technology solutions when it comes to product and services; and (5) The ability to become pragmatic and oriented to achieve the organizational objectives and take decisions in a timely manner.

**Visualizing digital wealth creation goodness:** Throughout the process of a digital transformation, the organization's strategic goals should be realigned according to the DT aims. Therefore, the rethinking of strategic processes in times of digitization is essential. As such, this dimension focuses on the ability of the leader to make decisions based on the positive impacts on organization and society sustainable growth. Three main abilities are linked to this competency: (1) The ability to see the big picture of value-creation, and doing what is good not only for the organization but for the community at large as well as humankind; (2) The ability to cultivate commitment and positivity, since being idealistic opens the possibility to create new and different futures; and (3) The ability to be ethical and righteous, because ethical leadership has a crucial role in an organization's success, particularly during digital transformation processes.

**Modelling a knowledge-creating context for digital transformation:** Organizations which undertake digital transformation should facilitate knowledge sharing and culture exchange for a better learning and growth. Four main abilities are linked to this competency: (1) The ability to create "shared context", since a digital transformative leader shapes the organizational capacity of constructing a an environment to nurture and exchange digital knowledge; (2) The ability to be open-minded, keep doors open, develop social interactions and promote the creation of real or virtual work-spaces to encourage connections and comparison; (3) The ability to create room for emotional and thinking sharing, fuel relationships, master team building and foster people's innovative spirit; and (4) The ability to act as a facilitator, stimulate comparisons, and make decisions that help achieve a learning environment.

**Sharing the essence of digital transformation:** Digital leaders of organizations working towards digital transformation's success have to communicate mission, vision and values of the essence of a digital transformation. This dimension is described by Nonaka and Takeuchi (2011) as "communicating the essence", suggesting that wise transformative leaders can interpret and express complex situations and problems through stories and lessons that help to extensively and effectively communicate to people. The critical question characterizing this competence is: how to inspire people to create new digital transformation knowledge? In answering this question, three main abilities are linked to this competency: (1) The ability to understand how people will perceive the messages and the reactions they will have, thus building the messages from the receivers' perspective; (2) The ability to influence the quality of organizational learning through storytelling, and creation of scenarios, codifying tacit knowledge, explaining ideas, smoothing the implementation of change and overcome mental obstacles people build against new knowledge; and (3) Ability to communicate through social media, adopting new communication approaches in the digital era, and leveraging Internet tools.

**Linking people with digital transformation:** Today, organizations are increasingly characterized by divergent teams, with people from different educational backgrounds, cultures, ages and countries of origin. Yet, people sometimes have difficulty in accepting and incorporating digital evolution. This competency is all about enabling people to act with DT concerns, overcoming the barriers, inspiring and holding together people from different ages, cultures, roles and primarily digital backgrounds. Three main abilities are linked to this competency: (1) The ability to understand people's perspectives, motivate them to action, and act as a catalyst to move forward in the complex digital landscape by using solid charismatic dominance; (2) The ability to engage in dialectical thinking, which is a kind of thinking that deals with disputations, converses and paradoxes in situations that emerge; (3) The ability to lead a group, with enthusiasm and energy, towards a shared direction, while encouraging team motivation, and enabling team members to bridge the gaps.

**Ensuring digital transformation is everyone's job:** The emergence of the digital age motivate organizations towards building an employee-base who are ready to embrace new working styles, filling roles that are just emerging, adjusting existing jobs, and cultivating soft and leadership skills. This competency is mainly embracing the capacity of the leader to spread digital transformation, as well as assisting people to enhance their leadership skills and digital knowledge competences. The critical question characterizing this competency is: how to foster DT competences in others? In 2011, Nonaka and Takeuchi described this ability as "fostering practical wisdom in others", suggesting the ability of wise leaders to spread wisdom as much as possible through the organization.

Five main abilities are linked to this competency: (1) The ability to diffuse energy and strength in the organization, encouraging all team members to work together without feeling intimidated, and inspiring people to attain the joint purpose; (2) The ability to understand that organizations are complex systems, thus merging both people-oriented and task-oriented behaviors of leadership; (3) The ability to be people-oriented, building mutual trust in relationships, respecting opinions and becoming compassionate about employees' emotions; (4) The ability to nurture critical thinking in subordinates, thus helping them make decisions that best suit a situation, as well as dealing effectively with social, scientific and practical problems that characterize digital transformation; (5) The ability to train leaders, nurture critical thinking, and promotes case-based learning environments to increase people thinking skills and knowledge attainment.

In conclusion, a digital transformative leader should foster people's development through personal and professional learning and mutual trust. He/she should be brave enough to assign them a challenging task that presumes responsibility and a sense of risk. Such a leader would also fosters delegation of power and encourages sustainability through which people, organization and communities acquire the capacity to change their environment to improve equity and the quality of their own life. A digital transformative leader also express trust to employees by encouraging them to manage talent, propose ideas and take initiatives for solving problems. Such a trust often stimulates people to exhibit performance levels that exceed their expectations (Schiuma et al., 2022). A digital transformative leader also creates an environment of inquiry where people can discuss their ideas, processes and practices.

## CONCLUSION AND IMPLICATIONS

The contribution of leadership can be mostly seen in enabling and facilitating digital transformation. As such, digital tools will not offset for the visionary and wise leadership. These qualities will have to be in place irrespective of the communication tools used. As the leadership pattern shifts from control to connection, from individual to group, and from competition to collaboration, the need has emerged for a new breed of leaders who possess a set of digital leadership competences, whom the literature is referring to as either "Digital Leaders" or "Digileaders". To successfully implement digital transformation, organizations need digital leaders who can grasp the opportunities of digitalization for their business and transform them into new business models. Digital leaders exhibit entrepreneurial behaviors, promote digital transformation, and foster timely and open communications. Yet, in line with the uncertainty and complexity of work duties in today's digital world, leaders also need to be able to manage risks while actively initiating and handling change in their organization. Moreover, the higher need for IT Competences and an increased need for life-long learning were also named as competency requirements for digital leaders.

To-date, empirical studies provide support for the impact of digitalization on leadership practices, such as the shift from ego-centric to altro-centric leadership in the knowledge economy, whereby sharing and inspiring leadership practices become relevant (Jakubik & Berazhny, 2017). Scholars also argue that the new leadership paradigm focuses more on active learning, creativity and innovation. This paradigm shift from classical leadership to digital leadership is fully supported by the author. In the search for an answer for the question: How digitalization is changing current and future leadership practices? trust, collaborative learning, sharing and communicating in teams, connecting people rather than imposing them, emerge as the most valuable competences for current and future leadership practices of the new paradigm for the digital era. Accordingly, human factor of leadership will remain fundamental regardless of the digital communication tools (Klein, 2020), because people will require face-to-face connections to discuss, share ideas and give/receive feedback.

In this regard, empirical studies are claiming that humans, not technology, drive DT and that organizations require leaders, and not necessarily technological experts, for managing the multi-phased changes that comprise an organization's DT. To-date, it is evident that a great variety of leadership skills and traits are expected to ensure successful DT. Competent digital leaders are expected to orchestrate a team of technology experts, business experts and entrepreneurs. Such leaders have to master a number of essential Competences, yet the strong emphasis is on communication skills, cross-functional collaboration, team leadership, customer orientation, and strategic thinking. Those competences can be easily grouped under four general categories: (1) cognitive, (2) interpersonal, (3) business, and (4) strategic skills.

Despite the fact that current literature provide evidence that digitalization causes disruptive changes in leadership practices, yet other implications are still deficient and need further evidences to be considered. First, and most evidently, the impact of contextual (i.e. external) factors of digitalization on leadership practices should be taken into consideration more seriously. More empirical studies should be devoted to the correlation between digitalization and the leadership styles and more attention should be given to the outcomes of those studies. Second, introducing leadership competences in education and training programs (both in schools and universities), which should be given higher priority by finding more ways to incorporate those competences into different curricular activities. Third, top executives and human resources professionals should develop approaches and programs for developing leadership competences of their current employees and potential recruits, provide the standards to design a performance system to evaluate a digital leader's Competences and perform benchmarking analysis with a radar onto the competences that are relevant for the future digital leadership practices.

What is lacking so far are empirical studies that analyse actual competency profiles for leaders of the DT and the behavioural indicators corresponding to those competency profiles. Among the other deficiencies prevailing in the current literature is the lack of inductive studies aiming at developing a taxonomy of leadership competence needed for managing DT successfully. Reasons for the lack of such studies in my opinion might be firstly; the difficulty of the inductive approach which requires the application of the grounded theory research methodology, and secondly; the fact that inductive studies are time-consuming which might be a barrier for many researchers.

## FUTURE RESEARCH DIRECTIONS

Research on digital leadership competences needed for Digital Transformation is still in its early stages, regardless all the attempts made by different scholars to identify, categorize and apply those competences in action. As such, suggestions for future research (both theoretical and empirical studies) can be made in many directions. Firstly, a more precise definition of the new terminology, such as; "Digital Leadership", "Digital Leaders", "Digital Transformative Leadership" and "Digileaders" is needed in order to create a common consensus among different business sectors as well as geographical scopes.

Secondly, in many studies, the main outcome is a comprehensive list of Competences defined broadly. As such, more empirical research is needed to identify behavioral indicators under those competences. Identification of such behavioral indicators will enable better understanding and conceptualization of those competences in action, and thus enable linking those competences with successful digital transformation projects and initiatives. Thirdly, longitudinal research studies are much encouraged at this point of time (especially in developing countries) to study the correlation between the different digital leadership competences (on one side), and the implementation of the different phases of digital transformation (on another side). Fourthly, more comparative studies between countries (both developed and under-developed) are also needed to understand the relationships and causalities between digital transformative leadership competences and digital transformation implementation in practice.

## REFERENCES

Berson, Y., & Avolio, B. J. (2004). Transformational leadership and the dissemination of organizational goals: A case study of a telecommunication firm. *The Leadership Quarterly*, *15*(5), 625–646. doi:10.1016/j.leaqua.2004.07.003

Bharadwaj, A., El-Sawy, O. A., Pavlou, P. A., & Venkatraman, N. (2013). Digital business strategy: Toward a next generation of insights. *Management Information Systems Quarterly*, *37*(2), 471–482. doi:10.25300/MISQ/2013/37:2.3

Bolden, R., & O'Regan, N. (2016). Digital Disruption and the Future of Leadership. *Journal of Management Inquiry*, *25*(4), 438–446. doi:10.1177/1056492616638173

Brown, R. B. (1993). Meta-Competence: A Recipe for Reframing the Competence Debate. *Personnel Review*, *22*(6), 25–36. doi:10.1108/EUM0000000000814

Brunner, M., Gonzalez-Castañé, G., & Ravesteijn, P. (2021). How Digital Leadership competences and IT Capabilities affect an organization's ability to digitally transform and adopt new technologies. *Journal of International Technology and Information Management*, *30*(4), 139–156.

Draganidis, F., & Mentzas, G. (2006). Competency Based Management: A Review of Systems and Approaches. *Journal of Information Management and Computer Security*, *14*(1), 51–64. doi:10.1108/09685220610648373

Dubois, D. (1993). *Competency-Based Performance Improvement: A Strategy for Organizational Change*. Harvard Press.

Dunkle, D., & Gurbaxani, V. (2019). Gearing up for Successful Digital Transformation. *MIS Quarterly Executive*, *18*(3), 209–220. doi:10.17705/2msqe.00017

Fenech, R., Baguant, P., & Ivanov, D. (2019). The Changing Role of Human Resource Management in an Era of Digital Transformation. *Journal of Management Information and Decision Sciences*, *22*(2), 166–175.

Frankenberger, K., Mayer, H., Reiter, A. & Schmidt, M. (2020). *The Digital Transformer's Dilemma: How to Energize Your Core Business While Building Disruptive Products and Services*. New Jersey. John Wiley & Sons.

Gebelein, S. H. (2001). Leadership Competency. Leadership. *Excellence*, *18*(3), 10.

Goleman, D., & Senge, P. (2014). The Triple Focus: A New Approach to Education. More than Sound Productions. Florence.

Gudergan, G., Mugge, P., Kwiatkowski, A., Abbu, H., Hoeborn, G., & Conrad, R. (2021). Digital Leadership - Which leadership dimensions contribute to digital transformation success? *IEEE International Conference on Engineering, Technology and Innovation (ICE/ITMC)*, 1-8. 10.1109/ICE/ITMC52061.2021.9570231

Hearsum, S. (2015). How to develop digital leadership capability. *Strategic HR Review*, *14*(5), 208. doi:10.1108/SHR-08-2015-0059

Imran, F., Shahzad, K., Butt, A., & Kantola, J. (2020). Leadership Competences for Digital Transformation: Evidence from Multiple Cases. *Proceedings of the AHFE 2020 Virtual Conferences on Human Factors, Business Management and Society, and Human Factors in Management and Leadership*, July 16-20, USA, 81-87.

Jackson, D. (2009). Profiling Industry-Relevant Management Graduate Competences: The Need for a Fresh Approach. *International Journal of Management Education*, *8*(1), 85–98. doi:10.3794/ijme.81.281

Jakubik, M., & Berazhny, I. (2017). Rethinking Leadership and It's Practices in the Digital Era. In Suzana Laporšek; Sedmak Suzana & Doris Gomezelj Omerzel (eds.), *Managing the Global Economy. Proceedings of the Management International Conference*, Monastier di Treviso, Italy, 471–483.

Jones, B., Harris, M. E., & Santana, M. (2008). Mastering developing new leadership for transformative change. *Journal of Academy of Business and Economics*, *8*(2), 66–74.

Juhro, S. M., & Aulia, A. F. (2019). New sources of growth: The role of frugal innovation and transformational leadership. *Bulletin of Monetary Economics and Banking*, *22*(3), 383–402. doi:10.21098/bemp.v22i3.1195

Juhro, S. M., Aulia, A. F., Hadiwaluyo, D., Aliandrina, D., & Lavika, E. (2020). The Role of Catalytic Collaboration in Leveraging Transformational Leadership Competences to Generate Sustainable Innovation. *International Journal of Organizational Leadership*, *9*(1), 48–66.

Kane, G. C., Phillips, A. N., Copulsky, J., & Andrus, G. (2019). How Digital Leadership Is(n't) Different. *MIT Sloan Management Review*, *60*(3), 34–39.

Kane, G. C. P. D., Phillips, A. N., Kiron, D., & Buckley, N. (2015). Strategy, not technology, drives digital transformation, 1-25. Deloitte University Press.

Klein, M. (2020). Leadership Characteristics in the Era of Digital Transformation. *Business and Management Studies International Journal*, *8*(1), 883–902. doi:10.15295/bmij.v8i1.1441

Le Deist, F. D., & Winterton, J. (2005). What is Competence? *Human Resource Development International*, *8*(1), 27–46. doi:10.1080/1367886042000338227

Libert, B., Beck, M., & Wind, Y. (2016). 7 Questions to ask before your next digital transformation. *Harvard Business Review*.

Mack, T. C. (2015). Leadership in the Future. In Sowcik et al. (Eds.) Leadership 2050. Challenges, Key Contexts, and Emerging Trends.

Mazurchenko, A., & Maršíková, K. (2019). Digitally-Powered Human Resource Management: Skills and Roles in the Digital Era. *Acta Informatica Pragensia*, *8*(2), 72–87. doi:10.18267/j.aip.125

McClelland, D. (1973). Testing for competence rather than for intelligence. *The American Psychologist*, *28*(1), 1–14. doi:10.1037/h0034092 PMID:4684069

Megahed, N. (2015). Capturing Competences and Behavioral Indicators of Diplomats for a Multiple-Jobs Competency Model. *Journal of Human Resources Management and Labor Studies*, *3*(1), 54–78. doi:10.15640/jhrmls.v3n1a4

Megahed, N. (2018). A Critical Review of the Literature and Practice of Competency Modelling. *KnowledgeE Social Sciences*, KnE Publishing, 104–126.

Megahed, N., Heijden, B. V., Shaker, M., & Wahba, K. (2012). A Framework for Developing a Multiple-Jobs Competency Model for Diplomats. *International Journal of Business and Social Science*, *3*, 42–55.

Nonaka, I., & Takeuchi, H. (2011). The wise leader. *Harvard Business Review*, *89*(5), 58–67. PMID:21548419

Prentice, W. C. H. (2004). Understanding leadership. *Harvard Business Review*, *82*(1), 102–109. PMID:14723181

Reis, J., Amorim, M., Melão, N., & Matos, P. (2018). Digital Transformation: A Literature Review and Guidelines for Future Research. *Proceedings of the World Conference on Information Systems and Technologies*, 411–421. 10.1007/978-3-319-77703-0_41

Sainger, G. (2018). Leadership in Digital Age: A Study on the Role of Leader in this Era of Digital Transformation. *International Journal of Leadership*, *6*(1), 1–6.

Salicru, S. (2015). The Global Leadership Psychological Contract Model – Actionable to Shape the Future to 2050. In Sowcik et al. (Eds.) 2015. Leadership 2050. Challenges, Key Contexts, and Emerging Trends, 159-173. Emerald Publishing.

Schiuma, G., Schettini, E., Santarsiero, F., & Carlucci, D. (2022). The transformative leadership compass: Six Competences for digital transformation entrepreneurship. *International Journal of Entrepreneurial Behaviour & Research*, *28*(5), 1273–1291. doi:10.1108/IJEBR-01-2021-0087

Shields, C. M. (2020). *Transformative leadership*. Oxford Research Encyclopedia of Education. doi:10.1093/acrefore/9780190264093.013.632

Spencer, E. M., & Spencer, S. M. (1993). *Competence at Work*. John Wiley & Sons, Inc.

Spencer, L. M., & Spencer, S. M. (1993). *Competence at Work: Models for Superior Performance*. John Wiley and Sons Inc.

Tabrizi, B., Lam, E., Girard, K., & Irvin, V. (2019). Digital transformation is not about technology. *Harvard Business Review*, *13*, 1–6.

Vial, G. (2019). Understanding digital transformation: A review and a research agenda. *The Journal of Strategic Information Systems*, *28*(2), 118–144. doi:10.1016/j.jsis.2019.01.003

Wilson, E. J., Goethals, G. R., Sorenson, G., & Burns, J. M. (2004). Leadership in the digital age. Encyclopedia of leadership, 4, 858-861.

Youn, S., Stepich, D., & Cox, D. (2006). Building a Competency-Based Curriculum Architecture to Educate 21st Century Business Practitioners. *Journal of Education for Business*, *81*(6), 307–311. doi:10.3200/JOEB.81.6.307-314

# Chapter 6
# The Challenge of Leadership Development in the Digital Era

**Hyung-Woo Lee**
*Hannam University, South Korea*

## ABSTRACT

*This chapter focuses on the challenge of developing effective leadership in the digital era. As technology develops, a growing trend emerges that interpersonal relationship in organizations is characterized by technology-based interactions. This chapter shows how this trend pose a challenge to developing effective leadership in organizations. In doing so, this chapter posits that effective leadership emerges thorough frequent in-person interactions between leader and followers. To establish this position, this chapter proposes a relationship-based model of leadership development, in which the methods of exerting interpersonal influence that leader uses evolve as relationship develops. Using these different methods results in follower's commitments of different kinds and qualities. With this model, the chapter aims to explain why prevalence of technology-based interaction in organization makes it difficult for leader to develop close interpersonal relationship with their followers, which is followed by the suggestions on how to overcome these barriers.*

## INTRODUCTION

Leadership is such an important factor for the success of today's organizations. The classic theories of organization have placed a greater emphasis on the design of organizational structure based on the belief that establishing one-fits-all approach can ensure the optimal productivity of an organization. According to these theories, the role of managers was mainly to implement the bureaucratic rules, formal regulations, and standardized procedures (Zaleznik, 1977). However, as the rate of changes in societal and market environment increases, timely organizational responses to the rapidly changing demands of various stakeholders has become a keyword for their survival and prosperity (Suarez & Oliva, 2005). In this context, the role of those occupying leadership positions to create the momentum for organizational change and adjustment to meet the environmental demands is increasing emphasized (Johnson, 1998). It

DOI: 10.4018/978-1-6684-5864-8.ch006

seems clear that organizations need leaders who can better mobilize their employees to achieve greater performance than just making sure their employees are fulfilling their routine tasks.

The concept of leadership involves a type of interpersonal interaction in which one person affect behaviors of others. A conceptual clarification is in order because there are some concepts similar to leadership in social science literature. One of which is the concept of management. Management also involves interpersonal influence. Managers determine what their subordinates should do and the subordinates follow the instructions from managers. The concept of management is predicated on the existence of organizational context in which hierarchical authority characterizes relationship among employees. In essence, manager's activity of influencing subordinate's behavior take place in the situation in which it is subordinate's formal responsibility to do so (Kerr & Jeremier, 1978). In contrast, leadership tend to focus on the ability of leaders inducing employees to make voluntary efforts to achieve tasks goals sometimes going beyond formal responsibility. The distinction between management and leadership is reflected in a line of current leadership studies. For instance, effective leadership is found to increase organizational citizenship behavior (OCB) indicating that people can do more work than they are required when they are inspired by an effective leadership (Bambale, Shamdusin, & Subramaniam, 2011; Dartey-Baak & Addo, 2018).

Another scholarly concepts similar to leadership is power. Power also refers to the situation where a person makes others to do what he/she wants. However, power is a broader term than leadership in that power can be exerted through coercive measure, whereas leadership tend to emphasize follower's voluntary compliance. This distinction is well shown in the notion of transformational leadership. Bass (1990) proposed a taxonomy of leadership by which he introduced a new concept of transformational leadership, positioning it in juxtaposition with a more traditional notion of transactional leadership. He goes on to argue that transformational leadership is more effective in that it enables to achieve extraordinary performance beyond expectation by transforming the follower' motivation tendency such that they voluntarily internalize the goals of leader or organization.

Also notable in the concept of leadership is its relational aspect. Leaders influence their followers through close and intimate relationship, which is reflected in the behavioral approach in the 1940-50's as well as the recent theory of leader-member exchange. The early scholars of leadership attempted to identify the types of leadership behaviors. In 1947, a group of researchers from University of Michigan conducted a research to find what specific behaviors can induce subordinate to follow their leaders (Ronald, 2014). In this study, they identified two types of leadership behavior, one of which is the behaviors of heeding to employee's personal needs. This indicates that employees want to follow leaders when they care about individuals in organizations. This further implies that leaders not only need to focus on improving the productivity of an organization but also to develop intimate relationships with individual followers. Leaders need to view their employees not only as one of their resources to get the job done but also treat them as humans with which task goal are shared.

The relational aspect of leadership is reflected in more recent studies as well. For instance, the multidimensional concept of transformational leadership contains the element of individualized consideration. This shows that it is necessary for leaders to show a genuine care about their employees in order to achieve extraordinary performance. Furthermore, a group of leadership scholars proposed the LMX theory (Graen & Uhl-Bien, 1995). The theory posits that how intimate a leader is with their subordinate determines the quality and magnitudes of influences he/she can exert on the subordinate. It can be drawn from these streams of leadership research that the effectiveness of leadership hinges on the quality of relationships between leader and followers.

Given this, the current changes in work environment pose some challenges to developing effective leadership. An increasing number of employees work from home. In addition, the current health crisis has expedited the transformation of workplace interactions toward technology-based. Hence, the emotional attachment among employees are increasingly weakening as the nature and quality of interpersonal interactions attenuate. This concern is expressed by a number of organization scholars. Spicer (2020) pointed this out from organizational culture perspective. He argued that the new norm of technology-mediated communication posed challenges to managers in building the culture of exploration and creativity in organization in which employee's obsession to safety leaves managers shorthanded. The work of Schein (1999) is informative in this regard that emphasizes the role of dialogues in transmitting organizational culture. Newman and Ford (2021) raised an apparent problem of limited personal contacts caused by transformation to the virtual work environment.

In this background, this article proposes an integrative model that elucidates why the current trend in the digital era hinders development of effective leadership. The integrative model develops by combining the theories regarding the two concepts: power and commitment. This article concludes with a number of suggestions to mitigate such negative effects resulting from the proliferation of technology-based communication in organizations.

## LEADERSHIP AND SOURCES OF POWER

Given that social science is investigation of social phenomena, interpersonal influence has always been a topic of interest for most social scientists. Political scientists have defined the concept of power in terms of asymmetric nature of influence in relationship between people (Dahl, 1957). The early conception of power tended to focus on the coercive nature of power making people follow those in the authority positions. However, as an increasing number of scholars realized the ubiquity of power in human relations, the concept has expanded to explain more implicit power disparity between people neither of which is under the other party's formal authority. Accordingly, the concept of power began to include more invisible and non-coercive measures by which people's behaviors are influenced by other's decisions or instructions.

In this vein, the concept of power can be said to embrace the concept of leadership in that the latter represents a particular type of the former. In other words, while power can be exerted through both coercive and non-coercive measures, leadership tends to refer to influencing others using non-coercive measure or at least using coercive power in a non-coercive manner (Fuqua, Payne, & Cangemi, 2000). Of course, the association between power and leadership has been posited in many different ways. Some view power as constituting the toolkit for leaders to use to influence their employees (Bal, Campbell, Steed, & Meddings, 2008), while others tend to view the two concepts as representing the different ends of a continuum (Brown, 2006). In addition, one can easily find that the concept of leadership is sometimes used interchangeably with the concept of power in the literature and theories of power are often applied to explain leadership (e.g, Erkutlu & Chafra, 2006). Having said that, although some may disagree, the above-mentioned position about the association between power and leadership was suggested to highlight the different foci of the concepts.

French, Raven, and Cartwright (2016) proposed a taxonomy of power, which suggests the following five different ways to exert power over others. Coercive power comes from the ability to punish or give negative reinforcement to those who refused to comply with the power holder. Reward power, to the contrary, depends on the ability to provide rewards for doing something wanted by the person with power. Legitimate power means that people follow another because he/she has the formal authority to order them to do something. This type of power resides in those occupying the official position in organization. Expert power can be exerted when the expertise and knowledge of leaders are the reason why subordinates seek their help or guidance. Referent power can be exerted when subordinates admire their leader or they voluntarily want to identify themselves with their leaders.

These five types of power can be located sequentially along a continuum indicating the differing extent of the volition of subordinates, with coercive power and referent power at both ends. Subordinates who comply with leader's direction because of coercive measure used by their leader likely act with the least degree of volition. To the contrary, subordinates who identify themselves with their leader are likely to comply with leader's direction with the greatest degree of volition.

The current literature on leadership tend to focus on the ability of leaders who can make their subordinates voluntarily follow them as discussed earlier. It is distinguished from the early conception of management which focused on the organizational authority as a primary source of interpersonal influence in organizational context (Bennis, 1989). The concept of management assumes that the primary source of cohesion in organization comes from the formal authority to make employees perform their tasks in compliance with organizational rules and hierarchical orders. In this vein, management is equivalent to the activity of leaders relying on coercive, reward, and legitimate power.

To the contrary, the concept of leadership highlights volitional action of subordinates. One of the most popular notion of leadership, transformational leadership, reflects the emphasis on subordinate's volition. What Bass (1990) proposed in his original book was the full range of leadership. His model is a full range model in that it contains both the traditional and less-effective notion of leadership and the new and more-effective notion of leadership. The traditional model of leadership was labelled as transactional leadership in that the relationship between leaders and followers are conceived as a give-and-take relation, and that the major role of leader is to carry out the transaction with subordinates according to the rules and regulation. In other words, the primary role of transactional leadership lies in their execution of the formal authority granted by their organization, including the authority to provides sanction for those who failed to deliver task outcomes and rewards for those who do so.

To the contrary, the newly suggested (in the time of Bass) and more effective leadership is labelled as transformational leaders. The major role of leaders is viewed as transforming the mindset of employees such that they voluntarily endeavor to achieve the organizational mission that has become their own. Since Bass (1990), many scholars have developed various leadership styles, such as authentic leadership and servant leadership, most of which also emphasize the ability to make their employees voluntarily committed to their tasks and missions. Thus, it is reasonable to argue that the notion of today's leadership highlights the ability to provoke the volitional desire of employees to achieve organizational tasks, goals, and missions.

Admittedly, the distinction between management and leadership is not clear-cut. For instance, the formal authority of leaders often helps them exert transformational leadership and induce employees to voluntarily pursue organizational missions as if those are their own. Also, some scholars like Fiedler (2015) posited that the availability of formal authority over employees can constitute a favorable condition for exerting an effective leadership. Nevertheless, it is reasonable to argue that the conceptional prototypes of management and leadership are sufficiently distinguishable based on the reliance on formal authority. Based on this position, the model of French et al. (2016) categorizing the sources of power also presents the distinction between the concept of management and that of leadership, which is presented in Figure 1.

*Figure 1. Source or Power and the Conceptual Distinction between Management and Leadership*

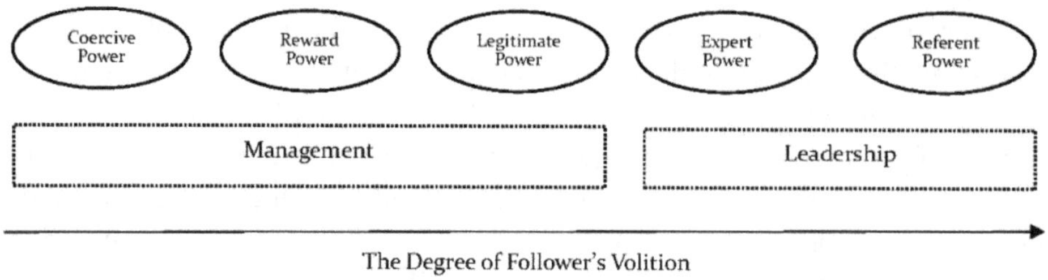


## TYPES OF COMMITMENT

Scholars have categorized the types of commitment as well. Allen and Meyer (1990) identified three types of organizational commitment, each of which is driven by distinct motives. Continuance commitment refers to employees who remain working in the organization or performing their tasks simply due to the lack of alternatives. Central to this type of commitment is employee's continuance to work in organization, in other words, not leaving the organization. No emotional attachment is involved in this type of commitment. Normative commitment refers to the situation in which employees working in organization due to the sense of obligation. This obligation can be towards both their coworkers, leaders, and their organization. Affective commitment is, on the contrary, takes place when employees are committed because they like their tasks or organizations. Emotional attachment plays a significant role in affective commitment. These three types of commitment can also be placed along a continuum indicating the degree of employee's volition. Continuance commitment and affective commitment are placed at each of the ends. This relation between the types of commitment and the degree of volition is presented in Figure 2.

## INTEGRATIVE MODEL OF LEADERSHIP

One of the key roles of leadership is to promote employee's commitment to their tasks and organizational goals. Most of leadership theories implicitly and explicitly highlights this ultimate role of leadership. The reason why LMX theory emphasizes the intimacy in relationship with employees is also because the intimacy is conducive to promoting employee's commitment and their work efforts, thereby ac-

*Figure 2. Types of Commitment and the Degree of Employee Volition*

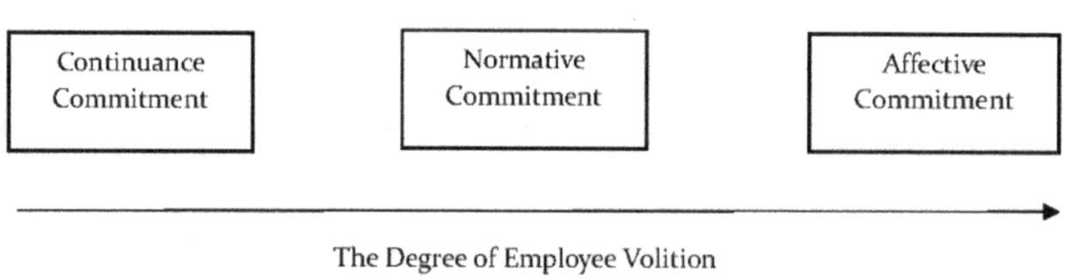

complishing organizational goals (Graen & Uhl-Bien, 1995). This role is particularly emphasized for lower- and middle-managers who have more frequent in-person contacts with street-level employees who are responsible for executing organizational tasks.

Therefore, based on the conceptual comparability, causal linkages, and the degree of employee's volition, these two models (Figure 1 and 2) can be integrated. First, when employees perceive that their leaders use coercive and reward power, they may be committed to their tasks and organizations. The main reason why they do so is because they either have no choice but to follow their leaders. Those who stay in current organization only because of the sanction and reward may leave the organization if they are offered better jobs in other organizations. In this vein, coercive and reward power lead to continuance commitment. Second, when leaders exert legitimate power, employee may commit to their tasks because it is a shared norm in organization to follow their legitimate orders. Hence, the use of legitimate power leads to normative continuance. The use of legitimate power also leads to continuance commitment because employees need to comply with the shared norm in organization to the extent that they want to remain as a member of organization. Third, the use of expert and referent power likely result in affective commitment on the part of employees. If employees perceive that their leaders are knowledgeable about their tasks, and hence, capable of providing insightful advices on how to effectively perform their tasks, they will respect and sometimes even admire their leaders (affective commitment). Moreover, if employees like their leaders personally, their affection will lead them to commit to their works and organizations.

Indeed, studies have provided evidence that the types of power exerted by leaders have differential effect on affective commitment. For instance, Teimouri, Izadpanah, Akbariani, Jenab, Khoury, and Moslehpour (2015) reported that the use of referent power showed the greatest correlation with affective commitment, and the use of coercive power showed the least correlation. Cogliser & Schriesheim (2000) found that expert and referent power had greater influence over relationship with their subordinates, and the remaining three types of power had less influence on the relationship. Similarly, Borchgrevink and Boster (1997) found that expert power positively affected intimate relationship which in turn laid the foundation for the use of referent power, while none of the other types of power significantly affected the relationship quality with leaders. Jalilvand and Vosta (2015) also corroborate with this finding by showing no significant relationship between coercive power and affective commitment among employees in sport organizations. Rahim and Afza (1993) also reported a similar finding. Erkutlu and Chafra (2006) showed the negative effects of the use of the first three types of power by leaders. They found that the use of coercive, reward, and legitimate power, which they labelled as position power, increases the stress-level of employees while the use of expert and referent power, labelled as personal power, alleviate it. Given the stress evoked by the use of positional power should have negative effect on affection of employees toward their leaders, this result implies that exertion of positional power may have a harmful effect on affective commitment. Expert power is also found to positive affect affective commitment. Pierro, Raven, Amato, and Bélanger (2013) soft power base, including the use of expert power, positively affects affective commitment.

Therefore, the following model can be suggested, as presented in Figure 3.

## THE QUALITY OF RELATIONSHIP AND THE TYPES OF COMMITMENT

The types of commitment not only represent different sources of commitment but also indicate different degrees of commitment. Let's start by looking at the literature on intimate personal relationship devel-

*Figure 3. Integrative Model of Leadership and Commitment*

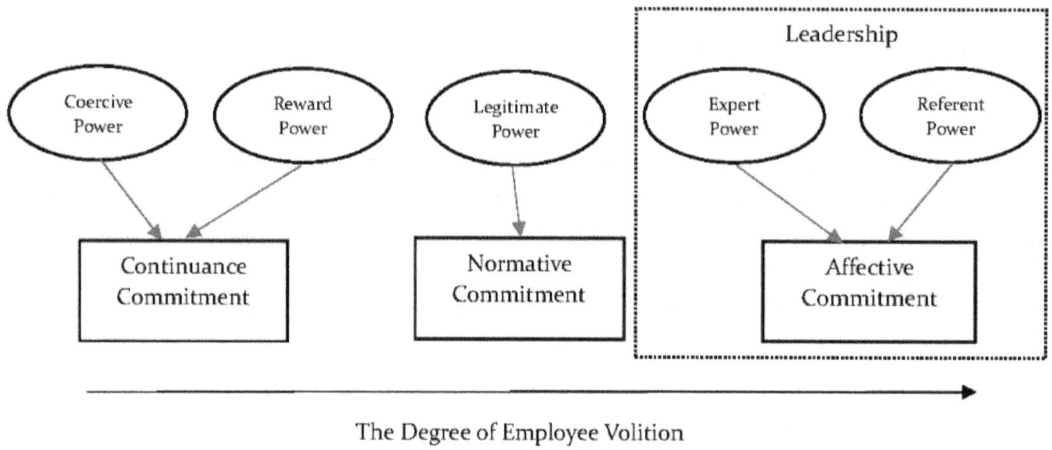


opment. Frank and Brandstätter (2002) differentiated the types of commitment in intimate relationship into two types: avoidance- and approach-based commitment. The former is similar to continuance commitment in that it makes people commit to their partner to avoid negative relational consequence such as losing partner, while the latter is similar to affective commitment since it comes from an actor's volition to gain pleasure from the sense of emotional attachment with his/her partner. This research confirmed that the parameters of the quality of relationship, such as satisfaction and positive emotions, was positively correlated with approach-based commitment and negatively with avoidance-based commitment. In organization studies, Iverson and Buttigieg (1999) reported a similar finding. They found that affective commitment is the most beneficial to organization by reducing turnover and absentees, and encouraging to accept organizational change, while continuance commitment is detrimental to organizational effectiveness.

The literature also suggests that commitment builds over time as the quality of relationship develops between people. The marketing literature points to the importance of developing quality relationship with customers such that customers have affective commitment toward sales person. The emergence of the concept of relationship marketing itself implies the importance of promoting affective commitment of customers toward sales persons (Sheth & Parvatlyar, 1995). Gruen, Summers, and Acito (2000) found that only the types of activities that lead to affective commitment enabled participants to engage in a more advanced type of cooperation (i.e., coproduction), whereas simply participating to the membership activity was possible with normative commitment. Boateng and Narteh (2016) also found that only that cooperative activities that increases mutual trust can eventually help build affective commitment, implying that developing affective commitment takes the effort to build trust in relationship over time. The importance of developing quality relationship for promoting affective commitment is also salient in the literature on interorganizational network. This literature commonly assumes that securing affective commitment from partner organizations are beneficial in the long run. It also assumes that it takes time and efforts to build affective commitment. Predicated on these assumptions, Agostini, Nosella, and Venturini (2019) suggested a few ways to facilitate affective commitment from their partner organizations.

## The Role of the Relationship Quality for Enhancing Leadership Effectiveness

The theory of leader-member exchange (LMX) posits that the quality of relationship between leader and follower increases positive attitudinal outcomes of followers (Dansereau, Graen, & Haga, 1975), suggesting that leaders should develop close relationship with their subordinates in order to exert effective leadership. Those employees with intimate relationship with their leaders tend to perceive that their organization treats them with care and respect (perceived organization support), thereby develops affective commitment to their leader and organization (Casimir, Ng, Wang, & Ooi, 2014). Moreover, organizational efforts to support their employees results in greater affective commitment when employees have intimate relationship with their leaders (Buch, 2015).

As previously discussed, transformational leadership is effective in helping employees achieve extraordinary performance. One of the reasons for this is also because transformational leadership cares about individuals in organization. Bass (1990) proposed individualized consideration as one of the components of transformational leadership, which refers to the extent to which leader attends to follower's needs and provides individually tailored coaching on how to improve their performance. Amin, Akram, Shahzad, and Amir (2018) showed that individualized consideration had a greater effect on affective commitment than other components of transformational leadership. Kim and Kim (2014) also reported the same result.

Another component of transformational leadership emphasizes the use of expert power. Bass (1990) identified intellectual stimulation as one of the key elements of transformational leadership. Transformational leaders can intellectually stimulate subordinates by proposing a new perspective on the matter using their expertise in the task. In addition, another element of transformational leader is inspirational motivation requiring the ability to articulate an attractive vision that is compelling enough to inspire their subordinates. Leaders cannot inspire and stimulate employees without expertise in the field. Without trusting leader's expertise, subordinates would see the vision proposed by the leader as unrealistic. Both inspirational motivation and intellectual stimulation depends on leader's expert power which will increase employees' affective commitment (Pierro et al., 2013).

## The Challenges to Developing Relationship in Virtual Workplaces

It seems undeniable that the recent advance of information technology shows the potential for teleworking to become the typical way of working in organization. Indeed, an increasing number of employees want their organization to expand teleworking and organizations are looking to do so. The recent public health crisis also contributed the surge of demands for teleworking. Due to the advance in the computer-aided virtual communication methods, it seems possible for teleworking to become typical work arrangement in organizations.

However, the experience of increased teleworking during the recent health crisis showed not only the potential benefits of this alternative work arrangement but also the challenges to expanding it. The effectiveness of work-related communication was not necessarily undermined during the COVID-19 with the help of using the advanced digital technology. Some scholars pointed to the potential of the current development of digital communication methods to improve the interaction quality between people (Liu, Baumeister, Yang, & Hu, 2019). However, the benefits of using digital communication which these scholars have discussed is mainly about reaching out to the general public and obtaining their feedback in the context of marketing (Nasir, 2015). To the contrary, in organizational context, replacing in-person communication with communication via digital media can cause problems of attenuating the quality of interpersonal interaction among workers and weakening groups cohesion.

A number of studies documented the difficulties associated with teleworking reported by participants. One of the most notable downsides is participant's isolation. Gainey, Kelly, and Hill (1999) pointed out that teleworkers tend to show a greater level of turnover due to the lack of social interaction with coworkers. Cooper and Kurland (2002) pointed out that teleworkers cannot benefit from career development opportunity such as network building, informal learning, and mentoring. Fireman (1999) found that teleworkers tend to stop teleworking because they feel isolated due to the lack of office social interactions and supervisor support. Even if teleworkers can communicate with their coworkers and supervisors without time lags with the help of video conferencing, teleworkers felt they lacked communication with their coworkers and supervisor (Lowry, 1996). Admittedly, some scholars such as Chen and Wei (2020) showed that the use of social media for work-related communication with supervisors and coworkers can increase work performance. However, their study examined the supplementary effect of social media use for communication among workers working onsite rather than the effect of replacing in-person communication in the workplaces.

It is obvious that computer-mediated communication enables to sharing information with those who reside remotely from each other. However, scholars have frequently reported that building intimacy and emotional attachment may not be possible. For instance, Hambley, O'Neil, and Kline (2007) found that the group in which participant doing face-to-face communication showed greater level of team cohesion than those communicating via video conferencing or text chat.

To the extent that effective leadership requires reliance on expert and referent power, teleworking or communicating via digital media can undermine the effectiveness of leadership. While exerting referent power conducive to promoting employee's affective commitment requires leader to invest on developing intimate relationship with their subordinates, attenuating interaction by increased use of digital media for communication can make it hard for leaders to develop quality relationship with their subordinates.

## CONCLUSION

If the practice of teleworking in organization is to expand in the future, it may pose challenge to developing work group cohesion and employee's emotional bond with supervisors. It may be better to start with those employees who have already developed close relationship with their supervisors. Given that strong group identity is one of the major sources of affective commitment (Marique, Stinglhamber, Desmette, Caesens, & De Zanet, 2012), organization should be prepared to take measures to maintain a strong group identity. In teleworking environment, the point of contact for teleworkers tend to reduce to supervisors or a limited number of coworkers. Hence, leaders need to convene a regular meeting where all team members participate to build and maintain group-oriented mindset.

Also important is leaders' effort to maintain close relationship with those working in virtual environment, given that employees have stronger affective commitment when leaders can use referent power. As Johnson, Bettenhausen, and Gibbons (2009) found, it may be necessary to attempt to frequently interact in-person with teleworkers such that at least ten percent of the total amount of interaction with their subordinates is through in-person contact.

Creating a positive organizational culture is also important. In general, organizational culture is another factor making employees behave in socially acceptable manner and remain committed to accomplish their task goals, and leader is better positioned to create or promote positive organizational culture than followers. The culture of accountability can help reduce the downsides of teleworking, for instance, the lack of task communication. Also, the culture of trust will also help leaders maintain social cohesion with teleworkers (Newman & Ford, 2021).

Of course, there are some people with positive view arguing that the transition toward digital communication can be an opportunity to better harness human capital rather than a crisis caused by the lack of group cohesion. Surely, encouraging to suggest novel idea through internet and collectively building a solution to wicked problems can lead to success. In addition, employees can perform their tasks without dealing with interpersonal conflict and office politics. However, any novel idea cannot be realized into realistic solution without refinement and development through the process of in-person communication among workers and with supervisors.

Computer-aided communication may become a typical mode of work-related communication in the future. If that is the future to come, leaders and organizations should prepare the paradigm of management suited for the new working environment. The points raised in this article and suggestions can be a starting point for the preparation.

## REFERENCES


Agostini, L., Nosella, A., & Venturini, K. (2019). Toward increasing affective commitment in SME strategic networks. *Business Process Management Journal*, *25*(7), 1822–1840. doi:10.1108/BPMJ-02-2018-0035

Allen, N. J., & Meyer, J. P. (1990). The measurement and antecedents of affective, continuance and normative commitment to the organization. *Journal of Occupational Psychology*, *63*(1), 1–18. doi:10.1111/j.2044-8325.1990.tb00506.x

Amin, W., Akram, U., Shahzad, F., & Amir, M. (2018). Impact of transformation leadership on affective employee's commitment. *European Online Journal of Natural and Social Sciences: Proceedings*, *7*(1(s)), pp-48.

Bal, V., Campbell, M., Steed, J., & Meddings, K. (2008). The role of power in effective leadership. *Center for Creative Leadership*. www. ccl. org

Bambale, A. J. A., Mohd Shamsudin, F., & Subramaniam, C. (2011). Stimulating organizational citizenship behavior (OCB) research for theory development: Exploration of leadership paradigms. [IJARBSS]. *International Journal of Academic Research in Business & Social Sciences*, *1*, 48–69.

Bass, B. M. (1990). From transactional to transformational leadership: Learning to share the vision. *Organizational Dynamics*, *18*(3), 19–31. doi:10.1016/0090-2616(90)90061-S

Bennis, W. G. (1989). Managing the dream: Leadership in the 21st century. *Journal of Organizational Change Management*, *2*(1), 6–10. doi:10.1108/09534818910134040

Boateng, S. L., & Narteh, B. (2016). Online relationship marketing and affective customer commitment–The mediating role of trust. *Journal of Financial Services Marketing*, *21*(2), 127–140. doi:10.1057/fsm.2016.5

Borchgrevink, C. P., & Boster, F. J. (1997). Leader-member exchange development: A hospitality antecedent investigation. *International Journal of Hospitality Management, 16*(3), 241–259. doi:10.1016/S0278-4319(97)00013-3

Buch, R. (2015). Leader–member exchange as a moderator of the relationship between employee–organization exchange and affective commitment. *International Journal of Human Resource Management, 26*(1), 59–79. doi:10.1080/09585192.2014.934897

Casimir, G., Ng, Y. N. K., Wang, K. Y., & Ooi, G. (2014). The relationships amongst leader-member exchange, perceived organizational support, affective commitment, and in-role performance: A social-exchange perspective. *Leadership and Organization Development Journal, 35*(5), 366–385. doi:10.1108/LODJ-04-2012-0054

Chen, X., & Wei, S. (2020). The impact of social media use for communication and social exchange relationship on employee performance. *Journal of Knowledge Management, 24*(6), 1289–1314. doi:10.1108/JKM-04-2019-0167

Cogliser, C. C., & Schriesheim, C. A. (2000). Exploring work unit context and leader–member exchange: A multi-level perspective. *Journal of Organizational Behavior, 21*(5), 487–511. doi:10.1002/1099-1379(200008)21:5<487::AID-JOB57>3.0.CO;2-P

Cooper, C. D., & Kurland, N. B. (2002). Telecommuting, professional isolation, and employee development in public and private organizations. *Journal of Organizational Behavior: The International Journal of Industrial. Occupational and Organizational Psychology and Behavior, 23*(4), 511–532. doi:10.1002/job.145

Dahl, R. A. (1957). The concept of power. *Behavioral Science, 2*(3), 201–215. doi:10.1002/bs.3830020303

Dansereau, F. Jr, Graen, G., & Haga, W. J. (1975). A vertical dyad linkage approach to leadership within formal organizations: A longitudinal investigation of the role making process. *Organizational Behavior and Human Performance, 13*(1), 46–78. doi:10.1016/0030-5073(75)90005-7

Dartey-Baah, K., & Addo, S. A. (2018). Psychological identification with job: A leadership-OCB mediator. *The International Journal of Organizational Analysis, 27*(3), 548–565. doi:10.1108/IJOA-10-2017-1262

Erkutlu, H. V., & Chafra, J. (2006). Relationship between leadership power bases and job stress of subordinates: Example from boutique hotels. *Management Research News, 29*(5), 285–297. doi:10.1108/01409170610674419

Fiedler, F. R. E. D. (2015). Contingency theory of leadership: Fred Fiedler. In J. B. Miner (Ed.), *Organizational behavior 1: Essential theories of motivation and leadership, (pp. 232-255).* Routledge.

Fireman, S. M. (1999). *A model of telecommuting withdrawal: Employee perceptions predicting the reduction or stopping of telework.* [Doctoral Dissertation] University of Washington.

Frank, E., & Brandstätter, V. (2002). Approach versus avoidance: Different types of commitment in intimate relationships. *Journal of Personality and Social Psychology, 82*(2), 208–221. doi:10.1037/0022-3514.82.2.208 PMID:11831411

French, J. R., Raven, B., & Cartwright, D. (2016). The bases of social power. In J.M., Shafritz, J. S., Ott, & Y. S., Jang (Eds.) Classics of Organization Theory, pp. 311-320. Cengage Learning.

Fuqua, H. E., Payne, K. E., & Cangemi, J. P. (2000). Leadership and the effective use of power. *National Forum of Educational Administration and Supervision Journal, 17*, 1-6.

Gainey, T. W., Kelley, D. E., & Hill, J. A. (1999). Telecommuting's impact on corporate culture and individual workers: Examining the effect of employee isolation. *S.A.M. Advanced Management Journal, 64*(4), 4.

Graen, G. B., & Uhl-Bien, M. (1995). Relationship-based approach to leadership: Development of leader-member exchange (LMX) theory of leadership over 25 years: Applying a multi-level multi-domain perspective. *The Leadership Quarterly*, *6*(2), 219–247. doi:10.1016/1048-9843(95)90036-5

Gruen, T. W., Summers, J. O., & Acito, F. (2000). Relationship marketing activities, commitment, and membership behaviors in professional associations. *Journal of Marketing*, *64*(3), 34–49. doi:10.1509/jmkg.64.3.34.18030

Hambley, L. A., O'Neill, T. A., & Kline, T. J. (2007). Virtual team leadership: The effects of leadership style and communication medium on team interaction styles and outcomes. *Organizational Behavior and Human Decision Processes*, *103*(1), 1–20. doi:10.1016/j.obhdp.2006.09.004

Iverson, R. D., & Buttigieg, D. M. (1999). Affective, normative and continuance commitment: Can the 'right kind' of commitment be managed? *Journal of Management Studies*, *36*(3), 307–333. doi:10.1111/1467-6486.00138

Jalilvand, M. R., & Vosta, L. N. (2015). Examining the relationship between managerial power and affective organizational commitment: An empirical study in the sport sector of Iran. *Sport, Business and Management*, *5*(4), 344–364. doi:10.1108/SBM-04-2011-0041

Johnson, J. R. (1998). Embracing change: A leadership model for the learning organisation. *International Journal of Training and Development*, *2*(2), 141–150. doi:10.1111/1468-2419.00042

Johnson, S. K., Bettenhausen, K., & Gibbons, E. (2009). Realities of working in virtual teams: Affective and attitudinal outcomes of using computer-mediated communication. *Small Group Research*, *40*(6), 623–649. doi:10.1177/1046496409346448

Kerr, S., & Jermier, J. M. (1978). Substitutes for leadership: Their meaning and measurement. *Organizational Behavior and Human Performance*, *22*(3), 375–403. doi:10.1016/0030-5073(78)90023-5

Kim, S. G., & Kim, J. (2014). Integration strategy, transformational leadership and organozational commitment in Korea's corporate split-offs. *Procedia: Social and Behavioral Sciences*, *109*, 1353–1364. doi:10.1016/j.sbspro.2013.12.637

Liu, D., Baumeister, R. F., Yang, C. C., & Hu, B. (2019). Digital communication media use and psychological well-being: A meta-analysis. *Journal of Computer-Mediated Communication*, *24*(5), 259–273. doi:10.1093/jcmc/zmz013

Lowry, T. (1996). *Alternative work arrangements: The effects of distance and media use on the supervisor-subordinate relationship.* [Doctoral Dissertation] Rice University.

Marique, G., Stinglhamber, F., Desmette, D., Caesens, G., & De Zanet, F. (2012). Organizational identification and commitment: The impact of POS and prestige. Universite catholique de Louvain.

Nasır, S. (2015). *Customer Relationship Management Strategies in the Digital Era*. Business Science Reference. doi:10.4018/978-1-4666-8231-3

Newman, S. A., & Ford, R. C. (2021). Five steps to leading your team in the virtual COVID-19 workplace. *Organizational Dynamics*, *50*(1), 100802. doi:10.1016/j.orgdyn.2020.100802

Pierro, A., Raven, B. H., Amato, C., & Bélanger, J. J. (2013). Bases of social power, leadership styles, and organizational commitment. *International Journal of Psychology*, *48*(6), 1122–1134. doi:10.1080/00207594.2012.733398 PMID:23072507

Rahim, M. A., & Afza, M. (1993). Leader power, commitment, satisfaction, compliance, and propensity to leave a job among US accountants. *The Journal of Social Psychology*, *133*(5), 611–625. doi:10.1080/00224545.1993.9713916

Ronald, B. (2014). Comprehensive leadership review-literature, theories and research. *Advances in Management*, *7*(5), 52.

Schein, E. H. (1999). Sense and nonsense about culture and climate. Massachusetts Institutes of Technology.

Sheth, J. N., & Parvatlyar, A. (1995). Relationship marketing in consumer markets: Antecedents and consequences. *Journal of the Academy of Marketing Science*, *23*(4), 255–271. doi:10.1177/009207039502300405

Spicer, A. (2020). Organizational culture and COVID-19. *Journal of Management Studies*, *57*(8), 1737–1740. doi:10.1111/joms.12625

Suarez, F. F., & Oliva, R. (2005). Environmental change and organizational transformation. *Industrial and Corporate Change*, *14*(6), 1017–1041. doi:10.1093/icc/dth078

Teimouri, H., Izadpanah, N., Akbariani, S., Jenab, K., Khoury, S., & Moslehpour, S. (2015). The effect of managerial power on employees' affective commitment: Case study. *Journal of Management*, *3*(2), 21–30.

Zaleznik, A. (1977). Managers and leaders: Are they different. *Houston Police Department Leadership Journal*, *17*(4), 47–63.

# Chapter 7
# The Value of Workplace Culture in the Digital Leadership Era

**Fleming Sampson**
https://orcid.org/0000-0003-1747-8644
*HCLTech, India*

## ABSTRACT

*In today's business world, digital leadership is needed to keep up with the speed of change. The digital workplace is centered on collaboration, communication, and human interaction. Corporate employees nowadays are looking for more than autonomy and productivity. Power and responsibility are both affected by technology, and this fact cannot be ignored. Leaders are required by everyone who is impacted by digital technology. In transitions, digital leadership is prevalent since neither technology nor process has a monopoly on the situation. The hybrid work model has become the most popular way for people to return to work. Every industry will need to develop its own methodology and determine its productivity. Using the findings of this study, leaders may better understand how technology is changing their workforces, markets, and whole industries. Leadership in the digital age should be based on a new set of values and rules. Future research must focus on digital leadership styles and traits. In this regard, a new empirical study should measure digital leadership's effectiveness.*

## INTRODUCTION

The digital era has accelerated the rate of change across industries. In today's fast-paced and ever-changing corporate climate, digital leadership has become a must for survival. As a result, cultivating habits that assist in comfort at work and accuracy at work has become increasingly important. Digital technology has had a profound effect on the world of business, and so this new period entails a revolutionary transition in terms of chosen business methods from the traditional to the digital era. There are several strategies for capitalising on the new market through digital techniques. Digital transformation has triumphed as a company ideology and strategic imperative. Globally, serious company executives recognise that their markets, customers and employees have migrated to the digital age. According to the most recent global management study, 93% of employees across industries and regions agree that being digitally savvy is

DOI: 10.4018/978-1-6684-5864-8.ch007

critical to performing well in their jobs (Cognizant, 2021). The idea that successful digital transformation leads to agility, flexibility and a focus on the customer has become a management policy and a way for executives to stay motivated.

Effective digital transformation, on the other hand, can come with additional risks and expenses that were not expected. Digitally savvy workers have taken issue with the emphasis on efficiency and productivity put on by leaders. Leadership in the digital age is expected to provide employees with more than just increased freedom, recognition and productivity-enhancing working conditions. According to studies by the MIT Sloan Management Review and Cognizant, digitally adept employees do not only anticipate enhanced company capabilities or prospects from digital transformation; they also want it to better represent and respect their concerns and beliefs (Schrage et al., 2021). Leaders' authority, influence and control are disrupted by these new standards of conduct. The new bottom line: leaders must tangibly alter themselves in order for digital transformation to be successful. Workplace success depends as much on data-driven agility and productivity as it does on leaders' own emotional digital transformation in order to be effective at leading the digital transformation of their organizations (Jim, 2021). Leaders must first undergo their own affective digital transformation.

Managing many identities with coworkers, family and friends is nearly impossible in the age of social media, making leadership in this environment even more difficult (Schrage et al., 2021). It is possible that this flattening of numerous identities could have unintended consequences for business executives in the digital age. As a result, leaders are unable to effectively tailor their messaging to diverse groups of stakeholders. In today's digital world, leadership activities are immediately visible and accessible to everyone. Individuals' desire to be perceived as authentic is hampered by the ability of digital platforms to allow for the interpretation of the same message by several audiences. Research shows how the expectations of digitally informed employees are changing the way leadership problems are framed as old boundaries disappear. Leaders can no longer dismiss the impact of digital transformation on power and accountability relations because the data is so obvious and overwhelming. The findings of this study give specific advice on how to lead people, markets and industries that have been changed by technology.

Despite the widespread adoption of digital business strategies, many organizations still fail to recognize the importance of digital leadership in these transformations (de Villiers et al., 2020; Abbu and Gopalakrishna, 2021). Digital leaders are supposed to have the essential tools to manage digital transformation, yet there are severe weaknesses in both technological dominance and process management. As part of this study, the researchers will look at how the digital leadership age has affected business practices by conducting an in-depth literature review. Global industrial strategies, on the other hand, are rethinking how digital leaders work so that they can better understand how this process changes based on their skills, expertise, experience and other factors, even though many sectors are moving more quickly through globalization. Hybrid workforce models can help promote organizational culture. Moving into a building does not instantly create culture. Remote and hybrid employees are happier with their company culture than on-site employees.

## DIGITAL WORKPLACE

The digital workplace is the natural transition of the workplace. It is made up of the technology that employees use on a daily basis. The "digital workplace" refers to all of the technologies that individuals use to accomplish tasks in today's workplace, including those that are already in use and those that are yet to be deployed. It includes human resource management and essential business applications, as well as e-mail, instant messaging, enterprise social media and virtual meeting tools. 64% would choose a lower-paying job if it allowed them to work remotely. Businesses that have robust online social networks are 7% more productive than those that do not. Internally implemented social networking tools resulted in a median 20% improvement in employee satisfaction. When employee engagement rises, staff retention increases by up to 87%. Information professionals favor more modern modes of communication (Cisco, 2010; Pentland, 2009).

Digitization is completely changing the way we work, the way we manage, where and when we work, how and why organizations are organized, what goods and services are offered, and how we communicate (Redwood et al., 2016). Organizations are constantly looking for better ways to do things, and the incorporation of cutting-edge technology into their operations has been shown to be advantageous. Such adoption continues to contribute to the digitalization of workplaces, and it is critical to understand how digital technologies are altering the ways in which employees perform their responsibilities, as well as how businesses may adapt to and evolve in the face of such technological adoption. Generally, it is a digital workplace that allows users to exchange files and information, get answers, solve issues, and seek information and expertise, as well as tap into the collective knowledge of customers, partners and peers from nearly any location.

The digital workplace is all about collaborating, communicating and engaging with people. Information exchange is encouraged in order to foster fruitful business partnerships within and outside of natural work groupings. The digital workplace is aided by technology. Every firm already has a digital workplace toolset. The technologies required to enable your digital workplace will vary by sector and company demands. The habit is to provide the staff with the correct tools. Controls enable the successful use of technology in the digital workplace (Mckinsey, 2009; HCI, 2009). It is needed to support the digital workplace with suitable governance and management. The organization's rules and industry requirements must also be followed. The digital workplace, like any key effort, must be driven by business needs. To maximize its benefits, digital workplace should follow organization's direction.

## DIGITAL LEADERSHIP ERA

Digital leadership is the strategic use of an organization's digital assets to accomplish organizational and individual goals (Dimitrios et al., 2013; Thomson et al., 2016). Many businesses have seen major changes in their competitive and organizational contexts and responsibilities as a result of recent digital technology. Numerous organizational adjustments are necessary, including changes in roles, work culture and technology. The idea is created by combining leadership skills with digital skills in order to get the most out of digital technology and improve the company's performance. Sandel (2013) defines digital leadership as the talents and capacities that enable the creation of an environment conducive to creativity via the optimization of technology and digital competence. The digital traits of a leader include innovation, inspiration, credibility, broader knowledge, collaboration, interaction and confidence in subordinates. Digital leaders must possess a set of abilities that will enable them to overcome these obstacles and assist enterprises in moving forward with change (Frank et al., 2019; Somerville, 2013). As a result, leaders have a tremendous impact, as a new skill set is necessary to effectively lead the business into an unpredictable, more dynamic future. The digital leaders of the future will have a hard time motivating their employees to work with a new set of technologies that may or may not be used in the digital future because the digital future itself is unprecedented.

*Figure 1. From Industrial to Hybrid revolution*

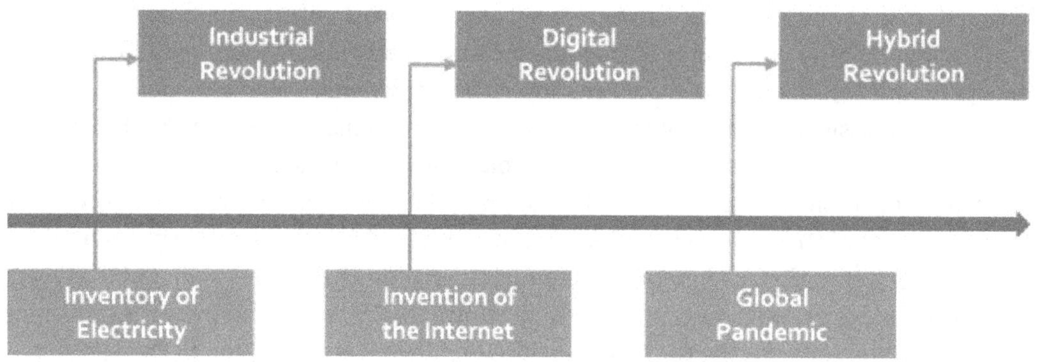


The Industrial Revolution in electricity technology has far-reaching consequences for industry and society. To begin with, the need for fuel compelled the coal industry, which had already expanded significantly by the early 18th century, to continue expanding and innovating. The steam engine, which increased the demand for coal, helped people get more efficient mine pumps and better ventilation systems. When mechanical and analogue electronic technology were replaced by digital electronics in the final years of the twentieth century, this was known as the "digital revolution." Using computers and other digital technologies has changed our relationship with our surroundings and continues to do so today. There have been a wide range of effects on the economy as a result of the digital revolution. For example, globalization would not be possible in today's world without the emergence of the internet. The revolution changed the way people and businesses interacted with one another and with the world around them. Small and medium-sized businesses now have access to large global markets. The widespread use of digital technology in recent years has been attributed to the rise in economic output and its associated activities. The digital revolution has led to a need for new work skills because of new technology (Gartner, 2021).

The fourth industrial revolution is known as "disruption." The disruptive phenomena that characterised the Industrial Revolution 4.0 period will usher in the technology revolution, which will indirectly alter our ways of living, thinking, working and socialising. Leadership means being able to lead through all changes and differences. Leadership in the 4.0 industrial revolution requires the ability to unify and offer clear direction, a vision that is broader than the organisation or firm, has an impact and benefits all members/teams, the surrounding environment and even the globe (Asri et al., 2020). The hybrid revolution is about empowering a culture of choice, not simply the tools that make hybrid work possible. There were so many people around the world who liked hybrid work that it caused a lot of change. The Internet's hybrid work optimization has spawned a new work culture standard. Secure mobile devices allow us to move and operate successfully anywhere. Remote teams may collaborate as if they were in a room using collaboration technologies. 5G/Wi-Fi 6 technology is blurring the barrier between home and corporate networking, much as streaming movies at home is challenging the movie theatre business model. But decisions have repercussions. This culture of choice must be based on accountability, trust and discipline (Lee, 2021).

## HYBRID WORKFORCE MODEL

The hybrid work model has become the most popular way for people to get back to work. Global companies like Nationwide, Citigroup, Ford Motor Company, IBM and General Motors Company have all chosen to combine the best parts of working in the office and working from home (Kingo, 2022). According to US research, 83% of CEOs want their employees to return, but only 10% want to return to their offices. The majority of them want to keep working from home or follow a hybrid model. Every organisation is debating whether working from home, the office, or a hybrid is better (Srinivasan, 2022). Many businesses have discovered a hybrid style of working to increase productivity, efficiency and output. However, there is no universal method that can be applied to all sectors. Every sector will need to devise their own methodology and determine their productivity. The hybrid work paradigm is here to stay since it provides advantages to both employees and businesses.

Antiquated beliefs about work design have been destroyed by the way people have adapted to working during the pandemic. These days, executive leaders have a unique chance to change how they work. They can move away from an industrial-era work model based on location constraints and build work around a human-centered model in order to attract digital-era talent and meet company goals. Hybrid workforce models provide an important opportunity to reinforce company culture. Employees do not instantly absorb culture just by walking into a building. So far, remote and hybrid employees have reported higher levels of satisfaction with their workplace culture than on-site employees. Whether or not employees are remote, success needs deliberate culture change and role modelling (Gartner, 2021). Shifting workers to job models that existed prior to the outbreak is a step backward. Furthermore, organizations will not be able to maintain their resilience until they revisit techniques like hybrid workforce models. Begin by

*Figure 2. Future of work reinvented*

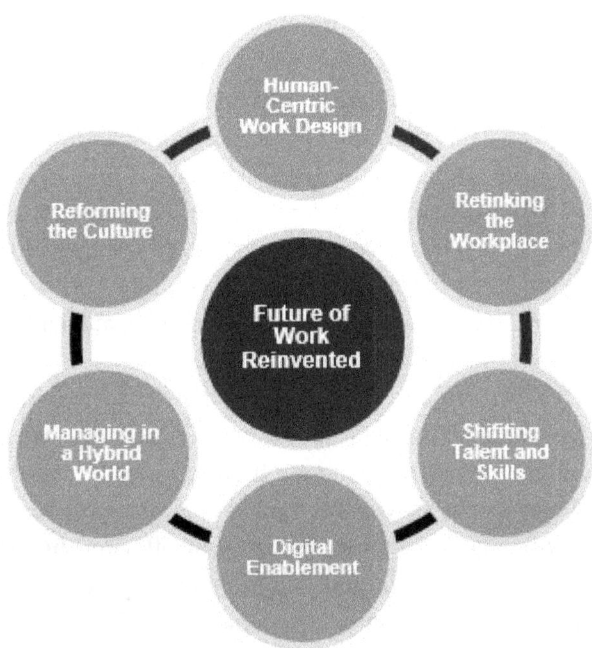

debunking the myths that are preventing from taking advantage of this once-in-a-lifetime chance. Then, to make hybrid working a good thing for both as an employer and employees, work together to try, learn and improve on six different fronts (Gartner, 2021).

- **Human-centric work design:** It is defined by flexibility and empathy, and it enhances employee empowerment, productivity and engagement. It also allows businesses to be more responsive to client needs, resilient to interruptions and productive. It can also save money on anything from real estate to travel to employee turnover. In short, the human-centric approach can benefit both individuals and enterprises, but it necessitates management commitment to a mixed workforce strategy. Give employees more control over their work and work environment to increase productivity and well-being.
- **Rethinking the workplace:** The COVID-19 crisis has radically altered our culture and economy. A worldwide pandemic affects all businesses, whether they're remote or they've had to furlough employees and lock their doors. Work has altered forever. The relaxation of stay-at-home laws in certain countries and states is encouraging businesses to welcome both staff and customers. The workplace is for, and think of it as a tool for getting people to talk to each other instead of a place where they can work.
- **Shifting Talent and Skills:** Flow-to-work operating models link limited capabilities to high-priority work, promote employee development and boost corporate responsiveness. As more technology experts are needed, the need for technical abilities, including high IT skills and fundamental digital skills, will grow. These developments will need workers all across the world to expand their present skill sets or learn new ones (Bughin et al., 2018). Organizations will need to rethink how work is organized within their organizations.
- **Digital Enablement:** People are at the center of all the solutions that technology providers need to enable. Companies are working towards keeping their employees connected and technologies such as augmented reality (AR) and virtual reality (VR) have found their use in this digital workplace era. Devices such as AR glasses are finding their use in workplace environments for virtual meetings and customer demonstrations (Kulkarni et al., 2021). However, to make the adoption of such technologies more sustainable and intuitive in the long run, companies need to work on providing employees with an experience that is more genuine and comfortable for them to use for long durations.
- **Managing in a Hybrid World:** Leaders must adopt the best strategy to keep employees connected and engaged in a hybrid workforce. Many jobs allowed for hybrid or remote work before the pandemic. However, many large corporations lacked remote work strategies and infrastructure. Companies that use a hybrid work environment model now have an advantage over their competitors when it comes to hiring the best people (Yativ, 2021).
- **Reforming the Culture:** Reforming organizational culture to maximize the benefits of hybrid work. The pandemic has changed the way people work and many see a hybrid future. The challenge of reimagining culture may inspire leaders. Imagine a leader orchestrating a hybrid based on duties, interactions and purpose. A successful hybrid workplace involves more attentive employee needs discussions. Many businesses will recognize that offering this greatly enhances the probability that their employees feel encouraged, motivated and productive. But hybrids are complicated. It takes greater thinking and planning (Hancock et al., 2021).

Although the world is moving towards a hybrid work model, challenges remain – duplicating the office environment in a remote setup, lack of learning through osmosis, lack of personalization in employee experience, to name a few. However, companies are rapidly innovating to make the hybrid model of working a reality, to make it comfortable for employees whether they operate from an office, home or while on the move (Kulkarni et al., 2021). Organizations need to be prepared to build a new workplace model that is balanced both structurally and culturally, and provides increased freedom and autonomy to the employees to work from the place they want and at a time that does not spill over into their personal lives.

## NEW NORMAL WORKPLACE AND CULTURE

Leadership has always been the key to running a successful business. However, the workplace has never changed so quickly in such a short amount of time. This is because digital innovations and changing customer habits are always changing the environment. Supporting your team through change is vital. Successful digital transformation projects usually have plans to ensure individual employees have the correct training to proficiently utilise technology at implementation. However, the recent instantaneous switch to a fully remote working environment was both unplanned and unpredictable. Business leaders and team leaders had to think on their feet throughout the crisis. Their teams' needs were met and they felt supported through the adaptation in terms of communication, collaboration, comfort, happiness and feelings incorporated within the team and organisation. Company culture has been key to attracting the best talent. External communications like this are commonplace and have been for a long time. However, there has been a recent rise in pride and the promotion of how companies have dealt with the crisis and maintained the happiness, cohesiveness and collaboration of their teams. While it is unclear what percentage of this has been truly agile adaptations and or employee attraction, it is clear that the digital workplace has been a vital element of navigating through the crisis and the digital first culture has enabled companies to prosper.

Remote working presents numerous challenges for teams and leaders. Having the right technology in place negates some of these but strong leadership, transparency, support and an encompassing company culture are required for lasting success. Empathy is a key element to consider when leading a team or business in a remote setting, understanding each individual role enables you to plan the resources, tools, permissions and support required. We need to bridge connection between teams in order to share resources but not overload certain employees by providing a clear and transparent view of ongoing projects each individual/team is involved with. Each role requires unique digital tools to achieve proficiency, whether these be specific programs to enable them to perform functions or collaboration software to work efficiently as a team. Permissions also need to be set to govern employees access to business critical documentation and information. Support is necessary to ensure individuals and teams are happy and able to consistently perform at high levels, this includes the correct training and opportunities of progression through the organization. All of these elements need to be considered to be an effective digital leader and all of these are also much more difficult to manage in a remote setting.

It is important to listen to employees in order to improve employee experience, if company is looking to utilize remote working as a new normal. It is important to research the current user experience of digital workplace. Feedback can be more difficult to attain whilst working remotely but helps instill a strong digital first culture by including all individuals within the digital strategy and planned improvements of current ecosystem. This also aided design, software development and architecture teams to deliver products which make an instant difference with shorter implementation time in terms of staff training. Having individuals and teams involved in the design enables them to understand and learn new software or processes easier, as they feel involved in the project. Similarly, as a leader we must understand new stresses effecting the teams on both a business and personal level. Remote working has been a completely new experience for some individuals, some of whom are less accustomed to using technology as part of their daily job, most are utilizing technologies they may have never used before. It is important to provide support for all roles with engaging training, this can be delivered online, one to one or as a team activity. Manager should be aware of all individuals within the team and check in on their proficiency with new technologies, creating a culture where no member regardless of age or digital literacy feels comfortable to share with the team.

It has also been a challenge to promote workplace happiness. Adapting to a new environment can be difficult emotionally, and this cannot be something that is overlooked. Management needs to look at ways to ensure employee satisfaction remains high and remote working as the norm makes it hard to provide similar benefits socially and in terms of comfort and emotional support, motivation, praise and unity (Sam, 2021). Leaders have needed to adapt quickly. They need to be supported by technology and financially in order to make quick decisions for the good of their team/organisation. Now is the time to look back on the internal innovations of the past few months, take in all employee feedback, and look to the future by making a digital leadership strategy that promotes a digital-first culture, remote support, collaboration and innovation. Further, the way to attract the young and new generation of talent into the working space of today would be to have the preparedness to accept remote working totally, have the latest in collaboration and meeting tools, providing infrastructure support for effective working besides clear goals focussed on outcomes, giving them space to experiment and high levels of empowerment and freedom. In addition, the way to attract young and new generations of talent into the working space of today would be to have the preparedness to accept remote working completely, have the latest in collaboration and meeting tools, provide infrastructure support for effective working along with clear goals focused on outcomes, give them space to experiment and have high levels of empowerment and freedom. These are some of the ways that they can attract younger and new generations of talent.

## SOLUTIONS

Digital leaders must use the appropriate technologies to ensure connectivity and performance regardless of location. Collaborate with all players on the digital transformation. Develop a better grasp of the technology and processes that employees appreciate the most and work on the collaboration tools necessary to deliver a seamless digital experience. Empathy, creativity, teamwork and resilience are all necessary human talents for leaders and their staff to succeed in the new hybrid world of work. To assist employees in coping with uncertainty and continual change, leaders must adopt more empathic, informal communication methods that foster debate, listening and feedback. Leaders must integrate learning and innovation into the digital workplace. They must increase their investment in staff training and provide them with the appropriate training on new software and technologies. It is critical to prioritise one-on-one or small group training to ensure a seamless and efficient transition. To create a fantastic digital workplace environment favourable to the growth and success of hybrid workforces, the approach must be employee-driven. A favourable digital working environment results in improved employee experiences. This, in turn, will help the business reach its most important goals, such as getting employees more involved, making customers happier and making the business run more efficiently and with more cooperation.

The Accenture Future of Work Study found that most individuals desire a hybrid approach where they work both remotely and onsite. 83% of workers prefer a mixed model. This new work style has benefited many organizations, especially those motivated by the concept of a virtual office. The greater use of technology has helped businesses prosper in this new world of employment. All daily procedures have been virtualized, allowing staff to work from anywhere on the globe. This opens up a larger talent pool, since geographical restrictions no longer hinder the hunt for the greatest talent. Also, using tech-based solutions may enable you to reach a larger client base (Rahman, 2021). The hybrid approach offers intriguing flexibility to employees. It improves work-life balance, producing a highly desired harmony between professional and personal lives. Employers use this method to retain female employees. A McKinsey survey found that 52% of employees want more flexibility post-pandemic. According to the report, 30% of employees would transfer employment if entirely on-site work was reinstated. Leaders must improve the employee experience to create a digital workplace that supports a hybrid workforce. They must emphasize innovative ways to support performance, culture and relationships. Personalized digital workplace experiences help employees be more productive and engaged.

While digital solutions to increase employee engagement and welfare, we must remember that technology is merely a tool. Leaders must constantly adapt tactics to foster employee connections. In the lack of physical space, the firm's culture and values must be integrated into employees' daily lives, and each organization must build its own initiatives and tactics. Businesses of all sizes still have a hard time making new employees feel like they belong in the world after a pandemic. During work from home periods, many employees' personal and professional lives become intertwined, leading to burnout and major mental health difficulties. "The absence of clear information about the future of post-pandemic employment has led to staff burnout," says the McKinsey survey report. Almost half of those polled said they were burned out at work. Finally, the well-being agenda takes on new dimensions in a hybrid workspace and no longer fits everybody. Catering to the different wellness requirements of the workforce is vital, yet difficult, given the increasing mental stress generated by the epidemic and the rapid, unexpected change in the workplace (Rahman, 2021). This calamity has given businesses a chance to review their policies and rethink how they treat remote employees and HR technology in the wake of a calamity.

## FUTURE RESEARCH DIRECTIONS

Digital leaders are meant to have the necessary skill set to manage digital change. However, traditional executives supporting digital transformation in many organizations suffer from significant gaps in technology dominance and process management. In order to succeed in this era, many organizations recognize the importance of digital transformation. Hence, they fail to recognize the importance of strong digital leaders, which frequently results in painful, incomplete digital transformations that have a negative impact on business performance and result in increased costs. Despite the fact that digital leadership has a positive influence on the operations of a firm, there has been little research on the issue in the organizational literature. Therefore, more academic study on digital leadership characteristics and styles will be necessary in the future. In this case, a new empirical study should be conducted to figure out how to measure the effectiveness of digital leadership.

## CONCLUSION

Organizations must recognise that leaders in the digital world require various talents and skills in order to succeed in a global digital transformation effort. Innovation and teamwork are the keys to success in the workplace. They need to rethink their leadership training and put an emphasis on empowering participants. Companies may gain a competitive edge in the digital age by empowering future leaders to think, act and react differently. As a result of the lack of models and strategies, businesses could fail if they do not have the right digital leaders in place. Leadership in the digital age should be led by a new set of values and principles. A digital leader must be adaptive and open to new ideas, as well as intellectually curious and hungry for information. Like other leaders, they must be able to find value in a variety of viewpoints, be able to handle ambiguity and be passionate about their work. In their quest for knowledge, they travel the world in search of problems to solve and new challenges to face. In contrast to their predecessors, they still have a more egalitarian and goal-oriented attitude. The new normal is all about providing flexibility to the employees while achieving the same levels of productivity as a fully in-person workforce. To lay the foundation of a hybrid workplace, the primary focus for employers is their workforce. Remote workers need to be equipped with the right devices, tools/applications and better connectivity, while those returning to the office need to be assured of a safer return by leveraging the right technologies.

## REFERENCES


Abbu, H. R., & Gopalakrishna, P. (2021). Synergistic effects of market orientation implementation and internalization on firm performance: Direct marketing service provider industry. *Journal of Business Research, 125*, 851–863. doi:10.1016/j.jbusres.2019.06.004

Bughin, J., Hazan, E., Lund, S., Dahlstrom, P., Wiesinger, A., & Subramaniam, A. (2018). *Skill shift: Automation and the future of the workforce*. McKinsey Global Institute.

Cisco (2010). The Cisco Connected World Report. *Cisco Systems*.

de Villiers, C., Kuruppu, S., & Dissanayake, D. (2020). A new role for business – Promoting the United Nations' Sustainable Development Goals through the internet-of-things and blockchain technology. *Journal of Business Research*.

Dimitrios, N. K., Sakas, D. P., & Vlachos, D. S. (2013). The Role of Information Systems in Creating Strategic Leadership Model. *Procedia: Social and Behavioral Sciences, 73*, 285–293. doi:10.1016/j.sbspro.2013.02.054

Frank, A. G., Mendes, G. H. S., Ayala, N. F., & Ghezzi, A. (2019). Servitization and Industry 4.0 convergence in the digital transformation of product firms: A business model innovation perspective. *Technological Forecasting and Social Change, 141*, 341–351. doi:10.1016/j.techfore.2019.01.014

Gartner (2021). C-Suite: Redesigning Work for a Hybrid Future. *Gartner*.

Hancock, B., Schaninger, B., & Weddle, B. (2021). Culture in the hybrid workplace. *Mckinsey*. https://www.mckinsey.com/business-functions/people-and-organizational-performance/our-insights/culture-in-the-hybrid-workplace

Jim, H. (2021). The Future of Leadership. *Reimagine Leadership.* https://www.reimagine-leadership.org/the-future-of-leadership-get-digital-or-get-out

Kingo, A. G. (2022). Secrets of a Successful Hybrid Work Model. *Toptal.* https://www.toptal.com/insights/future-of-work/hybrid-work-model#:~:text=The%20hybrid%20work%20model%20has,in%2Doffice%20and%20remote%20working

Kulkarni, N., & Bharadwaj, B. (2021). *Future of Work – The Arrival of the Hybrid Digital workplace.* Zinnov.

Lee, D. (2021). Hybrid work: Revolution or evolution? *Cisco Systems.* https://newsroom.cisco.com/c/r/newsroom/en/us/a/y2021/m10/hybrid-work-revolution-or-evolution-.html

McKinsey. (2009). How companies are benefiting from Web 2.0: McKinsey Global Survey Results. *The McKinsey Quarterly.*

Rahman, T. (2021). Surviving and thriving in the hybrid workplace. *People Matters Digital Magazine.* https://www.peoplematters.in/article/hr-technology/surviving-and-thriving-in-the-hybrid-workplace-31601

Redwood, S., Holmstrom, M., & Vetter, A. (2016). Transitioning to the future of work and the workplace embracing digital culture, tools and approaches. *Deloitte.* https://www2.deloitte.com/content/dam/Deloitte/us/Documents/humancapital/us-human-capital-transitioning-to-the-future-of-work.pdf

Sam, B. (2021). *Digital Leadership in a New Era: The constantly increasing importance of cultivating workplace culture.* Beyond Business Buzzwords.

Somerville, M. M. (2013). Digital Age Discoverability: A Collaborative Organizational Approach. *Serials Review, 39*(4), 234–239. doi:10.1080/00987913.2013.10766404

Srinivasan, G. (2022). The future of work: A Hybrid Model. *The Economic Times.* https://economictimes.indiatimes.com/news/company/corporate-trends/the-future-of-work-a-hybrid-model/articleshow/89561612.cms?from=mdr

## ADDITIONAL READING

Asri, A. A. S. M. A. N., & Darma, G. S. (2020). Revealing the digital leadership spurs in 4.0 industrial revolution. *International Journal of Business. Economics and Management, 3*(1), 93–100.

Cognizant (2021). New MIT Sloan Management Review Study Finds Many Leaders Lack Essential Skills to Effectively Lead Digital Transformation. https://news.cognizant.com/2021-01-26-MIT-Sloan-Management-Review-Leaderships-Digital-Transformation

HCI. (2009). *The Value and ROI in Employee Recognition.* Human Capital Institute.

Pentland, A. (2009). How Social Networks Network Best. *Harvard Business Review, 87*(2), 37. PMID:19227554

Sandel, S. (2013). *Digital Leadership: How Creativity in Business can Propel Your Brand & Boots Your Result*. Allen House Publishing Company Limited.

Schrage, M., Pring, B., Kiron, D., & Dickerson, D. (2021). Leadership' Digital Transformation: Leading purposefully in an Era of context collapse. *MIT Sloan Management Review*.

Thomson, N. B. III, Rawson, J. V., Slade, C. P., & Bledsoe, M. (2016). Transformation and Transformational Leadership: A Review of the Current and Relevant Literature for Academic Radiologists. *Academic Radiology*, *23*(5), 592–599. doi:10.1016/j.acra.2016.01.010 PMID:26971043

Yativ, R. (2021). How to manage a Global team in a hybrid world? *Forbes Business Council*. https://www.forbes.com/sites/forbesbusinesscouncil/2021/09/09/how-to-manage-a-global-team-in-a-hybrid-world/?sh=5a019c9f7662

## KEY TERMS AND DEFINITIONS

**Corporate Reformation:** People who work for big businesses and foundations are trying to change and improve education policy and the curriculum.

**5G/Wi-Fi 6 technology:** 5G brings new network speeds, reduced latency and quicker download rates to cellular. Wi-Fi 6 aspires to be different from previous generations, offering a new generational naming scheme, enhanced IoT capabilities and multiuser capabilities.

**Digital Leadership:** It is the strategic use of a company's digital assets to achieve commercial objectives. This may be addressed both organizationally and personally.

**Digital Communication:** The information is encoded digitally as discrete signals and sent electronically to the receivers.

**Human-centric leadership:** It prioritises people's surroundings, social connections and mental state. Uncertainty is inevitable, but a leader must be aware of it.

**Hybrid Workforce:** A hybrid workplace concept combines in-office and remote work to give employees flexibility.

**New Normal:** Workplaces must adapt to new conditions to keep employees safe, healthy and productive.

# Chapter 8
# Organisational Changes in the Age of Digital Transformation

**Anitha Kumari**
https://orcid.org/0000-0002-8343-8926
*Hindustan Institute of Technology and Science, India*

## ABSTRACT

*The organization's culture is a key part of its successful move into the digital age. Industrial organisations are implementing company-wide digital transformation programmes in response to new risks and opportunities provided by fast emerging digital technologies. There is a serious shortage of adaptable project and organisational teams with a well-defined implementation approach. Companies must assess their current competencies, organisational structure, and corporate culture to identify which technologies are crucial and how they will be implemented. This chapter focuses on technology-based attributes like strategy, leadership, and culture. Researchers, practitioners, and industrial organisations will benefit from the findings of this study because it provides a digital strategy for commercial organisations. It is imperative to review the relationship between a company and its partners and customers in light of digital technology's impact on business operations and market offerings. This chapter makes it possible for future research, which helps this field and theories move forward.*

## INTRODUCTION

Technology is a powerful facilitator in the digital age. People are at the forefront of successful companies. Organisations nowadays confront several challenges: new technology, enormous data, creative collaborations, and unexpected competitors (Accenture, 2016). Industrial organisations are reacting to new threats and possibilities posed by rapidly evolving digital technology by implementing company-wide digital transformation programmes. A deeper understanding of the main enablers of digital transformation efforts that improve operational performance is required. Digital innovations are transforming businesses (Chanias & Hess, 2016). Better goods and services, a competitive edge, increased customer experience, business model innovation, and new business processes are all possible through digital transformation

DOI: 10.4018/978-1-6684-5864-8.ch008

(Niemi et al., 2021). Because of these potential benefits, digital transformation has become a strategic requirement for industrial organisations (Vial, 2019).

Organizational agility is gained by simultaneously exploiting and investigating what it provides (Hess et al., 2016). Disruptive changes, defined as changes in a corporation and its operational environment driven by digitalization, can create digital transformations in many situations. These developments cause a lot of uncertainty, so sectors and businesses strive to react in various ways. To stay competitive, innovative, agile firms include change in their plans. They respond to new possibilities and danger by doing so (Bondar et al., 2017). However, previous studies have failed to provide a comprehensive understanding of organizational change by presenting an integrated approach (Sony and Naik, 2020; Warner and Wäger, 2019). Determining clear standards for research and practice in organizational change management requires a complete knowledge of digital transformation. It tries to find and study digital technology enablers for digital transformation strategies in organizations.

The digital transformation of organisations is one of the most significant problems that they face today. New business models necessitate that organisations use digital technology to build and implement new capabilities, organisational structure, and culture so that they can identify and implement the appropriate technologies, as well as how they will be enacted in the organization's processes and products, among other things. Digital transformation needs organisations to identify what technologies are important and how they will be implemented in business solutions. Digital technology will have an effect on business strategies as companies look at how they look and how they work with their partners and customers. This chapter discusses organisations and their attempts to make sense of digital transformation as new technological advances bring their digital concerns to execute management operations.

## BACKGROUND

The Industrial Revolution in electricity technology has far-reaching consequences for industry and society. To begin with, the need for fuel compelled the coal industry, which had already expanded significantly by the early 18th century, to continue expanding and innovating. The steam engine, which increased the demand for coal, helped people get more efficient mine pumps and better ventilation systems. When mechanical and analogue electronic technology were replaced by digital electronics in the final years of the twentieth century, this was known as the "digital revolution." Using computers and other digital technologies has changed our relationship with our surroundings and continues to do so today. There have been a wide range of effects on the economy as a result of the digital revolution. Globalization, for example, would not be possible in today's world without the emergence of the internet. The revolution changed the way people and businesses interacted with one another and with the world around them. Small and medium-sized businesses now have access to large global markets. The widespread use of digital technology in recent years has been attributed to the rise in economic output and its associated activities. The digital revolution has led to a need for new work skills because of new technology.

The fourth industrial revolution is known as "disruption." The disruptive phenomena that characterised the Industrial Revolution 4.0 period will usher in the technology revolution, which will indirectly alter our ways of living, thinking, working, and socialising. Leadership means being able to lead through all changes and differences. Leadership in the 4.0 industrial revolution requires the ability to unify and offer clear direction; a vision that is broader than the organisation or firm, has an impact and benefits all members/teams; the surrounding environment; and even the globe (Asri et al., 2020). The hybrid revolution is about empowering a culture of choice, not simply the tools that make hybrid work possible. There were so many people around the world who liked hybrid work that it caused a lot of change. The Internet's hybrid work optimization has spawned a new work culture standard. Secure mobile devices allow us to move and operate successfully anywhere. Remote teams may collaborate as if they were in a room using collaboration technologies. 5G/Wi-Fi 6 technology is blurring the barrier between home and corporate networking, much as streaming movies at home is challenging the movie theatre business model. But decisions have repercussions. This culture of choice must be based on accountability, trust, and discipline (Lee, 2021).

Digital leadership is the strategic use of an organization's digital assets to accomplish organizational and individual goals (Dimitrios et al., 2013; Thomson et al., 2016). Many businesses have seen major changes in their competitive and organizational contexts and responsibilities as a result of recent digital technology. Numerous organizational adjustments are necessary, including changes in roles, work culture, and technology. The idea is created by combining leadership skills with digital skills in order to get the most out of digital technology and improve the company's performance. Sandel (2013) defines digital leadership as the talents and capacities that enable the creation of an environment conducive to creativity via the optimization of technology and digital competence. The digital traits of a leader include innovation, inspiration, credibility, broader knowledge, collaboration, interaction, and confidence in subordinates. Digital leaders must possess a set of abilities that will enable them to overcome these obstacles and assist enterprises in moving forward with change (Frank et al., 2019; Somerville, 2013). As a result, leaders have a tremendous impact, as a new skill set is necessary to effectively lead the business into an unpredictable, more dynamic future. The digital leaders of the future will have a hard time motivating their employees to work with a new set of technologies that may or may not be used in the digital future because the digital future itself is unprecedented.

*Figure 1. Core Concepts of Digitalization*

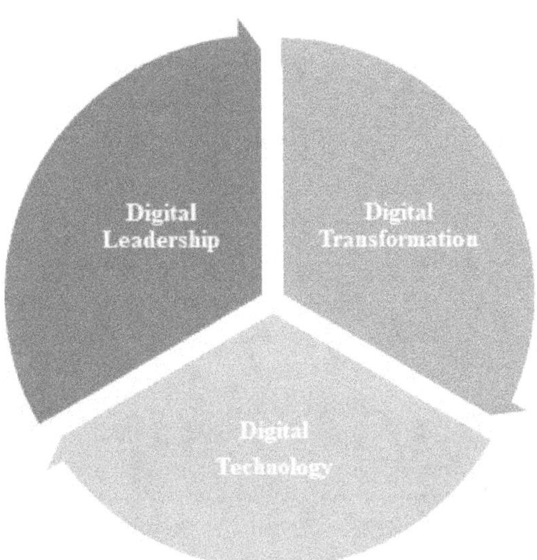

## DIGITAL TRANSFORMATION

The ability of an organisation to leverage digital technology to improve the efficiency and efficacy of its internal operations as well as the products and services it offers to external markets is referred to as digital transformation. Digital transformation is a comprehensive term that describes this ability (Vial, 2019). The sociocultural process of adapting businesses to the new organisational structures and skill sets required to be viable and relevant in a digital context is referred to as digital transformation. It goes further than ideas like change made possible by improvements in information technology, which seeks to improve upon existing processes. Previous research (Kohli and Grover, 2008) showed that the value of IT is seen in economic gains, process improvements, and improvements to the brand name that make customers feel more connected to the firm. The different ways that digital technology is thought to create value are in line with these findings.

For researchers and practitioners, digital transformation is a key phenomenon (Fitzgerald et al., 2013). The utilisation of digital technology is transforming industrial operations, ushering in a new age of industrialisation known as Industry 4.0. To remain competitive, organisations have had to change their value generation routes by incorporating a range of digital technologies (Vial, 2019). Gilchrist (2016) cites sophisticated algorithms, artificial intelligence, hyper-connectivity, self-learning systems, automation, big data, and analytics as a few examples (Gilchrist, 2016). Organisations are now designing plans that embrace the consequences of digital transformation and achieve greater operational performance (Hesse, 2018). These digital technologies are only a minor component of an organisation's digital transformation, which requires additional work from the organisation.

To generate business advantages and performance, IT expenditures must be used effectively (Gerth and Peppard, 2016). The creative industries may help foster innovation and entrepreneurship in several economic areas. According to Li (2020), digital technology not only enables but also changes

*Figure 2. Digital Transformation*

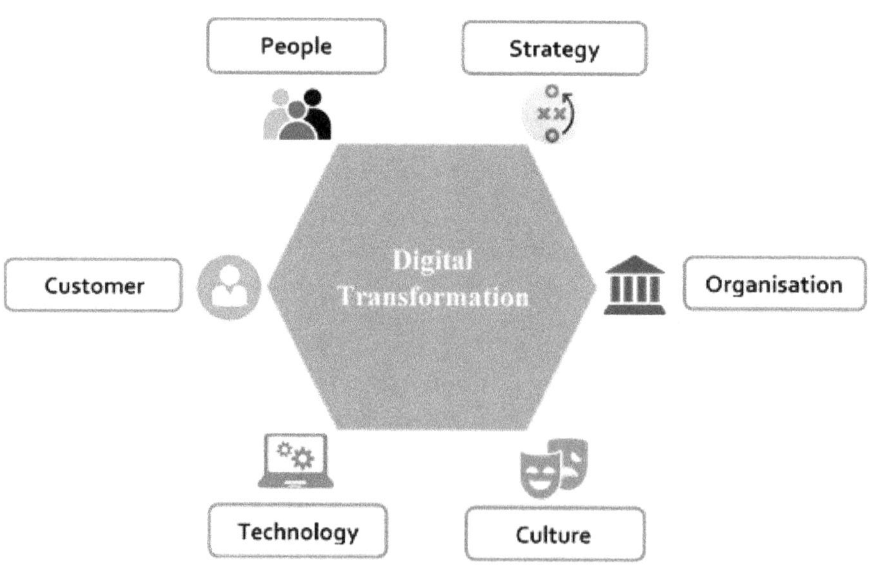

new business models. Business models can be automated or extended using digital technology. They enable new and old business models to coexist. Classical and digital business performance management methodologies are compared with digital transformation indicators. Digital technologies compel market actors to rethink their business models and their role in the digital ecosystem. Major hurdles to digital transformation include managerial, methodological, and information areas (Bruskin et al., 2017). Digital performance management systems may be built and used to promote corporate digital management.

- **Strategy:** A strategy is a plan of action that describes how a company should reposition itself strategically in the digital economy. The ways in which winning businesses operate evolve as client behavior changes. They innovate, transform operating and commercial paradigms, and capitalize on emerging technology. In the corporate sector, strategy is critical to developing a successful and technologically mature business. The natural ability of an executive or digital leader to think of a digital transformation strategy is a valuable asset.
- **Organization:** Digital transformation is the process of changing an organization's culture, structure, and operations by smartly integrating digital technologies, processes, and skills across all levels and functions in a strategic way. Most businesses rely heavily on digital systems and solutions these days, both to improve internal processes and to make the customer experience better on the outside.
- **Culture:** Organizational culture manifests itself in people's actions and attitudes, which influence and are influenced by the organization's practices and ideals. The transformation of technology and business models by digital transformation. The organization's culture is also crucial to its successful transition into the digital age. In fact, the success of a digital transition depends on a comprehensive grasp of cultural complexities. This trend has been amplified by the epidemic, making digital transformation essential to company success.
- **Technology:** Digital transformation is the use of digital technology to reinvent a process in order to make it more efficient or effective. Rather than simply recreating an existing service in digital form, the objective is to use technology to transform that service into something considerably more helpful. In today's digital environment, huge volumes of information can be compressed and saved on small, portable storage devices.
- **People:** Digital transformation entails more than merely embracing new technologies. It is about transforming corporate processes, business models, and organizational culture via the use of technology. It is about taking advantage of the insights provided by technology to envisage new business models, markets, and more efficient methods of attracting, engaging, and providing value to consumers, among other things. Successful digital transformation initiatives are more likely to be achieved if organizations focus on putting skilled people in important roles at the start of their transformation projects.
- **Customer:** Customer experience is a critical aspect in every organization, and it is even more important in the context of digital transformation. It is crucial to recognize that innovation and improvement in customer experience are significant factors in the growth and success of a company. Technological improvements and outstanding customer experience have raised the bar for the digital consumer experience. The success of a business is very dependent on things like new ideas and making the customer experience better, among other things.

## DIGITAL TECHNOLOGY

With the rise of mixed work in recent years, the introduction of digital workplace components helps to accelerate and succeed in flexible work. Companies all over the world have been able to grow and expand their operations by using a variety of new hiring tools and ways to work together.

- **Seamless coworker communication:** Smartphone technology has made it easier for remote workers to stay in touch with co-workers. This helps people who need frequent touch with headquarters or team members. Digital workplaces do not require on-site project meetings. Software delivers asynchronous and synchronous channels and stakeholder insights. Using special software and apps, workers can quickly send and receive project papers, messages, and other files from their mobile devices. This makes the digital office experience more seamless.
- **Digitalization increased efficiency:** The digitalization of workplaces maximises efficiency and technology. Digital workplaces can make duties and challenges easier. Digitalizing the workplace can reveal difficulties the company had not considered. Digital technologies will benefit internal and external actors in both scenarios. Schnuck Markets uses technology to help employees and customers (Lumapps.com, 2022). Before cloud computing, employees checked email and placed orders from their breakrooms. This required personnel to move between counters and back rooms. Meanwhile, consumers waited at the counter. Employees may now monitor orders, check emails, and help clients without leaving their stations.
- **Digital Innovation:** Many firms are focusing on digital transformation to streamline and automate their processes to keep up with the rapidly changing digital landscape. Digital technologies like robotic process automation, artificial intelligence, and machine learning can help digitize complicated or time-consuming corporate processes. This frees up personnel for more critical activities that would ordinarily demand human effort or time. Digital technology can provide proactive systems that examine data streams for potential errors and automate corrective steps before problems occur. Digital transformation can revolutionize how firms function and yield huge productivity and cost benefits.

## DIGITAL LEADERSHIP

Digital transformation necessitates the adoption of new methods of functioning rather than simply new technologies. Many firms find that the most precious resource is not necessarily technical expertise, but rather leadership. To succeed in this age of digital transformation, leaders must have the capacity to sift through an avalanche of digital initiatives, manage rapidly increasing innovation cycles, and rebuild their organizations around new techniques like agile. (Danoesastro et al., 2017). Only change is constant. We need purpose, speed, inclusion, and behavior change to confront the digital forces and trends impacting work and the workplace. Instead of seeing change management as a one-time effort that takes a month or a year to complete, a continuous procedure is required and the greatest way to achieve it is to put people first.

### Adopting A Digital-Era Approach to Change Management

There are four people-centric digitization change management methodologies that arose in response to many corporate changes.

- **Purpose:** In the digital age, information and resources are brought together into a single set of tools for business. For a business to grow and flourish, it needs to be able to respond quickly to shifting conditions and plans as a result of digital transformation. Work attitudes have altered. They desire meaningful work and to feel valued. Giving employees a sense of purpose can help them cope with the stress of constant change, which can be confusing, stressful, and discouraging (BCG, 2017).
- **Speed:** The pace of technological change is escalating steadily and explosively, with new technologies being brought out more rapidly each year. Work attitudes have altered. They desire meaningful work and to feel valued. Giving employees a sense of purpose can help them cope with the stress of constant change, which can be confusing, stressful, and discouraging. A feeling of workplace community is more crucial as digital technologies diminish face-to-face interactions with coworkers and consumers (BCG, 2017).
- **Inclusiveness:** Openness and innovative use of digital technology can help close the digital divide and promote a more inclusive digital transformation that upholds and defends human rights. This will be done through a comprehensive approach that includes building up employees' skills, keeping an eye on risks, giving advice on policy, and raising people's awareness. Crowdsourcing and social media have increased the desire for a more open and honest way of working together, just like text messaging conditioned people to desire speedier real-time interactions. In the workplace, employees want to feel involved and empowered. Today's workers, regardless of their age, demand clear, authentic, and individualised relationships, as well as the feeling that their opinions are being heard.
- **Transformative Behavior Change:** Adapting to the digital world may need a completely new way of doing things for organizations. However, significant change is not always simple to achieve. In addition to taking a training or learning a new skill, a company's organizational structure, team structure, workforce, or product and service mix may need to be revised. Changing basic habits and building new standards for everyone involved, from top-level leaders to customers and shop floor workers, is essential to achieving such a transformation. It is no surprise that technology plays a role in some methods of behavior modification. Google frequently pushes its employees to adopt new practices in order to increase productivity and operational efficiency (Garvin, 2013).

## Adopting A People-First Approach to Change

It's important for companies to think of people as their most important asset and use these strategies to help them deal with changes in the way they do business.

- **Catalytic Leadership:** Change initiatives are ongoing and complex, so leaders must be determined and tenacious to keep up. They must also instill a feeling of purpose in the company's mission that encourages individuals to embrace change. Traditionally, leaders delivered instructions and followers obeyed. Leaders now inspire and enable their staff, creating an environment that energizes and excites them about work. Engaged employees are more productive, efficient, agile, and enthusiastic. To encourage change in employees and throughout the organization, senior leaders must present a cohesive front. They must learn to listen to and work with each other, as well as with others in the organization. The training made senior executives become the type of catalysts the firm required. Managers collaborated better, making decisions faster and uniting around the company's reorganization. That accelerated transformation efforts. Despite the layoffs, the company was able to fill important roles, an indication that the management's new outlook was shared by the whole staff, providing valuable people a reason to stay.

- **Agile Ways of Working:** As demonstrated by Tesla, businesses in the digital age must be able to adjust quickly to changing client needs and market situations. By slashing time spent on procedures, making decisions easier, and engaging and empowering individuals and teams, agile ways of working make it happen (BCG, 2016). Because of the frequent in-process check-ins that allow workers to identify possible problems and fix them early in the process, agile methodologies stress speed through the use of minimal viable products (MVPs). While agile emphasizes early and frequent feedback gathering, it also aims to improve the end product. Individuals and groups working with Agile have the ability to operate independently inside predefined structures or procedures, which we refer to as "freedom within a frame." Encouraging innovation and creativity by allowing employees some degree of self-direction is a sure way to keep them engaged and motivated. In addition, agile organizations use management structures that allow teams to form and operate at a sprint, or a quicker pace, whenever they are needed. Multidisciplinary teams have a lot of advantages, like being able to communicate in real time with people from different departments or jobs.

## DIGITAL TRANSFORMATION STRATEGY

With regard to this chapter's topic of "digital transformation," there are both possibilities and risks (Moreno et al., 2015). Organisations income and earnings will suffer greatly if they do not respond to digital disruption, or do so just partially (Bughin et al., 2017). Having a clear strategy and putting "digital" at the centre of your company strategy is essential for a successful digital transformation (Gill and Vanboskirk, 2016). According to various studies (Ismail et al., 2017; Kane et al., 2015), a successful organisation's competitive advantage is based on the tactics its leaders employ rather than the technology they use. As a result, strategy, rather than technology, is the driving force behind digital transformation. There are both advantages and disadvantages to adopting a company-wide overall digital transformation strategy that goes beyond functional thinking (Singh & Hess, 2017). This approach may also serve as a unifying framework to manage, prioritise, and implement all of an organisation's digital transformation initia-

*Figure 3. Digital Transformation Strategy*

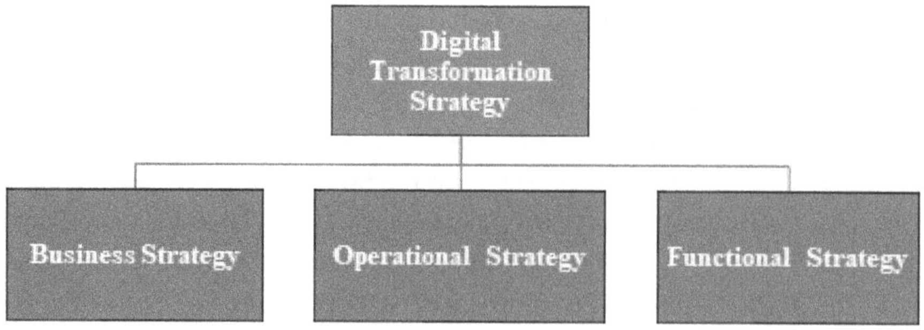

tives. As a result, the research suggests that digital transformation be treated as an enterprise strategy. Organisations should be able to make use of the many possibilities offered by the digital environment in a way that their rivals will find it difficult to duplicate (Ross et al., 2017). Figure 2 shows how the digital transformation strategy is linked to other business, functional, and operational strategies.

- **Business Strategy:** Business strategies assist businesses in developing dynamic capabilities to compete in a volatile business environment (Pavlov and El Sawy, 2010). As small businesses reorganise to adapt to the digital era, understanding digital business strategy and principles is critical to development and success. According to a 2019 Tech Pro Research report, 70% of corporate executives are devoting more time and attention to digital strategy. A digital company strategy may enhance customer experience, increase efficiency, and utilise business analytics. Everyone seems to be running a digital company nowadays. However, prominent business executives have differing views on what "digital" implies.
- **Operational Strategy:** Different types of technology in use have a significant impact on the operational side of the business process as well. Because of the supportive structure of digital firms, company processes are not restricted to a rigid, slow-moving nature, allowing for fluidity, agility, and flexibility to be introduced into the organisation, which can then work together seamlessly to operate the business smoothly (Desmet et al., 2015). The focus of a digital transformation strategy is on enhancing existing capabilities while also expanding the scale of the business through the use of underpinning technologies and business processes. This must be accompanied by increased speed in business operations and decision-making in order to generate new value propositions for the business.
- **Functional Strategy:** Strategic planning is a logical approach for separating management activities at the corporate, business, and functional levels. Digital strategy is a separate strategic element that should be part of both functional and corporate level organisational strategy. However, the other school of thought says that DX (digital transformation) strategy should support both operational and functional level strategy, which functions should be aligned with the corporate business strategy (Matt et al., 2015). One of the main ideas of digital business strategy is that businesses can make money and have unique experiences by making the best use of the resources they already have (Bharadwaj et al., 2013).

## PEOPLE CENTRIC DIGITISATION

Technology is everywhere, pervasive, and unavoidable. It is designed to make lives and work easier, less boring, and safer while expediting business interactions. People-Centric Digitalization can help achieve and retain a competitive advantage. The combination of technical data and user input can offer fresh insights into how the plant is working, ease the operators' work by giving them trustworthy information when they need it, and help them prevent human mistakes and improve safety.

**Teamwork:** Digitalization is a difficulty and solution. It facilitates hybrid teamwork, simplifies and automates complicated and expensive processes, and enables new business models. It disrupts old occupations and company sectors and requires a new corporate culture and innovation cycles. The digital world of work requires innovation to keep up with fast changing conditions and to foresee and shape new trends. These teams define their own criteria for the new working world, including a management style that gives them ample flexibility and responsibility to generate lasting ideas. Managers and employees encourage each other, share expertise, and work on new solutions, ideas, and innovations. This method can dissolve corporate pyramid hierarchies. This digital company culture values courage and experimentation (Haufe, 2021). Companies and employees must support daily learning. Successful digitization requires collaboration, openness, and adaptability.

**Engagement:** Employees need to feel heard, included in the dialogue, and that interactions are personal. To attain that degree of participation, organizations must personalize information sharing and receiving from their employees. People expect to be engaged more personally. They like tailored messages and are more inclined to reply. Employees want faster and more bite-sized communication now that more people have cellphones. It also makes individuals feel more connected, which may help change management initiatives succeed. The app, the bank claims, enhanced communications, increased staff engagement, knowledge exchange, and increased sales of digital services. Crowdsourcing enabled senior executives and frontline workers to agree on a fundamental strategic change from selling to corporations to selling directly to consumers. Managers liked the adjustment, but not executives. The corporation built a crowdsourcing stage where higher management could exchange business news and problems while frontline managers could add their own perspectives. Managers asked questions that senior executives answered in all-hands sessions. Top executives held hackathon-style meetings to tackle corporate concerns.

**Communications:** Communication is a critical leadership ability, and digitalization has transformed how people communicate. While technology can be distracting, it can also improve communication. Business executives must embrace technology to better communicate in the digital age. Communications help firms adapt to the shifting business landscape caused by remote workers. This desire to collaborate from anywhere spurred enterprise digital transformation (Alcatel-Lucent, 2022). Digital communication is intended to facilitate productivity rather than hinder it, particularly when interacting with business partners or coworkers in different time zones. This makes it tough for individuals to unwind. Managing the internet task is a further difficulty posed by digital communication. The proliferation of digital platforms makes it difficult for employees and companies to determine what is important. Businesses need to have a strong digital presence both inside and outside of the company, but many do not know how to do this, and doing it wrong could hurt the business.

**Digital Nudges:** It might be challenging for an organization's ability to adapt to today's digital world. A study found that people tend to go back to their old ways. Behavioral economics-based cues, known as nudges, are being used by organizations to support long-term behavioral changes. When nudges are used correctly, they can help individuals make better decisions. Organizational behavior changes may be transmitted more rapidly and widely via digital nudges like emails, text messages, and push alerts. The data generated by digital nudges may also be utilized to assess the effectiveness of the prompts and, if necessary, to adjust them. Personalized emails reminding someone to finish a job or form are examples of basic digital nudges (BCG, 2017). A digital nudge's message should be delivered in a method that is convenient for the person receiving it and at a time when they are ready to hear it. Social nudges, such as checking in with a goal or publishing successes on a workplace intranet or internal newsfeed, can be used to hold individuals responsible. For example, a member of a team may send a group SMS to their co-workers to motivate them to achieve their own work objectives.

## RECOMMENDATIONS

Companies throughout the world are reforming at varying rates and outcomes. Researchers believe that the transition process is hard (McConnel, 2018), and that effective transformative programmes rely on people, not technology. Pressure on businesses and organisations to modify technology, systems, established ways of working, and solutions has resulted in rapid changes that involve more than just the formal organisational structure since they involve a group of perspectives (Andersson et al., 2018). To survive and compete, businesses must adjust their internal organisation to the continuously changing external environment. They must invest in creating and equipping a staff capable of meeting the demands of a digital organisation. In today's digital world, when digital may be both an opportunity and a danger, digital transformation is critical to developing a company that can thrive (Solis, 2017).

There is a severe shortage of project and organizational teams that are quick to adapt and have a well-defined implementation strategy. If it is not addressed, the mismatch between traditional business practices and agile methods might be a problem. A lack of communication and cooperation among the many units and levels organized into functional silos might result as a consequence of this. It is not uncommon for projects to use the services of change managers to aid in the adoption of agile and change mindsets. To ensure future success, companies must examine their present organizational structures and assess if adding new digital technologies to their existing organizational skills would suffice. In order to successfully implement change, organizations need to be more flexible and modular.

## FUTURE RESEARCH DIRECTIONS

Technology-based traits like strategy, leadership, and culture are the focus of this research. Business management, new technology, and business practises are all discussed extensively in this research. This study contributes to the progress of this field and the growth of theories by creating opportunities for future research. Disruptive innovations should be put into their own new groups that work with the people who will use this technology in the future. More research is being done on digital transformation agents like customer-centric approach, technology-centric dimension, digital business process transformation, and digital structural agility, which are seen as defining pillars of digital transformation projects.

## CONCLUSION

For many firms, large and small, the new digital era is both a threat and an opportunity. These businesses would be left behind if they ignored digitization. Companies must quickly adapt to new procedures, agile techniques, organizational structures, and staff training to support their digital strategy. Digital transformation requires organizational change on a broad scale, in addition to the use of digital technology. Successful digital transformation requires a framework that describes the various dimensions that must be considered when developing a digital transformation strategy. This literature review identified and analyzed frameworks that describe the various dimensions that must be considered when developing a digital transformation strategy. Organizations in the industrial sector are organizing and managing their digital transformation drives. The study provided light on the most critical digital sources that are critical to incumbent organizations' digital transformation. It demonstrates how optimizing each of the specified digital sources together might assist incumbent organizations in achieving common goals. This study develops a digital strategy for business organizations, guiding researchers, practitioners, and industrial organizations on their digital transformation drives.

## REFERENCES

Alcatel-Lucent. (2022). Digital Age Communications. Alcatel-Lucent. https://www.al-enterprise.com/en/solutions/digital-age-communications

Andersson, P., Movin, S., Mähring, M., Teigland, R., & Wennberg, K. (2018). *Managing digital transformation*. SSE Institute for Research, Stockholm School of Economics.

Bharadwaj, A., El Sawy, O. A., Pavlou, P. A., & Venkatraman, N. (2013). Digital business strategy: Toward a next generation of insights. *Management Information Systems Quarterly*, *37*(2), 471–482. doi:10.25300/MISQ/2013/37:2.3

Bondar, S., Hsu, J. C., Pfouga, A., & Stjepandić, J. (2017). Agile digital transformation of system-of-systems architecture models using Zachman framework. *Journal of Industrial Information Integration*, *7*, 33–43. doi:10.1016/j.jii.2017.03.001

Bruskin, S. N., Brezhneva, A. N., Dyakonova, L. P., Kitova, O. V., Savinova, V. M., Danko, T. P., & Sekerin, V. D. (2017). Business performance management models based on the digital corporation's paradigm. *European Research Studies Journal*, *20*(4), 264–274.

Bughin, J., & Van Zeebroeck, N. (2017). The Best Response to Digital Disruption. *MIT Sloan Management Review*, *58*(4), 80–86.

Chanias, S., & Hess, T. (2016). Understanding digital transformation strategy formation: Insights from Europe's automotive industry. *PACIS 2016 Proceedings*, Chiayi, Taiwan, 296. https://aisel.aisnet.org/pacis2016/296

Desmet, D., Duncan, E., Scanlan, J., & Singer, M. (2015). *Six building blocks for creating a high performing digital enterprise*. McKinsey & Company.

Fitzgerald, M., Kruschwitz, N., Bonnet, D., & Welch, M. (2013). Embracing digital technology: A new strategic imperative | Capgemini consulting worldwide. *MIT Sloan Management Review*, *55*(1), 1–13.

Garvin, D. A. (2013). How Google Sold its Engineers on Management. *Harvard Business Review*. https://hbr.org/2013/12/how-google-sold-its-engineers-on-management

Gerth, A. B., & Peppard, J. (2016). The dynamics of CIO derailment: How CIOs come undone and how to avoid it. *Business Horizons*, *59*(1), 61–70. doi:10.1016/j.bushor.2015.09.001

Gilchrist, A. (2016). Industry 4.0: The industrial internet of things. *Apress*. doi:10.1007/978-1-4842-2047-4

Gill, M., & Vanboskirk, S. (2016). The Digital Maturity Model 4.0. Cambridge, Massachusetts.

Hess, T., Matt, C., Benlian, A., & Wiesbock, F. (2018). Options for formulating a Digital Transformation Strategy. *MIS Quarterly Executive*, *15*(2), 123–139.

Ismail, M. H., Khater, M., & Zaki, M. (2017). *Digital Business Transformation and Strategy: What Do We Know So Far?* Cambridge Service Alliance.

Kane, G. C., Palmer, D., Phillips, A. N., Kiron, D., & Buckley, N. (2015). Strategy, not technology, drives digital transformation. *MIT Sloan Management Review and Deloitte University Press*, *14*, 1–25.

Lumapps (2022). What is a Digital Workplace? Definition and Examples. https://www.lumapps.com/digital-workplace/

Matt, C., Hess, T., & Benlian, A. (2015). Digital transformation strategies. *Business & Information Systems Engineering*, *57*(5), 339–343. doi:10.100712599-015-0401-5

McConnell, J. (2018). How Digital Leaders Inspire Engagement. *MIT Sloan Management Review*.

Moreno, J. P., Gera, P., Colangelo, M., Proverbio, M., Skan, J., Busch, W., & Caroll, G. (2015). *The Everyday Bank a New Vision for the Digital Age*. Accenture.

Parviainen, P., Tihinen, M., Kääriäinen, J., & Teppola, S. (2017). Tackling the digitalization challenge: How to benefit from digitalization in practice. *International Journal of Information Systems and Project Management*, *5*(1), 63–77. doi:10.12821/ijispm050104

Pavlou, P. A., & El Sawy, O. A. (2010). The "third hand": IT-enabled competitive advantage in turbulence through improvisational capabilities. *Information Systems Research*, *21*(3), 443–471. doi:10.1287/isre.1100.0280

Ross, J. W., Sebastian, I. M., & Beath, C. M. (2017). How to Develop a Great Digital Strategy? *MIT Sloan Management Review*, *58*(2), 7–9.

Solis, B. (2017, December). The Digital Change Agent's Manifesto, 1–29. https://marketing.prophet.com/acton/media/33865/he-digital-change-agents-manifesto--altimeter

Sony, M., & Naik, S. (2020). Industry 4.0 integration with socio-technical systems theory: A systematic review and proposed theoretical model. *Technology in Society*, *61*, 101248. doi:10.1016/j.techsoc.2020.101248

Vial, G. (2019). Understanding digital transformation: A review and a research agenda. *The Journal of Strategic Information Systems*, *28*(2), 118–144. doi:10.1016/j.jsis.2019.01.003

Warner, K. S. R., & Wäger, M. (2019). Building dynamic capabilities for digital transformation: An ongoing process of strategic renewal. *Long Range Planning*, *52*(3), 326–349. doi:10.1016/j.lrp.2018.12.001

## ADDITIONAL READING

Accenture. (2016). Digital transformation: people are the irreplaceable changemakers. *Accenture.* https://www.accenture.com/nl-en/blogs/insights/digital-transformation-people-are-the-irreplaceable-changemakers

Danoesastro, M., Freeland, G., & Reichert, T. (2017). A CEO's Guide to Leading Digital Transformation, *BCG.* https://www.bcg.com/publications/2017/digital-transformation-digital-organization-ceo-guide-to-digital-transformation

Kohli, R., & Grover, V. (2008). Business value of IT: An essay on expanding research directions to keep up with the times. *Journal of the Association for Information Systems*, *9*(1), 1. doi:10.17705/1jais.00147

Li, F. (2020). The digital transformation of business models in the creative industries: A holistic framework and emerging trends. *Technovation*, *92-93*, 102012. doi:10.1016/j.technovation.2017.12.004

Mingardon, S., Wolfgang, M., Keenan, P., Krief, A., Doust, A., & Adida, F. (2017). Digital-Era Change runs on People Power: The new way of working series. *BCG.* https://www.bcg.com/publications/2017/change-management-organization-digital-era-change-runs-people-power

Niemi, M. K., Dan, S., Kalliokoski, J., Shahzad, K., Shakeel, S. R., Alagirisamy, R., & Laurila, I. (2021). Talent retention and the development of digital skills: A study of the ecosystem-based digitalisation academy located in Vaasa, Finland. *Publications of the Ministry of Economic Affairs and Employment.* http://urn.fi/URN:ISBN:978-952-327-840-0

Singh, A., & Hess, T. (2017). How Chief Digital Officers Promote the Digital Transformation of their Companies. *MIS Quarterly Executive*, *16*(1), 1–17.

## KEY TERMS AND DEFINITIONS

**Agility:** Agility in the digital age refers to the capacity to detect and grasp market possibilities created by digital technology.

**Catalytic Leadership:** The catalytic leader brings together people from many agencies to solve interrelated public challenges.

**Customer-Centric:** Customer centricity is the capacity of an organization's employees to understand and meet the needs and expectations of its customers.

**Digital Trend:** The digital trend represents significant shifts in the way marketers should communicate with their target audiences.

**Digital Nudges:** Digital nudging is a method that uses user interface (UI) design features to influence users' choices in digital settings. UI design elements include graphics, text, and minor features.

**Employee Engagement:** Employee engagement defines a worker's excitement and commitment to their job. It is connected to work happiness and morale, and it's vital to a company's success.

**Technology Centric:** Technocentrism is a value philosophy based on technology and its capacity for environmental control and protection.

# Chapter 9
# One Brain, One Heart, One Body:
## Technological Stress and Health in Organizations of the Digital Era

**Evgeny Rudnev**
*Moscow Economic Institute, Russia*

## ABSTRACT

*The chapter reveals the problem of health in the context of digitalization and building an organizational culture based on hybrid communication, workplace practices, and burnout prevention. Health is the main human resource, which is becoming a predictor of organization success in the 21st century; and it is the responsibility of business to create conditions conducive to the health of employees. The problem of technological stress and understanding of health based on medical and psychological approaches are considered. It is concluded that the psychological approach allows a broader consideration of health in relation to conditions of digitalization - social context and role of emotions. An overview of health research results in various countries is presented, taking into account the factors of education, gender, age, and culture. Recommendations are given for building an organizational culture based on hybrid communication, behavior in the workplace. and prevention of emotional burnout.*

## HEALTH OF WORKERS AS A PREDICTOR OF ORGANIZATION SUCCESS IN 21 CENTURY

*Health is the main resource of human. In recent decades, the problem of safety becomes relevant (Zinchenko, 2011), and a new scientific direction "psychology of health" is developing. (Health Psychology, 2006). 85% of the managers professional activity consists communication and correlated with intellectual loads. The solution of various problems, increased responsibility and stress attract risks for leaders that depend on health. together with that business plays a significant role in creating a healthy environment, meaningful work and well-being of people. (Pitts at el, 2022)*

DOI: 10.4018/978-1-6684-5864-8.ch009

Modern leaders work in an environment of uncertainty, which increases the health risks associated with the strategic development of organization. And in the era of information technologies intensive development in organizations, the impact of which on human health has not been fully studied.

Traditionally, at the household level and among professionals, there is an opinion "health is the absence of disease". This is due to the fact that the medical approach dominated in science for a long time. Research by psychologists at the early stages of ontogenesis - preschool children showed such an idea of health in Russia is formed from an early age (Fedorenko, 2009). The children were asked to describe their health. An analysis of the children's stories included descriptions of a medical nature dominated in their content: to be healthy - not to take pills, not to go to doctor. Less often - eat fruit, wash hands, play sports. Thus, the medical approach to health is quite common in Russia. However, back in 1948, the World Health Organization determined a definition of health, indicated its the social nature, human well-being - "health is a state of complete physical, mental and social well-being, and not just the absence of diseases and physical defects." (http://www.who.int)

*The issue of stress is described in detail in the psychological literature. (Bodrov, 2012) Nevertheless, there is a new type of stress in 21 century - technological. Technological stress is a stress that occurs in a person from exposure to special devices (laptop, smartphone and others used in the workplace and in everyday life), the impact of which on a person has not been fully studied.*

At present, the only way to deal with technological stress is to establish norms of behavior, to increase the importance of a person using technical devices. No one, except the owners of technical means, can set these standards and control them.

Some norms that reduce the level of technological stress:

- turn off all devices that emit signals before going to bed;
- warn acquaintances, relatives, colleagues that after 22.00 technical means of communication and devices, including e-mail, are not used;
- warn colleagues that on weekends technical means of communication are not used;
- establish norms for response time to messages and introduce them to acquaintances, relatives, colleagues;
- do not use communication devices while playing sports.

The task of leadership and top management of organizations is to support these rules and develop health behavior of workers.

In the 21st century, the psychological approach to understanding health is becoming increasingly popular. Obviously, a person is arranged in such a way that with age he ages. However, often a person enters the profession healthy, and leaves it - sick. A child born in Brazil or Burma (Myanmar) today can expect to live 20 years longer than one born only 50 years ago. In Iran, only around one in ten of the population is currently older than 60 years. In only 35 years' time, this proportion will have increased to around one in three. And the pace of change is much faster than was the case in the past, but little evidence exists that older people today are experiencing better health than their parents (Beard *at el,* 2017) The psychological understanding of health lies in the fact that it largely depends on our attitude and perception of life. The task of modern organizations is for a person to come to the workplace healthy, and after leaving the organization, to go on a well-deserved rest also healthy. In many respects, it also depends on whether health is a value for leader of the organization. Research by psychologists shows that employees of Russian organizations do not think about health as a value, including young professionals. (Bogacheva, 2010). According to mental health research, mental illness is the #1 health threat. The well-being and productivity of young people before the age of 25 are associated in 75% of cases with mental disorders. In addition, over 50% of youth experienced at least one period of poor mental health by their 25th birthday. (Krisberg, 2020)

To maintain health in modern science, simple and fairly effective methods have been developed. One of the methods was proposed by Canadian psychologist (coach) Marilyn Atkinson. Her understanding of health is based on how a person perceives his\her own life. Many people go through life and then turn around and ask the question: My life - how was it?

According to Atkinson, life includes work, career, money, friends, travel, family. Thus, the life of an adult is not limited to work. Understanding life in terms of "work-home-work" narrows the idea of life and increases the risks associated with emotional burnout and poor health. And only the diversity of life, the severity of all its segments makes a person's life rich, full, healthy. However, M.Atkinson[1] emphasizes different stages of life and its segments can be important to varying degrees. At one stage of life, a family may be more important for a person, at another, a career.

Obviously, in order to relax, a person needs to travel in order to better understand himself and own values. Traveling requires money. To have money for travel and recreation, need to make a career. Family support and communication with friends are important for a successful career. Furthermore, social isolation hurts health. "People with a small community of friends and family — or none at all — are much more likely to develop serious illness and have short life expectancies" - Dr. A. Komaroff (Harvard Health Letter, 2020) Thus, all segments of life are interconnected, and the task of a person is to turn the "wheel of life".

A fairly common phenomenon, studied, including in Russian studies, among people employed in the "person-to-person" sphere is emotional burnout. A condition characterized by a loss of meaning, loss of interest in work, and even sometimes a negative attitude - unwillingness to go to work. Psychologists have developed effective ways to prevent emotional burnout. (Semizdralova, 2010).

*A very common way to prevent emotional burnout is to move with music outside of work. It combines an emotional impact on the human psyche and physical activity aimed at supporting the human body in good shape. Bibliotherapy allows to give an emotional impulse. Works in poetic form contain the emotional color laid down in them by the author - emotional settings. Therefore, reading can be an effective tool for preventing burnout. In addition, exhibitions, theatre, and cinema set an intellectual and emotional impulse and allow to look at existing problems in a different way. Moreover, Canadian Scientific Studies, each additional hour spent on fresh air per day was associated with 7.0 minutes of moderate to vigorous activity, 762 individual steps, and 13 minutes less sedentary time. In addition, each case on the open air was associated with a lower chance of negative psychosocial outcomes (particularly with peers) problems compared to those who spent less time on the fresh air. (Larouche at el, 2016)*

Many longitudinal studies have found that a person needs to be productive at work, and laughter helps in this. The digital era is characterized by a high rate of information technology adoption in the workplace. Neuroscience shows that changes make it hard to control emotions. They help to understand where a person is moving and how to respond to other people accordingly. It is always important to manage emotions at work. But this task is even more important during times of change, when sensitivity to threat and negativity increases.

Part of leadership's responsibility is not only to manage their own emotions, but to help others do the same. (Scarlett, 2019) Emotions usually arise when people deal with thoughts, actions, and interactions with other people. They are different in the mood in which they arrive after their manifestation. Emotions are physiologically responsible for stimuli, help move in the direction of reward and avoid threats. In other words, their role is to promote a person to behave in a certain way that is in his interest. People constantly generate emotions, but mostly do not perceive them.

Emotions activate areas of the brain that they mostly associate with its limbic area. This part of the brain plays a role in perceiving emotions and influencing how a person responds to them physically and mentally.

The study of 142 countries showed that emotions have a greater impact on health than hunger, homelessness, and the threat to safety around the world. However, the relationship between emotions and health was stronger in countries with low gross domestic product than in countries with high gross domestic product. (Pressman *et al,* 2013)

In addition, the study of 1,567,295 individuals in 165 countries found that negative affect (anxiety, sadness, stress, and anger) showed the strongest association with subjective health and life satisfaction. (Joshanloo and Jovanović, 2021)

Positive emotions give the team a better chance of better work doing. In this case, mirror neurons play a special role. It may be to help people understand the actions and behavior of others so that they are better able to live, work and survive with others. They are significant in learning and allow to imitate the actions of others. It was found that people with emotional control had higher grades in school, higher salaries and were less likely to be overweight. As a rule, live better.

The prefrontal cortex, the main control center of the brain, which is also important for thinking, decision making and self-control, is also responsible for stress hormones. Those who are constantly under stress may develop fear and anxiety, which then easily trigger off to a lesser provocation.

The brain struggles to stay focused when nothing is variable and things are monotonous. And it's a source of stress. In the process of change, people can experience stress. Long-term stress has a negative effect on the immune system. Mental health conditions declared for employers (CIPD, 2018). Neuroscience researchers emphasize that stress hormones are long-term toxic to neurons, especially in areas that are considered key to high-quality job performance. The hippocampus has many receptors for adrenaline and cortisol and cortisol damage and destroy brain cells. Control helps lower cortisol levels. The act of detecting emotion expands activity in the prefrontal cortex and reduces activity in the amygdala. The definition of emotion (labeling) provides "a symbolic conversation where putting emotion into words creates a distance effect and so reduces it." (Scarlett, 2019; 98) There is a danger that the ability to create or overwrite memory will be impaired when a person experiences too much stress.

"Neuroscience for Organizational Change: An Evidence-based Practical Guide to Managing Change" offers for leaders: setting clear goals and guidelines; to become open to challenge and different views; identify own values and potential biases; form groups: set broad goals; create opportunities for face-to-face communication.

Wherein communication is critical during change. If workers don't understand a change, don't support it, or feel it can't be communicated, it won't happen. The brain is constantly comparing incoming information with predictable information. If the incoming information matches, all is well - the brain pays little attention to it. But if the incoming information does not meet expectations, attention is redirected so that the person decides - finds a way out. There is a limit to how much information the brain can take in. Emotionally intense events are recorded strongly in the sensory cortex and hippocampus.

Physical activity has a positive effect on the state of the body. However, it is worth remembering that by themselves they do not solve psychological problems. In recent years, wellness (from English "well" - good) is gaining momentum in the world - healthy lifestyle programs that include physical activity, special movements aimed at muscle and emotional relaxation, as well as healthy nutrition.

*A key factor in the development of physical activity: the global burden of non-communicable diseases, especially cardiovascular diseases, cancer and diabetes. These diseases cause more than 41 million deaths each year, of which a third occur before the age of 70. (Rutter at el, 2019)*

At the same time, according to the latest nutrition report, it is recommended to increase the amount of potassium in the diet and reduce the intake of sodium to reduce blood pressure and the risk of cardiovascular disease. It is also recommended to reduce the level of fats, which make up more than 30% of all food intake energy, replace foods saturated with trans fats with unsaturated fats, include vitaminizing salt with iodine, general strengthening wheat, corn flour and flour with vitamins and minerals everywhere. (Warnick, 2019)

In addition, socializing while eating has more health benefits than general socializing without food. Physiological health is affected not only by the choice of food, which affects mental health, but also with whom a person eats food. Those who ate in groups were less likely to have symptoms of depression. (Ruscigno, 2018)

*I emphasize that the psychological approach to understanding health does not exclude the medical one. However, the psychological approach not only expands the concept of health, but also allows a person to be more productive in the workplace, to build a full, vibrant, emotionally rich life. Knowing some information on stress, physical activity and eating allows to keep health of each adult person (Table 1)*

*Table 1. Predictors of health and ill health of adults*

| Fact | Knowledge |
|---|---|
| The most stressful factor | is a loss of spouse |
| Most stressful job | is an librarian |
| Stress can motivate to work | a distress destroys health |
| Time heals | but does not fix the problem |
| Every member of the organization has the right | to rest |
| The norm of fresh fruits and vegetables | is 400 grams per day |
| Salt plays a role in metabolism | do you add salt to food without tasting it? |
| Juices are sold in regular stores | they contain a lot of sugar |
| Caffeine stimulates the activity of the cardiovascular system | tea contains more caffeine than coffee |
| Office has physical and air volume limitations | it must be ventilated and filled with fresh air |
| Biking, skiing and walking | are alternative to physical activity in the gym. |

Furthermore, the prevention of technological stress does not mean complete isolation from society. According to Hilary Scarlet (2019), the brain has a social nature. Therefore, it is important to take into account knowledge both in the implementation and use of information technologies. In particular, change doesn't happen when there isn't a strong enough bond with and trust in workers. During times of change, workers need to connect with others. However, sometimes there are situations when leaders pay little attention to relationships. In this case, people have many questions, no answers, and are worried about the future. A significant role in communication, stress reduction and helping people lies in the identification of the object of influence. The ability to think and work in the best way is influenced by the assessment of "doing well". The other side of the sociality of the brain is increased cooperation. Learning from each other and expanding ideas leads to competitive advantage. The idea is not realized when people do not communicate with each other. The brain is driven by the goal of survival and the need for social connection. The person feels connected to others and feels the need to belong. Therefore, community resources in social networks and communication based on them can be actively used. Leaders can communicate through information technology and provide employees with information resources to establish communication and thus reduce stress levels.

*A person experiences illness from reduced social connection. This means that he always strives for connection and a sense of belonging. Identity within a group quickly leads to a boundary between team members. This is a behavioral benefit and is used to increase productivity. Social skills promote teamwork and collective intelligence.*

Dopamine as a neurotransmitter is responsible for transmitting signals between neurons in the brain. It affects brain functions, including cognition, voluntary movement, motivation, mood, working memory, and learning in a variety of ways. Dopamine also provides a learning signal to the parts of the brain that are responsible for enabling new behaviors to be acquired. It expands new connections in the brain, is associated with reward, and especially with its expectation. Decreased dopamine increases the desire to do something special and has a negative impact on the ability to think creatively.

When a person's thinking about being able to do something increases, he believes that he can do it best in practice. But not everyone has the potential to be excellent at anything. However, a person can get better if he tries to do it. People have a way of thinking about anything. During change, they face difficulties and setbacks. In the case when they have a way of thinking and do something badly, fail - then their intellect judges this.

Based on the difficulty, the person accepts a less difficult task until he experiences a positive feeling again. But when the brain is at rest, it works freely. Connections are created, and a person comes to a new idea. During this period, insight arises. The solution seems to come out of nowhere. While the brain works with options for possible solutions. From point of view, a culture of transformation, leaders take the initiative.

*Achieving a goal generates dopamine in the brain and makes a person feel good. For these, leaders show kindness – praising people and recognizing accomplishments. According to neuroscience, the human brain doesn't like much change, but likes to do some innovation. Too much uncertainty is a threat, while some innovation keeps a person motivated to create new - better environments and resources. The brain starts to fight in the case when something new and different happens every day. It cannot predict and goes to the threat model. People resist stress more when they feel they have some control. Events that are uncontrollable and unpredictable are very stressful for people.*

## TRANSFORMED ECONOMY – STRESS, HUMAN BEHAVIOR AND HEALTH IN CONDITIONS OF DIGITALIZATION

The subject of health is a global trend. However, there are not so many research results in various countries of the world on this topic.

Consider some of the conclusions made by scientists in the field of health psychology.

### Values, Education and Stress

It has been proven that being the main source of income and other material goods, as well as a source of social integration, prestige and meaning, employment is positively associated with health. At the same time, with physical and psychosocial stressors. (Burgard and Lin, 2013)

People with low levels of education reported significantly poorer health after retirement than people with higher education. Less educated workers had more physical activity and fewer psychosocial demands, a significant difference in tasks, and a higher level of autonomy in work compared to workers with higher education. (Breij *et al.*, 2019), These characteristics have been found to define differences between education and health after leaving a job around the world.

*Partially confirmed the causal relationship between work motivation and psychological health after six months. (Dagenais-Desmarais et al., 2018) In the study of feedback, it has been proven that psychological well-being at work contributes more to self-determination - motivation in action, namely its internal and identified types. Only psychological well-being at work and established regulation are fully correlated. In other words, working in accordance with self-values and goals leads to psychological well-being and vice versa. This process has the potential to lead to an upward spiral where workplace well-being and established regulation complement each other.*

The potential benefits of high status have been shown to improve health. For example, highly educated and higher status workers have greater access to creative work. In turn, creative self-expression can improve psychological well-being and cognitive function, as well as reduce stress and dysregulation of the hypothalamic-pituitary-adrenal axis, which increases the chances of a successful career.

### Timing and Regularity of Work

Another aspect of work and health researched is the timing and regularity of work. In particular, the transition to a round-the-clock economy - hours and schedules, an increase in the number of non-standard work hours can both positively and negatively affect health. For example, coronary and peptic ulcer diseases are associated with sleep disturbance during shift work.

It is emphasized that with the development of post-industrial economies, the professional structure, labor protection and safety rules are changing. Examples of commonly studied psychosocial stressors are work stress, insecurity, and the negative side effects of work. Tension is a combined experience of poor task control and maintaining a small amount of social media in the workplace. It has been associated with mental illness, musculoskeletal symptoms, insomnia, and coronary heart disease.

*In some studies, workload is associated with neuroendocrine and cardiovascular responses, which over a long period of time can lead to cardiovascular complications. It has been found that women employed in jobs with high work stress or low managerial support exhibit higher levels of fibrinogen, which is also associated with an increased risk of cardiovascular disease. Workers who believe they may lose their jobs in the near future have shown worsening mental and physical health. Moreover, those undergoing restructuring or layoffs, that is, exposed to job uncertainty, also exhibited worse biomedical outcomes, such as rising blood pressure and worsening overall health due to perceived insecurity. Together with that, an increase in sleep scores on the four dimensions - satisfaction, alertness, timing, efficiency by only one unit of measurement leads to a significant decrease in the expression of depressive symptoms.* (Appleton *at el, 2022)*

One of the popular dyads in health research is "the negative impact of work and family". This is a type of role conflict that occurs when responsibilities in one area interfere with responsibilities in another. Most of the research in this area is associated with negative associations—negative side effects from work and family and depressive symptoms, stress and distress, anxiety, poor self-reported health, hypertension, obesity, and musculoskeletal problems.

The impact of stress is also associated with an increase in risky behavior. For example, with increased tobacco use and lower levels of physical activity, less consumption of healthy or increased consumption of fatty foods - a shortening of life.

It is emphasized that flexible work policies and control over the work schedule of employees contribute to the reduction of the conflict between work and family - health promotion, greater sleep opportunities and regular sports.

*Simultaneously, highly educated workers may be at relatively greater risk of psychosocial stress. One of the latest hypotheses is that autonomy or power, previously seen as resources, may exacerbate the relationship between work and the family sphere.*

## Gender, Age and Informational Technologies on the Workplace

Some studies show that women are less prone to problems at work than men because their personality is not as strongly associated with job roles. For example, the ratio between labor force participation and mortality is higher among men.

Withal, women are found to be more likely than men to experience negative mental health outcomes as a result of feelings of guilt at work.

Theories of cumulative advantage and disadvantage describe how initial disadvantages can disqualify people from promotion, and how negative turning points, such as involuntary loss of a job, can block further progress, "traumatizing" workers in terms of their wage trajectory.

Breaks in work history can also lead to loss of seniority and benefits within the same organization, loss of pensions and health insurance, and flatter pay trajectories that exacerbate career-long social disadvantage.

*Unfavorable career trajectories predict health changes, in particular a higher risk of mortality for men who held a range of unrelated jobs, as well as for those who excelled in promotions early in their careers, but not later, compared to more stable successful career trajectories . Downward mobility between the ages of 25 and 50 associated with poor self-reported mental health has been found in English men. At the same time, overskilled Canadians with university education were at significant risk of lowering their self-reported health over a four-year period. Persistent exposure to a psychosocial stressor at work in relation to mental health was found in those who could not advance to jobs with better working conditions, and their career had a significant impact on health and mortality. Studies conducted in Sweden in the public sector (Håkansson et al., 2020) showed that imbalances in daily life due to excessive obligations predicted a decrease in women's ability to work, and a low educational level predicted a decrease in men's ability to work. However, the strongest predictor of work ability for both sexes was poor self-reported health. This multifactorial nature of work capacity (combination of poor self-reported health, imbalance in daily life and excessive commitment, reduced work capacity) should be taken into account when designing health promotion programs.*

The change of employer for older workers is accompanied by an improvement in work, health and working capacity. (Garthe and Hasselhorn, 2021). In other words, inclusive labor market policies, high job mobility have the potential to significantly improve individual working conditions, health and work capacity of workers, thereby increasing work participation. However, these results may be due to cultural differences. In particular, Russia does not belong to countries with a high level of mobility, unlike the United States.

*Research on a sample of 1,070 Swiss leaders showed - health is affected by work stressors, private factors and work resources. Work stressors, but not personal stressors, predicted emotional commitment, job satisfaction, and change intent. While personal stressors are emotional exhaustion, health status and psychosomatic complaints. Workforce predicted both attitudes and health outcomes. A stronger link between personal stressors and emotional exhaustion was found in men. At the same time, no tripartite influence has been established - between work stress factors, personal factors and gender. The conflict of confidentiality and work is confirmed as a mediator between personal stressors and job satisfaction, emotional exhaustion, psychosomatic complaints and health status.*

As a preventive measure to reduce stress factors at work and achieve a balance between work and family requirements, the development of an accepting and supportive organizational culture for both men and women is proposed. (Galliker *et al.*, 2020)

German studies showed that women in leadership positions did much more housework than men in leadership positions, even when they worked full-time.

Comparisons between job stressors and occupational stressors were larger for health-related variables, but smaller for attitude variables. Private stressors were more strongly associated with emotional exhaustion in men. In other words, women can handle stressors better than their male counterparts. In addition, private family stressors are more strongly associated with men's life satisfaction, as they are less effective at coping with family stressors. The hypothesis of differential vulnerability that women are more susceptible to life events than men has not been confirmed. It is likely that men react more strongly to events in the private sphere.

At the same time, it has been shown women who are less effective in coping with stress in their personal lives tend to leave leadership positions or refuse to take them in the first place. Female leaders are less likely to become parents and partners than male peers.

Nevertheless, having children is associated with better health and well-being.

In addition, women suffered from a higher burden of overall levels of stressors.

To prevent stress, it is proposed to harmonize the requirements of work and personal life - for example, flexibility of the schedule; home office days; services of a full-time "concierge" who deals with private matters (cleaning, shopping, repair or brokerage of craftsmen, universal child care facilities).

*One of the topical aspects of health at work is the impact of information and communication technologies (ICT), in particular on the older generation. The results of studies on the use of ICTs show that it does not in itself have a negative impact on older workers.*

Deterioration in mental health and work capacity may be associated with the intensification of digital work. (Borle *et al.*, 2020)

High levels of ICT use have been proven to cause no harm when not tested as an intensification of digital work. However, occupational health and organizational development professionals need to monitor digitalization processes to assess the extent to which they are implemented in order to intensify work. Because digitalization processes can lead to unequal health and social consequences.

It is emphasized that along with technological changes over time, digital proximity, the use of ICTs and their consequences may also change. Therefore, the problem of technological stress is not removed from the agenda.

A study on the health of women aged 45–55 years (Rindner *et al.*, 2020) showed - quality of life improves through good relationships with a partner, social support, and work-life balance in personal life. For balance, women are encouraged to set realistic goals in work and social life.

At the same time, practice and research into the implementation of lactation spaces in organization creates policies to support mothers and families and promote wellness in the workplace. (Hickey *at el*, 2022)

## Influence of National Culture, Visualization and Leaders Self-Regulation in Time of Changes

On a sample of Dutch and Japanese workers, mental health was studied from the point of view of the influence of culture. The first culture is characterized by a focus on a high level of individualism and quality, the second - a high level of collectivism and success. It was previously known that high mental well-being was associated with higher performance and achievement, while mental disorders were associated with lower performance and achievement (Royal College of Psychiatrists, 2011).

Both samples found that mental health problems were positively associated with shame and mental health demotivation and negatively with work engagement and intrinsic motivation. However, differences between Dutch and Japanese workers were that age and self-compassion were negative predictors of mental health problems in Japanese workers, while in Dutch workers, work engagement was a negative predictor of mental health problems. These differences are explained by the cultural emphasis on shame in Japan and the quality of life in the Netherlands. (Kotera *et al.*, 2020).

Perceived stress is negatively correlated with mental health, while at the same time there is a positive relationship between work stress and burnout. (Ghorbani *et al.*, 2018)

In a study conducted in Germany on a sample of school principals, was found - the strongest predictors of all outcomes in relation to health and work - the breadth of decision-making and self-efficacy. (Dadaczynski *et al.*, 2020)

*One way to reduce stress is visualization. The brain loves the known, and people trust familiar faces more than faces they don't know—the visual effect makes the difference. People need to set goals carefully: expectations that don't happen lead to a drop in dopamine and increased activity in the amygdala. Meeting and exceeding expectations leads to an expansion of dopamine.*

*Change is difficult for the brain as it prefers to live with old habits and conserve energy. Whereas change requires more energy. Managers who focus people and give them boundaries strike the right balance between certainty and autonomy. The feeling of brain fatigue can be caused by many things: hard work, boredom, lack of variety in work, planning, decision making, holding back emotions, feeling anxious, focusing attention, blocking out distractions, long and difficult cognitive tasks (i.e. thinking hard), lack of sleep, resistance to the consumption of sweet foods. (Scarlet, 2019)*

*The management of mental work includes a priority of tasks for the day and their recording; allocating time to study email; avoidance of small talk; decisions making in advance; scheduling time for reflection; writing down thoughts on paper - using the release of memory; taking a break; not working on several tasks at the same time; setting intentions, choosing filters: fueling yourself; learning to stay in a state of reward.*

*To ensure connection between the mind and body is recommended to: maintain blood sugar levels; learn to calm the brain on demand; develop the ability to say stop - take a breath; laugh; sleep / take a nap; exercise stress; be good at one or two things.*

*Along with this, it is indicated that comprehensive health literacy is a critical, direct determinant of health. But it's measurement should be standardised in every country to allow for designing adequate measures for the specific situation of the country. (Pelikan at el, 2018) Moreover, a study conducted on a sample of 25 adults (13 males, 12 females) aged 18-70 years old from 10 countries showed that people can get acquainted with health literacy using an avatar.(McElhinney at el, 2018)*

## BUILDING AN ORGANIZATIONAL CULTURE BASED ON HYBRID COMMUNICATIONS, WORK PLACE PRACTICES AND BURNOUT PREVENTION

### Development of the Optimal Mode of Operation Using Hybrid Communications

*With the efforts of digitalization of processes in organizations, the task is to develop hybrid communications - the development of the most optimal procedures for health with the inclusion of information technology. One option is three working days at the office and two at home or in free mode, where a person can focus more on completing tasks. With such an organization of work, the working week begins with a meeting of employees, where everyone talks about what tasks he\she solves, and what help or support he\she may need from other employees, what has been done and what tasks are still being solved. This approach allows to increase mutual control, transparency, responsibility and health.*

In this case, employees also determine on their own the days when they will be at the workplace and, if necessary, they can choose the general days of presence at the workplace. This approach means that the meeting can be held using remote technologies, and emerging issues can be discussed jointly. Working outside the office allows to increase the autonomy and responsibility of the employee for the execution of the task.

*In the case when the organization has a branched structure, such meetings can be held by subdivision, where their leaders can independently determine when such collaborations are held. At the same time, the CEO, together with top managers, can hold a similar meeting with the heads of departments.*

*A significant problem in increasing digitalization is the different experience of using information technology. Most modern workers use them. However, any software is a procedure laid down by the developer. In this regard, even experienced users of information technology can experience cognitive dissonance and technological stress. The task of the organization leader or heads of departments is to jointly train the selected software with the subsequent socialization of new employees in the workplace. This means that when starting to solve professional problems using new software or hardware, it is advisable to work out a new interaction experience, ask questions in case of misunderstanding of an action or procedure, and conduct action learning.*

*This will significantly reduce technological stress and create a healthy climate. The experience of the pandemic showed that the burnout of workers during this period was associated with the lack of social experience of hybrid communication in the majority. With the introduction of hybrid communication in an organization, norms of behavior associated with a flexible presence in the workplace can be developed – use the potential and abilities of people and information technologies that allow connections building in real time - leader in the workplace and remote workers, workers in the workplace and remote leader, face-to-face and remote communication of groups led by a leader, solving one or more tasks, several people at a distance, several people and a leader at the workplace, several people and a leader in removal and several people at the workplace.*

## Workplace Practices – Health Climate and Organizational Effectiveness

The study of relationship of health in an organization with support practices (St-Hilairea *et al.*, 2019) conducted with distinguishing two categories of competencies: performing any tasks and helping to solve a task. This is reflected in the methods of work relating to the fulfillment of one's own task and to contribution of subordinate to the organization's mission achievement - common to all.

Almost a third of managers said that their subordinates replace their leader for certain tasks (32%) or change work schedules when necessary (32%). One of the ways to increase the level of health is the practice of affiliation. It includes the ability to create a favorable climate at work and recognize it. The behavior of subordinates may indicate that they are acting in solidarity with their supervisors and colleagues, creating a healthier environment and expressing appreciation for each other. Another option is facilitating practices.

Facilitating practices are methods in that subordinates participate to improve work to make it more efficient by making suggestions, trying new ways of doing things, and taking initiative through the practice of accepting responsibilities. 44% of managers reported this practice, and only 18% of subordinates mentioned it. In contrast, more subordinates (27%) than managers (8%) spoke of taking on authority or responsibility.

The next type is relationship practices. The theme of relationships manifests itself in practices that allow to establish a relationship with manager, or rather, through interaction and development of relationships.

Information practices are mainly concerned with the behavior of subordinates in engaging in dialogue and inviting others to participate, mainly with the manager, in the dissemination of information and in self-expression.

Almost 47% of subordinates report that they provided their supervisor with the necessary information, while only 20% of managers mentioned this practice.

Ethical practices reflect norms in competencies that demonstrate integrity - honesty and transparency.

Such studies of organizational practices are the most promising for the future, as they describe actions that subordinates can take to reduce the impact of stressors and assist managers. In them, the problem of health is considered from the point of view of behavior - an organizational culture that contributes to the preservation of mental health.

Moreover, scientific results contribute to the advancement of knowledge of organizational behavior and organizational health and safety, in addition to the integrated perspective of these two areas of human resource management, the development of mental health-promoting competencies in both - subordinates and leadership competencies development.

It is emphasized that in order to reduce stress, first actions can be initiated by the manager. While subordinates can take the initiative in stressful situations. Thus, mental health in the organization is determined by reciprocity - it is the responsibility of everyone.

Also identified are two organizational factors that influence the construction of the role of a passive or proactive follower: leadership style and organizational climate.

Subordinates may claim to be always ready to help, but not necessarily take any action. Leadership can encourage subordinates to go beyond the desired motivation, use the strategy of empowering subordinates.

Thus, promoting an organizational culture of shared responsibility between management and subordinates can have a positive impact on the stress and mental health of others, and keep people at work. At the same time, the development of culture of democracy and trust contributes to the formation of healthy relationships - clarity and transparency of the behavior norms in organization and increase the effectiveness of management. Including using the resources of social networks and other tools in digital era.

## HOBBIES, FREE TIME AND WORKPLACE BURNOUT PREVENTION

*When hiring, most often pay attention to the level of competencies development to perform the job - an advanced level of information technology knowledge or networking. However, one of the working capacity factors and hence the reliability of a person, is his\her ability to effectively organize time outside of work. That is hobbies and interests. The more hobbies and interests a person has, the more intense and intellectually rich his\her life is. A person who has all his\her thoughts and time concentrated only on work is more prone to emotional burnout, less flexible, and therefore less effective. In addition, personal interests make informal communication between colleagues more diverse and rich, and people more interesting in the eyes of each other. When employees stop seeing each other as just a function, conflicts and strained relationships are less likely to occur. Sometimes, a passion or hobby can become the main activity, such as knowledge of foreign languages or artistic abilities.*

To make sure that a person knows how to organize his\her free time, just ask at the interview (when applying for a job) if he\she has any hobbies.

An ideal option is when an organization provides employees with food or sports for the physical tone of the body. However, when this is not in the organization, people must have the time and opportunity to eat right to maintain the body. One of the options for norms in subdivisions is playing sports in the morning or evening.

*Invitations to the theater, cinema, exhibitions are much more effective than joint (corporate) events outside of work. It is important for people to understand that they have free time, which they can dispose of at their own discretion, that contributes to both a change in activity and environment, have the opportunity to spend time with family and in the fresh air, will reduce the level of emotional burnout in workplace and would contribute to improving the health of workers.*

## REFERENCES

Appleton, S. L., Melaku, A. Y., Reynolds, C. A., Gill, T. K., De Batlle, J., & Adams, J. R. (2022). Multidimensional sleep health is associated with mental well-being in Australian adults. *Journal of Sleep Research, 31*(2), e13477. doi:10.1111/jsr.13477 PMID:34622511

Beard, J. R., Officer, A., Araujo de Carvalho, I., Sadana, R., Pot, A.-M., Michel, J.-P., Lloyd-Sherlock, P., Epping-Jordan, J., Peeters, G., Mahanani, W.-R., Thiyagarajan, J. A., & Chatterji, S. (2017). The World report on ageing and health: A policy framework for healthy ageing. *Lancet, 387*(10033), 2145–2154. doi:10.1016/S0140-6736(15)00516-4 PMID:26520231

Bodrov, V. A. (2012). *Psychological stress. Development and overcoming*. Per Se.

Bogacheva, T. Yu. (2010) Health in the system of life values of a modern specialist. Ranepa. Moscow.

Borle, P., Boerner, F., Susanne, Z., Mahlknecht, V., Hasselhorn, H. M., & Ebener, M. (2020). The social and health implications of digital work intensification. Associations between exposure to information and communication technologies, health and work ability in different socio-economic strata. *International Archives of Occupational and Environmental Health*. doi:10.100700420-020-01588-5 PMID:33084928

Breij, S., Qvist, J. Y., Holman, D., Mäcken, J., Seitsamo, J., Huisman, M., & Deeg, D. J. H. (2019). Educational inequalities in health after work exit: The role of work characteristics. *BMC Public Health, 19*(1), 1515. doi:10.118612889-019-7872-0 PMID:31718592

Burgard, S. A., & Lin, K. Y. (2013). Bad Jobs, Bad Health? How Work and Working Conditions Contribute to Health Disparities. *The American Behavioral Scientist, 57*(8), 1105–1127. doi:10.1177/0002764213487347 PMID:24187340

Dadaczynski, K., Paulus, P., & Horstmann, D. (2020). The predictive value of individual and work-related resources for the health and work satisfaction of German school principals. *Health Education Journal, 79*(2), 225–236. doi:10.1177/0017896919867118

Dagenais-Desmarais, V., Leclerc, J.-S., & Londei-Shortall, J. (2018). The relationship between employee motivation and psychological health at work: A chicken-and-egg situation? *Work and Stress*, *32*(2), 147–167. doi:10.1080/02678373.2017.1317880

Fedorenko, E.Yu. (2009) Health as a result of education. *National education, 4*, 257-261

Galliker, S., Nyffenegger, D., Semmer, N. K., & Elfering, A. (2020). Women and men in leadership positions: Health and work-related attitudes and their associations with work-related stressors, private stressors, and privacy-work conflict. *Z. Arb. Wiss*, *75*(1), 29–45. doi:10.100741449-020-00203-0

Garthe, N., & Hasselhorn, H. M. (2021). Leaving and staying with the employer— Changes in work, health, and work ability among older workers. *International Archives of Occupational and Environmental Health*, *94*(1), 85–93. doi:10.100700420-020-01563-0 PMID:32893311

Ghorbani, N., Pourhosein, R., Armita, G.S. (2018) Self-compassion, mental health and work ethics: mediating role of self-compassion in the correlation between work stress and mental health. *Middle East Journal of Family Medicine*, 16(1), 113-121

Håkansson, C., Gard, G., & Lindegård, A. (2020). Perceived work stress, overcommitment, balance in everyday life, individual factors, self-rated health and work ability among women and men in the public sector in Sweden – a longitudinal study. *Archives of Public Health*, *78*(1), 132. doi:10.118613690-020-00512-0 PMID:33317600

Harvard Health Letter. (2020) *Are you healthy enough to age in place?* Harvard.

Health Psychology. (2006). *Textbook for universities*, G. S. Nikiforov (ed.). St. Petersburg, Russia. p. 607

Hickey, A., Henning, M., & Sirois, L. (2022). Lessons Learned During Large-Scale Implementation Project Focused on Workplace Lactation Practices and Policies. *American Journal of Health Promotion*, *36*(3), 477–486. doi:10.1177/08901171211055692 PMID:34806416

Joshanloo, M., & Jovanović, V. (2021). Subjective health in relation to hedonic and eudaimonic wellbeing: Evidence from the Gallup World Poll. *Journal of Health Psychology*, *26*(3), 438–448. doi:10.1177/1359105318820104 PMID:30582374

Kotera, Y., Van Laethem, M., & Ohshima, R. (2020). Cross-cultural comparison of mental health between Japanese and Dutch workers: Relationships with mental health shame, selfcompassion, work engagement and motivation'. *Cross Cultural & Strategic Management*, *27*(3), 511–530. doi:10.1108/CCSM-02-2020-0055

Krisberg, K. (2020). Global framework works to improve youth mental health, well-being. *The Nation's Health*, (August), 15.

Larouche, R., Garriguet, D., Gunnell, E. K., Goldfield, G. S., & Tremblay, M. S. (2016). Outdoor time, physical activity, sedentary time, and health indicators at ages 7 to 14: 2012/2013 Canadian Health Measures Survey. Statistics Canada, Catalogue no. 82-003-X *Health Reports*, *27*(9), 3–13. PMID:27655167

McElhinney, E., Kidd, L., & Francine, M. C. (2018). Health literacy practices in social virtual worlds and the influence on health behavior. *Global Health Promotion*, *25*(4), 34–47. doi:10.1177/1757975918793334

Pelikan, J. M., Ganahl, K., & Roethlin, F. (2018). Health literacy as a determinant, mediator and/or moderator of health: Empirical models using the European Health Literacy Survey dataset. *Global Health Promotion*, *25*(4), 57–66. doi:10.1177/1757975918788300 PMID:30427258

Pitts, J. S., Milstein, B., & Saha, S. (2022, July). The Role of Business in Supporting Vital Conditions Necessary for the Well-Being of People, Places, and Racial Justice. *American Journal of Health Promotion*, *36*(6), 1050–1060. doi:10.1177/08901171221092576c PMID:35699324

Pressman, S. D., Gallagher, M. W., & Lopez, S. J. (2013). Is the Emotion-Health Connection a "First-World Problem"? *Psychological Science*, *24*(4), 544–549. doi:10.1177/0956797612457382 PMID:23443305

Rindner, L., Nordeman, L., Strömme, G., Svenningsson, I., Premberg, A., Hange, D., Gunnarsson, R., & Rembeck, G. (2020). Prognostic factors for future mental, physical and urogenital health and work ability in women, 45–55 years: A six-year prospective longitudinal cohort study. *BMC Women's Health*, *20*(1), 171. doi:10.118612905-020-01015-4 PMID:32787825

Ruscigno, M. (2018) Health Benefits of Shared Meals. Environmental Nutrition, 41(11).

Rutter, H., Cavill, N., Bauman, A., & Bull, F. (2019). Systems approaches to global and national physical activity plans. *Bulletin of the World Health Organization*, *97*(2), 162–165. doi:10.2471/BLT.18.220533 PMID:30728623

Scarlett, H. (2019) Neuroscience for Organizational Change: An Evidence-based Practical Guide to Managing Change, (2nd ed.). Kogan Page Ltd, London. p. 274

Semizdralova, O.A. (2010) Psychological health of the teacher and ways to preserve it. *National education, 1*, 130-135

St-Hilairea, F., Gilbertb, M.-H., & Brunb, J.-P. (2019). What if subordinates took care of managers' mental health at work? *International Journal of Human Resource Management*, *30*(2), 337–359. doi:10.1080/09585192.2016.1276090

Warnick, A. (2019) WHO: Better nutrition standards needed to improve global health. *The Nation's Health, 19.*

http://www.who.int

Zinchenko, Yu. P. (2011). Methodological foundations of security psychology. *National Psychological Journal*, (2), 11–14.

## ENDNOTE

1 From the report on the meeting with practical psychology "Planet of People", April 22-26, 2011, Moscow, Presidium of the Russian Academy of Sciences

# Chapter 10
# Sustainability of the School Leadership in the Digital Era Under the Shadow of Crisis

**Ramazan Atasoy**
https://orcid.org/0000-0002-9198-074X
*Harran University, Turkey*

## ABSTRACT

*Today, 'innovative era' paradigm waves of 4th Industrial Revolution (4thIR) have deeply changed and prominently affected many lifestyles, organizational structures, and job profiles, including educational setting which cannot be considered independent from the environment, institutions, and their school leaders. In this digital era where the lifestyle has been reshaped, school systems and leadership should be redesigned expediently. This chapter aims to shed light on school leadership's unpredictability and uncertainty under the shadow of the Covid-19 crisis that will possibly overtake all parameters that were known before on the topic. In this paradigmatic change, school leaders' behaviors have been playing a pivotal role in school improvement, revealing the vision and mission of the school. However, Covid-19 pandemic has turned all the known facts about school and face-to-face education upside down. In this context, school leaders have had to take precautions setting directions and improving teaching and learning environment for sustainable educational development.*

## INTRODUCTION

Today, the fount of learning goes beyond the scope of schools and teachers. With the increasing use of digital technology in social life, learners find the opportunity to reach information whenever and wherever they want. Although Industry 4.0 ensures golden opportunities for people who are well educated and prepared to develop skills, it also presents various challenges for disadvantaged students, traditional educational systems, and routine professions. Thanks to information and communication technologies, we can experience new knowledge. However, they change repeatedly and continuously. Thus, the focus is now on school leadership in the complex and dynamic school environment in the 21st century. In

DOI: 10.4018/978-1-6684-5864-8.ch010

this respect, the main issues are to adapt to the new normal, straighten the challenges, cope with the Covid-19 pandemic, and transform schools. The global world, changing dynamically with developments in information and communication technology, has resulted in a new term called Industry 4.0. This era has led to transform the industrial society into a knowledge society. Because its scope was very broad and worldwide, the winds of change blew hard in the field of education, as well (Leahy, Holland, & Ward, 2019). The world of education has endeavored to react to this revolutionary phenomenon with Education 4.0 to harmonize and integrate digital technology into instructional processes (Priatmoko, 2018). Today, the waves of this 'innovative era' paradigm named the 4th Industrial Revolution ($4^{th}$IR) have deeply changed and prominently affected many lifestyles, organizational structures, and job profiles. It also includes an educational setting which cannot be considered independent from the environment, institutions, and school leaders. In this digital era, the lifestyle has been reshaped. Therefore, school systems and leadership should be redesigned expediently according to Education 4.0.

The society in which we live and school organizations in which individuals are shaped according to the educational goals require its citizens/students to exhibit several competencies such as 21st-century skills to deal with the challenges of today and the future. Without a doubt, digital technologies are configured to attain these goals. Thus, the education systems worldwide have to actualize their educational transformation according to the $4^{th}$IR as the workforce is extremely the tendency to change with the advancement of digital life, the internet of things (IoT), robotics, artificial intelligence, and automation technology. The great news is that there is an increasing interest concerning the application of Education 4.0 and its management in educational settings. However, very limited research by now has been realized about its advantages, limitations, effectiveness, challenges, and characteristics in educational environments.

The educational challenge of an unusual era, the twilight process of the Covid-19 epidemic which changed the normal functioning of education systems and the nature of schools and completely turned the flow upside-down, requires taking some radical decisions, changes in education policy, precisely calls for the school leaders as well as the teachers to follow an open-minded approach towards the changes caused by expeditious progres in technology in the context of school improvement. However, for the past two decades, although school leaders in many education systems have wanted to follow their professional development (Machado & Chung, 2015) in parallel with Education 4.0, some antecedent studies have exhibited that school leaders could not reach appropriate professional development for effective and sustainable school leadership. Researchers reveal that the crucial limitation of digital adoption is the deficiency of an educational platform in which school leaders and educators can build customized digital experiences or lack of the time for thinking and discussing the pedagogical value of digital content and activities (Munoz-Cristobal et al., 2015). Through this approach, the school leaders transform into the main actors in the educational system. In Education 4.0 context, school leaders have to not only transform themselves into leaders but also, by promoting a positive school climate, orient their teachers for the contemporaneous education system to be renovated in line with the new educational policy based on $4^{th}$IR and educational goals. Earlier last year, as the 'undeniable chaos' (Hargreaves & Fullan, 2020) of the COVID-19 pandemic caused to slam doors, shut on all aspects of everyday and workplace life, and disrupt economic growth in educational institutions globally, school leaders undertook a new and unusual challenge collaborating with teachers and searched for technology-based new opportunities. In a way, under the shadow of the Covid-19 pandemic crisis and challenges of technological changes, this is the projection of efforts to recognize a school improvement for sustainable school development (SED), revising classic understandings related to school and the footsteps of new education service beyond the perception of the traditional school inherited from the industrial society.

## EDUCATION 4.0

Education 4.0 can be defined as the capability to respond to new learning strategies, teaching methods and techniques, materials, educational content, and leadership styles. It also includes considering the needs of 4thIR where individuals and technology are combined. Burner (2018) expounds on Education 4.0 as the reorganization of a spiritual state of leadership and functional versatility. He also focuses on the greater capacity of adaptability to relevant technological advances and changes of 4thIR during leading/teaching processes. It is a new learning strategy that improves students' ability to perform new digital sources, enables them to adapt to changes in the workplace, and meets the market requirements to conform to international development trends. It is not only adequate to explain the concept with 21st-century skills. Scholars also consider focusing on the management of skills, school environment, school climate, resistance to change in schools, changing nature of schools, constituting a professional learning community, and collaboration in the aspect of learning and teaching process. In this sense, Education 4.0 is more than just traditional educational approaches. It is rather related to the strong changing behavior with the special characteristics of parallelism, connectivity (Goldie, 2016), and visualization.

Harkins (2008) divided education into four eras, splitting it into the agrarian society as Education 1.0, industrial society as Education 2.0, globalization as Education 3.0, and innovation as Education 4.0. Education 1.0 addressed the needs, demands, and requirements of the agricultural society, transferring the knowledge from the teacher who focused on explaining the main method to the students. In this paradigm, it comes to the forefront of an expository approach (traditional model) in which the teacher is dominant in classroom management. Education 2.0 replies to the need of the industrial society in which individuals focus on the notion of teaching to learn. The learning process is focused on acquiring the technologies required in work life. In this educational era, schools have taken an important role, and technology has been utilized as a tool for mass production (Pooworawan, 2015). Though it changes according to the state of development of the country's education systems, this paradigm period shows the importance of the group projects applying the open technologies (i.e. Arduino) in the context of school and classroom activities. In this period, educational institutions have been identified with a factory metaphor and the students are like products. So, outcomes are the same qualifications and not so creative. School principals are identified as task controllers of the school. Education 3.0 is related to the requirements of the 'technology society' such as social networks, digital social media, and a more open environment. It is characterized by self-learning using learning technology in the forms of teaching materials and interactive learning. It has evolved education to meet the wants of society through the advantage of technology. Education 4.0 is finally defined as an arising new paradigm, covering artificial intelligence (AI), (Popenici & Kerr, 2017), IoT, Virtual Reality (VR), and Augmented Reality (AR) (Shahroom & Hussin, 2018). It is expected to meet the demands and needs of the innovation age. Harkins (2008) conceptualized Education 1.0 to Education 4.0 respectively as 'download education', 'open access education, 'knowledge-producing education', and 'innovation producing education'. To understand school improvement and school leadership effectiveness, it may be helpful to look at how school leaders can move their institutions to educational paradigms. Where do school leaders and teachers position their institutions on the spectrum, from download education to innovative product education paradigms? In other words, it is necessary to know that school leaders' practices concerning distance education during the Covid-19 pandemic do not mean adapting technology to education. Moreover, it can be a useful measure to understand whether school leaders are engaged in an organizational development effort based on 'knowledge-producing education', and 'innovation-producing education'. It can also help us see school leaders, who take the school beyond the second half of the spectrum of education 4.0 paradigms, as successful school leaders and innovative leaders who bring technology to education. This means that the perceived school concept and its usual nature are changed, and the roles and responsibilities of school leadership have been altered radically.

## Education 4.0 and Context of School Leadership

Although most of the school leaders and teachers are familiar with the term 4$^{th}$IR, a deeper understanding of the concept and its relevance to any activity is necessary for many schools due to the lack of detailed knowledge. So, the chances of this paradigm are not yet integrated into educational organizations. Research on the Education 4.0 reveals that it has not been sufficiently discussed in the field of educational administration yet. This lack or inadequacy of research in the literature affects negatively the way of directing school improvement studies and understanding the changing school nature and its structure. In this perspective, it is a recent challenge to redefine Education 4.0 and sustainable school leadership in this innovative paradigm. It is also a new but difficult task to reveal the roles and responsibilities of school leaders who cannot maintain former leadership practices during this period while administering educational institutions, specifically in the context of understanding, leading, implementing, and managing the changes in schools.

Education 4.0 paradigm based on 4$^{th}$IR technologies paves the way for a new educational horizon of the school organizations where school leaders lead in different ways, teachers teach via multifaceted methods and materials, and students of Gen Z learn in different multi-channel ways. It is a new vision innovative, initiative and response to the needs and expectations of 4$^{th}$IR where humans and technology are collocated and aligned to allow new developments and new possibilities. This vision change consubstantiated with Education 4.0 has some implications and reflections for learning, teaching and school management. Teachers are identified as the facilitators of the teaching process while the school principals as transformational leaders, distributed leaders, or instructional leaders assume the role of mentors in their school management. In this point, the authors care about school leadership, which refers to a broader and inclusive combination of leadership among the many contemporary leadership styles.

School leaders carry countless and intensive responsibilities to cope with the school administration matters such as school budget, teaching and learning materials, students' discipline and attendance, safety, monitoring of teachers, assessments and curriculum, professional development, relationships with teachers and students, communication with parents and the school community. However, Drake and Roe (2005) reported that the main task of school leaders is to perform instructional leadership because it concerns the implementation of supporting and improving student learning innovation programs. Lahui-Ako (2001) also revealed that the role and duty of school leadership are related very closely to instructional leadership such as developing school, radiating school goals, determining school standards, coordinating all administrative mecanismes, improving curriculum, evaluating teachers' classroom instructions and practices (Beycioglu, 2014), boosting teachers' professional development, and stimulating students to academic achievement.

Related to school leadership, foregoing studies were previously focused on leadership, its nature, and efficacy such as leadership skills, leader behaviors (Tan, 2010), and the role of school leaders (Fisher & Waller, 2013). However, studies on the professional development needs of school leaders have been neglected (Grissom & Harrington, 2010). Fisher and Waller (2013) indicated that the professional development components of school leaders should be investigated as research variables. Although there are many leadership styles such as transformational, technological, and distributed leadership supporting transformation, collaboration, and change as a 21st Century key characteristic in the leadership domain, many of today's school leaders were brought up on the traditional leadership styles and the mindset. In this innovative environment, rather than tackling Industry 4.0 challenges and opportunities alone, the authorities expect from today's school leaders that they could lead challenges with courage at their school, let their traditional mindset ways go away, allow Generation Z to step up, give inspiration to their followers, collaborate within and beyond their schools, motivate their school community, and be comfortable with transformation and change. This viewpoint requires having a culture of open innovation and a change of mindset for school leaders.

As a reflection of transformative leadership behavior, school leaders are anticipated to follow what students, teachers, and society need today. This means that successful school leaders and innovative teachers have to understand that they need to rethink school models, contents, materials, methods of education, and redesign school and their educational environments so that it is more student-centered. This refers not only to allowing and adopting new educational technologies at school but also giving up obsolete forms of attitudes toward what constitutes educational success. They also recognize the reality of international competition among countries, and educational innovativeness. Bill Gates, who gives the direction and codes of future education, was able to predict that the best internet-based lessons that could support the function of the school could be reached in 2015. Bill Gates suggested that "five years from 2010, students will be able to find the best lectures on the Web for free, which are better than any single university." To ensure educational transformation at their school and achieve qualified learning management, leaders are expected to regulate and reform the school administration process. Adam Bunting [school leader of Champlain Valley Union High School] aimed to drive his school *"not through top-down 'push' energy* hierarchically, but rather *'pull' energy"* where teachers, students, staf and the stakeholders focused on change (www.forbes.com).

The 21st century of school leadership based on technology is related to all technology-based educational and administrative activities at school consisting of organizational decisions, policies, and technology implementation (Dexter, 2011). Today, school leaders should address online knowledge and learning resources offered in an online format for a fee or for free, based on sustainable school development and support the use of these resources for school purposes. In this context, they are expected to act as mentor and focus on vital skills for students such as critical thinking, creativity, communication, and collaboration in the digital era. School leaders are also expected to emphasize specifically learning and innovation skills which are increasingly being recognized as domains that different teachers, innovative or traditional, and that distinguish students who are prepared for more complex life and workplace from those who are not. It necessitates that the use of the digital materials and tools recognizes some changes in roles, attitudes and beliefs of students, teachers and school principals concerning the teaching-learning process and administration of the school. Bughin et al. (2018) recommend that it is beneficial to secure that future knowledge workers will be deeply trained in emerging technologies, but also to improve interdisciplinary skills that will serve them to cultivate reflective thinking. In an interview, Turkish Minister of National Education, Selcuk mentions that "we are heading towards a period in which digital content works within the human being employing chips, and at the same time, the physical content is integrated into the human body". The Minister emphasizes that "if the necessary transformation is not achieved in education, children who start pre-school education and primary school will start working life soon, but they will most likely be fired due to this new system brought about by robots and mechanization" (www.hurriyet.com.tr, 2018). Islam (2018) state that the major challenge for new learners of nations could be

*Figure 1. School leadership model and its capabilities framework*

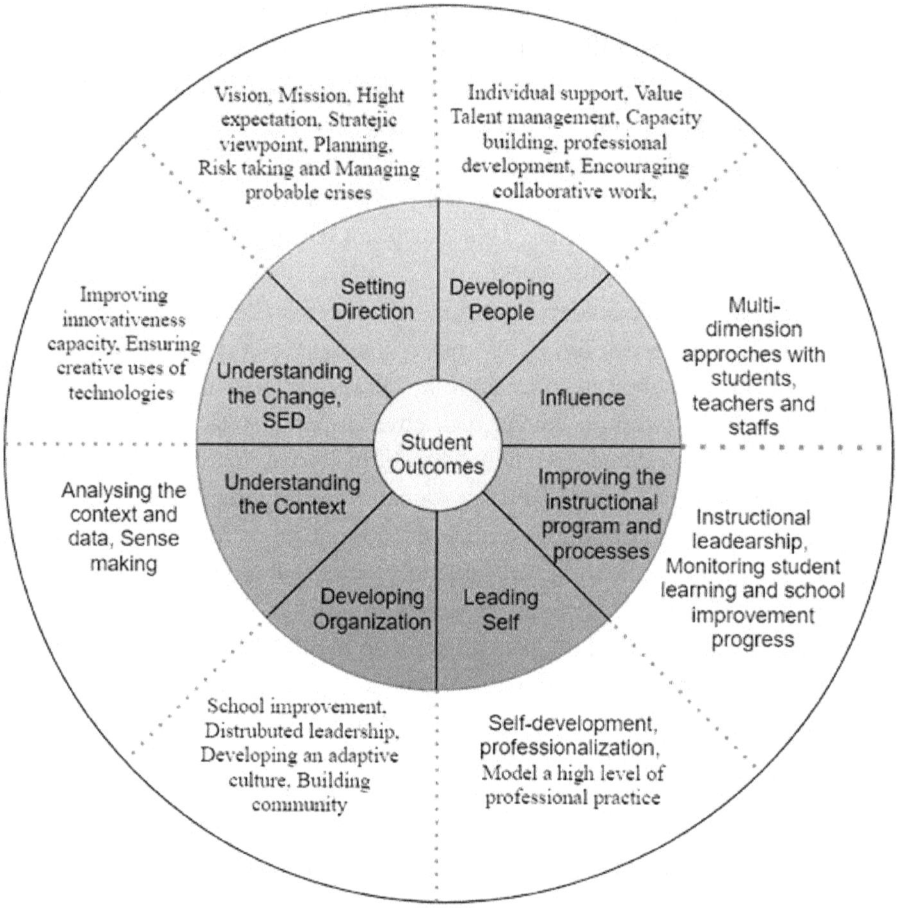


to utilize such various knowledge and skills for innovative solutions in the digital era. School leaders should aim to benefit from these adaptive learning technologies and contribute to students' learning with technological support. However, it is difficult to say that there is a clear policy and consensus in the literature on exactly how to do this. Figure 1 is the framework of the school leadership model for sustainable educational development.

The school leadership framework model in Figure 1 was derived from the Ontario Leadership Framework (Printy, Marks & Bowers, 2009), which includes evidence-based effective school leadership components and was redesigned based on current school leadership studies in the literature (Day & Leithwood, 2007; Gurr & Drysdale; 2020; Leithwood, 2012; Leithwood, 2019; Leithwood, Harris & Hopkins, 2020; Leithwood & Sun, 2012).

With Education 4.0, school leadership skills have also changed increasingly within the framework of 21st-century skills at school organizations. School leaders should be able to catch up with technological developments because this will affect their school outcomes and their students' life. In this context, school principals are expected to be school leaders who know the needs and demands of the society, think about the future of the country to transform its current status, analyze data, and follow the practices in other countries. They should also follow what is done globally, and catch up with the age (Balyer &

Öz, 2018). The constantly transforming and rapidly changing school ecosystems have complex impacts on today's schools to reshape the future.

School leaders, related to the Education 4.0 era, can mostly exhibit transformative, instructional, distributed, and technological leadership behaviors rather than transactional leadership. School leaders are expected specifically to behave as technology leaders and teachers as mentors and facilitators (Roblyer & Doering, 2014), to ensure the skills and knowledge needed for 21st-century schools. They should closely follow the changes in technology and contribute to the integration of the school by its educational objectives. However, the authors found strong arguments in the literature that school leaders as technology leaders contribute to the professional development of teachers, and facilitate and enhance technology integration in the classroom (Thannimalai & Raman, 2018). Transformative school leaders who inspire teachers to integrate technology and who are connected with innovative practices could be able to lead the way in promoting the divergent thinking of Generation Z, boost their creativity, and help have skills in response to the trend of globalization expected from the workforce for the 21st century. In this sense of empowering human and material resources, school leaders who have a direct and/or indirect impact on the school outcomes, are seen as the predictors/contributors of the technical competency of the school. This means that training and supporting teachers by school leaders in line with the needs of the technology-based innovative era can contribute to have a solid basis of human resources.

As well as education itself, school leadership is one of the most key concepts to ameliorate school capacity and the quality of humans to be able to face the globalization and 21st century of the 4$^{th}$IR era. School principals in today's 4$^{th}$IR era engage in an important role in envisaging many administrative roles and designing various activities such as encouraging multicultural students, boosting culture of entrepreneurship, disseminating life-long learning, promoting distance learning, and establishing global network lines for new learning envirements. School leaders must have the ability to read, analyze and use big data information in the digital educational era. This also means that they have to demonstrate not only the capacity of technology literacy skills and human literacy to produce quality education but also to develop their competencies as a facilitator and agent of change (Schneider, 2013). Therefore, school leaders can dominate enough digital skills and knowledge to spearhead, motivate and lead initiatives for teachers to adopt and harmonize digital technology in the classroom management processes in line with Education 4.0. To reach this educational goal, school leaders must focus primarily on teacher capacity investing in developing professional teachers who can prepare students for the education of the future.

Due to the challenges of educational environments in the era of the industrial revolution such as disruptive innovativeness, 21st-century skills, globalization, and competition, school leaders have to exhibit more efforts in facing the challenges of the educational needs for student learning development through new literacy, numeracy, and problem-solving in technology-rich environments and, they have to encourage their teachers to take more responsibility about student learning and school improvement. They can help and empower teachers to build and develop individual abilities. They can also guide teachers with the potential to be creative and innovative and create learning environments responding to the changing social and economic environment. This means that school leaders are in the role of the knowledge manager or mentor leadership behavior as well as meeting human capital requirements.

School leaders should pay attention to two basic attributes of the Education 4.0 paradigm, which are personalization and flexibility (Bartolomé, Castañeda & Adell, 2018) by opening doors in a large spectrum and promoting students to discover their model and speed of learning in/out school environments. In this context of personalization and flexibility, school leaders can allow, encourage, support, and authorize teachers to utilize adaptive learning models (Kara & Sevim, 2013) such as virtual learning environments, artificial intelligence, and big data according to the exclusive wants/needs of each student and school's goals.

Schools that lived with technology-based education during the pandemic had the opportunity to closely test the limitations and advantages of face-to-face education at traditional schools. Digital sources and technological materials that transcend time and space barriers have significant potential to improve student application and comprehension skills. Digital learning environments based on Education 4.0 have many positive contributions to student learning such as flexible learning times, reducing physical space constraints, and learning anytime, anywhere. Although some traditional leaders and parents may have different worries and negative views about educational digitalization, technology-based education might ensure a lot of advantages (e.g. flipped classroom education model, personalized learning environments, online learning, big data, and access to the digital knowledge). It can also facilitate a better understanding of the students and their learning needs (Al-Emran, Mezhuyev, & Kamaludin, 2018). However, it is reported that technological developments could cause some inequality within and between schools. During the pandemic period, the researchers witnessed inequality in distance education applications between countries and schools in the same country. Therefore, school leaders in poverty regions faced lots of challenging problems such as lack of technological sources, high level of inequality, and connection to the internet.

In the literature, several assumptions are discussed about how school leaders and teachers can adapt to the changes and can solve challenges brought about by Education 4.0 which is to meet the wants and expectations of an innovative society. Aberšek and Flogie (2017) suggested that Education 4.0 has given rise to new challenges which are evident by two big demands and expectations in the 4$^{th}$IR such as a new way of problem-solving skills and new thinking strategies in education environments. These challenges are determinant to evaluate the effects of various teaching-learning methods and tools that are still being explored at the present. Therefore, Education 4.0 procures unbounded opportunities and possibilities for multiple teaching and learning practices that allow every individual to acquire knowledge and skills for a lifetime in the innovative era (Ishak & Mansor, 2020). Virtual Learning Environments (VLEs), Learning Management Systems (LMSs), and Smart Learning Environments (SLEs) are important in the context of interactive and collaborative educational components (Richert, Plumanns, Gross, Schuster & Jeschke, (2015) inside or outside school. In this point, VLEs, LMSs and SLEs, which are the transition process of Educational 1.75 (Salmon, 2019) can be seen as a new, unlimited and wellness school. Learning with these tools has gained an independent, exploratory, and adaptable ground for students (Barker & Gossman, 2013; Richert et al., 2015). Although it does not reflect the lower levels of each education system, it is claimed that traditional learning models (Education 1) and administration styles were called into question. Therefore, every education paradigm continues to transform school systems gradually and significantly. The debate about the school systems in which some groundwork was done, began to gather force (Levin & Riffel, 2019) and caused fractures in long-held assumptions of learning and teaching. However, these debates remained at the higher education level. Initially, reflections on high school, middle school, and primary school levels were rather individual and limited.

Education 4.0 is supported by the emergence of synchronous or asynchronous e-learning practices and fostered appreciable innovations in teaching methods inside and outside the classroom in educational contexts. This means that games, perceived playful creative activities in educational environments, promote students' learning and develop their skills. In this context, school leaders are expected to provide the administrative and instructional support that teachers need to organize their classroom activities. They have a responsibility to realize several efforts to face challenges caused by 4$^{th}$IR such as transforming school and teachers, prioritizing collaboration with all followers and partners, developing critical and creative thinking skills, rethinking student assessment methods, improving curriculum, and focusing on learning processes rather than only on learning outcomes. Some researchers state that school leaders and teachers must consider learners' expectations and their learning strategies in this era of the 4thIR, which supports every student to equip themselves with their best skills.

For school leaders, 4thIR presents a new dimension to coping with global educational challenges such as human resources development, qualified human capital outcomes, improvement of school capacity, and teachers' professionalism. However, the main challenges are related to the adaptation of this new paradigm in school systems and school principals' confusion over the Education 4.0 approach. Another challenge in Education 4.0 is about the sustainability of school systems or the future of schools. It is known that the greatest transformations in education are slow. Although the contribution of digital technology gives us clues as to the future of educational change, it could be said that school organizations expect an uncertain future due to rapid changes in education technology and accessibility of the technology itself (Puncreobutr, 2016). Moreover, it is still unclear to education researchers worldwide how to adopt Industry 4.0 and Education 4.0 in school systems. How ready are school leaders to face the challenges of Education 4.0 anytime and anywhere? How will school leaders manage their schools and integrate them into this boundless learning opportunity offered as free in virtual environments in the internet age? It is possible to add more questions related to the future of the school. But, it is also necessary to focus on the waves of digital technologies which threaten school structures. One should think over the responsibilities of school leaders, and how to transform the school by integrating it into the huge changes of 4thIR. Depending on how principals position technology and school within the education system, the answers can vary. It is revealed that many studies on integrating technology into teaching and learning processes at schools (Fullan, 2001) agree that school leaders play a key role in the use of ICT. This analytic ability of school leaders is related to their capacity to understand the statistical and physical conditions of school administration such as student behavior, teacher motivation, and school climate. Nevertheless, in the recent decade, it has also been interestingly debated by some traditional researchers if technology leadership is one of the issues in the literature that should be accentuated in the professional development of school leaders.

Rapid and continuous changes in social systems force education systems to change (Atasoy & Güçlü, 2019). Similarly, Dunwill (2016) claims that the progress of technologies relies on changing traditional methods and transforming the teaching-learning process and school administration. This situation brings about the questioning of the existing structure in the education system and dragging it towards a new order. As stated in the SETA report (2019), the conflict of order and disorder in schools is experienced through the concepts of 'school management' and 'instructional and distributed leadership. School systems are mostly political, and school principals are in the administrative clamp of legislation and their top executives. On the one hand, school principals are given the responsibility of maintaining order as a role of the administration. With this aspect, the powers of school principals to adopt innovations are determined by rules, regulations, and directives from top management. On the other hand, they are expected to go beyond this conventional order and improve the school. With this perspective, school principals are expected to exhibit transformational and instructional leadership behaviors. Responsibilities corresponding to these two different concepts create tension for the school principal and the difficulty of managing this tension lies behind the administrative problems in schools. While the concept of "school management" evokes a responsibility for ensuring order in schools, the term "instructional leadership" requires constant renewal, change and transformation because of its features. This implicit conflict in schools leads to the discussion of school principals over their responsibilities (SETA, 2019). Consequently, there is a need to evaluate Education 4.0 at the macro level throughout the education system and top managers as well as at the micro level evaluation like the school organization and school leaders. In other words, the success of the educational transformation depends on the "educational policies", which have been holistically restructured by the top managers, following the conditions of the time and context, on the 'school administrators' who take the most critical responsibilities in the implementation phase of these policies, and on the skills of the teachers. There is currently no need for so much theoretical knowledge and accumulation for an educational transformation. However, the authorities certainly require proactive, idealistic but at the same time realistic, universal, and innovative top managers, policymakers at the macro level, and strong school leaders who will implement these educational policies in schools at the micro level. Like the metaphor of Tolstoy, school leaders can transform their organizations just like a foreign person coming to a city.

## Education 4.0 Within the Context of School Improvement

In the 21st century, education and school systems are on the verge of tremendous changes. Schools are undergoing phenomenal transformation and school leaders have to adapt to these challenges within the framework of the 4$^{th}$IR, particularly in times of crisis such as working from home, lockdown, and responding to the pandemic (Bush, 2021). The triggering role of the technology on one hand and the pandemic process on the other have helped form an important context for school development. During the pandemic, with the leadership of school principals who facilitated teacher collaboration, educators have often been able to adapt quickly to this unpredicted situation. They have to use a variety of technology in teaching and learning techniques to provide distance learning and focus on e-learning tools.

4$^{th}$IR has provided a new approach and an educational perspective in which humans and information and communication technologies grow more closely together (Zheng, Wang, Sang & Zhongm, 2018). Information age technologies have various implications for school systems and school management. It seems that skills and competencies imposed by 4$^{th}$IR will reshape the educational policies which are the first source of modeling of the human resources of tomorrow (Ishak & Mansor, 2020) as we know or probably predict it. However, it is expected that this new paradigm would cause a huge decrease in human-intensive labor because the 4$^{th}$IR's environment would tend to eliminate routine jobs and focus more on highly educated human resources and highly skilled jobs (Brynjolfsson & Mcafee, 2014). Today, it could be seen anywhere that robots that are replacing human resources could perform not only routine tasks but also complex and sophisticated tasks beyond the routine. It has characteristics that blend particularly human and digital technologies. Its implication for the teaching and learning process has generated several applications such as Kahoot, Socrates, Google Class, Edmodo, Sevima, Moodle, E-learning, blended learning, and Collaborative Based Learning as a manifestation in improving the quality of education. Notice or not, the challenges due to the 4$^{th}$IR, which involves the advancement of smart technologies and provides a huge availability of information with seamless interconnectivity such as IoT (Bonekamp & Sure, 2015) have influenced many components of education. The Artificial Intelligence, IoT, Big Data and Analytics, Horizontal and Vertical System Integration, Cyber Security, and Cloud Computing factors lead to not only rapid changes based on ICT production, but also, these innovative technology tools have been forced to change education systems.

Industry 4.0 would revolutionize the educational systems with the social structure of countries so much that instructional techniques, processes, structures and practices and the jobs which reside today would no longer exist in 50 years (Gabriel & Pessl, 2016). Developments in information and communication technologies (ICT) will certainly be a crucial and key determinant in how education in the future varies from education today. Thus, there is a strong acquiescence that 4thIR technologies would not only change professions or put an end to current jobs but also create new ones (Salmon, 2019). In this new innovative era symbolized by extremely interconnected and complex organizational networks within a creative, technological and knowledge-based economy of 4thIR, education should go beyond learning critically and traditional learning approaches. Fisk (2017) points out that the new perspective of learning in the Education 4.0 era encourages students to learn not only skills and knowledge that are needed but also to identify the source to learn these skills and knowledge, to collaborate with their peers, to build learning process around them. This educational transformation taking place as a result of 4thIR not implies only changes in the activity of students, teachers and school leaders, but also necessitates the creation of a digital educational environment, using new learning materials, methodological support and taking instructional reinforcement.

## THE CONTEXT OF SCHOOL LEADERSHIP AND GENERATION Z

Another point that school leaders should take into account while studying school improvement is today's student profile and their changing demands (Al-Kahtani & Allam, 2013). For the Gen Z students who can learn and reach the knowledge anywhere/anytime, and have unlimited access to it, learning has no boundaries. Generation Z prefers online education, opting for social media and blogs as digital environments. These media enable them to collaborate easier and perform learning while still connected to the internet. For a sustainable education in schools, leaders should consider the preferences of Gen Z students who are mostly connected and online. As these students communicate via industrial equipment, learn, and share their knowledge in a virtual environment, they become so revolutionized by technology and innovativeness. Teachers also have to be provided with opportunities to integrate them more into current technologies in their teaching methodology. As an instructional leadership behavior, they have to consider that the preferences of the 'innovative era' students differ from the students of 10 years ago. School leaders should brace teachers by integrating more current technologies that will make them more creative in designing their lessons. For, these teachers make learning more interesting, more attractive, more developing, and more effective, which match Gen Z students' preferences.

Over the last decade, the workplace markets, their job configurations, demands, expectations and many of the jobs for which people have been educated or trained have changed considerably depending on the emergence of new digital technologies. The challenges of the educational transformation concerning adaptability and competition based on technology require the attention of decision-makers from the political, economic and social levels, especially from the perspective of educational policies. In the perspective of the Education 4.0 paradigm, the role of the human factor in future workplace skills defined as 21st-century skills has a great significance in the innovative competition of nations. The main focus of relevant educational actors, policymakers, and school leaders in a transformative and instructional leader role in school environments is to identify how to get over and/or adapt to these new technological paradigms using a diagnosis of contemporary Generation Z skills, motivations, attitudes, values, and characteristics.

For Generation Z flourishes in full diversity, globalization, online entertainment, social trends, and technology-rich environments, innovations and changes are not considered disruptive. The new normality of the 21st century based on technology does not surprise this generation who wants to take a role in the innovative process. They want to play a part in all learning processes, to participate in all activities, including job processes of planning, coordinating, designing, producing, and marketing at least (Allam, 2018; Allam, 2020; Allam & Malik, 2020). The goal orientation of Generation Z who wants to make sense and be accountable is inspired by surfing the internet, establishing social networks, social rewards, mentoring, flexible hours and constant feedback (Bencsik, Horváth-Csikós & Juhász, 2016).

Key and defining characteristics unique to Gen Z can assist school leaders in their role in developing school organizations and human resources. Gen Z has the potential to think outside the box in different ways, perceive something with a new perspective, and come out of conventional patterns. Thinking outside the box often is related to innovativeness and creative thinking processes. This refers to the unusual approach to the structure of traditional problem solving and logical thinking. This means that the educational perspective of Gen Z is moving from formal education to interactive environments and education is no only longer limited to one stage of school life, but a lifelong learning reality. Another characteristic of Gen Z is individualism which is related to their competitiveness. They focus on their projects and take responsibility. They contribute to problem-solving, finding solutions, implementing coping strategies, and being more engaged in diverse knowledge and job experiences. However, they are identified by low concentration because of the multiple tasks conducted with various data sources of distraction, and by depending on more consumption of information. For building a successful school climate, school principals have to better analyze the characteristics of generation Z, their behavior models, attitudes and values. We can simply summarize that the main challenges of the school principals who faced Gen Z students are the unusual approach to learning and thinking styles and strategies, innovativeness and creative thinking processes.

## The Context of School Improvement, Orientation of Profession and Business World

Because traditional school systems respond to the needs of industrial society, it is doubtful to what extent they can respond to the dynamics of today's knowledge-intensive society. The main problems and challenges faced by school leaders are due to the gap between business and education. School leaders should have precaution about necessities technologic among schools and its usibilty by teachers and students, lack of skill recognition, lack of a common expectation and objectives mutually agreed upon among all stakeholders and the inability to establish a structure that can integrate 21st-century skills into education.

According to the predictions of the World Economic Forum (WEF), Industry 4.0 would likely cause a loss of over five million jobs specifically with the greatest losses in white-collar office and administrative roles in 15 major developed and developing countries in the next five years (Cann, 2016). However, $4^{th}$IR is to present new job and employment opportunities with Education 4.0 approaches. This remarkable aspect of Education 4.0 could be a positive impact on employment. Although there is a considerable debate about the increase or decrease of employment as a consequence of Industry 4.0, researchers highlight that the functionality of Education 4.0 has a serious impact and positive effect on the employability of future learners (Müller, Kiel & Voigt, 2018). What seems to be clear for educational policymakers, schools, and school leaders is aware of these challenges. They have to be proactive and innovative to transform educational challenges based on technological transformation. At this point, governments and educational policymakers have to take urgent and targeted action today to lead changes, manage the near-term and long-term transition of $4^{th}$IR, construct a labor force with 21st-century skills, and cope with ever-growing unemployment and inequality. Educational policymakers and school leaders also need to have longer-range strategies and take ad-hoc approaches to Industry 4.0 to leverage new technologies that reach across school systems with Education 4.0. In many countries, the pace of technological development is several times ahead of the speed of changes in their education systems.

It is expected the school leaders to provide their teachers and students with broadly leveraging technologies throughout their instructional process and educational operations. School leaders have to lead their schools with the awareness that education is not only a function to shape one, raise morale and dignity, nor ensure a better life (Gerhana, Mardiyana & Pramudya, 2017). But, it also could provide one with a good carrier in the future. However, school leaders have a long way to go regarding school strategies of Education 4.0 to improve their schools. First, they need to have comprehensive knowledge of Education 4.0 strategies. However, it can be seen that many educational systems lack educational policies and formal strategies to cope with technological innovativeness. School leaders who have no idea about Education 4.0 strategies and their potential benefits are far from appreciating the implications of Industry 4.0 for their school's improvement. In this sense, the only way to get out of the destructive nature of Industry 4.0 may be a new educational vision that takes the functionality of school organizations and workplace expectations into account. Andiyana, Maya, and Hidayat (2018) argue that education has an important role in influencing one's abilities. Research shows that most undergraduate students will be employed in middle-skilled jobs, which raises the concern of whether these diplomas will be able to secure jobs upon graduation. Therefore, to provide high employability, school leaders need to inform top managers of the teaching and learning activities of students so that they can meet employers' expectations from the graduates in the $4^{th}$IR.

The school systems of the 21st century must be equipped with multidimensional perspectives and/or must be designed with digital information technology that is more innovative, more creative, more critical, and more sophisticated and fit to be competitive. School leaders, specifically vocational and technical school leaders need an interdisciplinary understanding of information technology, systems, production processes, automation technology, and business processes in the context of Education 4.0. This awareness of school leaders concerning Education 4.0 is crucial for school outputs. It is probably possible that learners or knowledgeable employees of the future can confront technological problems if the schools' educational policies could not be transformed by the school leaders. Because, today's job requirements of workplaces are based on information and technologies, purely qualified and highly educated knowledgable citizens who could use such technologies as automation programmers, robot programmers, informatics specialists, big data analysts, and cyber security specialists (Benešová & Tupa, 2017).

## CONCLUSION

This book chapter is framed by conceptualizing the volatile, uncertain, and key roles in the digital era of school leadership behavior, both inside and outside the school under the shadow of all stages of societal crisis. It seems that the Covid-19 pandemic, which has possibly overshadowed all the facts about school leadership practices, has been the precursor to the paradigm shift in education. This unexpected phenomenon deeply affected the school leadership practices and broke the resistance to change. School leadership was reinterpreted with the closure of schools, and the roles and responsibilities of school principals were revised by the new normal. As transformational, distributed, and instructional leaders in the Education 4.0 era, the role of school leaders is to set direction, improve the capacity of human resources, and develop the organization. With this viewpoint, they can canalize teachers to teach by educational goals, which are well defined and beyond the comfort zone. They can guide educational opportunities for teacher development and student learning and cultivate mental harmony among teachers. Thus, they can avoid being predictive and contribute to teachers' and students' creativity. In the context of Education 4.0, school leaders can improve some helpful strategies in dealing with the disruptive era of 4$^{a}$IR, such as developing digital skills for teachers and students and applying new technologies in the field of education. To support and strengthen teaching and learning processes, school leaders can emphasize high-level critical and creative thinking skills, and encourage teachers by permitting digital education sources, e-learning tools, materials, and new practices in school areas. They can also encourage the teachers to prioritize focusing on the instructional contents and learning processes rather than learning outcomes (Tan, Choo, Kang & Liem, 2017). They can also overcome learning difficulties in students by supporting them through their learning journey and increasing their motivation.

During the Covid-19 pandemic period which brought about rapid changes, every extra expectation, demand, pressure, or problem arising from teachers, staff, and students asks more of school leaders both professionally and personally. In the context of school improvement and SED, everything done at school organized by the Education 4.0 concept by school leaders should be in line with the vision and mission of the school including team collaboration and their innovativeness, learning planning, teaching-learning process, students' success, school well-being, organizational objectives, activities, school environment, media, and the facilities provided at the school. School leaders should inspire teachers and relevant stakeholders by infusing a shared vision and lead the implementation of a shared vision for the integration of digital technology to hearten excellence and encourage the changes needed in the school settings. They have also to engage education for all students. School leaders can also bear the responsibility to promote an environment of professional learning and innovative thinking that empowers teachers to offer student learning through digital educational resources and follow emerging educational trends regarding the utilization of digital educational technology. Through the effective use of ICT sources such as access to digital tools, local and/or global network-based communication systems, and technology-based instructional practices that have been embedded into school life and daily routines, school leaders of the Education 4.0 era have been assumed a great roles and responsibilities. This type of digital age leaders can ameliorate their schools permanently and continually and exert effort so that the school infrastructure bolster teaching and learning environments. Kurland, Peretz, and Hertz-Lazarowitz (2010) have reported that school leaders who build a school vision for the integration of effective digital technology resources and ensure sustained professional development have been noticed to be most effective in influencing teachers to integrate technology into the school.

It is a challenge for school leaders to plan and design the educational requirements and contents in the rapid change environments and the era of 21st-century learning. School leaders as educational leaders should focus primarily on the teaching and learning process which is the act of acquiring new learning, enriching existing knowledge, characters, and values, improving students' soft skills, touching a potential change of the students toward creativity and innovation beyond the physical capacity of the school. They also have some roles and responsibilities to promote school learning climates such as inculcating an optimum learning environment, protecting instructional time, enriching professional development, maintaining high visibility, and providing incentives for teachers and learning. School leaders who create a positive school climate which will consolidate their achievements and productive efforts also inspire indirectly optimum student learning environment. They can do it by explaining to the students and teachers clearly, focusing on the educational vision and school mission, explicating the school's expectations, school rules and goals and supporting the implementation of teachers' professional development. The number of school leaders who take into account the changing needs of students and pioneer innovative practices is increasing. *"Stacy Kane is a school leader, visionary and steadfast in her conviction that all students should have a high school education that prepares them not only academically but also for the complex contexts of her students including the need to be able to earn money during the education process. Instead of locating those needs beyond the scope of the school, she insists to meet these needs in school. To that end, she is building a school that brings Computer Science (CS) and the ability to create coding-related side gigs like web design to all WLA students, not just those in advanced classes"* (www.forbes.com).

School leaders faced an unexpected crisis, have passed, and continue to take this difficult test. During the Covid-19 pandemic, school leaders have faced many problems such as access to the internet, uncertainty about program continuity and practice, issues concerning the assessment integrity, educational inequities for low-income families, and discontinuity in education, especially in rural remote areas, workload and work intensification for teachers. Schools were closed all over the world due to this compelling crisis, but the authors have witnessed that the education solutions are not exhausted and that the strong cooperation of school leaders and teachers in overcoming the difficulty with technology-based, online, distance education systems gives schools a breath of fresh air. Considering the digital era under the shadow of the crisis, such as those encircling open forms of learning spaces, IoT, AR technologies, metaverse and AI, we need to be careful, as reported by Milojevic (2005), not just of future educational contents and improvements, but also focus on the studies of influences or resistance leading to the rise or fall of innovations in education.

Leadership emerges at difficult times and real leaders are those who can anticipate difficulties, take necessary precautions, and manage change in line with organizational goals. Sustainable educational development is closely related to the school leaders' actions, who have a collaborative and distributed leadership approach within the framework of a common vision shared by their staff and external stakeholders. Nowadays, people frequently talk of going back to school in educational settings. In the abyss of rapid change and under the shadow of the pandemic crisis, school leaders seem to walk on a tight rope without a safety precaution. It is still uncertain what the impact of opening schools under the shadow of the Covid-19 pandemic might be. Some research reveals the negative effects of e-learning in many schools. It is evident that rather than the virus itself, the physical and mental health of students who are confined at home constitutes a real problem for students' psychological development. In the time of turbulence fed by Covid-19 and disruptive technological change, proactive solutions are required in the 21st-century world. Thus, school leaders have to swiftly set direction by encouraging collaborative work. To meet high expectations, they should develop themselves and the people at the organization, improving teaching and learning beyond the traditional methods. They should also understand the context, change, and SED. However, it should not be forgotten that the main thing behind all these administrative processes is to highlight the policies and practices that prioritize the well-being of the students, who are the seeds for the future.

## REFERENCES

Aberšek, B., & Flogie, A. (2017). Evolution of competences for new era or education 4.0. In *XXV Conference of Czech Educational Research Association (CERA/ČAPV) "Impact of Technologies in the Sphere of Education and Educational Research."* Czech.

Al-Emran, M., Mezhuyev, V., & Kamaludin, A. (2018). PLS-SEM in information systems research: A comprehensive methodological reference. *4th international conference on advanced intelligent systems and informatics.*

Al-Kahtani, N. S., & Allam, Z. (2013). Supportive and defensive communication climate among subordinate staff of Salman bin Abdulaziz University: An empirical assessment. *Life Science Journal, 10*(4), 502–509.

Allam, Z. (2018). Students' perception of quality in higher education: An empirical investigation. *Management Science Letters, 8*(5), 437–444. doi:10.5267/j.msl.2018.4.002

Allam, Z. (2020). Demystifying the aspect of quality in higher education: Insights from Saudi Arabia. *SAGE Open, 10*(1), 2158244019899057. doi:10.1177/2158244019899057

Allam, Z., & Malik, A. (2020). Exploring the Predictors of Student Satisfaction: A Case of Undergraduate Business School in King-dom of Saudi Arabia. *Universal Journal of Educational Research, 8*(11B), 5760–5767. doi:10.13189/ujer.2020.082210

Andiyana, M. A., Maya, R., & Hidayat, W. (2018). Ability analysis thinking creative creative student mathematics students in material building construction. *Journal of Innovative Mathematics Learning/ Jurnal Pembelajaran Matematika Inovatif, 1*(3), 239.

Atasoy, R., & Güçlü, N. (2020). Evaluation of numeracy skills of adults according to the results of PIAAC 2015 in Turkey. *World Journal of Education, 10*(2), 1–123. doi:10.5430/wje.v10n2p27

Balyer, A., & Öz, Ö. (2018). Academicians Views on Digital Transformation in Education. *International Online Journal of Education & Teaching, 5*(4), 809–830.

Barker, J., & Gossman, P. (2013). The learning impact of a virtual learning environment: Students' views. *Teacher Education Advancement, 5*(2), 19–38.

Bartolomé, A., Castañeda, L., & Adell, J. (2018). Personalisation in educational technology: The absence of underlying pedagogies. *International Journal of Educational Technology in Higher Education, 15*(14), 1–17. doi:10.118641239-018-0095-0

Bencsik, A., Horváth-Csikós, G., & Juhász, T. (2016). Y and Z Generations at Workplaces. *J. Compet., 8*, 90–106.

Benešová, A., & Tupa, J. (2017). Requirements for Education and Qualification of People in Industry 4.0. *Procedia Manufacturing, 11*, 2195–2202. doi:10.1016/j.promfg.2017.07.366

Beycioglu, K. (Ed.). (2014). *Multidimensional perspectives on principal leadership effectiveness.* IGI Global.

Bonekamp, L., & Sure, M. (2015). Consequences of industry 4.0 on human labour and work organisation. *Journal of Business and Media Psychology*, *6*(1), 33–40.

Brynjolfsson, E., & Mcafee, A. (2014). *The second age machine*. W.W Norton & Company.

Bughin, J., Hazan, E., Lund, S., Dahlström, P., Wiesinger, A., & Subramaniam, A. (2018). *Skill Shift: Automation and the Future of the Workforce*. McKinsey Global Institute.

Burner, T. (2018). Why is educational change so difficult and how can we make it more effective? *Forskning og forandring, 1*(1), 122-134.

Bush, T. (2021). Leading through COVID-19: Managing a crisis. *Educational Management Administration & Leadership*, *49*(3), 373–374. doi:10.1177/1741143221997267

Cann, O. (2016). Five million jobs by 2020: The real challenge of the fourth industrial revolution. World Economic Forum. *International Organisation for Public Private Cooperation,* Geneva, Switzerland.

Day, C., & Leithwood, K. (Eds.). (2007). *Successful School Leadership in Times of Change*. Springer-Kluwer. doi:10.1007/1-4020-5516-1

Dexter, S. (2011). School technology leadership: Artifacts in systems of practice. *Journal of School Leadership*, *21*(2), 166–189. doi:10.1177/105268461102100202

Drake, T. L., & Roe, W. H. (2005). *The principalship* (6th ed.). Merrill/Prentice Hall.

Dunwill, E. (2016). *4 changes that will shape the classroom of the future: Making education fully technological*. https://elearningindustry.com/4-changes-will-shape-classroom-of-the-future-making-education-fully-technological

Fisher, D. M., & Waller, L. R. (2013). The 21st century principal: A study of technology leadership and technology integration in Texas K-12 schools. *The Global E Learning Journal, 2*(4), 1-44.

Fisk, P. (2017). *Education 4.0 … the future of learning will be dramatically different, in school and throughout life*. https://www.thegeniusworks.com. https://www.forbes.com/sites/barbarakurshan/2019/11/12/profiles-in-innovation-leading-at-the-edge-of-education/?sh=520401ad6109

Fullan, M. (2001). *Leading in a culture of change*. Jossey-Bass.

Gabriel, M., & Pessl, E. (2016). Industry 4.0 and sustainability impacts: Critical discussion of sustainability aspects with a special focus on future of work and ecological consequences. Annals of the Faculty of Engineering Hunedoara. *International Journal of Engineering*, *14*(2), 131–136.

Gerhana, M., Mardiyana, M., & Pramudya, I., (2017). The Effectiveness of Project Based Learning in Trigonometry. *Journal of Physics: Conference Series, 895*, 012-027.

Goldie, J. G. S. (2016). Connectivism: A knowledge learning theory for the digital age? *Medical Teacher*, *38*(10), 1064–1069. doi:10.3109/0142159X.2016.1173661 PMID:27128290

Grissom, J. A., & Harrington, J. R. (2010). Investing in administrator efficacy: An examination of professional development as a tool for enhancing principal effectiveness. *American Journal of Education*, *116*(4), 583–612. doi:10.1086/653631

Gurr, D., & Drysdale, L. (2020). Leadership for challenging times. *International Studies in Educational Administration*, *48*(1), 24–30.

Hargreaves, A., & Fullan, M. (2020). Professional capital after the pandemic: Revisiting and revising classic understandings of teachers' Work. *Journal of Professional Capital and Community*, *5*(3/4), 327–336. doi:10.1108/JPCC-06-2020-0039

Harkins, A. M. (2008). Leap frog principles and practices: Core components of Education 3.0 and 4.0. *Futures Research Quarterly, 8*, 1-15. https://www.hurriyet.com.tr/gundem/bakan-selcuktan-pns-cagi-uyarisi-40969660

Ishak, R., & Mansor, M. (2020). The Relationship between Knowledge Management and Organizational Learning with Academic Staff Readiness for Education 4*.0. Eurasian Journal of Educational Research*, *20*(85), 169–184. doi:10.14689/ejer.2020.85.8

Islam, I. (2018). Automation and the future of employment: Implications for India. *SA Journal of Human Resource Management*, *5*(2), 234–243.

Kara, N., & Sevim, N. (2013). Adaptive learning systems: Beyond teaching machines. *Contemporary Educational Technology*, *4*(2), 108–120. doi:10.30935/cedtech/6095

Kurland, H., Peretz, H., & Hertz-Lazarowitz, R. (2010). Leadership style and organizational learning: The mediate effect of school vision. *Journal of Educational Administration*, *48*(1), 7–30. doi:10.1108/09578231011015395

Lahui-Ako, B. (2001). The instructional leadership behaviour of Papua New Guinea high school principals. A provincial case study. *Journal of Educational Administration*, *39*(3), 233–265. doi:10.1108/09578230110392875

Leahy, S. M., Holland, C., & Ward, F. (2019). The digital frontier: Envisioning future technologies impact on the classroom. *Futures*, *113*, 102422.

Leithwood, K. (2012). *The Ontario Leadership Framework 2012 with a discussion of the research foundations*. Institute for Educational Leadership and the Ontario Ministry of Education.

Leithwood, K. (2019). Characteristics of effective leadership networks: A replication and extension. *School Leadership & Management*, *39*(2), 175–197. doi:10.1080/13632434.2018.1470503

Leithwood, K., Harris, A., & Hopkins, D. (2020). Seven strong claims about successful school leadership revisited. *School Leadership & Management*, *40*(1), 1–18. doi:10.1080/13632434.2019.1596077

Leithwood, K., & Louis, K. S. (2012). *Linking leadership to learning*. Jossey-Bass.

Leithwood, K., Sun, J., & Schumacker, R. (2019). How school leadership influences student learning: A test of "The four paths model". *Educational Administration Quarterly*, *56*(4), 570–599. doi:10.1177/0013161X19878772

Levin, B., & Riffel, J. A. (2019). *Schools and the changing world: Struggling toward the future*. Routledge. doi:10.4324/9780203046562

Machado, L. J., & Chung, C. J. (2015). Integrating Technology: The Principals' Role and Effect. *International Education Studies*, *8*(5), 43–53. doi:10.5539/ies.v8n5p43

Milojevic, I. (2005). *Educational futures: Dominant and contesting visions*. Routledge. doi:10.4324/9780203413982

Müller, J. M., Kiel, D., & Voigt, K. I. (2018). What Drives the Implementation of Industry 4.0? The Role of Opportunities and Challenges in the Context of Sustainability. *Sustainability*, *10*(1), 247. doi:10.3390u10010247

Munoz-Cristobal, J. A., Jorrin-Abellan, I. M., Asensio-Perez, J. I., Martinez-Mones, A., Prieto, L. P., & Dimitriadis, Y. (2014). Supporting teacher orchestration in ubiquitous learning environments: A study in primary education. *IEEE Transactions on Learning Technologies*, *8*(1), 83–97. doi:10.1109/TLT.2014.2370634

Pooworawan, Y. (2015). *Challenges of New Frontier in Learning: Education 4.0*. Document by Innovative Learning Center, Chulalongkorn University.

Popenici, S., & Kerr, S. (2017). Exploring the impact of artificial intelligence on teaching and learning in higher education. *Research and Practice in Technology Enhanced Learning*, *12*(22), 1–13. doi:10.118641039-017-0062-8 PMID:30595727

Priatmoko, S. (2018). Memperkuat eksistensi pendidikan islam di era 4.0 [Strengthening the existence of islamic education in 4.0 era]. *Jurnal Studi Pendidikan Islam*, *1*(2), 1–19. doi:10.52166/talim.v1i2.948

Printy, S. M., Marks, H. M., & Bowers, A. (2009). Integrated leadership: How principals and teachers share instructional influence. *Journal of School Leadership*, *19*, 504–532. doi:10.1177/105268460901900501

Puncreobutr, V. (2016). Education 4. 0: New challenge of learning. *St. Theresa. Journal of the Humanities and Social Sciences*, *2*(2), 92–97.

Richert, A., Plumanns, L., Gross, K., Schuster, K., & Jeschke, S. (2015). Learning 4.0: Virtual immersive engineering education. *Digital Universities: International Best Practices and Applications*, *2*, 51–66.

Roblyer, M., & Doering, A. (2014). *Integrating educational technology into teaching*. Pearson.

Roy, S., & Edan, Y. (2018). Investigating joint-action in short-cycle repetitive handover tasks: The role of giver versus receiver and its implications for human–robot collaborative system design. *International Journal of Social Robotics*.

Salmon, G. (2019). May the fourth be with you: Creating Education 4.0. *Journal of Learning for Development-JL4D, 6*(2).

Schneider, R. (2013). Research Data Literacy, *Commun. Comput. Inf. Sci, vol. 397. CCIS*, (October), 134–140.

SETA [SİYASET, EKONOMİ VE TOPLUM ARAŞTIRMALARI VAKFI]. (2019). *Öğretim Lideri, vs. Okul Müdürü*. İstanbul. SETA Yayınları.

Shahroom, A., & Hussin, N. (2018). Industrial revolution 4.0 and education. *International Journal of Academic Research in Business and Social Sciences*, *8*(9), 314–319.

Tan, J. P. L., Choo, S. S., Kang, T., & Liem, G. A. D. (2017). Educating for twenty-first century competencies and future ready learners: Research perspectives from Singapore. *Asia Pacific Journal of Education*, *37*(4), 425–436.

Tan, S. C. (2010). School technology leadership: Lessons from empirical research. In C. H. Steel, M. J. Keppell, P. Gerbic, & S. Housego (Eds.), *Curriculum, technology & transformation for an unknown future. Proceedings Ascilite Sydney 2010,* (pp. 896–906).

Thannimalai, R., & Raman, A. (2018). The Influence of Principals Technology Leadership and Professional Development on Teachers' Technology Integration in Secondary Schools. *Malaysian Journal of Learning and Instruction*, *15*(1), 201–226. doi:10.32890/mjli2018.15.1

Zheng, P., Wang, H., Sang, Z., & Zhongm, R. Y. (2018). Smart manufacturing systems for industry 4.0: Conceptual framework, scenarios and future perspective. *Frontiers of Mechanical Engineering*, *13*(2), 137–150.

## KEY TERMS AND DEFINITIONS

**School Leadership:** School leadership can be defined as all administrative and management tasks focusing on student outcomes. Its main responsibilities include empowering teachers, building and developing individual potentials, creating organizational learning environments, responding to the changing social and economic environment, integrating many leadership styles to improve the school, individuals, information technologies, and instructional capacity.

**Education 4.0:** Education 4.0 can be defined as the period in which the education settings integrate ICTs to develop instructional, pedagogical, and technological processes. It also improves operational processes through new learning and teaching methods, innovative solutions to current and future challenges in society. In addition, it aims to reveal management tools, and smart infrastructure.

**Industry 4.0:** Industry 4.0 is a new innovative level and collective term for technologies combining many intelligent machines, systems production, and processes of the value of chain organization and management across the lifecycle of products. It can also be defined as the integration of complex physical machinery and devices with networked sensors and software, used to better outcomes.

**School Improvement:** It can be defined as multidimensional development efforts that include all effective school practices to improve the human, material and instructional capacity of the school.

**Generation Z:** Generation Z mostly refers to individuals born between 1995 and 2009.

# Chapter 11
# Exploring Work Constructs Driving Satisfaction in the Digital Era with Special Reference to Millennials

**Poonam Arora**
https://orcid.org/0000-0001-8578-3638
*St. Kabir Institute of Professional Studies, India*

**Nidhi Arora**
*Full Stack Technology, India*

## ABSTRACT

*Generation Y, also known as Millennials, are twined to be job-hoppers. This generation interacts tremendously well with technology and known to use it to shape their efforts in leading an organization. With projections of Millennials forming 75% of the workforce by 2027, employers in the technology driven era are putting in tremendous efforts to win loyalty of Millennial workers towards the organization. In this VUCA world, employers are trying to explore key workplace drivers to maintain and manage this generation. The goal of businesses is to exercise technology for maximizing the satisfaction of the talented employees, resulting in loyalty and patriotism towards the organization. This chapter aims to explore the factors affecting the work satisfaction of Millennial employees leading extreme patriotism towards the organization steering to long term retention. The chapter includes a quantitative study following a descriptive research design covering 398 Millennials. The main purpose is to find broad constructs which can facilitate satisfaction level of Millennials in this technology led era.*

DOI: 10.4018/978-1-6684-5864-8.ch011

## INTRODUCTION

Businesses in the current competitive world are making significant profits by virtue of the most strategic asset which is its people. Human resources of an organization facilitate a business and garner tremendous profits through their innovative and diverse ideas. Satisfied employees of an organization are highly motivated, have good morale and work more effectively and efficiently. Satisfied employees are devoted to ceaseless improvement and better work quality. But employees with their unfulfilled psychological contract feel detached from their organization and start planning to hop to another job in no time.

Generational cohorts provide the researchers an opportunity to analyze changes with respect to a specific generation. Strauss Howe's generational theory says that "an era in which a person is born affects the development of his view about the whole world and his value systems are shaped by observing the working pattern of his immediate previous generation" (Strauss & Howe, 1991). The change in generations over years of time promote the understanding of impact of events, social shifts and changes in technology on people's views about the world. Every generation is different and their views differ from one another based on the surrounding environment they grew up in. Among all the three generations referred after World War III, Millennials is a generation born between 1981 and 1996 (Dimock, 2019). So the most critical cohorts of new recruits – Millennial are considered as an imperative commodity. Not only India, all over the world the workforce is dominated by this younger generation (Arora & Kshatriya, 2017). This generation is seen to acquire striking values and characteristics which are found to be very different and difficult to tackle. Delloitte Millennial Survey 2016 reveals that this generation at all the stages is directed by values which are strong and sound and has shaped their views on workplace expectations which if not fulfilled motivate them to leave their jobs (Deloitte Millennial Survey, 2016). The survey in 2016 revealed that around 50 per cent of Millennials are already looking for a new job (Business wire, 2016). So, the most important question of the era that HR managers are toggling with is to find what satisfies a Millennial employee. The challenge is to know the presence of factors that make Millennials happy and satisfied at work steering them to stick at the same place. Managers understand that happy and satisfied Millennials can become more committed to the organization showcasing loyalty towards the job if they are satisfied with job.

With the forecast of 75 per cent increase in Millennials by 2025, Kohl in 2019 reported that employers are toggling with the strategies to win job satisfaction of Millennial employees thereby making them more loyal (Kohl, 2019). Employers want to explore key constructs driving Millennials' job satisfaction to maintain and manage them; winning loyalty of this generation towards the organization (Stahl, 2019).

As compared to generation X, Millennials do not live so that they can work, rather they work so that they can earn and live life to the fullest. This is the most critical workforce in today's era with uniquely contrasting work preferences but still organizations are struggling to manage this generation and their organizational prospects. Managing young talent is challenging as their work habits need to be incorporated in the existing culture of the corporate melting pot.

There is a need to understand working style of every generation so that their working strengths can be utilized for overall business efficiency. Millennials, not only in India; but around the world are making their existence felt, forcing businesses and supervisors to re design their working systems and policies for easy adaptation of the generation (Arora, 2020). Fulfilling demand of Millennials is one of the greatest challenges that employers are facing in the twenty first century. In Indian context too, the workforce is dominated by Millennials. Divergent work demands and unusual characteristics and nature of this generation is insisting employers to bring techno structural changes in their organization balancing the existing culture with the work habits of this new generation. Following the trend of hiring Generation Y, workplaces are now pouring in with this generation but what is challenging for employers is maintaining and managing job satisfaction of Millennial employees (Burgess, 2008). So, it is crucially relevant to study Millennials clearing all fade clouds and find their right work characteristics.

Information technology is critical in dealing with dynamic things at workplace. Technology aids in exchange of information by providing set of techniques that boosts the speed of work. It helps in making processes faster through speedy decision making and problem solving at work. It facilitates enhancing efficiency of systems, products and services by streamlining processes, maintain optimized data flow and manage contacts and employee records by tracking right set of data. The increase in efficiency enable the business to grow rapidly. It has provided a level of communication never experienced before. Employees can connect with each other in a team, their supervisors and other stakeholders, anywhere at any time. So employees can communicate better collaborate more. Millennials are known to be the most tech savvy generation which has not seen an era without technology. Theirs is a generation which has grown in the digital era amidst all sorts of electronic gadgets like tablets, phones and video games. They have not seen or completed any work in absence of portable PCs. They have completed their educational years learning on laptops. And so, the working style of this generation is also impacted by their ease of use of technology. Millennials stands different from previous all other generations in terms of technology needs as well and hence they also have higher work expectations. They have a strong affinity towards workplaces rich in latest technology so as to deliver challenges which require them to have collaborative approach along with multi-tasking way of working (Shaw & Fairhurst, 2008). Generation Yers are independent, entrepreneurial thinkers who relish a working environment rich in technology.

Millennials do not want to adapt in an organization rather they want the organization to adapt according to their needs (Arora, 2019). They are very choosy about the kind the employer they want to work with. Millennials want freedom at work and strive for an environment wherein they have systems running on MIS based systems. This generation doesn't like to report their supervisors on every small thing. They demand IT enabled systems which allow them to plan their own work and let them decide how the next set of work can be taken ahead. They want the freedom to attend online meetings over electronic support systems without lamenting the hierarchy of organization. Generation Y prefers to work with superiors who are approachable and believe that views of every one is important and should be heard. Working with the aim of organizational productivity, Millennials are also conscious about their personal development and so they continuously seek learning opportunities. Generation Y has unique characteristics that affect their learning style as they want to learn over technology based systems (Naim & Lenka, 2018). Generation Y are known to be very focused about their studies and are known to be lifelong learners making their future secure. Millennials prefer to work on profiles which are challenging but not monotonous and require them to do aimless paperwork. The generation like to work with the organizations which provide equal compensation for equal work and more pay for more work, offering competitive salary following the market trend (Arora, 2019). Generation Y want to work for companies which are adopting new systems of technology and implementing them into work processes. They have a deep understanding that technology needs to be with humans and so they have a well-developed idea of their workspace specifications and mode of work along with other expectations in terms of brand, profile, salary and incentives. To ensure retention success, employers need to understand that Millennials cannot be forced to adapt to the traditional work culture and policies rather to get them molded, employers need to rethink the organizational policies as this generation of Millennials is crucial to business which in turn is going to impact the economy (Pasco,

Maellaro & Stodnick, 2020). In Indian context as well, Millennials need to be studied afresh with a new angle so that businesses can offer them what they desire and are ready with the policies and the tactical strategies to retain them well.

According to Gallup report published in October 2019, 60% of millennials were open to a new job, while only 29% are engaged at work (Robison, 2019). This increasingly common trend have tagged millennials to be the "job-hopping generation." Businesses because of this effect of low retention of Millennials tend to bear high cost of induction trainings thereby resulting into high turnover rates. In this competitive job market, only those organizations which can save money on recruitment costs and can avoid turnover rates can only experience better performance and productivity. This chapter clearly is a business case citing factors that develop work satisfaction of Millennials in the era of technology which in turn may develop loyalty thereby helping the organization in retaining talented employees for a longer tenure. Reasons of Millennials leaving a job can relate to their demands being unfulfilled. But fortunately, organizations can address these issues by reviewing their retention strategies to match expectations of Generation Y from their workplace (Arora & Kshatriya, 2018). The main goal of organizations is to design such a culture that can interest and fulfil requirements of this generation while keeping in mind the dominant factors that impact the overall job satisfaction among them leaving them loyal. Patriotism is the feeling of dedication, devotion, love and attachment that can be developed in an employee; fulfilling his unsaid unwritten yet expected need. This attachment towards one's organization can be an evolved by providing the employee with a combination of the work constructs relating to various tangible and intangible aspects of workplace. An employee who is happy and satisfied when dedicatedly works for the organization become a patriot for the same. Extreme and aggressive patriotism i.e. Jingoism, towards the organization happens when an employee is work satisfied and committed. The quality of work then offered, is backed by trust and loyalty of the employees for their organization and the productivity is marked by positive aggression. Employee satisfaction, therefore, directly influences sustainable relations. From a theoretical to managerial perspective, therefore, it is crucial to identify the key drivers of employee work satisfaction, to monitor continuous satisfaction and to take the right measures to foster satisfaction and loyalty thereby winning extreme patriotism towards the organization.

Earlier, all the preliminary studies linking Millennials and HR practices have generally been conducted focusing on the aspects of attracting, engaging and retaining this talented but not linking it with technology. However, in the current digital era, where a single operation in the company does not move without availability of internet services, there seems to be limited research in relation to businesses in the growing economies, like India wherein work values are strongly influenced by technology which may have an impact on expectations of employee from the workplace.

India's changing demographics and the technology aspirations makes it more important to study India's Millennial generation (Raina, 2016). Employers need to seek greater understanding and generate more ideas relating to factors engaging of this generation as some economic and legal issues are expected to emerge in a workplace populated by this new generation (Cole, Smith, & Lucas, 2002). Hence, it is important that the Indian Millennial talent should be studied in a new light and with a new perspective leaving behind the shadows of their working myths so that the management of an organisation should have proper knowledge about the work practices, ways and expectations of this generation in this digital era. Therefore, there are a lot of factors driving loyalty of an employee towards their organization in today's millennial workforce. This chapter aims to explore factors affecting loyalty of Millennials thereby increasing their satisfaction levels in the digital era.

## LITERATURE REVIEW

Generations prior to Generation Y have spent their entire life working in one organization only. In their times there was no such agile working environment and even work-life balance was not a priority. Factors like employee satisfaction, work environment, work culture, trust, loyalty, monetary benefits, non-monetary rewards, recognition from the employer, work-life balance, flexible working hours and many more were not considered as some of the strongest drivers of working and staying in the organization. As the current work offices are already majorly composed of this generation, it is worthy to take up a literature review and understand the factors affecting Millennials and their job satisfaction (Bobek & Wicham, 2015).

### Characteristics of Millennials

Millennials is the generation which is found to be uniquely different from its previous generations as they see the world differently owing to varied values, distinct perceptions, preference and have a discrete outlook to view the world (Lyons & Kuron, 2014; Garcia et al., 2019). Millennials are socially conscious and optimist towards life. They are known to be the most knowledgeable generation of the time (Cheng, 2019). This generation is hardworking and they like working with a team as they are collaborative workers (Bhatnagar, 2017). Millennial generation as employees are dynamically super active and always believe in solving their own problems using their experiences and knowledge by giving the problem a good thought (Zaharee et.al, 2018). This is the generation which is always active and ready to learn more (Cheng, 2019). Millennials need a job that allow them to personally develop, achieve their goals, give them a chance to prove their abilities and help them in expanding their creativity and responsibility (Hansen & Leuty's, 2012)

They are going to stay longer in an organization if they will find their job meaningful and their profile challenging (Kong et al. 2016) which will keep them job satisfied (Garcia, 2016).

### Job Satisfaction

Job satisfaction is defined as how people feel about their job and the different facets of their jobs. Ellickson and Logsdon (2002) backs this view by defining job satisfaction as "the extent to which employees like their work and it's a response which is emotional and affective towards the work of an employee. The feeling that a worker has about his job is job satisfaction. Job satisfaction has manifold facets and thus is a complex mechanism (Xie & Johns, 2000); which is impacted by the factors of empowerment, freedom, work culture and organizational loyalty (Lane, Esser, Holte & Anne, 2010; Vidal, Valle and Aragón, 2007; Fisher & Locke, 1992; Xie & Johns, 2000).

A few similar research papers have discovered that employee satisfaction is a solid determinant of corporal responsibility and dependability (Mak & Sockel, 2001). The idea of workplace is a genuinely broad one as it includes the physical, mental and social perspectives that increase the working condition.

### Factors Affecting Job Satisfaction

Trust empowers cooperative conduct, advances network-based types of culture, decreases clashes and encourages viable reactions to crisis. Employee trust in their leaders enhances job satisfaction (Asencio, 2016). Interpersonal trust means the willingness of one party to accept the actions of other party. Employees of an organization can be efficient if they can have trust on their supervisors which may lead to and high level job satisfaction (Gucer and Serif, 2014). There are three principle aspects of trust: first, trust in someone else considered as an individual's desire or conviction that the their partner will also reciprocate kindly; also, trust includes the ability to be unshielded and the conjecture that the other individual may not live up to their expectations; and thirdly, trust includes a specific degree of reliance which implies that an individual is influenced by the activities of others (Whitener et al., 1998). Thus, in work environment associations, representatives will feel more secure and increasingly positive about their supervisors and friends when they accept that their pioneers and companions are reliable.

Apart from the factors that Millennials need at the workplace, they expect the absence of policies that does not allow employee engagement and prevents them to collaborate closely with the supervisor. They hate micromanagement, hazy planning and vision and work without proper directions (Glazer et.al, 2019). Millennial employees in presence of the above factors or in the absence of factors that satisfy them at workplace are more prone to leaving their jobs and switch to a more promising job opportunity. Absence of job satisfaction lead them to switch their jobs (Tsai, 2017). But the satisfied Millennial employee stay longer and loyal to the organization promising more fruitful association with the employer (Annakis et al., 2011) though it's also known that this generation is the most difficult generation to satisfy (Marston, 2019).

The positive side is job satisfied Millennial employee showcases a positive behavior at workplace reducing absenteeism and grievances at workplace. This positively affects the retention ratio of employees (Celik and Oz 2011; Garcia et al. 2019). Van der Westhuizen et al. (2012), Pacheco and Webber (2016) in their studies have shown that Millennials want autonomy at workplace. They expect to be involved in strategic decision making where their voices are heard and respected. They believe in the policy of employee empowerment (Westhuizen et al., 2012; Pacheco &Webber, 2016). Active contribution at workplace ensures that this generation is satisfied. Millennials prove to be highly satisfied at workplace when they are given the freedom to participate more in the tasks and the decision making at workplaces (Westhuizen et al., 2012; Pacheco & Webber, 2016). To inculcate the feeling of involvement and expressive addition in various work profiles, Millennial employees should be given frequent honest feedbacks on their work. They expect this feedback to be genuine and honest so that they can bring in improvement in their performance (Zhang & Li, 2020) which thereby brings more vigor in their work. Brannan et al. (2015) showed that there exists a significant impact of constant feedbacks on performance and job satisfaction which creates job meaningfulness for Millennials (Shantz & Booth, 2014). They consider their peers as friends and their seniors as their guides. They need constant feedbacks to learn and adapt to the current culture (Campione, 2015). Dominant factors as rated by Millennials themselves that they want at workplaces are job security, employment prestige and reputation, challenging job profile, starting salary and employer location (Arora & Kshatriya, 2017). The more challenging and tasking a job is, the more is the job satisfaction (Garcia, 2016).

Salary is associated with worldwide employee work satisfaction and even more closely with the aspect of monetary satisfaction leading to loyalty. Although money is important to individuals, research has shown that, Individuals who earn more are not necessarily satisfied in their jobs. In a Chinese study it was revealed that salary raise impacts job satisfaction and pay is an important.factor affecting overall job satisfaction. Promotions provide opportunities for personal growth. More responsibilities and increased social status. Job satisfaction is said to be experienced by those employees who get promotional opportunities which are fair (Yang, Miao, Zhu, Sun, Liu & Wu, 2008).

In this Gig economy, the employees hardly stay in one organization for as long as 5 years. The millennials today prefer freelancing over a 9 to 5 job, so in the times of more flexible working hours and less job security, how do you build employee loyalty and trust for the organization? The job of HR has become more and more difficult as how do they identify the right talent in this world of freelancers. Non-tangible incentives awarded as recognition is more sought by Millennials and even make them happier (Urban & Wood, 2015). Along with the tasking profiles, this generation also have high need for strong work-life balance in comparison with all the previous generations (Weeks et al., 2017). Presence of this has positive influence on their job satisfaction and retention rates at work. Workforce. Work-life balance has majorly become a key construct factor to millennial employees affecting their job satisfaction and retention (Philip et al., 2017).

Technology at workplace can help ease the work systems. Millennials are tagged to be tech-savvy, as they use technology in every aspect to make the lives easier (Bannon, Ford & Meltzer, 2011). Digital technology has profoundly impacted Millennials and has impacted their work life Technology is the factor that has united Millennials all over the globe (Raines, 2002). HR managers can manage their millennial workforce more effectively by harnessing technology appropriately at workplace. This can help managers gain overall confidence, support and loyalty of millennial workforce in the organization (Jha, Sareen & Potnuru, 2018). Millennials has been the generation which in their growing years have tablets and computers as their childhood toys. There were always surrounded by the digital technology (Kadakia, 2017). Understanding that for Millennials, technology is not desire but a need will help employers make them job satisfy and will also help them in motivating and guiding Millennial employees (Towler, 2020). Millennials is a generation which can handle technology better than the previous generations and are multitaskers when supported or provided with technology based systems or gadgets (Weeks et al., 2017). Because of the environment that this generation spent their growing years, they are always curious to work so as to improve their technical skills. They are always anxious to upgrade their digital expertise necessary in this online world. Millennials have not known a world without technology and hence want smartphones, tablets, laptops and other wireless gadgets and systems to make the workflow smoother (Cheng, 2019). Interest in technology based systems have made this generation more independent, curious and of course tech savvy. These employees cannot imagine a world in the absence of technology (Cheng, 2019). Need of technology in the time to come will become a necessity at workplaces contributing in the overall success and satisfaction of employees (Nakagawa & Yellowlees, 2020).

Literature reveals that here are different factors studied by different authors and researchers that determine the patriotism of employees towards their organization. In this study, we further analyze and find out if all those factors are true and to find out other factors then the ones given above.

## MATERIAL AND METHODS

### Research Methodology

Research method is the technique which is employed in generating detailed understanding of the given topic forming the base for collection of data and generating the evidence for concluding the research. The study adopted descriptive method as the research was conducted to know the state of affairs by examining the respondents in detail as it exists. Descriptive studies are used to summarize and describe the characteristics of a group and this research studies the generation of Millennials to understand their job satisfaction work constructs. Descriptive studies are based on surveys and in this study the data was collected through structured tool and survey on Millennials was taken to achieve the aim of the study.

This research has adopted primary as well as secondary source of data collection. The data from published works, research papers from various national and international journals and articles from newspapers forms the secondary source of data collection. On the other hand primary data was collected through a structured questionnaire which was drafted by the researcher based on the study topic. The research followed convenience sampling method to access respondents for this study as the researcher relied on accessibility of working Millennials to determine the variables in the research sample. The population in reference is Management field Millennials from the city of Ahmedabad. Cochran's formula was used to calculate the sample size. The standard normal; sample size of 385 was finalized for the study with level of confidence to be 95% in the current case.

## Data Collection

The chapter aims to explore the factors affecting Millennials' work satisfaction leading to extreme patriotism towards the organization steering to long term retention pertaining to digital era. To achieve the objective, the author conducted this research on Millennials through quantitative approach of data collection. For taking the opinions of the respondents, a well-structured questionnaire was prepared, containing twenty two questions associated with factors relating to work satisfaction. Different questions on different scales were asked in questionnaire. There were two demographic questions both asked in nominal scale. Gender was asked as a dichotomous question while work experience was asked as a multiple choice single response scale. Twenty two questions were asked on factors affecting job satisfaction using Likert scale.

The data collection took total one month to be completed and study ended up with 13 more responses in comparison to planned sample size. To know the opinion of Millennials over job satisfaction, data from 398 employees was collected. The main aim of the questionnaire was to find the factors affecting work satisfaction of Millennials by exploring the broad constructs that affect the loyalty of this generation. For exploration of data, exploratory factor analysis was used to find the broad constructs.

## Data Analysis

To check the data suitability and model appropriateness, initial values of KMO and Bartlett's were observed. KMO value of 0.861 confirmed the sample adequacy while Bartlett's test proved that there is a significant correlation between the variables and application of exploratory factor analysis is suitable. Communalities of all the statements as asked in the tool came out to be greater than 0.60 which shows that there is a good amount of variance that variables of the study share with each other.

To know the amount of deviation created by the factors in overall job satisfaction, total variance as generated by SPSS output is analyzed.

*Table 1. Showing Total Variance Explained for Factor Analysis*

| Component | Initial Eigenvalues | | | Extraction Sums of Squared Loadings | | | Rotation Sums of Squared Loadings | | |
|---|---|---|---|---|---|---|---|---|---|
| | Total | % of Variance | Cumulative % | Total | % of Variance | Cumulative % | Total | % of Variance | Cumulative % |
| 1 | 4.808 | 34.346 | 34.346 | 4.808 | 34.346 | 34.346 | 3.273 | 23.376 | 23.376 |
| 2 | 2.39 | 19.068 | 53.414 | 2.39 | 19.068 | 53.414 | 2.497 | 17.821 | 39.197 |
| 3 | 1.508 | 13.771 | 67.815 | 1.508 | 13.771 | 67.815 | 2.465 | 15.608 | 56.805 |
| 4 | 1.306 | 11.611 | 79.426 | 1.306 | 11.611 | 79.426 | 1.677 | 12.976 | 69.781 |
| 5 | 1.204 | 2.218 | 81.644 | 1.204 | 2.218 | 81.644 | 1.311 | 8.231 | 78.012 |
| 6 | 1.101 | 2.008 | 83.652 | 1.101 | 2.008 | 83.652 | 1.210 | 5.64 | 83.652 |
| 7 | 0.595 | 2.623 | 86.275 | | | | | | |
| 8 | 0.494 | 2.528 | 88.803 | | | | | | |
| 9 | 0.439 | 1.135 | 89.938 | | | | | | |
| 10 | 0.415 | 1.000 | 90.938 | | | | | | |
| 11 | 0.415 | 0.967 | 91.905 | | | | | | |
| 12 | 0.266 | 0.902 | 92.807 | | | | | | |
| 13 | 0.139 | 0.995 | 93.802 | | | | | | |
| 14 | 0.111 | 0.791 | 94.593 | | | | | | |
| 15 | 0.494 | 0.788 | 95.381 | | | | | | |
| 16 | 0.494 | 0.778 | 96.169 | | | | | | |
| 17 | 0.439 | 0.694 | 96.863 | | | | | | |
| 18 | 0.415 | 0.692 | 97.555 | | | | | | |
| 19 | 0.266 | 0.691 | 98.246 | | | | | | |
| 20 | 0.139 | 0.685 | 98.931 | | | | | | |
| 21 | 0.111 | 0.68 | 99.611 | | | | | | |
| 22 | 0.057 | 0.389 | 100 | | | | | | |

## TOTAL VARIANCE EXPLAINED

Table 1 shows the factors with Eigen value greater than 1 and therefore six factors are extracted out of all the statements. Total 84 percent variance is explained by all the extracted factors. The rotation component matrix with varimax rotation and principal component analysis segregated the statements in six factors.

Rotated component matrix helps in exploring major set of factors creating variance in the model.

## ROTATED COMPONENT MATRIX

The rotated component matrix as per table 2, revealed that there are six major factors explaining the work satisfaction of Millennials.

As per table 2, first four statements that are clubbed under the first factor are:

*Table 2. Showing Rotated Component Matrix*

| | Component | | | | | |
|---|---|---|---|---|---|---|
| | 1 | 2 | 3 | 4 | 5 | 6 |
| My superior is a person I can trust. | 0.892 | | | | | |
| I am loyal to my organization considering it is the best. | 0.877 | | | | | |
| I feel I can trust the organization in my career development | 0.824 | | | | | |
| My supervisor gives me constructive feedbacks in a way that emphasizes positives rather than negatives. | 0.738 | | | | | |
| I am able to attend social gatherings in family. | | 0.871 | | | | |
| I get time to go on vacations with my family/friends. | | 0.865 | | | | |
| I feel my work is recognized and appreciated by my superior. | | 0.774 | | | | |
| My work gives me a feeling of personal accomplishment. | | | 0.802 | | | |
| My efforts are recognized and acknowledged in tangible ways. | | | 0.735 | | | |
| The cultural and emotional climate of the organization is positive | | | 0.672 | | | |
| The cultural and emotional climate of the organization is supportive. | | | 0.660 | | | |
| My efforts are recognized and acknowledged in intangible ways. | | | 0.609 | | | |
| I don't have to worry about pushing my assigned tasks to next level | | | | 0.782 | | |
| I don't have to report my supervisor again and again for status of my work | | | | 0.765 | | |
| I can focus on more productive tasks than doing mechanical tasks | | | | 0.671 | | |
| I enjoy my work because actionable data is always readily available | | | | 0.662 | | |
| I enjoy confidentiality, integrity and availability of authorized information | | | | | 0.833 | |
| Technology and processes control vulnerability and potential threats | | | | | 0.801 | |
| Data security policies at work gives me peace of mind | | | | | 0.772 | |
| Management systems are transparent and secure | | | | | 0.706 | |
| I have confidence in the fairness of my organization. | | | | | | 0.829 |
| I feel I am being paid a fair amount for the work I do. | | | | | | 0.712 |
| Extraction Method: Principal Component Analysis.<br>Rotation Method: Varimax with Kaiser Normalization. | | | | | | |
| a. Rotation converged in 6 iterations. | | | | | | |

This signifies that the statements shown in table 3 are strongly related and they are measuring relatively the same thing. All the statements here reveal that an employee is satisfied at work if they trust their employer. Millennial when trust their superior, take feedbacks in a constructively positive way. Feeling of Jingoism prevails when the employee trusts the organization and increases the certainty that the organization is taking every measure to develop their career. So all these statements are pointing towards the feeling of trust and certainty increasing the security towards the job. Hence, the new factor is termed as: Job Security.

The next 3 statements are clubbed under the second factor that creates 17.8 per cent of the variance.

This signifies that all the above statements in table 4 are highly correlated and they are measuring relatively the same concept. All the statements here are trying to measure whether an employee is able to give time to his family and can go on vacations and attend social gatherings. Hence, the new factor is termed as: Work Life Balance. An organization working to maintain balance between the personal and professional space of their employees win extreme patriotism from them.

The next 5 statements are clubbed under the third factor as shown in table 5.

All the statements here are clubbed under the third factor which points towards the recognition that an employee receives from an employer. Good work; when is appreciated and recognized gives a feeling of accomplishment leading to satisfaction. This recognition can be tangible or intangible but it creates an overall positive climate which leads to work satisfaction enhancing loyalty. Hence, the new factor is termed as: Recognition.

The next 4 statements are clubbed under the fourth factor are shown in table 6.

Millennials are so habituated of using technology led smart gadgets in their daily lives that they also prefer technology dependent work systems. Micromanagement and frequent reporting prevent Millennials to be constructive and so they prefer workplaces where systems are automated which eliminates the need to report the daily work status and submit the work done to be sent for the next step. This avoids wasting time on mechanical work. The readily available data from the automated systems aids towards enhanced productivity of Millennials leaving them satisfied from their jobs.

Hence, the new factor is termed as: Automated Workflows.

*Table 3. Showing statements belonging to Factor 1*

| Statement | Factor Loading |
|---|---|
| My superior is a person I can trust. | .892 |
| I am loyal to my organization considering it is the best. | .877 |
| I feel I can trust the organization in my career development | .824 |
| My supervisor gives me constructive feedbacks in a way that emphasizes positives rather than negatives. | .738 |

*Table 4. Showing statements belonging to Factor 2*

| Statement | Factor Loading |
|---|---|
| I am able to attend social gatherings in family. | .871 |
| I get time to go on vacations with my family/friends. | .865 |
| I feel my work is recognized and appreciated by my superior. | .774 |

*Table 5. Showing statements belonging to Factor 3*

| Statement | Factor Loading |
|---|---|
| My work gives me a feeling of personal accomplishment. | .802 |
| My efforts are recognized and acknowledged in tangible ways. | .735 |
| The cultural and emotional climate of the organization is positive | .672 |
| The cultural and emotional climate of the organization is supportive. | .660 |
| My efforts are recognized and acknowledged in intangible ways. | .609 |

*Table 6. Showing statements belonging to Factor 4*

| Statement | Factor Loading |
|---|---|
| I don't have to worry about pushing my assigned tasks to next level | .782 |
| I don't have to report my supervisor again and again for status of my work | .765 |
| I can focus on more productive tasks than doing mechanical tasks | .671 |
| I enjoy my work because actionable data is always readily available | .662 |

*Table 7. Showing statements belonging to Factor 5*

| Statement | Factor Loading |
|---|---|
| I enjoy confidentiality, integrity and availability of authorized information | .833 |
| Technology and processes control vulnerability and potential threats | .801 |
| Data security policies at work gives me peace of mind | .772 |
| Management systems are transparent and secure | .706 |

*Table 8. Showing statements belonging to Factor 6*

| Statement | Factor Loading |
|---|---|
| I have confidence in the fairness of my organization. | .829 |
| I feel I am being paid a fair amount for the work I do. | .712 |

The next 4 statements are clubbed under the fourth factor as per table 7.

With automated systems in use and default data gathering happening at workplaces, this poses a lot of data security challenges. Issues such as tempering with the private data, data theft, falsifying identities of users and unauthorized access to confidential data makes employees vulnerable at workplace. One of the crucial factor that satisfy Millennials at workplace in this digitized world is security and privacy of their data leading to more commitment towards organization.

They want to work with a system which is transparent, holds data security and is accountable for authorized information. Millennials want employer to have specific data security policies which avoid individual data being vulnerable thereby helping them to work without stress at workplace.

So, Information Security is the fifth factor that may lead to job satisfaction.

The last two statements are shown in table 8.

Both the statements here are clubbed under the last factor which points towards fairness that an employee expects from an employer. Work satisfaction in an employee is instilled when they know that their organization is fair. Hence, the new factor is termed as: Equality.

## CONCLUSION

In the digital era of constant competition, where companies are struggling to retain the best talent, using the best employee engagement activities, Millennial employee has their own set of expectations from the employer which if fulfilled, results into high degree of trust and extreme patriotism towards the organization. The study explores key constructs which are responsible for Millennials' fulfilment of expectations directing to work satisfaction. The six major constructs can lead to sustainable relation between the two parties. Feeling of Jingoism develops with the constant rise of employee's trust in their employer which can be achieved when employer takes measures to develop its employee which ultimately leads to job security. Security in job motivates an employee to perform better. Work Life balance is considered equally important by Millennials as with constant work and career development they expect their employer to give them space, time and opportunity to fulfil their social responsibilities. Also, with recognition and appreciation on good work, Millennials expect the employer to be fair in the matters relating to them, be it providing with career shaping opportunities, time to self-heal, take a break or giving right compensation. Equality is the factor that increases work satisfaction and meets the workplace expectations of Millennials. As regards to the culture at workplace, fairness in work related decisions is the highest expectation of Millennials. They being impatient in nature, can take responsibility of work if given the equity in work related matters. Fairness and equality at workplace, treating every employee equally by putting in more confidence in their work and paying them fairly brings more work satisfaction.

In the digital world, Millennials demand automated workflows and systems to minimize constant supervision and reporting making them more dynamic. Automated work flows can facilitate employee experience that can potentially drive competitive advantage radiating through Millennials. Secure information ensures that employees are saved from potential threats of Adware and Ransomware eliminating the risk of work slowdown due to system viruses. Information security at workplace curbs theft of critical organizational and employee information protecting its systems and processes from cyber theft. The feeling of security brings extreme satisfaction and hence a feeling of loyalty towards the employer.

For maintaining long term relations with the employees and steal the feeling of Jingoism, employers need to review their retention strategies to win trust of its employees.

## RECOMMENDATIONS

This is the time that employers need to perceive that Millennials is the generation which is potentially very crucial for work but difficult to retain. Keeping this fact in consideration, they need to provide Millennial employees with meaningful work profiles, leadership tasks and added responsibilities leading to more career development opportunities so as to offer them a secured job. The untold fact about Millennials is that they need frequent constructive feedbacks from the supervisor they trust and this is the mantra to successfully manage Millennials.

While it is not necessary for employers to offer extra luxuries to Millennials but by providing a right balance between their work and lives will make them happy, more satisfied and loyal towards the organization. Optimum degree of work life balance will help them in fulfilling their family responsibilities also that can enhance their productivity and will aid them to work with a free mindset.

Simple policies of regular recognition and fair treatment can be introduced at workplaces to keep this generation motivated. Ease of work through automated workflow can help enhance this generation in being more productive by not wasting their efforts in manually managing and administrating the tasks. Use of Information technology to run the system can help this tech savvy generation to excel and perform higher and be more satisfied at workplace.

Human Resource seniors and managers need to be actively proactive, seeking and sharing opportunities with their Millennial employees to give them a chance to develop themselves before they quit. Winning a Millennial employee is not that difficult as they don't expect loaded perks but they want to see is a better future at an organization.

## MANAGERIAL IMPLICATIONS

With Millennials flooding the workplaces, it is important for organizations to understand and apply retention strategies for this generation. To manage and retain Millennials in the world of transforming digitization, employers need to win the satisfaction quantum of this job hopping generation to maintain a proper flow of fresher candidates joining the workplace so that the balance between the supply and demand can be maintained.

Thus, knowledge about the factors important for Millennials' satisfaction as found out in this research can be useful for any organization affiliated in any sector to make sure that the management is providing the right kind of environment as expected by employees and is crucial for the long term sustenance of this generation. Application of work satisfaction constructs as concluded here will help employers in winning the work satisfaction degree of the Millennial employees thereby retaining them for a longer period of time.

Furthermore, with the onset of digital technologies, managers can use this study results to redesign or amend their working environments jeweled with automation and embedded in information technology in such a way that they meet the expectations of newer generations of workers.

## REFERENCES

Annakis, J., Lobo, A. and Pillay, S. (2011) 'Exploring Monitoring, Work Environment and Flexibility as Predictors of Job Satisfaction within Australian Call Centers.' *International Journal of Business and Management, 6*(8), pp. 75-93, Research Gate. doi:10.5539/ijbm.v6n8p75

Arora, C. R. P. (2019). Predicting Job Expectations of Millennials: A Generation with Soaring Work Projections. *SKIPS 1*(1).

Arora, P. (2020). *Understanding and Analyzing the Determinants of Millennials' Workplace Expectations: A Study on Management Aspirants With Special Focus on Gujarat State*. [Doctoral Dissertation] GLS University. http://hdl.handle.net/10603/308037

Arora, P., & Kshatriya, K. P. (2017). Millennials: The new generation with high employment expectations. *International Journal (Toronto, Ont.), 5*(8), 101–109.

Arora, P., & Kshatriya, K. P. (2018). Redefining Millennials: Understanding characteristics and Perceptions of Generation Y. *International Research Journal of Human Resources and Social Sciences, 5*(03), 181–199.

Bannon, S., Ford, K., & Meltzer, L. (2011). Understanding millennials in the workplace. *The CPA Journal, 81*(11), 61.

Bhatnagar, D., Singh, S., Yadav, S., Kumar, A., & Kaur, I. (2017). Experimental and theoretical investigation of relative optical band gaps in graphene generations. *Materials Research Express*, *4*(1), 015101. doi:10.1088/2053-1591/4/1/015101

Bobek, A., & Wickham, J. (2015) *Working Conditions in Ireland Project; Employment in the Irish Financial Services Sector: A preliminary Background Report*. https://www.tasc.ie/assets/files/pdf/20150929160149.pdf

Brady, M. (2016). *Better Quality of Work Life is Worth a $7,600 Pay Cut for Millennials*. https://www.businesswire.com/news/home/20160407005736/en/Quality-Work-Life-Worth-7600-Pay-Cut

Brannan, M. J., Parsons, E., & Priola, V. (2015). Brands at Work: The Search for Meaning in Mundane Work. *Organization Studies*, *36*(1), 29–53. doi:10.1177/0170840614553382

Burgess. (2008). Managing the new workforce Generation Y (Millennials). *Red Fusion*.

Campione, W. (2015). Corporate Offerings: Why aren't Millennials Staying? *Journal of Applied Business & Economics*, *17*(4), 60–75.

Canedo, J. C., Graen, G., Grace, M., & Johnson, R. D. (2017). Navigating the new workplace: Technology, millennials, and accelerating HR innovation. *AIS Transactions on Human-Computer Interaction*, *9*(3), 243–260. doi:10.17705/1thci.00097

Celik, D.A. and Oz, E.U. (2011). The Effects of Emotional Dissonance and Quality of Work Life Perceptions on Absenteeism and Turnover Intentions among Turkish Call Center Employees. *Procedia Social and Behavioral Science, 30*(1), pp. 2515– 2519, Research Gate. . doi:10.1016/j.sbspro.2011.10.491

Cheng, M. (2019) *8 Characteristics of Millennials That Support Sustainable Development Goals (SDGs)* https://www.forbes.com/sites/margueritacheng/2019/06/19/8-characteristics-of-millennials-that-support-sustainable-development-goals-sdgs/?sh=66e01a7029b7

Cole, G., Smith, R., & Lucas, L. (2002). The debut of Generation Y in the American workforce. *Journal of Business Administration Online*, *1*(2), 1–10.

Deloitte (2016). *The 2016 Deloitte Millennial Survey winning over the next generation of leaders*. Deloitte Touche Tohmatsu Limited, United Kingdom.

Dimock, (2019). *Defining generations: Where Millennials end and Generation Z begins*. Pew Research Centre. https://www.pewresearch.org/fact-tank/2019/01/17/where-millennials-end-and-generation-z-begins/

Ellickson, M. C., & Logsdon, K. (2002). Determinants of job satisfaction of municipal government employees. *Public Personnel Management*, *31*(3), 343–358. doi:10.1177/009102600203100307

Fisher, C. D., Locke, E. A., & Henne, D. L. (1992). The new look in job satisfaction theory and research. In *Job satisfaction: Advances in research and applications,* (pp. 165–194). The Free Press.

Garcia, G.A., Gonzalez-Miranda, D.R., Gallo, O. & Roman-Calderon, J.P. (2019) Employee Involvement and Job Satisfaction: A Tale of the Millennial Generation. *Employee Relations: The International Journal, 41*(3), pp. 374-388. Emerald Insight. . doi:10.1108/ER-04-2018-0100

Garcia, J. (2016) Passing the Torch: What Motivates Millennials? *Resources Magazine*, pp. 26-27, http://eds.b.ebscohost.com/eds/pdfviewer/pdfviewer?vid=5&sid=adadf2dc-c848- 4ce8-bcbd-2319ec31e273@pdc-v-sessmgr03 .

Glazer, S., Mahoney, A., & Randall, Y. (2019). Employee development's role in organizational commitment: A preliminary investigation comparing generation X and millennial employees. *Industrial and Commercial Training*, *51*(1), 1–12. doi:10.1108/ICT-07-2018-0061

Hansen, J., & Leuty, M. (2012). Work Values Across Generations. *Journal of Career Assessment*, *20*(1), 34–52. doi:10.1177/1069072711417163

Jha, N., Sareen, P., & Potnuru, R. K. G. (2018). Employee engagement for millennials: Considering technology as an enabler. *Development and Learning in Organizations*.

Kadakia, C. (2017). *The Millennial Myth: Transforming Misunderstanding into Workplace Breakthroughs*. Berrett-Koehler Publishers.

Kong, H., Sun, N., & Yan, Q. (2016). New Generation, Psychological Empowerment: Can Empowerment Lead to Career Competencies and Career Satisfaction? *International Journal of Contemporary Hospitality Management*, *28*(11), 2553–2569. doi:10.1108/IJCHM-05-2014-0222

Lane, K. A., Esser, J., Holte, B., & McCusker, M. A. (2010). A study of nurse faculty job satisfaction in community colleges in Florida. *Teaching and Learning in Nursing*, *5*(1), 16–26. doi:10.1016/j.teln.2009.05.001

Lyons, S. and Kuron, L. (2014). Generational Differences in the Workplace: A Review of the Evidence and Directions for Future Research. *Journal of Organizational Behavior, 35*(1), pp. 139-157, JSTOR Journals. . doi:10.1002/job.1913

Mak, B. L., & Sockel, H. (2001). A confirmatory factor analysis of IS employee motivation and retention. *Information & management, 38*(5), 265-276.

Marston, C. (2019). Tips for keeping Millennial Employees: Understanding Myths about Millennials. https://www.thebalancecareers.com/tips-forretaining-millennial-employees-1918679.

Naim, M. F., & Lenka, U. (2018). Development and retention of Generation Y employees: A conceptual framework. *Employee Relations*, *40*(2), 433–455. doi:10.1108/ER-09-2016-0172

Nakagawa, K., & Yellowlees, P. (2020). Inter-generational Effects of Technology: Why Millennial Physicians May Be Less at Risk for Burnout Than Baby Boomers. *Current Psychiatry Reports*, *22*(9), 45. doi:10.100711920-020-01171-2 PMID:32661817

Pacheco, G. and Webber, D. (2016). Job Satisfaction: How Crucial is Participative Decision Making? *Personnel Review, 45*(1), pp. 183-200. Emerald Insight. . doi:10.1108/PR-04-2014-0088

Philip, J., Najmi, H., Orudzheva, L., & Struckell, E. (2017). Work life overlap in the millennial generation: The role of ubiquitous technology. *Journal of Strategic Innovation and Sustainability*, *12*(1), 80–98.

Pierce, J. (2019). *Minimizing Employee Turnover in a Changing Workforce*. Forbes. https://www.forbes.com/sites/forbeshumanresourcescouncil/2019/09/05/minimizing-employee-turnover-in-a-changing-workforce/?sh=54b470c73884

Raina, (2016). *What's different about the Indian Millennial?* Strategic HR.Gurgaon. New Delhi

Raines, C. (2002). Managing millennials. *Connecting Generations: The Sourcebook, 16.*

Robison, J. (2019). Why Millennials Are Job Hopping. https://www.gallup.com/workplace/267743/why-millennials-job-hopping.aspx%20OCTOBER%2028,%202019%20JENNIFER%20ROBISON

Rousseau, D. M., Sitkin, S. B., Burt, R. S., & Camerer, C. (1998). Not so different after all: A cross-discipline view of trust. *Academy of Management Review*, *23*(3), 393–404. doi:10.5465/amr.1998.926617

Shantz, A., & Booth, J. E. (2014). Service Employees and Self-verification: The Roles of Occupational Stigma Consciousness and Core Self-evaluations. *Human Relations*, *67*(12), 1439–1465. doi:10.1177/0018726713519280

Shaw, S., & Fairhurst, D. (2008). Engaging a new generation of graduates. *Education + Training*, *50*(5), 366–378. doi:10.1108/00400910810889057

Stahl, A. (2019). *5 Keys to Retaining Millennial Employees, the 'Job-Hopper' Generation.* https://www.forbes.com/sites/ashleystahl/2019/09/17/5-keys-to-retaining-millennial-employees-the-job-hopper-generation/?sh=6701baf63bdd

Towler, A. (2020). *The Job Characteristics Model: What it is and Why it Matter More Than Ever.* https://www.ckju.net/en/dossier/job-characteristicsmodel-what-it-is-and-why-it-matters-more-ever

Tsai, M., (2017). *Attracting and Retaining Millennial Workers in the Modern Business Era.*

Urban, B., & Wood, E. (2015). The Importance of Opportunity Recognition Behavior and Motivators of Employees When Engaged In Corporate Entrepreneurship. *Journal of Business Economics and Management*, *16*(5), 980–994. doi:10.3846/16111699.2013.799087

Van der Westhuizen, D., Pacheco, G., & Webber, D. (2012). Culture, Participative Decision Making and Job Satisfaction. *International Journal of Human Resource Management*, *23*(13), 2661–2679. doi:10.1080/09585192.2011.625967

Vidal, M. E. S., & Valle, R. S. (2007). Antecedents of repatriates; job satisfaction and its influence on turnover intentions: Evidence from Spanish repatriated managers. *Journal of Business Research*, *60*(12), 1272–1281. doi:10.1016/j.jbusres.2007.05.004

Weeks, K. P., Weeks, M., & Long, N. (2017). Generational perceptions at work: In-group favoritism and out-group stereotypes. *Equality, Diversity and Inclusion*, *36*(1), 33–53. doi:10.1108/EDI-07-2016-0062

Xie, J. L., & Johns, G. (2000). Interactive effects of absence culture salience and group cohesiveness: A multi-level and cross-level analysis of work absenteeism in the Chinese context. *Journal of Occupational and Organizational Psychology*, *73*(1), 31–52. doi:10.1348/096317900166868

Zaharee, M., Lipkie, T., Mehlman, S., & Neylon, S. (2018). Recruitment and Retention of Early-Career Technical Talent. *Research Technology Management*, *61*(5), 51–61. doi:10.1080/08956308.2018.1495966

Zhang, T. and Li, B. (2020). Job Crafting and Turnover Intention: The Mediating Role of Work Engagement and Job Satisfaction. *Social Behavior and Personality: An international journal, 48*(2), pp. 1-9. Psychology and Behavioral Sciences Collection. . doi:10.2224/sbp.8759

## ADDITIONAL READING

Asencio, H. (2016). Leadership, trust, and job satisfaction in the public sector: A study of US federal employees. *International Review of Public Administration*, *21*(3), 250–267. doi:10.1080/12294659.2016.1237342

Güçer, E., & Şerif, A. D. (2014). Organizational trust and job satisfaction: A study on hotels. *Business Management Dynamics*, *4*(1), 12.

Kohll, A. (2018). *The Evolving Definition of Work-Life Balance*. Forbes. https://www.forbes.com/sites/alankohll/2018/03/27/the-evolving-definition-of-work-life-balance/?sh=11a9c25b9ed3

Pasko, R., Maellaro, R., & Stodnick, M. (2020). A study of millennials' preferred work-related attributes and retention. *Employee Relations: The International Journal*.

# Chapter 12
# Resilience as a Moderator Between Perceived HR Digitalization and Positive Employee Outcomes

**Reyhan Baykara**
*Istanbul Bilgi University, Turkey*

**Deniz Kantur**
*Istanbul Bilgi University, Turkey*

## ABSTRACT

*This study investigates the moderating role of employee resilience on the relationship between perceived HR digitalization and positive employee outcomes such as work effort (WE) and affective commitment (AC). A combination of qualitative interviews with 6 employees and survey data collected from 248 participants were analyzed. The results showed a positive relationship between perceived HR digitalization and positive employee outcomes such as AC. This relationship was moderated by resilience such that satisfaction with HR digitalization predicted AC in employees with low resilience. A positive correlation was found between perceived digitalization and resilience. No strong relationship was found between perceived digitalization and WE. Perceived digitalization of HR tools that enabled communication and training opportunities positively impacted outcomes such as commitment and motivation. Employees with experience working digitally and with a higher perceived digitalization reported the most favorable WFH experience. These employees had a more positive view of HR digitalization.*

## INTRODUCTION

Digitalization has been one of the most popular topics of the last decade, and its popularity is increasing more than ever. In the organizational context, the digitalization of human resources (HR) had already started to gain more attention as companies realized its importance in terms of strategic consequences.

DOI: 10.4018/978-1-6684-5864-8.ch012

However, it was still not the priority for many organizations until recently. The Covid-19 pandemic, which stroke the world in 2019, significantly impacted the employees' lives and increased the importance of HR's digitalization.

The Covid-19 pandemic served as a driving force in the adoption of digitalization at an "unprecedented" speed and extent (Aurelia & Momin, 2020). According to a survey conducted on behalf of McKinsey (LaBerge et al., 2020), participants reported that their organizations digitalized 20 to 25 times faster than they had foreseen. This pace exceeded their expectations by 40 times. The investment into HR digitalization increased to triple the amount of the investments in 2017 by reaching 3.1 billion dollars, and it is expected to reach 30 billion dollars by 2025 (Aurelia & Momin, 2020). Moreover, employees' expectation for an implementation process was one year, whereas it only took 11 days to implement digital solutions in reality (LaBerge et al., 2020).

During the pandemic period and the lockdown situations in many countries, it came to the surface that many organizations were not ready to ensure business continuity in times of unexpected, massive, sudden changes such as this. Some organizations needed to find quick-fix solutions for the unforeseen technological needs of long-term homeworking. Many large organizations which have a diverse workforce with many different national backgrounds, cross-border workers, distant team members as well as immigrants, and ex-pats had to implement digital solutions in order to be able to continue their businesses. The accuracy of the data in the HR systems showed to be the resource that helped the organizations to be prepared for the lockdown situation in a very short time. The organizational practices which were done face-to-face had to be replaced with new remote practices. The lengthy discussions on organizational matters and longsome bureaucratic processes had to be cut shorter to reduce the effort on communication. All of these new conditions required employees to adjust to many changes, which created various implications on employee well-being and related business outcomes (De-la-Calle-Durán & Rodríguez-Sánchez, 2021).

With the working conditions imposed by the unexpected pandemic regulations, it has become apparent to many people and organizations that digitalization is indispensable in the globalized world. Moreover, the digital way of working is seen as the "new way of working" (Fogarty et al., 2020), and the winnings of digitalization are expected to be kept and built upon.

Throughout the pandemic, the physical danger of the virus, the psychological impact of the traumatic event, and the atmosphere of uncertainty created stress globally. Along with this, employees had to change their daily routines, working styles, social interactions, and relations to technology among many other workplace practices. Away from the habitual work environment, establishing work routines became a challenge while the border between private and professional life got blurry. For example, parents had to take care of their children while working from home. Some employees had difficulties in finding a proper physical space that allows productivity. Managing time was challenging for some employees, and they found themselves working more than before. For many organizations, the business expectations from the employees remained the same while the issues that the employees had to deal with increased. These factors, along with their psychological outcomes such as emotional exhaustion or burnout (King & Sethi, 1997), brought attention to positive employee outcomes such as well-being as well as organizational commitment, motivation, and productivity.

Even though the situation was experienced globally, the consequences were not the same for everyone. During this time, two concepts have become more distinctive than ever: the importance of digitalization and the importance of resilience. The extensive diffusion of digitalization during Covid-19 has been a cornerstone and started a new era with a lot of changes in the way of working. This created an urgent need to explore the employee-related concepts and consequences of digital HR practices in order to draw a future direction for organizations with regards to this reality. As this period showed, resilience is an essential factor that can bring competitive advantage as well as helping employees and organizations during times of crisis. Therefore, this research investigates the moderating role of resilience between digitalization of HR and positive employee outcomes.

## HR DIGITALIZATION

Previous literature suggests numerous different definitions for Electronic Human Resource Management (e-HRM) (Alghafri, 2015; Sareen, 2012). In the earlier definitions, e-HRM was described as a *"specialized information system within the traditional functional areas of the organization, designed to support the planning, administration, decision-making, and control activities of human resource management"* (DeSanctis, 1986). However, such IT-based definitions with an operational HRM focus were seen as a simplification of e-HRM's role in transformational outcomes such as employee involvement and workforce alignment. Alternatively, more recent definitions emphasized its role in transformational business functions such as strategic management and defined e-HRM as *"an umbrella term covering all possible integration mechanisms and contents between HRM and Information Technologies aiming at creating value within and across organizations for targeted employees and management."* (Bondarouk and Ruël, 2009).

HR is one of the drivers of the success of organizations in the "knowledge economy" (Chakraborty & Mansor, 2013). People and information technology are considered as the two resources which can "dramatically" affect the success of the business (Teo et al., 2007), and proper adoption of e-HRM systems is claimed to stimulate organizational success by combining these two resources; people and technology (Sareen 2012, Teo et al., 2007). Bandrouk and Ruel (2013) argue that e-HRM is expected to bring two strategic advantages to the human resources function; transforming HR's role into a strategic business partner and bringing HR's time investment in strategic HR issues. The main goals attributed to e-HRM in the literature are reducing costs, improving HR services, and improving the strategic orientation of the HR function (Bandrouk & Ruel, 2013; Bondarouk et al.,2017). Moreover, properly implemented and consciously used e-HRM systems are often associated with the potential to create this competitive advantage (Lippert & Swiercz, 2005; Campbell et al., 2012; Troshani et al., 2010; Pfeffer et al., 2002; Al Kahtani et al., 2016).

Organizational success comes from a combination of capabilities of HR management, agility, learning potential, speed, and employee competence (Huselid et al., 1997; Saha et al., 2017; Brockbank, 1999; Ulrich, 1998). In a similar way, competitive advantage is closely attached to innovation, customer service, efficiency, quality, and competitive advantage strategies such as low cost, differentiation, and focus (Beckers & Bsat, 2002). e-HRM system can add value to the organization by developing organizational agility, learning, and innovation (Marler, 2009).

In addition, "innovative work practices" such as e-HRM are claimed to increase work efficiency by allowing employees to redesign their own way of doing their jobs and future careers based on their first-hand knowledge and experience. Such collective knowledge management can reduce the workload of supervisors and middle managers in return while maintaining employee performance and motivation with the help of immediate feedback from the supervisors (Ichninowski et al., 1996; Rothwell & Arnold, 2005; Huselid et al., 1997; Ederer, 2010; Sailer et al., 2013).

By enabling employees to enter and update data by themselves, e-HRM ensures more accurate data in less time, reduces the work of the HR personnel (Chakraborty & Mansor, 2013; Hendrickson, 2003), decrease the chances of human error (Panayotopoulou et al., 2007) and prevent the overlapping work (Nivlouei, 2014). As a result, it helps reduce the costs and effort of HR, which can leave the time and resources for analytical positions and strategical plans of the organization (Marler, 2009; Beckers & Bsat, 2002). e-HRM practices such as e-recruiting and e-learning can help organizations obtain unimitable, rare, valuable human resources in a faster manner by enabling access to a broader pool of potential talents (Wright & McMahan, 1992; Strohmeier, 2007; Huselid et al., 1997; Mukherjee et al., 2014).). e-HRM also helps improve employee skills through broad training and development activities (Huselid & Delaney, 1996), which enable them to determine their career developments based on web-based HR tools (Bondarouk et al., 2004).

Thanks to digitalization, employees can get informed about organizational updates and join online conversations (Bondarouk et al., 2004). e-HRM stimulates new ways of thinking (Kovach & Cathcart, 1999) and encourages initiative-taking (Chakraborty & Mansor, 2013). Such learning opportunities help increase employee well-being and, as a result, employee health, productivity and performance (Van Dam et al., 2020; Erim, 2018)

As well as connecting team members around the same goals, e-HRM also ensures continuity of interpersonal relationships. During times of crisis, communication between colleagues and the guidance from leaders and mentors become even more critical. Under remote working conditions, e-HRM offers means to ensure continuous communication and support between the leaders, mentors as well as other team members. As shown in resilience research, such HR practices can enhance employee resilience and promote proactive employee behaviors (Bardoel et al., 2014; Wu & Parker, 2016). This communication is also vital in the case of new employees. Employee orientation includes teaching new employees the organizational culture, philosophies, and initiatives (Akdere & Schmidt, 2008), which helps new employees settle into their environment and understand their responsibilities while helping the organization to have well-trained, highly motivated employees as quickly as possible (Robinson, 1998). e-HRM serves as a link between the employees and the team in such a situation and helps the new joiners adapt to the company and the teams.

Information technology is expected to bring transparency into the employee's labor, interactions, and performance (Avolio et al., 2014). Transparency about rewards and compensation, standardization of HR practices increase employee confidence, pride and trust (Martin et al., 2008;), which is associated with supporting employee well-being during Covid-19 (De-la-Calle-Durán & Rodríguez-Sánchez, 2021). Such organizational investments help employees feel justice and might produce positive outcomes such as employee identification with the company and increased commitment (Erim, 2018; Allam, 2019; 2017). e-HRM also enables employers to respond to changing business environments by targetted compensation programs or arranging better salary and benefit options, optimize the training needs and costs (Lippert & Swiercz, 2005).

In addition to the administrative tasks, the most common HR practices include planning, recruitment, training and development, performance management, compensation and benefits, along with protecting employees in terms of legal aspects as well as health and safety (Fındıklı & Bayerçelik, 2015). As summarized above, E-HRM offers a lot of potentials to improve organizational success at the firm level and employee level in each of these areas.

## RESILIENCE

The physical threat of the Covid-19 pandemic includes two-week-long quarantine periods, hospitalization due to the virus, and in the most extreme cases, death (Jones, 2021). As a result, employee mental health was threatened as well (Jones, 2021). A lot of employees reported psychological difficulties such as stress, loneliness, anxiety, depression, issues with domestic relationships, job insecurity, and financial problems (Jones, 2021; Killgore et al., 2020; Caligiuri, 2020). In this context, resilience became an essential topic for businesses.

Resilience comes from the study of physics and describes the process of elastic material which changes shape by pressure, coming back to its previous form after the pressure is removed. This term is also used to metaphorically describe a person's ability to bounce back after a strong hit by a difficulty (Webster, 1977). As it can be concluded from this definition, resilience requires having enough space to protect the previous form. This means having resources already set in place, which enables the organization and the employees to sail through organizational traumas, and economic recessions (Williams & Vorley, 2014), human errors (Sheridan, 2008), natural disasters (Barasa et al., 2018), human resources issues (Al-Ayed, 2019) or other sudden changes with the least harm. Resilience is often considered as a "reflex" -which is deeply carved into someone's mind and soul (Coutu, 2002). Therefore, it is not likely to be built in the course of terrible events and successfully assist the organization. It has to be considered as a part of the strategic agenda during times of relative calm (Bardoel et al. 2014).

According to a literature review in 2011, as many as 122 definitions were identified for the resilience construct (Meredith et al., 2011). The basic understanding of resilience is constructed around three types of dominant defining categories 1- describe resilience as a process or capacity which develops over time, 2- emphasize adapting and returning to a baseline after an adverse situation, 3- involve growth after the adversity (Meredith, 2011; Luthans et al., 2006). Kuntz and colleagues define employee resilience as "the capacity of employees, facilitated and supported by the organization, to utilize resources to positively cope, adapt and thrive in response to changing work circumstances" (Kuntz et al., 2015). The more resources the individuals have, the less vulnerability they show in the face of adversity, and the better they accumulate further resources (Shin et al., 2012).

Individual factors such as positive coping, positive affect, positive thinking, a positive view of the self, self-regulation, intrinsic motivation, realism, behavioral control, physical fitness, and altruism; family-level factors such as emotional ties, communication, support, closeness, nurturing, and adaptability; unit-level factors such as positive command climate, teamwork, and cohesion; community-level factors such as belongingness, cohesion, connectedness and collective efficacy constitute important elements of resilience (Masten, 2001; Meredith et al., 2011).

Positive emotions such as joy, interest, and contentment might broaden the span of attention, thoughts, and actions of an individual as well as encourage them to be open to new information or invoke creativity. These emotions can motivate individuals to foster better social relations and long-lasting interpersonal bonds, which can contribute to the individuals' physical, intellectual and social resources (Fredrickson, 2001). These factors can be very important in surviving stressful situations, maintaining employee health, sustaining business continuity, managing well-being during stressful times and increase the resilience of the individuals (Hobfoll et al., 2015; Avey et al., 2010; Luthans & Youssef., 2007).

Conservation of Resources theory argues that individuals operate on the basic principle of obtaining, retaining, and protecting their resources which refers to the things that they value (Hobfoll et al., 2015). These resources can be objects such as the individual's physical belongings, conditions such as job stability, personal characteristics such as self-esteem, and energies such as credits or money. Individuals experience psychological stress when these resources are threatened, lost or when they do not obtain the benefits that they hope for in exchange for their investments in the resource (Hobfoll, 2001; Golembiewski et al., 2001).

Resilient employees differ from non-resilient employees in stressful situations by their resources such as flexibility, motivation, perseverance, and optimism (Bhamra & Burnard, 2011). Johnson and Wiechelt (2004) support that resilience helps individuals preserve hope and health despite the difficulty. Resilient employees are less prone to the negative impacts of job insecurity, emotional exhaustion, or burnout and more motivated to adapt to new situations. They are expected to show less counter-productive work behavior tendencies, and they tend to be less suspicious of their organizations in terms of keeping promises (Shoss et al., 2018). As they can have a more positive view of the situation as well as their organizations, they can survive difficulties with less harm, show better performance (Cooper et al., 2018) and commitment (Meng et al., 2017).

Resilient employee behaviors consist of network leveraging, learning, and adaptability (Kuntz et al., 2017). Sinclair and colleagues make a distinction between the capacity for resilience and the demonstration of resilience. In their integrative framework for employee resilience, processes that reflect the capacity for resilience include an appraisal of adversity, coping with adversity, and seeking help from others. The positive adaptation -demonstration of resilience- is reflected through job performance, low symptoms, high well-being, and healthy relationships. (Sinclair et al., 2016). Coutu (2002) defines resilient people with a capacity to accept harsh realities, finding meaning in difficult times, and being able to improvise with whatever is at hand. For organizations, employees who can maintain their optimism, hope, and effort despite difficulty can be valuable resources in the face of adversity.

More recently, within the frame of Positive Psychology, resilience started to be seen as a developable capacity rather than a merely innate trait (Duchek, 2019; Luthans et al., 2006). The theory advocates for focusing on the strengths and psychological capital (PsyCap) of the employees in order to improve the performance instead of trying to fix the negative aspects. This view is centered on promoting positive organizational behavior and claims that resilience can be increased through certain practices that aim to motivate and lead poorly performing employees or change their non-productive attitudes and behaviors (Luthans, 2002). According to this view, resilience capacity can be an enhancing factor of other psychological capital traits such as confidence (self-efficacy), optimism or hope (Luthans et al., 2006; Avey et al., 2010; Luthans & Youssef, 2007).

As a developable capacity, resilience is claimed to be enhanced through strategic human resources management (Luthans et al., 2006; Avey et al., 2009). By building knowledge, skills, abilities, and other such attributes as well as establishing collective routines and processes, Strategic HR practices can lead to enhanced resilience (Lengnick-Hall et al., 2011). For example, by increasing the opportunities for connection between employees and their mentors as well as their peers, well-being-oriented HRM practices can be a way to increase employee resilience (Guest, 2017). Alternatively, training opportunities are mentioned as an effective way to increase employee resilience (Avey et al., 2010) by increasing hope or self-efficacy (Alqurashi, 2016). Also, internal communication solutions can provide the social support opportunity for the employees by which resilience can be increased (Longstaff & Yang, 2008). Within this frame, it is important to investigate the relationship between e-HRM practices and employee resilience.

## POSITIVE EMPLOYEE OUTCOMES

The factors that affect employee productivity and performance have been an area of great interest in organizational studies. Among these factors, employee motivation, work effort, and commitment have received great attention as they are thought to lead to increased productivity by bringing out positive outcomes such as job satisfaction or performance (Allen & Meyer, 1996; Erim, 2018; Kanfer, 1990).

Performance refers to any behavior that is focused on achieving a goal or completing a task (Campbell & Pritchard, 1976). It is important to understand how employees get motivated to exhibit such efforts during difficult times such as the period of the pandemic. Reinforcements, drives/needs and incentives such as promotions, increase in salary, job security are seen as the main determinants of why people work (Campbell & Pritchard, 1976; Erim, 2018). However, psychological needs such as recognition and respect, being among amicable colleagues and having good interpersonal relationships also motivate people (Campbell & Pritchard, 1976; Erim, 2018; Donkin, 2010) and lead to increased organizational productivity and competitiveness (Brown & Leigh, 1996).

Motivation consists of three determinants which are the choice to start the effort on the task, the choice to spend effort, and the choice to keep this effort in the long run (Campbell & Pritchard, 1976). The work effort as a component of motivation is defined as "the means by which motivation is translated into accomplished work" (Parson, 1968, cited in Erim, 2018). The determinants of effort are defined as duration, intensity, and direction (Brown & Leigh, 1996; Erim,2018). The increase in the work requirement is defined in two ways; longer hours and increased effort spent at work (Green & McIntosh, 2001). These factors create an emotional burden on the employees and a decrease in their level of motivation. During the pandemic, even though the official working hours stayed the same, with the involvement of personal life-related contexts in the working hours, the working hours got longer for many employees. To balance the increased work hour needs with the official requirements and time frame of the work, employees needed to increase their efforts. Moreover, additional work intensification was created due to the non-routine tasks (Avgoustaki & Bessa 2019) and requirements of the new context, such as increased written communication.

The performance-related workplace behaviors which are associated with organizational effectiveness are considered in two separate categories, which are task performance and contextual performance. Task performance refers to the "core technical behaviors and activities involved in the job" (Griffin et al., 2000). These behaviors depend on factors such as ability, self-efficacy, goal setting, and task strategies (Locke et al., 1984). Contextual performance, on the other hand, refers to the "behaviors that support the environment in which technical core operates" (Griffin et al., 2000). It assists the organization's effectiveness by shaping the organizational, social, and psychological contexts that enable the actualization of the task performance through voluntary efforts or cooperation (Borman & Motowidlo, 1997).

Organizational Citizenship Behavior refers to the positive behaviors that do not have a direct correspondence with the official reward system but support the effective functioning of the organization (Organ, 1997). How the employee will perform these behaviors depends on their perception of what constitutes extra-role behaviors and in-role behaviors. These include voluntarily helping others (helping behavior), openness to endure impediments without dissenting (sportsmanship), standing by the organization in external contexts and maintaining commitment (organizational loyalty), relating to the rules and policies of the organization (organizational compliance), attempting to contribute to the job and the organization and improve them (individual initiative), commitment and the feeling of being a part of the organization (civic virtue) and the efforts and interest of the employees in terms of building on their knowledge and skills (self-development) (Podsakoff et al., 2000).

Being able to utilize a variety of skills and participating in diverse activities, having the autonomy to decide how to perform their job and receiving adequate feedback might increase employee work effort by making employees enjoy their jobs more (Erim, 2018; Yu & Frenkel, 2012). These can be achieved through innovative practices such as e-HRM (Ichniowksi et al., 1996). Digital HR practices that allow employee-supervisor, leader, and mentor communication might increase employee work effort by giving a sense of empowerment (Conger & Kanungo, 1988).

Previous research (Brockner et al., 1992) shows that job insecurity has a moderating impact on employee turnover. However, when the job insecurity is too high, employees are not motivated to work hard as the consequence seems inevitable. Considering the large amount of layoffs that occurred during the Covid-19 period, moderating the level of this insecurity becomes important to ensure the work effort. HR practices that endorse employee involvement and commitment are claimed to increase work effort (Green, 2004). Perceived online connection with colleagues and leaders can strengthen the employee's sense of relatedness, which might motivate them to be more willing to exert effort on external demands and needs (Yu & Frenkel, 2012).

Positive perception of work experiences can help reduce the turnover intention of the employees (Langkamer & Ervin, 2008; Allen & Meyer, 1996), which is explained by organizational commitment. As one of the most important employee management and strategic HR goals, organizational commitment has been one of the most widely researched organizational behaviors (Ulrich et al., 2019; Dey et al., 2014). Along with socialization and morale, it constitutes one of the three main performance dimensions (Borman Motowidlo, 1997). Organizational commitment is defined as the "strength of an individual's identification and involvement with a particular organization", and it refers to a strong belief and acceptance of the goals and values of the organization, willingness to exert a fair amount of effort on behalf of the organization, and a desire to maintain organizational membership (Porter et al., 1974; Allen & Meyer, 1996). Affective commitment is found to be positively correlated with performance, organizational citizenship behaviors, extra-role behaviors, willingness to express suggestions concerning improvements, accept things as they are in addition to work attendance and negatively correlated to ignoring dissatisfying situations (Allen & Meyer, 1996). As a part of the organization, employees who are committed to their organizations try to build their organization's success as well as their own. This means that organizations also benefit from their investments in the employees in return (Huselid, 1995). e-HRM innovations are expected to ameliorate employee trust by improving the relationship between employees, HR and employers, providing transparency and perceived fairness (Bissola & Imperatori, 2013; Avolio et al., 2014) which can increase the affective commitment of the employees.

Change is perceived as the biggest threat to organizational commitment (Meyer et al., 2009). Due to the sudden and big changes during the pandemic, there was a need for additional support for employees with the help of distant communication means. According to the Perceived Organizational Support theory (POS) (Yu & Frenkel, 2012), felt-obligation, group identification, and outcome expectancy are three mechanisms that organizational support can impact employee outcomes. Certain strategic HRM practices are known to create a "mutually beneficial environment" where organizations invest the employees and employees "reciprocate" that investment by organizational outcomes (McClean & Collins, 2011). These strategic HRM practices can include digital HR services that can benefit employees in terms of effort, socialization, development, and other such aspects. Organizational factors, which include procedural justice, change, perceived organizational support, and psychological climate, are also known to increase affective commitment, work effort as well as job involvement and performance (Langkamer & Ervin, 2008; Sharma & Dhar, 2016; Griffin & Rafferty, 2006; Brown & Leigh, 1996).

Within the context of the pandemic period and involuntary working-from-home situation, the question was to understand how do employees maintain the effort to exhibit these behaviors? How can digitalization be related to bringing out these efforts? The accelerated digitalization, as a technological change, created increased work intensification (Green, 2004). In the circumstances which were prepared by a global emergency, autonomous motivation (Bidee et al., 2013) was more relevant than other types of motivation. The situation was shared by all, and the reason for the strain was not related to one single organization. Therefore, the effort that the employee spent on showing positive organizational behaviors had a voluntary aspect to it.

## RESEARCH MODEL & HYPOTHESIS

During the time of the pandemic, digital tools that enabled growth such as online training options, that provided easier communication opportunities with mentors and colleagues, that allowed better orientation opportunities, that enabled immediate feedback and performance evaluations are thought to increase the employee's motivation and work effort as a result. The positive perception of employees with regards to HR's digitalization is expected to contribute to this process. When employees perceive that they have the means to communicate with their colleagues remotely or when the organization organizes online team-building activities, maintaining a positive climate is expected to be easier. The role stress can be reduced within this sharing environment, and harmony is expected to happen more easily. Moreover, perceived digitalization might give a sense of autonomy to the employees, which can help them face job-related challenges more smoothly. Having access to immediate feedback from supervisors or support from mentors, employees can avoid feeling lost or disconnected. In addition, they can avoid role ambiguity, which is known to be positively correlated with stress (Stout & Posner, 1984) and negatively correlated with job satisfaction (Chang & Hancock, 2003). As the emotional difficulties are reduced in the positive climate, the resources which are spent on regulating these difficulties can be directed towards more productive results while employee well-being is improved (Jamal, 1999).

As explained earlier, employees spend their resources both on task performance and contextual performance (Griffin et al., 2000). During the time of Covid-19, a lot of employees started working with digital tools that they had never used before. Some of these employees were not habitually familiar with remote working conditions. In the technology acceptance literature, it is well-known that the technical difficulties experienced or perceived by employees cause stress (Kim & Park, 2018). These difficulties increase the demands of the immediate tasks. When this is the case, it is not unexpected that the increase in the task demands might lead to a decrease in the resources that an individual can spend on contextual activities (Griffin et al., 2000). For example, an employee who perceives difficulty in managing the tasks in an inefficient digital context might not have the motivation to help others or might experience low motivation to stay in the organization. e-HRM practices that focus on increasing resilience are claimed to enhance employees' psychological capital, attitudes as well as behaviors, and organizational performance (Bardoel et al., 2014). Also, it is claimed that individuals with a higher level of resilience might have stronger commitment to their organization (Garg & Paul, 2012). As a result of these, they might put more effort into exhibiting citizenship behaviors.

*Figure 1. Conceptual Framework*

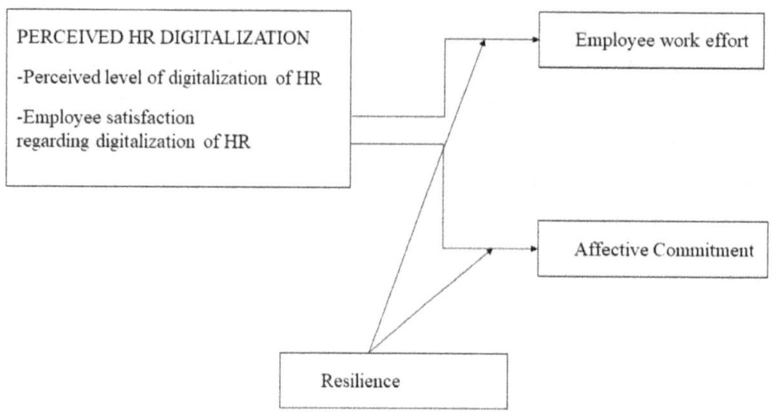


As suggested by previous research (Tusaie & Dyer, 2004), resilient employees who have more resources to deal with stressful situations might find it easier to canalize their efforts more effectively. This way, they might show higher motivation and effort towards their tasks. As the importance of contextual performance increases (Borman & Motowidlo,1997), investing the role of resilience gains weight as well. As digital working is considered a new way of working, it is necessary to investigate resilience in the context of digitalization.

It is argued that people's interaction with their work environments depends on how they perceive these environments (James & James, 1989). Therefore, understanding employee perceptions regarding HR digitalization is accepted as a good method of understanding employee-related consequences of digitalization. In order to contribute to the literature, this research aims to understand and assess if there is a relationship between perceived HR digitalization and positive employee outcomes such as work effort and affective commitment based on employees' resiliency. The model proposed by this research is illustrated below (See: Figure 1).

To contribute to the literature, this research proposes the following hypothesis.

**Hypothesis One:** There is a positive correlation between perceived digitalization and employee work effort in resilient employees.

**Hypothesis Two:** There is a positive correlation between perceived digitalization and the affective commitment of resilient employees.

**Hypothesis Three**: The positive relationship between perceived HR digitalization and work effort is moderated by resilience.

**Hypothesis Four:** The positive relationship between perceived HR digitalization and affective commitment is moderated by resilience.

## METHOD

The methods used in research consist of a quantitative survey and a qualitative semi-structured interview. To have a better understanding of the period of the pandemic, establish the research ground better, and structure the quantitive study questions, 6 semi-structured interviews were conducted before the quantitative study. The interview questions were mainly addressed to employees' understanding of HR's digitalization, perception of their organization's HR digitalization, and their experiences during the Covid-19 pandemic period within the last 9 months, from June 2020 to February 2021.

In the semi-structured interviews, sample interview questions included the questions below.

1. What do you understand when I say HR digitalization? How would you define it?
2. How digitalized is your organization's HR department?
3. How do you evaluate the digitalization of your organization's HR department?
4. How did you experience HR's digitalization during Covid 19 pandemic period in the last 9 months? Were there any changes in your organization or work? How did it affect you?

The total number of participants in the qualitative study was 6 (female=5, male=1). The interview participants worked in different positions in various sectors from finance to tourism (Finance=1, Education=1 MNC=2, Tourism=1, Industrials=1). All of the participants were white-collar employees who were working in private organizations. The participants consisted of 1 manager, 4 specialists and 1 professor. The age of the participants differed from 28 to 43. All of the participants were university graduates, 3 of them had a master's degree, 1 of them had a doctorate degree. The participants' average tenure was 4.83 years.

The data collected in voice recordings were transcribed later on. The names of the participants and their organizations were kept confidential during the transcriptions. Each participant was given a participant number. The main/recurring themes were analyzed.

Issues reported in the interviews mainly focused on difficulties with keeping a healthy working schedule, social challenges due to lack of interaction with colleagues in small organizations, challenges due to lack of proper technological implementation and integration in small organizations. Digital HR practices offered by the organizations mainly focused on administrative functions for small organizations, communication and training functions for the bigger organizations. HR digitalization was associated with positive employee outcomes such as motivation and work effort, resilience, affective commitment.

The main findings of the study suggested that working from home situation during the pandemic brought a lot of changes at different scales. Managing any kind of change is known to be stressful (Griffin & Rafferty, 2006). However, employees who had previous working from home experience reported positive experiences regarding the situation. As mentioned earlier, resilience is a "reflex" (Coutu, 2002) that needs to be built in time before unfortunate events take place. The comments from the participants show that the digital HR practices that were already in-place, helped them survive through these changes with less harm. Therefore, after the pandemic period, digitalization should continue to be carefully implemented and improved, employees should be trained and supported to be able to make use of these technologies in times of difficulty.

As indicated by some participants, the organizations' approach to HR digitalization had an impact on how the employees related to it. Organizations that were able to have a holistic approach toward HR digitalization and make it a part of their strategy used digital solutions as a means to communicate and guide their employees. By increased communication and activities, they showed their focus on their employees' well-being, which was reflected on employees' happiness, well-being, affective commitment, motivation and work effort. This is an indication of how a strategic approach to digitalization can support the employees while creating an advantage for the organization in return. In order to gain benefits in terms of employee outcomes, digitalization should be taken as a strategic HR practice. Otherwise, it can get stuck at the administrative level (Bondarouk & Ruel, 2009), which can make working "very hard", as one of the participants reported.

From the responses of the participants, it is understood that digitalization had a certain positive contribution to the lives of the employees during this period. Some employees obtained small benefits from the situation, such as "spending less time in traffic" or on "dressing up", which might make the lives of the employees easier. Even though these examples are small, it shows that digitalization and partial working from home can save time of the employees and reduce stressors.

It is important to note that the compulsory nature of the pandemic should be taken into consideration while interpreting the negative comments about digitalization. Working from home 7 days a week created a need for a specific working space and adjustment of all the relevant aspects of employees' lives to the situation. With the social restrictions in general, the worrying atmosphere due to the virus can also be among the reasons for some employees to feel stuck at home or not being able to socialize enough. Moreover, the stress that was related to domestic issues might be increased because of the long periods of staying inside the home. Some of the stressors might be the result of a life change rather than merely a change of platforms.

In the quantitative part of this research, a survey was sent out via the online survey tool Survey Monkey on various social media. The data was collected for 3 weeks between February 2021 and March 2021. The quantitative survey consisted of 2 sections and an additional part which addressed the demographic information of the participants. The first section of the survey consisted of questions directed to understanding the perception of digitalization, including well-being-oriented human resources practices (Celma et al., 2018). Employees were asked how digitalized they thought their organizations' HR departments were both in general and in terms of its specific functions. These questions were assessed based on earlier research published by Zhou et al. (2020). They were followed by questions addressing how happy the employees were with the digitalization of their organizations' HR departments, both in general and with regards to specific HR functions. The satisfaction was rated on 5-item Likert scale (Sullivan & Artino Jr., 2013) with an additional option of "not digital". Following the perception questions, the employees were asked if they had a flexible working arrangement or not within the last 9 months in order to set a time frame, based on the earlier research by Avgoustaki & Bessa (2019).

The second part of the survey contained questions regarding the behavioral consequences of HR's perceived digitalization, specifically in terms of work effort and affective commitment, as well as employee resilience status. The questions focused on resilience were assessed based on the 9-item Employee Resilience scale (EmpRes) proposed by Kuntz et al. (2015). Work effort questions were evaluated based on the 10-item Work Effort Scale (WESC) (Cooman et al., 2009). Lastly, the affective commitment was assessed with the help of Meyer and Allen's 8-item commitment scale focused on affective commitment (Meyer & Allen. 1990).

For the purposes of this study, non-probability (convenience) sampling was used. The aim was to reach a random pool of participants, all of whom were actively working at the time of the survey regardless of their sector or seniority. The participants who were not actively working were disqualified from the survey.

In order to understand the context better, the survey had 9 demographic questions, including the sector in which the participant's organizations operated and the age of their organization.

The scales used in this research are:

**Digitalization Scale:** The scale used to assess digitalization was designed based on the earlier study by Zhou et al. (2020). As it was in their research, "To what extent is digital HRM systems used in your enterprise?" was the main question of the research. This question was first asked for HR department in general. After this, the same question was modified for 6 specific HR functions, including recruitment, training and development, talent management, performance management, compensation and benefits, and administration functions. These were followed up with the functions that are associated with employee well-being in the literature (Celma et al., 2018). In the next 4 questions, employees were asked to what extent they thought their enterprise was digitalized in terms of the tools and platforms that enable training/personal development, internal communication, flexible working and leadership/mentoring.

**Satisfaction with Digitalization Scale:** The employees were asked for their level of satisfaction with the digitalization of their organization's HR department. The 11 questions covered HR department in general and with regards to specific functions, which are recruitment, training and development, performance management, compensation and benefits, and administration functions. These functions were followed by the tools and platforms that enable training/personal development, internal communication, flexible working and leadership/mentoring.

**Resilience Scale:** Kuntz et al. (2015) define resilience within the frame of "resilient behaviors that employees engage in" rather than a personal "trait-like capacity". Based on this view, the scale to assess resilience was developed in accordance with employee behaviors taken from the 9-item Employee Resilience Scale (EmpRes) (Kuntz et al., 2015). The 3rd item in the scale "I resolve crisis competently at work" and the 7th item "I seek assistance to work when I need specific resources" were reversed.

**Work Effort Scale:** The common view in the literature is that work effort is a difficult concept to measure (Green & McIntosh, 2001); therefore, the research into work effort has been very limited due to the lack of measures (Green, 2004). With its broad definitions, work effort can be assessed by objective and subjective measures, which are based on either the reports of other people or self-reports of the individuals (Erim, 2018).

This research investigates the work-effort-related consequences based on employees' self-reports based on Cooman and colleagues' (2009) 10-item Work Effort Scale (WESC). For the purposes of this study, the 4th, item "I do my best to do what is expected of me", the 7th item "I think of myself as a hardworker" and the 10th item "I always exert equally hard during the execution of my job" were reversed and asked in order to prevent any potential biases.

**Affective Commitment Scale:** The affective commitment questions in this research were taken from the well-known scale developed by Allen & Meyer in order to assess organizational commitment. The original Organizational Commitment scale consists of three parts which are affective commitment (8-item), continuance commitment (8-item) and normative commitment (8-item) (Meyer & Allen, 1990). For the purposes of this research, the 8-items in the affective commitment were presented to the participants in the original order.

## DATA ANALYSIS AND RESULTS

Data was analyzed in SPSS 25. To test the normality of the data, skewness and kurtosis were calculated. As skewness and kurtosis results were distributed between -1.96 and +1.96, variables were assumed to be normally distributed and parametric tests were used. Relationships between the variables digitalization, satisfaction with digitalization, resilience, work effort and affective commitment were assessed with Regression analysis. Lastly, moderation analysis was conducted with affective commitment as the dependent variable, satisfaction with digitalization as the independent variable and resilience as the moderator.

## Results

The demographic information with regards to the 248 total number of participants is illustrated below (See. Table: 1)

The mean score of digitalization in the participant's work environments was 6.21 (SD = 2.49) (See Table 3).

## Reliability of Measures

The scales used in this study are summarized below (see Table 2).

Results revealed strong correlation between digitalization and participants' satisfaction with digitalization ($r = .74$, $p < .05$). There was a weak positive correlation between satisfaction with digitalization and resilience ($r = .23$, $p < .05$) as well as satisfaction with digitalization and work effort ($r = .18$, $p < .05$). Resilience had positive strong correlation with work effort ($r = .63$, $p < .05$), and weak positive correlation with affective commitment ($r = .34$, $p < .05$). Affective commitment and work effort was moderately correlated with each other ($r = .43$, $p < .05$). Digitalization was not significantly correlated with resilience, work effort or affective commitment.

*Table 1. Sociodemographic characteristics of Participants*

| | | |
|---|---|---|
| **Work situation** | Actively working | 232 |
| | Unemployed | 10 |
| **Work schedule (last 9 months)** | Flexible (working without time and place constraints) | 62.9% |
| | Part-time | 8.9% |
| | Compressed schedule (working 3-4 work days instead of 5-6 days for the equal amount of work) | 15.3% |
| | Working from home (WFH) | 69% |
| **Tenure (years)** | 5 or below | 46,8% |
| | 6-10 | 17.3% |
| | 11 above | 4.4% |
| **Age** | 25 or below | 1.6% |
| | 26-35 | 49,1% |
| | 36-45 | 14.1% |
| | 46 or above | 3.6% |
| **Gender** | | |
| | Female | 35.5% |
| | Male | 33% |
| | Another/No answer | 31.5% |
| **Highest education level** | Bachelor | 33% |
| | Master | 31% |
| | Doctorate | 4.4% |
| | Other/No answer | 31.6% |

*Table 2. The scales used in the study*

| Scales | Cronbach's Alpha |
|---|---|
| Digitalization scale (11 items) | .956 |
| Satisfaction with digitalization scale (11 items) | .953 |
| Resilience scale (9 items) | .767 |
| Work effort (7 items) | .866 |
| Affective Commitment (7 items) | .873 |

*Table 3. Means, Standard Deviations and Correlations*

| Variable | M | SD | 1 | 2 | 3 | 4 |
|---|---|---|---|---|---|---|
| 1. Digitalization | 6.21 | 2.49 | | | | |
| 2. Work Effort | 4.32 | 0.47 | 0.06 | | | |
| 3. Affective Commitment | 3.18 | 0.83 | 0.12 | 0.43* | | |
| 4. Resilience | 3.91 | 0.47 | 0.10 | 0.63* | 0.31* | |
| 5. Satisfaction With Digitalization | 3.41 | 1.22 | 0.74* | .18* | 0.13 | 0.23* |

## Regression

Two multiple linear regression analyses were conducted. First regression analysis was calculated to predict affective commitment based on satisfaction with digitalization and resilience. A significant regression equation was found ($F(2, 177) = 9.75$, $p < .01$) with an $R^2$ of .107. Resilience was found as a significant predictor of affective commitment, $t = 4.06$, $p < .01$. Participants' affective commitment score increased 0.53 points with one-point increase in resilience score. However, satisfaction with digitalization was not found as significant predictors of affective commitment. (See: Table 4)

Second regression analysis was conducted to predict work effort based on satisfaction with digitalization and resilience. Regression equation was found as significant ($F(2, 175) = 57.48$, $p < .01$ with an $R^2$ of .40. Resilience significantly predicted the work effort, $t = 10.26$, $p < .01$. Participants' affective commitment score increased 0.61 points with one-point increase in resilience score. However, satisfaction with digitalization was not found as significant predictors of affective commitment. (See Table 5)

To test the hypothesis that the resilience of employees moderates the relationship between satisfaction with digitalization and affective commitment, multiple regression analysis was conducted. Satisfaction with digitalization, resilience, and the interaction of these two variables were included in the analysis.

*Table 4. Regression Analysis Summary Dependent Variable as Affective Commitment*

| | B | 95% CI | ß | t | p |
|---|---|---|---|---|---|
| (Constant) | 0.98 | [0.48 1.48] | | 1.95 | 0.05 |
| Satisfaction | 0.04 | [-0.01 0.09] | 0.06 | 0.71 | 0.43 |
| Resilience | 0.53 | [0.40 0.66] | 0.30 | 4.06 | < .01 |

*Table 5. Regression Analysis Summary Dependent Variable as Work Effort*

| | B | 95% CI | ß | t | p |
|---|---|---|---|---|---|
| (Constant) | 1.86 | [1.66 2.12] | | 8,23 | 0.00 |
| Satisfaction | 0.02 | [0.00 0.04] | 0.04 | 0.64 | 0.52 |
| Resilience | 0.61 | [0.55 0.67] | 0.62 | 10.26 | < .01 |

Regression equation was found as significant ($F(3, 171) = 8.01$, $p < .01$ with an $R^2$ of .12). Satisfaction, resilience, and the interaction of them were revealed as significant predictors (Table 6). The hypothesis was supported. To decompose the interaction, simple intercepts and simple slopes were calculated with Quantypsy tool. Satisfaction with digitalization was a significant predictor of affective commitment among employees who had low resilience ($B = .15$, $SE = .14$, $t(171) = 2.30$, $p < .05$). However, affective commitment could not be predicted by satisfaction with digitalization for employees who have high ($B = -.04$, $SE = .05$, $t(171) = -0.91$, $p = .37$) or moderate ($B = .05$, $SE = .03$, $t(171) = 1.56$, $p = .12$) resilience levels. So, being satisfied with the digitalization of their company predicts greater affective commitment for people who have low resilience but not for people who have high or moderate resilience (Figure 2).

To test the hypothesis that the resilience of employees moderates the relationship between work effort and satisfaction with digitalization, multiple regression analysis was conducted. Satisfaction with digitalization, resilience, and the interaction of these two variables were included in the analysis. Regression equation was found as significant ($F(3, 174) = 39.77$, $p < .01$. Resilience was found as a significant predictor ($t = 5.33$, $p < .01$). Satisfaction with digitalization and interaction was found to be nonsignificant. The hypothesis was rejected (See: Table 7).

*Figure 2. Visualization of the Moderation Effect*

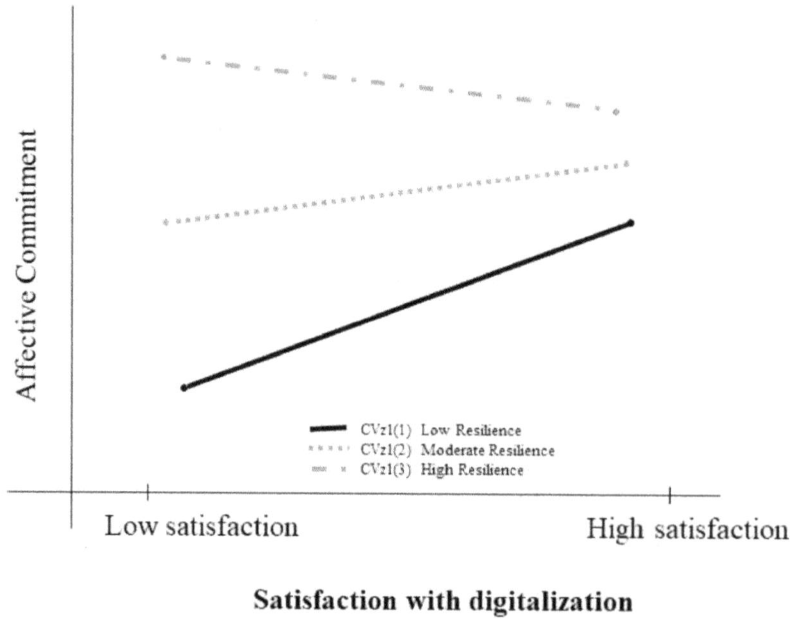

*Table 6. Moderation Analysis Summary Dependent Variable as Affective Commitment*

| | B | 95% CI | ß | t | p |
|---|---|---|---|---|---|
| Constant | -1.72 | [-3.13 -0.31] | | -1,22 | 0.23 |
| Satisfaction | 0.85 | [0.45 1.25] | 0.94 | 2.13 | 0.04 |
| Resilience | 1.21 | [0.86 1.57] | 1.45 | 3.38 | 0.001 |
| Interaction | -0.21 | [-0.31 -11] | -0.90 | -2.04 | 0.04 |

*Table 7. Moderation Analysis Summary Dependent Variable as Work Effort*

| | B | 95% CI | ß | t | p |
|---|---|---|---|---|---|
| Constant | 0.84 | [0.20 1.48] | | 1,31 | 0.19 |
| Satisfaction | 0.33 | [0.15 0.51] | 0.87 | 1.80 | 0.07 |
| Resilience | 0.88 | [0.72 1.04] | 0.89 | 5.33 | 0.001 |
| Interaction | -0.08 | [-0.13 0.03] | -0.94 | -174 | 0.08 |

## DISCUSSION ON FINDINGS

According to the results, there is a strong correlation between digitalization and employee satisfaction with digitalization. As also supported in the qualitative study, employees working in organizations with highly digitalized HR have a more positive perception of HR digitalization. The perceived digitalization showed a positive correlation with resilience, even though this correlation was not strong. There was also a weak correlation between satisfaction with digitalization and work effort. Affective commitment and work effort were moderately correlated as well.

Resilience moderated the impact of satisfaction with HR digitalization on affective commitment. As suggested, satisfaction with HR digitalization in combination with resilience had a positive impact on affective commitment. This relationship was stronger in employees who had a low level of resilience.

As explained earlier, resilience impacts how much individuals are affected by environmental factors. Individuals with high resilience are expected to be affected less by environmental factors. On the other hand, employees with low resilience are expected to be affected more by environmental factors and changes. This might explain the increasing affective commitment level of low-resilient employees thanks to their level of satisfaction with HR digitalization.

The moderation effect of resilience on satisfaction with digitalization and work effort was not observed. Resilience was found to be a predictor of work effort. Satisfaction with digitalization also had a weak correlation with work effort. However, employee satisfaction with digitalization and its interaction with resilience was not found to impact employees' work effort. Hypothesis 4 was rejected. In this part, the compulsory nature of the digitalization practices during Covid-19 might be a factor that affected employee work effort. For example, as mentioned earlier, employees might not have perceived enough difference in terms of the consequences of increasing their work effort. This aspect should be investigated with further study.

## CONCLUSION

In this research, both the qualitative study and the quantitative study implicated that there is a relationship between perceived digitalization and positive employee outcomes. Also, the employees whose organizations were already digitalized avoided the negative psychological impact of the pandemic period comparatively. This shows a promising future for digitalization and resilience as well as related research.

In a Resilience survey conducted in 2015, the last cause people expected to affect the businesses in the following 3 years was "Risk of disease and epidemics by 10% of total participants (The Economist Intelligence Unit, 2015). However, it emerged as the event which had the biggest impact on all businesses in 2020. The future cannot be foreseen. Therefore, resilience and digitalization need to be investigated thoroughly, so as to be ready for any future disruption. Protecting employee well-being during such a time is equally important.

This research contributes to the literature by investigating resilience in the context of digitalization and providing evidence. It was also important to do this research during the course of the pandemic in order to provide insights regarding the crisis situation and rapid digitalization while the situation is ongoing.

However, as the study was conducted while the pandemic period is still going on, there were methodological limitations. First of all, due to the working from home situation, it was difficult to access enough participants for long interviews. Therefore, the survey method was chosen. The survey was sent out by using platforms such as social media. The data was collected by convenience sampling method. If the situation allowed, case studies or in-depth interviews would have enabled a broader understanding of the topic.

Another limitation was that the previous research regarding the consequences of the Covid-19 pandemic is very young and not sufficient. Moreover, research on resilience was very limited in the context of digitalization. Therefore, it was difficult to structure the study and draw the direction. In order to refine the methodology, a qualitative study was conducted before the survey was created. As the data accumulates, it is expected to be easier for further research to gather the data together and build on these previous studies.

It is suggested that further research investigates the relationship between digitalization and work effort from a different angle. In this study, the relationship between perceived digitalization and work effort was not found significant in the survey. However, the qualitative study indicated a kind of relationship between satisfaction from digitalization and positive employee outcomes such as work effort and motivation. Therefore, further qualitative research can uncover the missing parts and might help improve the direction of the survey used in this research.

In addition, it was shown that fully integrated administrative solutions and higher digitalization had an impact on employee perceptions of digitalization as well as employee outcomes. There were differences between the perception and experience of the employees working in different sectors and organizational scales. In order to investigate the concept of resilience better, the level of actual digitalization can be included as a variable in a case study as well. This way, employee perception and the reality of digitalization can be compared, which might help identify the role of resilience better. A comparative study focusing on small and large-scale organizations might give insights with regards to tailored digitalization options for organizations at both scales and contribute to the innovation diffusion research. It might be useful to investigate the strategic approaches in small and big companies with regards to the pandemic period. This way, as indicated by this research, resilience can be investigated as a developable capacity in a deeper context and the practices that supported this capacity can be identified.

Lastly, the digital HR practices that contributed to employee satisfaction focused on training opportunities and communication-related strategies. Further research needs to be conducted to specify these practices.

It is inarguable that the pandemic had great consequences on employee well-being and working conditions. Some of the concepts discussed in this research were investigated in different forms in previous research; however, it was important to carry these arguments to the digital context as per the requirements of our time. Investigating these concepts and consequences broadly will determine the direction of digitalization in the future.

## REFERENCES


Akdere, M., & Schmidt, S. W. (2008). Employee Perceptions of Quality Management Effects of Employee Orientation Training. *Paper presented at the Academy of Human Resource Development International Research Conference in the Americas,* Panama City. https://eric.ed.gov/?id=ED501643

Al-Ayed, S. I. (2019). The impact of strategic human resource management on organizational resilience: An empirical study on hospitals. *Business: Theory and Practice*, *20*, 179–186. doi:10.3846/btp.2019.17

Al Kahtani, N. S., Nawab, A. K., & Allam, Z. (2016). Unfair HRM practices in the telecom sector in Saudi Arabia. An empirical investigation of selected public and private sector companies. *International Journal of Applied Business and Economic Research*, *14*(10), 6377–6396.

Alghafri, A. A. (2015). Literature Review on: 'The Advantages and Disadvantages of Implementing E-HRM for an Organisation, E-Learning as an Example.'. *American Journal of Economics*, *5*(2), 51–55. doi:10.5923/c.economics.201501.02

Allam, Z. (2017). Employee Disengagement: A Fatal Consequence to Organization and its Ameliorative Measures. *International Review of Management and Marketing*, *7*(2), 49–52.

Allam, Z. (2019). Exploring ambient discriminatory HRM practices: An insight from Kingdom Telecom Company. *The Journal of Social Sciences Research*, *5*(3), 646–654. doi:10.32861/jssr.53.646.654

Allen, N. J., & Meyer, J. P. (1996). Affective, Continuance, and Normative Commitment to the Organization: An Examination of Construct Validity. *Journal of Vocational Behavior*, *49*(3), 252–276. doi:10.1006/jvbe.1996.0043 PMID:8980084

Alqurashi, E. (2016). Self-Efficacy In Online Learning Environments: A Literature Review. [CIER]. *Contemporary Issues in Education Research*, *9*(1), 45–52. doi:10.19030/cier.v9i1.9549

Aurelia, S., & Momin, M. M. (2020). Global reverberation and prediction for HRM amid and after COVID-19: A technological viewpoint. *Materials Today: Proceedings*. doi:10.1016/j.matpr.2020.11.544

Avey, J. B., Luthans, F., & Jensen, S. M. (2009). Psychological Capital: A Positive Resource For Combating Employee Stress And Turnover. *Human Resource Management*, *48*(5), 677–693. doi:10.1002/hrm.20294

Avey, J. B., Luthans, F., Smith, R. M., & Palmer, N. F. (2010). Impact of positive psychological capital on employee well-being over time. *Journal of Occupational Health Psychology*, *15*(1), 17–28. doi:10.1037/a0016998 PMID:20063956

Avgoustaki, A., & Bessa, I. (2019). Examining the link between flexible working arrangement bundles and employee work effort. *Human Resource Management*, *58*(4), 431–449. doi:10.1002/hrm.21969

Avolio, B. J., Sosik, J. J., Kahai, S. S., & Baker, B. (2014). E-leadership: Re-examining transformations in leadership source and transmission. *The Leadership Quarterly*, *25*(1), 105–131. doi:10.1016/j.leaqua.2013.11.003

Barasa, E., Mbau, R., & Gilson, L. (2018). What Is Resilience and How Can It Be Nurtured? A Systematic Review of Empirical Literature on Organizational Resilience. *International Journal of Health Policy and Management*, *7*(6), 491–503. doi:10.15171/ijhpm.2018.06 PMID:29935126

Bardoel, E. A., Pettit, T. M., Cieri, H. D., & Mcmillan, L. (2014). Employee resilience: An emerging challenge for HRM. *Asia Pacific Journal of Human Resources*, *52*(3), 279–297. doi:10.1111/1744-7941.12033

Beckers, A. M., & Bsat, M. Z. (2002). A dss classification model for research in human resource information systems. *Information Systems Management*, *19*(3), 1–10. doi:10.1201/1078/43201.19.3.20020601/37169.6

Bhamra, R., Dani, S., & Burnard, K. (2011). Resilience: The concept, a literature review and future directions. *International Journal of Production Research*, *49*(18), 5375–5393. doi:10.1080/00207543.2011.563826

Bidee, J., Vantilborgh, T., Pepermans, R., Huybrechts, G., Willems, J., Jegers, M., & Hofmans, J. (2012). Autonomous motivation stimulates volunteers' work effort: A self-determination theory approach to volunteerism. *Voluntas*, *24*(1), 32–47. doi:10.100711266-012-9269-x

Bissola, R., & Imperatori, B. (2014). The unexpected side of relational e-HRM. *Employee Relations*, *36*(4), 376–397. doi:10.1108/ER-07-2013-0078

Bondarouk, T., Parry, E., & Furtmueller, E. (2017). Electronic hrm: Four decades of research on adoption and consequences. *International Journal of Human Resource Management*, *28*(1), 98–131. doi:10.1080/09585192.2016.1245672

Bondarouk, T., & Ruël, H. (2009). Electronic Human Resource Management: Challenges in the digital era. *International Journal of Human Resource Management*, *20*(3), 505–514. doi:10.1080/09585190802707235

Bondarouk, T., & Ruël, H. (2013). The strategic value of e-HRM: Results from an exploratory study in a governmental organization. *International Journal of Human Resource Management*, *24*(2), 391–414. doi:10.1080/09585192.2012.675142

Bondarouk, T., Ruël, H., & Looise, J. K. (2004). E-HRM: Innovation or Irritation. An Explorative Empirical Study in Five Large Companies on Web-based HRM. *Management Review*, *15*(3), 364–380. doi:10.5771/0935-9915-2004-3-364

Borman, W. C., & Motowidlo, S. J. (1997). Task Performance and Contextual Performance: The Meaning for Personnel Selection Research. *Human Performance*, *10*(2), 99–109. doi:10.120715327043hup1002_3

Brockbank, W. (1999). If hr were really strategically proactive: Present and future directions in hr's contribution to competitive advantage. *Human Resource Management*, *38*(4), 337–352. doi:10.1002/(SICI)1099-050X(199924)38:4<337::AID-HRM8>3.0.CO;2-5

Brockner, J., Grover, S., Reed, T. F., & Dewitt, R. L. (1992). Layoffs, Job Insecurity, And Survivors' Work Effort: Evidence Of An Inverted-U Relationship. *Academy of Management Journal*, *35*(2), 413–425. doi:10.2307/256380

Brown, S. P., & Leigh, T. W. (1996). A new look at psychological climate and its relationship to job involvement, effort, and performance. *The Journal of Applied Psychology*, *81*(4), 358–368. doi:10.1037/0021-9010.81.4.358 PMID:8751453

Caligiuri, P., De Cieri, H., Minbaeva, D., Verbeke, A., & Zimmermann, A. (2020). International HRM insights for navigating the COVID-19 pandemic: Implications for future research and practice. *Journal of International Business Studies*, *51*(5), 697–713. doi:10.105741267-020-00335-9 PMID:32836500

Campbell, B. A., Coff, R., & Kryscynski, D. (2012). Rethinking sustained competitive advantage from human capital. *Academy of Management Review*, *37*(3), 376–395. doi:10.5465/amr.2010.0276

Campbell, J. P., & Pritchard, R. D. (1976). Motivation theory in industrial and organizational psychology. In M. Dunette (Ed.), *Handbook of Industrial and oeganizational psychology*, (pp. 63–130). Rand-McNally.

Celma, D., Martinez-Garcia, E., & Raya, J. M. (2018). Socially responsible HR practices and their effects on employees' wellbeing: Empirical evidence from Catalonia, Spain. *European Research on Management and Business Economics*, *24*(2), 82–89. doi:10.1016/j.iedeen.2017.12.001

Chakraborty, A. R., & Mansor, N. N. (2013). Adoption of Human Resource Information System: A Theoretical Analysis. *Procedia: Social and Behavioral Sciences*, *75*, 473–478. doi:10.1016/j.sbspro.2013.04.051

Chang, E., & Hancock, K. (2003). Role stress and role ambiguity in new nursing graduates in Australia. *Nursing & Health Sciences*, *5*(2), 155–163. doi:10.1046/j.1442-2018.2003.00147.x PMID:12709171

Conger, J. A., & Kanungo, R. N. (1988). The Empowerment Process: Integrating Theory and Practice. *Academy of Management Review*, *13*(3), 471–482. doi:10.2307/258093

Cooper, B., Wang, J., Bartram, T., & Cooke, F. L. (2018). Well-being-oriented human resource management practices and employee performance in the Chinese banking sector: The role of social climate and resilience. *Human Resource Management*, *58*(1), 85–97. doi:10.1002/hrm.21934

Coutu, D. L. (2002). How resilience works. *Harvard Business Review*, *80*, 46–55. PMID:12024758

De Cooman, R., De Gieter, S., Pepermans, R., Jegers, M., & Van Acker, F. (2009). Development and validation of the work effort scale. *European Journal of Psychological Assessment*, *25*(4), 266–273. doi:10.1027/1015-5759.25.4.266

De-la-Calle-Durán, M. C., & Rodríguez-Sánchez, J. L. (2021). Employee Engagement and Wellbeing in Times of COVID-19: A Proposal of the 5Cs Model. *International Journal of Environmental Research and Public Health*, *18*(10), 5470. doi:10.3390/ijerph18105470 PMID:34065338

Desanctis, G. (1986). Human Resource Information Systems: A Current Assessment. *Management Information Systems Quarterly*, *10*(1), 15. doi:10.2307/248875

Dey, T., Kumar, A., & Kumar, Y. L. N. (2014). A New Look at the Antecedents and Consequences of Organizational Commitment: A Conceptual Study. *International Journal of Humanities and Social Science*, *4*(1).

Donkin, R. (2010). *The history of work*. Palgrave Macmillan. doi:10.1057/9780230282179

Duchek, S. (2019). Organizational resilience: A capability-based conceptualization. *Business Research, 13*(1), 215–246. doi:10.100740685-019-0085-7

Ederer, F. P. (2004). Feedback and Motivation in Dynamic Tournaments. SSRN *Electronic Journal*. doi:10.2139/ssrn.691384

Erim, T. (2018). *Expanding the Conceptual Boundaries of Work Effort*. Springer Fachmedien Wiesbaden.

Fındıklı, M. A., & Bayarçelik, E. (2015). Exploring the Outcomes of Electronic Human Resource Management (E-HRM)? *Procedia: Social and Behavioral Sciences, 207*, 424–431. doi:10.1016/j.sbspro.2015.10.112

Fogarty, P., Frantz, S., Hirschfeld, J., Keating, S., Lafont, E., Lufkin, B., Mishael, R., Ponnavolu, V., Savage, M., & Turits, M. (2020, October 23). *Coronavirus: How the world of work may change forever*. Bbc.com. BBC. https://www.bbc.com/worklife/article/20201023-coronavirus-how-will-the-pandemic-change-the-way-we-work

Fredrickson, B. L. (2001). The role of positive emotions in positive psychology: The broaden-and-build theory of positive emotions. *The American Psychologist, 56*(3), 218–226. doi:10.1037/0003-066X.56.3.218 PMID:11315248

Garg, P., & Paul, H. (2012). Elevating organizational consequences through employee resilience. *In conference proceeding of National Conference on Emerging Challenges for Sustainable Business held at IIT Roorkee during June, 1*(2), 811-828

Golembiewski, R. T. (2001). *Handbook of Organizational Behavior*. Marcel Dekker.

Green, F. (2004). Why Has Work Effort Become More Intense? *Industrial Relations, 43*(4), 709–741. doi:10.1111/j.0019-8676.2004.00359.x

Green, F., & McIntosh, S. (2001). The intensification of work in Europe. *Labour Economics, 8*(2), 291–308. doi:10.1016/S0927-5371(01)00027-6

Griffin, M., Neal, A., & Neale, M. (2000). The Contribution of Task Performance and Contextual Performance to Effectiveness: Investigating the Role of Situational Constraints. *Applied Psychology, 49*(3), 517–533. doi:10.1111/1464-0597.00029

Griffin, M., & Rafferty, A. E. (2006). Perceptions of organizational change: A stress and coping perspective. *The Journal of Applied Psychology, 91*(5), 1154–1162. doi:10.1037/0021-9010.91.5.1154 PMID:16953776

Guest, D. E. (2017). Human resource management and employee well-being: Towards a new analytic framework. *Human Resource Management Journal, 27*(1), 22–38. doi:10.1111/1748-8583.12139

Hendrickson, A. R. (2003). Human resource information Systems: Backbone technology of contemporary human resources. *Journal of Labor Research, 24*(3), 381–394. doi:10.100712122-003-1002-5

Hobfoll, S. E. (2001). The Influence of Culture, Community, and the Nested-Self in the Stress Process: Advancing Conservation of Resources Theory. *Applied Psychology, 50*(3), 337–421. doi:10.1111/1464-0597.00062

Hobfoll, S. E., Chen, S., & Westman, M. (2015). The Commerce and Crossover of Resources: Resource Conservation in the Service of Resilience. *Stress and Health, 31*(2), 95–105. doi:10.1002mi.2574 PMID:25873421

Huselid, M. A. (1995). The Impact Of Human Resource Management Practices On Turnover, Productivity, And Corporate Financial Performance. *Academy of Management Journal, 38*(3), 635–672. doi:10.2307/256741

Huselid, M. A., & Delaney, J. T. (1996). The Impact Of Human Resource Management Practices On Perceptions Of Organizational Performance. *Academy of Management Journal, 39*(4), 949–969. doi:10.2307/256718

Huselid, M. A., Jackson, S. E., & Schuler, R. S. (1997). Technical and strategic human resources management effectiveness as determinants of firm performance. *Academy of Management Journal, 40*(1), 171–188. doi:10.2307/257025

Ichniowski, C., Kochan, T. A., Levine, D. I., Olson, C., & Strauss, G. (1996). What Works at Work: Overview and Assessment. *The American Workplace,* 1–37. doi:10.1017/CBO9780511620027.002

Jamal, M. (1999). Job stress and employee well-being: A cross-cultural empirical study. *Stress Medicine, 15*(3), 153–158. doi:10.1002/(SICI)1099-1700(199907)15:3<153::AID-SMI809>3.0.CO;2-0

James, L. A., & James, L. R. (1989). Integrating work environment perceptions: Explorations into the measurement of meaning. *The Journal of Applied Psychology, 74*(5), 739–751. doi:10.1037/0021-9010.74.5.739

Johnson, J. L., & Wiechelt, S. A. (2004). Introduction to the Special Issue on Resilience. *Substance Use & Misuse, 39*(5), 657–670. doi:10.1081/JA-120034010 PMID:15202803

Jones, L. W. (2021). COVID-19 and Employee Mental Health: What Employers Can Do. *Employee Relations Law Journal, 47*(1).

Kanfer, R. (1990). Motivation theory and Industrial/Organizational psychology. In M. D. Dunette and L. Hough (Eds.), Handbook of industrial and organizational psychology, Volume 1: Theory in industrial and organizational psychology, (pp.77-170). Palo Alto, CA. Consulting Psychologists Press.

Killgore, W. D., Cloonan, S. A., Taylor, E. C., & Dailey, N. S. (2020). Loneliness: A signature mental health concern in the era of COVID-19. *Psychiatry Research, 290,* 113117. doi:10.1016/j.psychres.2020.113117 PMID:32480121

Kim, K., & Park, H. (2018). The Effects of Technostress On Information Technology Acceptance. *Journal of Theoretical and Applied Information Technology, 96*(24), 1817-3195

King, R. C., & Sethi, V. (1997). The moderating effect of organizational commitment on burnout in information systems professionals. *European Journal of Information Systems, 6*(2), 86–96. doi:10.1057/palgrave.ejis.3000259

Kovach, K. A., & Cathcart, C. E. Jr. (1999). Human resource information systems (HRIS): Providing business with rapid data access, information exchange and strategic advantage. *Public Personnel Management, 28*(2), 275–282. doi:10.1177/009102609902800208

Kuntz, J. R., Malinen, S., & Näswall, K. (2017). Employee resilience: Directions for resilience development. *Consulting Psychology Journal, 69*(3), 223–242. doi:10.1037/cpb0000097

LaBerge, L., O'Toole, C., Schneider, J., & Smaje, K. (2020, October 5). *McKinsey Digital and Strategy & Corporate Finance Practices.* McKinsey & Company. https://www.mckinsey.com/business-functions/strategy-and-corporate-finance/our-insights/how-covid-19-has-pushed-companies-over-the-technology-tipping-point-and-transformed-business-forever

Langkamer, K. L., & Ervin, K. S. (2008). Psychological Climate, Organizational Commitment and Morale: Implications for Army Captains' Career Intent. *Military Psychology, 20*(4), 219–236. doi:10.1080/08995600802345113

Lengnick-Hall, C. A., Beck, T. E., & Lengnick-Hall, M. L. (2011). Developing a capacity for organizational resilience through strategic human resource management. *Human Resource Management Review, 21*(3), 243–255. doi:10.1016/j.hrmr.2010.07.001

Lippert, S. K., & Swiercz, P. M. (2005). Human resource information systems (HRIS) and technology trust. *Journal of Information Science, 31*(5), 340–353. doi:10.1177/0165551505055399

Locke, E. A., Frederick, E., Lee, C., & Bobko, P. (1984). Effect of self-efficacy, goals, and task strategies on task performance. *The Journal of Applied Psychology, 69*(2), 241–251. doi:10.1037/0021-9010.69.2.241

Longstaff, P. H., & Yang, S. U. (2008). Communication management and trust: Their role in building resilience to "surprises" such as natural disasters, pandemic flu, and terrorism. *Ecology and Society, 13*(1). doi:10.5751/ES-02232-130103

Luthans, F. (2002). The need for and meaning of positive organizational behavior. *Journal of Organizational Behavior, 23*(6), 695–706. doi:10.1002/job.165

Luthans, F., Vogelgesang, G. R., & Lester, P. B. (2006). Developing the Psychological Capital of Resiliency. *Human Resource Development Review, 5*(1), 25–44. doi:10.1177/1534484305285335

Luthans, F., & Youssef, C. (2007). Positive Organizational Behavior in the Workplace: The Impact of Hope, Optimism, and Resilience. *Journal of Management, 33*(5), 774–800. doi:10.1177/0149206307305562

Marler, J. H. (2009). Making human resources strategic by going to the net: Reality or myth? *International Journal of Human Resource Management, 20*(3), 515–527. doi:10.1080/09585190802707276

Martin, G., Reddington, M., & Alexander, H. (2008). *Technology, outsourcing and transforming Hr.* Elsevier. doi:10.4324/9780080560984

Masten, A. S. (2001). Ordinary magic: Resilience processes in development. *The American Psychologist, 56*(3), 227–238. doi:10.1037/0003-066X.56.3.227 PMID:11315249

McClean, E., & Collins, C. J. (2011). High-commitment HR practices, employee effort, and firm performance: Investigating the effects of HR practices across employee groups within professional services firms. *Human Resource Management, 50*(3), 341–363. doi:10.1002/hrm.20429

Meng, H., Luo, Y., Huang, L., Wen, J., Ma, J., & Xi, J. (2017). On the relationships of resilience with organizational commitment and burnout: A social exchange perspective. *International Journal of Human Resource Management, 30*(15), 2231–2250. doi:10.1080/09585192.2017.1381136

Meredith, L. S., Sherbourne, C. D., Gaillot, S. J., Hansell, L., Ritschard, H. V., Parker, A. M., & Wrenn, G. (2011). Promoting psychological resilience in the US military. *Rand Health Quarterly, 1*(2). PMID:28083176

Meyer, J. P., Klein, H. J., & Becker, T. E. (Eds.). (2009). *Commitment in Organizations: Accumulated Wisdom and New Diretions,* (1st ed.). Routledge. doi:10.4324/9780203883122

Mukherjee, A. N., Bhattacharyya, S., & Bera, R. (2014). Role of Information Technology in Human Resource Management of SME: A Study on the use of Applicant Tracking System. *IBMRD's. Journal of Management Research, 3*(1).

Näswall, K., Kuntz, J., Hodliffe, M., & Malinen, S. (2015). *Employee resilience scale (EmpRes) measurement properties*. Resilient Organizations Research Programme.

Nivlouei, F. B. (2014). Electronic Human Resource Management System: The Main Element in Capacitating Globalization Paradigm. *International Journal of Business and Social Science, 5*(2), 147–159.

Organ, D. W. (1997). Organizational Citizenship Behavior: It's Construct Clean-Up Time. *Human Performance, 10*(2), 85–97. doi:10.120715327043hup1002_2

Panayotopoulou, L., Vakola, M., & Galanaki, E. (2007). E-HR adoption and the role of HRM: Evidence from Greece. *Personnel Review, 36*(2), 277–294. doi:10.1108/00483480710726145

Parsons, T. (1968). *The Structure of Social Action*. Free Press.

Pfeffer, J., Anderson, P., Arthur, M. B., Baruch, J. J., Bowen, D. E., & Bessant, J. (2002). Competitive Advantage Through People (J. Henry & D. Mayle, Eds.). In Managing Innovation and Change, (2nd ed.), pp. 61-73). London, MK. SAGE Publications.

Podsakoff, P. M., MacKenzie, S. B., Paine, J. B., & Bachrach, D. G. (2000). Organizational Citizenship Behaviors: A Critical Review of the Theoretical and Empirical Literature and Suggestions for Future Research. *Journal of Management, 26*(3), 513–563. doi:10.1177/014920630002600307

Porter, L. W., Steers, R. M., Mowday, R. T., & Boulian, P. V. (1974). Organizational commitment, job satisfaction, and turnover among psychiatric technicians. *The Journal of Applied Psychology, 59*(5), 603–609. doi:10.1037/h0037335

Robinson, G. W. (1998). New Teacher Induction: A Study of Selected New Teacher Induction Models and Common Practices.

Rothwell, A., & Arnold, J. (2005). How hr professionals rate 'continuing professional development'. *Human Resource Management Journal, 15*(3), 18–32. doi:10.1111/j.1748-8583.2005.tb00151.x

Saha, N., Gregar, A., & Sáha, P. (2017). Organizational agility and hrm strategy: Do they really enhance firms' competitiveness? *International Journal of Organizational Leadership, 6*(3), 323–334. doi:10.33844/ijol.2017.60454

Sailer, M., Hense, J., Mandl, H., & Klevers, M. (2013). Psychological Perspectives on Motivation through Gamification. *Interaction Design and Architecture(s). Journal, 19*, 28–37.

Sareen, P., & Subramanian, K. V. (2012). E-HRM: A Strategic Review. *International Journal of Human Resource Studies, 2*(3), 119. doi:10.5296/ijhrs.v2i3.2100

Sharma, J., & Dhar, R. L. (2016). Factors influencing job performance of nursing staff: Mediating role of affective commitment. *Personnel Review, 45*(1), 161–182. doi:10.1108/PR-01-2014-0007

Sheridan, T. B. (2008). Risk, Human Error, and System Resilience: Fundamental Ideas. *Human Factors, 50*(3), 418–426. doi:10.1518/001872008X250773 PMID:18689048

Shin, J., Taylor, M. S., & Seo, M.-G. (2012). Resources for Change: The Relationships of Organizational Inducements and Psychological Resilience to Employees' Attitudes and Behaviors toward Organizational Change. *Academy of Management Journal, 55*(3), 727–748. doi:10.5465/amj.2010.0325

Shoss, M. K., Jiang, L., & Probst, T. M. (2018). Bending without breaking: A two-study examination of employee resilience in the face of job insecurity. *Journal of Occupational Health Psychology, 23*(1), 112–126. doi:10.1037/ocp0000060 PMID:27786505

Sinclair, R. R., Britt, T. W., Shen, W., Grossman, M. R., & Klieger, D. M. (2016). How Much Do We Really Know About Employee Resilience? *Industrial and Organizational Psychology: Perspectives on Science and Practice, 9*(2), 378–404. doi:10.1017/iop.2015.107

Stout, J. K., & Posner, J. L. (1984). Stress, Role Ambiguity, and Role Conflict. *Psychological Reports, 55*(3), 747–753. doi:10.2466/pr0.1984.55.3.747 PMID:6522540

Strohmeier, S. (2007). Research in e-hrm: Review and implications. *Human Resource Management Review, 17*(1), 19–37. doi:10.1016/j.hrmr.2006.11.002

Sullivan, G. M., & Artino, A. R. Jr. (2013). Analyzing and interpreting data from Likert-type scales. *Journal of Graduate Medical Education, 5*(4), 541–542. doi:10.4300/JGME-5-4-18 PMID:24454995

Teo, T. S., Lim, G. S., & Fedric, S. A. (2007). The adoption and diffusion of human resources information systems in Singapore. *Asia Pacific Journal of Human Resources, 45*(1), 44–62. doi:10.1177/1038411107075402

The Economist Intelligence Unit. (2015).Organizational Resilience: Building an Enduring Enterprise. *The British Standards Institution.* https://www.bsigroup.com/en-GB/our-services/Organizational-Resilience/Organizational-Resilience-research-EIU/

Troshani, I., Jerram, C., & Gerrard, M. (2010). Exploring the organizational adoption of human resources information systems (HRIS) in the Australian public sector. *Proceedings of the 21st Australasian Conference on Information Systems (ACIS2010)*, Brisbane, Australia.

Tusaie, K., & Dyer, J. (2004). Resilience: A Historical Review of the Construct. *Holistic Nursing Practice, 18*(1), 3–10. doi:10.1097/00004650-200401000-00002 PMID:14765686

Ulrich, D. (1998). A New Mandate for Human Resources. *Harvard Businee Review, 01.*

Ulrich, D., Storey, J., & Wright, P. M. (2019). *Strategic human resource management: A research overview.* Routledge.

Van Dam, A., Noordzij, G., & Born, M. P. (2020). Linking the Fit Between Achievement Goal Orientation and Learning Opportunities With Employee Well-Being and Absenteeism. *Journal of Personnel Psychology*, *19*(4), 184–196. doi:10.1027/1866-5888/a000260

Webster, N. (1977). *The Merriam-Webster dictionary*. Pocket Books.

Williams, N., & Vorley, T. (2014). Economic resilience and entrepreneurship: Lessons from the Sheffield City Region. *Entrepreneurship and Regional Development*, *26*(3-4), 257–281. doi:10.1080/08985626.2014.894129

Wright, P. M., & McMahan, G. C. (1992). Theoretical perspectives for Strategic human resource management. *Journal of Management*, *18*(2), 295–320. doi:10.1177/014920639201800205

Wu, C.-H., & Parker, S. K. (2016). The Role of Leader Support in Facilitating Proactive Work Behavior. *Journal of Management*, *43*(4), 1025–1049. doi:10.1177/0149206314544745

Yu, C., & Frenkel, S. J. (2012). Explaining task performance and creativity from perceived organizational support theory: Which mechanisms are more important? *Journal of Organizational Behavior*, *34*(8), 1165–1181. doi:10.1002/job.1844

Zhou, Y., Liu, G., Chang, X., & Wang, L. (2020). The impact of HRM digitalization on firm performance: Investigating three-way interactions. *Asia Pacific Journal of Human Resources*, *59*(1), 20–43. doi:10.1111/1744-7941.12258

## KEY TERMS AND DEFINITIONS

**Affective Commitment:** Employee's emotional attachment towards the organization.

**Covid-19:** Covid-19 pandemic which broke out in 2019.

**Digital HR:** Online information system of human resources.

**E-HRM:** The general term used for specialized information system of HR processes.

**Organizational Citizenship Behaviors:** Positive employee behaviors regardless of direct rewards from the organization.

**Organizational Commitment:** Employee's attachment towards the organization which indicates negative correlation with negative consequences such as turnover intentions.

**Positive Psychology:** The new approach in psychology which focuses on the strengths rather than weaknesses.

**Psychological Capital (Psycap):** Employee's psychological resources such as optimism, self-efficacy, hope, and resilience.

**Work Effort:** The effort spent by the employee in the achievement of a goal or a task.

**WFH:** Working from home

# Chapter 13
# Innovation Leadership:
## Understanding Its Potential for Adoption of Big Data Analytics in Healthcare Organizations

**Jyoti Motwani**
*Malviya National Institute of Technology, India*

**Aakanskha Kataria**
*Malaviya National Institute of Technology, India*

## ABSTRACT

*Motivated by the significant role and importance of big data analytics in health care sector and the critical influence of innovation leadership, the authors study the impact of innovation leadership on adoption of big data analytics in Indian health care sector. Besides, the authors study the mediating effect of organization readiness on the relationship of innovation leadership and big data analytics adoption. The conceptual framework is built keeping in view the organization information processing theory as the theoretical lens. To conduct the study, the authors adopted survey method that was administered to the sample of general managers, senior and junior managers and other healthcare professionals acting as decision authorities for adopting new technologies within organization.*

## INTRODUCTION

Across industries, there has been rapid digitalization over the last decade. With the increasing penetration of Electronic Medical Records (EMRs), Healthcare Information Systems (HIS), handheld wearables, and smart devices, healthcare has also undergone this digital change. As a result, other than clinical data, a vast amount and variety of health-related data is now available in digital form, including omic data, socio-demographic data, and insurance claims data. This digital data can potentially improve healthcare

DOI: 10.4018/978-1-6684-5864-8.ch013

delivery by offering high-quality information. Unfortunately, this huge amount of data i.e., *"big data"* is still seen as a "by-product" of healthcare delivery rather than a strategic tool for competitive advantage (Mehta & Pandit, 2018).

The necessity for turning raw data into valuable and actionable information exists because electronic health data is frequently underutilized and thus wasted. Unstructured or semi-structured data makes up a large portion of instrumental healthcare data. Furthermore, typical data analyzing methods and methodologies struggle to extract usable information due to the data's complex, dynamic, and heterogeneous properties. In fact, without proper decision support, a human's ability to process this data is limited (Wang & Hajli, 2017; Cyganek et al., 2016). Therefore, to help solve this problem, '*Big Data Analytics'* is increasingly seen as a promising solution that *is continuously being integrated into healthcare.*

Big data analytics (BDA), in its broadest sense, can be elucidated as the analytical process deploying techniques to analyze large and diverse sets of structured, semi-structured, and unstructured data from different sources, and in various sizes from terabytes to zettabytes (Zakir et al., 2015). It can analyze a variety of complex data as well as provide useful insights that otherwise would be impossible to obtain. When applied to healthcare data, it has the potential to uncover trends, resulting in enhanced healthcare quality and cost savings, as well as the ability to make timely decisions. As per the report by McKinsey Global Institute, by utilizing big data effectively, healthcare can create a value of more than $300 billion every year, of which two-thirds would reduce healthcare expenditure by about 8%. Big data technologies can reveal hidden knowledge and automated examination of outcomes. Easy access to longitudinal patient data is now possible, thanks to advancements in cloud computing and the greater adoption of EMRs. Integration of longitudinal patient data with data from heterogeneous, structured, and unstructured big data sources opens up the possibility of a much better and faster comprehensive understanding of diseases. Big data analytics capacity to detect illness heterogeneity helps for speedy and accurate diagnosis and therapy evaluation. The predictive capability of big data analytics can also be utilized to transform continuous real-time data into meaningful information by integrating data from many sources and recognizing trends. In emergency medical settings, this is critical since it can mean the difference between life and death.

The promising value of big data technology in healthcare has created an increasing interest in academic & industry investigators. However, the adoption of big data analytics is still in its early stages and must be coordinated to address healthcare delivery problems and improve healthcare quality. Besides, there are certain enabling factors that affect the derived value from big data analytics such as data capturing and storage capabilities, data integration capabilities, top management's willingness to adopt big data analytics, financial feasibility, organization structure, and change management programs etc. Most importantly, '*organizational leadership*' acts as backbone to the process for the potential application of these enablers and execution of such change management programs (Bag et al., 2021; Ajmal et al.,2012).

More specifically, amongst all other leadership styles, innovative leadership includes the proper way to encourage individuals to take various initiatives, develop a transparent performance measurement system, and build an environment in which quality relationships would be treasured. Innovation is related to "out-of-the-box" thinking and introducing something new, such as new ideas, methods, or devices. Good innovation leadership will lead to increased creativities and readiness in the organization to adopt new technology, in our case, big data analytics. Besides, innovation leadership motivates individuals to be risk tolerant and readily accept any form of change management programs occurring within organizations.

Notwithstanding the significant potential impact of innovative leadership on adoption of big data analytics, the extant literature has failed to contemplate on this particular construct (Toufaili et al., 2021).

Hence, in an attempt to address this issue, our study based upon the "upper echelons" perspective argues that managerial background characteristics shape firm performance and innovation adoption. "Upper echelons"-based leadership theory can shed light on the leader's observable managerial characteristics to bring about circumstances such as technology adoption. Carmeli et al., (2010) argued that innovation leadership could improve strategic fit and further enhance the firm performance via adoption of big data analytics. Applying innovative thinking to leadership tasks can spur the whole organization to begin thinking in innovative ways, thereby leading to organizational readiness and further successful adoption and implementation of big data analytics.

Observing the crucial role of big data analytics in the healthcare sector and the critical influence of innovation leadership for its adoption, we study the impact of innovation leadership on adopting big data analytics in Indian healthcare sector. We further aim to explore the role of organization readiness in the relationship of innovation leadership and big data analytics adoption. The conceptual framework is built keeping in view the organization's information processing theory as the theoretical lens.

Consequently, the main research questions that our study intends to answer include;

RQ1: What is the role of innovation leadership in the adoption of big data analytics in Indian health care sector?

RQ2: How does organization readiness impacts the relationship between innovation leadership and adoption of big data analytics?

## THEORETICAL BACKGROUND AND HYPOTHESIS DEVELOPMENT

### Organization Innovation Processing Theory

According to IPT theory, in order to survive in an increasingly uncertain business environment, businesses must improve their information processing capacity. The COVID-19 pandemic has led to turmoil and dynamicity in both human and business lives. These uncertainties are forcing the business organizations to develop information processing capabilities, and adopt disruptive Industry 4.0 technologies like BDA that can assist them in scanning, collecting, organizing, and analysing data and make strategic decisions. The information processing theory explains how managers can build up and improve their information processing capability to assess external data such as supply crises, market demands, sales and competitors' distribution activities, rate of infection spread, number of infected cases, number of recoveries, number of deaths, and clinical trial monitoring and outcomes. OIPT has been used in the past to explain supply chain issues. During these unpredictable epidemic times, we propose that BDA improves firms' information processing capability.

#### Innovative Leadership

Innovative leadership is one of the most prevalent yet least understood phenomena, despite substantial research on it (Sen & Eron, 2012). In literature, leadership has been described as a function of an individual's, a group's, and an environment's personality. It is described as a mechanism for getting people to unanimously understand what has to be done efficiently and for facilitating individual and group efforts to realise an organization's common goal. As an alternative to the style of leadership where command and control have traditionally been at the forefront, a number of models have recently been developed. These models include transformational leadership (Rost, 1993), charismatic leadership (Conger & Kanungo, 1988), self-leadership (Manz & Sims, 1987), visionary leadership (Nanus, 1992), and democratic leadership (Ackoff, 1994).

Our study elucidates leadership as a process whereby leaders aim to develop a shared vision to achieve the goals, analyze external and internal conditions, develop and implement leadership strategies for solving problems, and readily accept the innovations as per the organization's needs. Considering this framework, innovative leadership is implementing radical changes through one or more innovations to address challenges in the areas of politics, economics, society, technology, and the environment and to better serve and thrive in the market. Innovative leaders have a clear vision for transforming and improving existing political, social, economic, and technological conditions in order to address current needs and predict future problems, thereby prescribing the potential solutions in advance. They are aware of the past, the present, and the future (Blanchard et al., 2004). They have a clear vision for the future and are determined to act bravely and take calculated risks to make that vision a reality. As mentioned, innovative leaders believe in a shared vision that is the reflection of fundamental beliefs and expressions of strong desires, aspirations, and dreams of an organization and its employees to achieve something great. These shared visions help innovative leaders in creating focus, identifying direction, inspire and unite people in a common effort, and aligning core values of people for successful implementation.

## BIG DATA ANALYTICS

In a recent article, Forbes while discussing a survey from Deloitte, revealed that 49% of respondents stated analytics helps them in better decision making, 16% responded, it enables key strategic initiatives and 10% said it helps to improve relationship with both customers and business partners. In this customer driven market, information is pre-requisite for the success of business organizations. Big data is characterized by its large size (volume) high speed (velocity) and heterogeneity (variety) that requires advanced techniques and tools for analysis. Big data analytics, along with its tools extract and analyse the systematic and relevant data from the chunks of data available to unveil the hidden trends and relations. Big data analytics helps to get the answers for various queries; it helps in creating various alternatives and choosing the best alternative for the purpose of timely decision making. Perhaps it is best to think of Big Data in multidimensional terms, in which three dimensions relate to the primary aspects of Big Data (Russom, 2011). These dimensions can be defined as follows:

- ***Volume-*** Volume refers to the size of data. With real-time inflow of information, the size of data which organizations receive is very large
- ***Variety-*** Variety refers to the heterogeneity of data; Data comes in various forms and hence is unstructured.
- ***Velocity-*** It is defined as the speed at which data flows. With increasing no. of platforms and user awareness data inflow takes at high speed which sometimes gets unmanageable if not handled with proper tool.

In this highly competitive market acquiring, recording analysing and interpreting data requires new and faster techniques. Big Data Analytics is proving itself to be a competitive edge and a resource that

*Table 1. Stages of Data Analytics*

| Descriptive Analysis | Diagnostic Analysis | Predictive Analysis | Prescriptive Analyis |
|---|---|---|---|
| This type of analysis answers what is happening. Its most common in all forms of business and is the first step towards decision making. | It answers why it happened, what is the root cause of a problem. This is the second step in the complexity of data analytics. | Predictive models help in forecasting the happening of events. These models are the most utilized tools across many fields. | This is the most critical stage whereby organization after considering all the data generated at previous stages looks for best alternatives available and choses the best course of action. |

promotes innovation and creativity along with timely decision making (Zakir et al.2015). Organizations have realised that data is no less than gold which has to be mined to find the nuggets of value to have positive impact on bottom line and overall performance of the organization.

## Innovation Leadership and Big Data Analytics

Support from top management is critical in creating a supportive environment and allocating enough resources for the adoption of new technology (Lin and Lee, 2005; Wang et al., 2010; Paley, 2017). As advancement in technology is precipitating complexity in technology adoption, senior management leadership can give the vision, support, and motivation needed to promote innovation (Lee and Kim, 2007; McAfee and Brynjolfsson, 2012). In our context, because BDA technologies demand proper resources, data and architecture integration, and user coordination, top management leadership is much more important. Carmeli et al. (2010) made the case for innovation leadership, asserting that it can increase strategic fit and boost company performance. The innovative nature of organisation leaders can be defined as prioritising and encouraging teamwork, clarifying individual roles and responsibilities, providing clear feedback to employees, emphasising task orientation, supporting initiatives, and creating trust among employees, among other things. Forecasting and planning activities in an uncertain corporate environment under COVID-19 is extremely tough. Disasters and pandemic events add to the uncertainty, and if executives continue to work in the same way they do under normal circumstances, their firms will not survive. When dealing with business issues during pandemics, innovative leadership can be quite beneficial. Applying innovative thinking to leadership activities can encourage staff to think outside the box and adopt new technology such as big data analytics (Horth and Buchner, 2014). As a result, we propose the following hypothesis:

*H1: Innovation leadership significantly impacts adoption of big data analytics*

## Innovation Leadership and Change Readiness

One of the crucial factors in the context of organizational change management program is the influential role of leaders (Nordin, 2011). Given the pervasiveness and constant need for change, extant literature has identified different leadership behaviours to have significant impact on individual effectiveness while implementation of change management programs (Lyons et al., 2009). Organizational support in the form of innovative leadership may play a crucial role in developing change readiness among employees in multiple ways. First, the social support may aid in developing the feeling of control while the change is taking place (Gigliotti, 2019). Opining similarly, Kirrane et al., (2017) supported the proposition by demonstrating a positive association between managerial support and readiness for change in their study. Also, organizational support fosters positive feelings towards change implementation and allows individuals to take greater risks with comfort, thereby, positively reciprocating to change management programs. Neves & Eisenberger (2014) suggested leadership styles stimulate psychological safety of individuals during the situations of uncertainties, such as organizational changes. In this sense, leadership behaviours have proved to provide significant positive results for employee productivity and readiness for change adoption (Leban & Zulauf, 2004; Gigliotti et al., 2018). Therefore, we propose;

*H2: Innovation leadership significantly impacts change readiness levels within organizations*

### Organization Readiness and Big Data Analytics Adoption

The introduction and adoption of new technology is a costly process in context to time invested, human expertise required, and organizational energy applied. Organizations while upgrading or changing the technological solutions in their business processes, often find individual resistance and reluctance as major obstacle in achieving the desired change. According to Jones (2003) organizational resistance to change implementation is one of the significant reasons behind failure to IT innovation and new technology adoption. In solution to such resistance, findings from literature suggest that the individual's perception of the technology's complexity (Rogers, 1995), attitude toward the technology (Burkhardt and Brass, 1990), personal innovativeness (Agarwal and Prasad, 1998), or anxiety about using a technology (Simonson et al., 1987) must be properly addressed before implementing new technology. This in turn would result in greater willingness and readiness for undergoing the change and adopting new IT solutions. Thus, it is believed that successful technology innovation and adoption is result to organizational change represented by individual willingness and readiness to innovation, and modification of activities in response to planned change management program (Lippert and Davis, 2006).

*H3: Organization readiness significantly impacts big data analytics (BDA) adoption*

*H4: Organization readiness mediates between innovation leadership and big data analytics adoption*

## PROPOSED RESEARCH MODEL

This research intends to address one of the major gaps in the literature and empirically examines the relationship between innovative leadership and big data analytics adoption in the presence of organization readiness.

*Figure 1. Research Model*

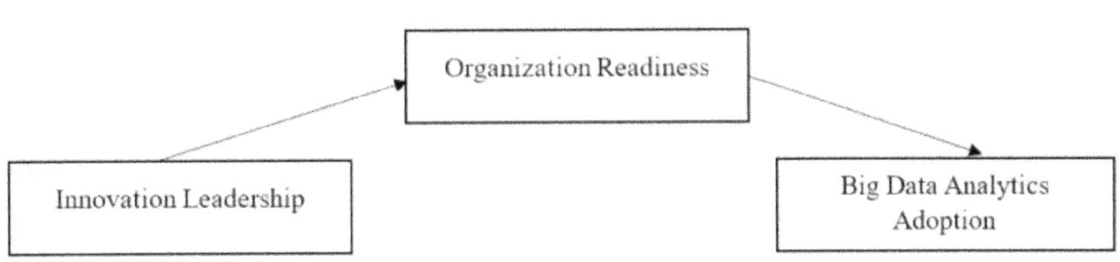

## Research Methodology

### Sampling

To address the stated research questions, we adopted survey method that was administered to the sample of general managers, senior and junior managers and other healthcare professionals acting as decision authorities for adopting new technologies within organization. Besides, this sample also included HR managers responsible for implication of change management program within organization. Besides, only those healthcare organizations were taken into consideration that are capable enough for investing in BDA technologies.

We targeted a total of 550 potential respondents using convenient sampling method. The final questionnaire was prepared and sent using Google Forms. The first cycle of data collection was performed in March, 2022 and we received 175 responses without any follow-up. However, after a round of follow-up we received 123 more responses by mid-April which provided us with total of 298 responses representing a response rate of 54%. On screening the responses, there were no incomplete responses, as the google forms were designed with all questions as mandatory. The demographic details of respondents are presented in Table 2.

### Measures

The administered survey questionnaire consisted of 27 items. A 4-item scale developed by Yoon et al., (2016) was used to measure the construct of innovation leadership. Dunham et al. (1989) proposed a 13- item scale to measure organization readiness and the same is used in our context. Lastly, to assess BDA adoption, we used the scale developed by Raguseo & Vitari (2018).

*Table 2. Demographical Information of Respondents*

| Category | | Frequency | Percentage |
|---|---|---|---|
| Gender | Male | 139 | 46.64 |
| | Female | 159 | 53.36 |
| | **TOTAL** | 298 | 100 |
| | | | |
| Age | 25-30 | 105 | 35.23 |
| | 30-35 | 92 | 30.87 |
| | 35-40 | 49 | 16.44 |
| | 40 & above | 52 | 17.45 |
| | **TOTAL** | 298 | 100 |
| | | | |
| Education | Bachelor | 145 | 48.66 |
| | Master | 124 | 41.61 |
| | Doctoral | 29 | 9.73 |
| | **TOTAL** | 298 | 100 |

## RESULTS FOR EXPLORATORY FACTOR ANALYSIS

Exploratory factor analysis was conducted using principal component analysis and varimax rotation (SPSS-26). We set the minimum factor loading criteria to 0.4. Consequently, the results were assessed on the basis of the threshold values recommended by Hair et al. (2010). The KMO measure of sampling adequacy came out to be 0.892 which is considered appropriate to be acceptable; the results of Bartletts' Test of Sphericity, that shows the probability of correlation among the components came out to be significant at $p < 0.00$ (Table 2). Further, the communalities that represent the amount of variance shared was greater than 0.50 for each dimension representing acceptable levels of explanation. The rotated component matrix yielded seven factors (Table 3). The first factor talks about the strategic and transformational values of big data analytics adoption, the second factor represents the attributes of innovation leadership, the third, fourth, fifth, and seventh factor depicts different attributes of organization readiness, and lastly, the sixth factor states the informational values for adoption of big data analytics.

### CFA and Path Analysis

Prior to performing path analysis, we undertook the reliability and validity test for the factors generated. The Cronbach's alpha values for all the factors were greater than 0.7 depicting acceptable values. For composite reliability (CR) and AVE values ranged between 0.7 to 0.9 and 0.6 to 0.85 respectively, which were again within the defined and acceptable ranges (Flynn B, 1990; Hair et al., 1998). Subsequently, CFA was performed through AMOS-26 to examine the consistency and validity of the proposed framework for the study. CFA results generated the following values; CMIN/DF= 2.689, root mean square error of approximation (RMSEA)= 0.072, PGFI= 0.680, and Tucker-Lewis ft index (TLI) = 0.9. All the CFA values stood in line with the given threshold values by Hair et al. (2010).

After analysing the goodness of fit of the model, we further moved on to check the results of structural model. The results of structural model depict that the indirect effect of innovation leadership on adoption of big data analytics through the mediation impact of organization readiness is significant with path coefficient value of 0.68 ($p < 0.05$). Whereas, the direct influence of innovation leadership on adoption of big data analytics holds the path coefficient value of 0.24 with significant p value ($p < 0.05$). Thus, it can be concluded that organization readiness partially mediates the relationship between innovation leadership and organization's adoption of big data analytics. Therefore, this study supports all the proposed hypothesis by presenting the positive relationship between the given variables (innovation leadership, organization readiness, and big data analytics). Table 5 presents the results of structural model.

*Table 3. KMO and Bartlett's Test*

| | | |
|---|---|---|
| Kaiser-Meyer-Olkin Measure of Sampling Adequacy. | | .892 |
| Bartlett's Test of Sphericity | Approx. Chi-Square | 5515.675 |
| | df | 351 |
| | Sig. | .000 |

*Table 4. Rotated Component Matrix*

| | Component | | | | | | |
|---|---|---|---|---|---|---|---|
| | 1 | 2 | 3 | 4 | 5 | 6 | 7 |
| IL1 | | .822 | | | | | |
| IL2 | | .642 | | | | | |
| IL3 | | .676 | | | | | |
| IL4 | | .868 | | | | | |
| OR1 | | | .817 | | | | |
| OR2 | | | .762 | | | | |
| OR3 | | | .840 | | | | |
| OR4 | | | | | .454 | | |
| OR5 | | | | .686 | | | |
| OR6 | | | | .761 | | | |
| OR7 | | | | .698 | | | |
| OR8 | | | | .463 | | | |
| OR9 | | | | | .625 | | |
| OR10 | | | | | .600 | | |
| OR11 | | | | | .781 | | |
| OR12 | | | | | | | .567 |
| OR13 | | | | | | | .790 |
| SV1 | .723 | | | | | | |
| SV2 | .712 | | | | | | |
| SV3 | .725 | | | | | | |
| TV1 | .632 | | | | | | |
| TV2 | .732 | | | | | | |
| TV3 | .748 | | | | | | |
| TV4 | .679 | | | | | | |
| IV1 | | | | | | .527 | |
| IV2 | | | | | | .688 | |
| IV3 | | | | | | .651 | |

*Extraction Method: Principal Component Analysis.*
*Rotation Method: Varimax with Kaiser Normalization.*

*Table 5. Hypothesis Summary*

| Structural Path | Effect | p Value | |
|---|---|---|---|
| Innovation ⟶ Readiness | .166 | *** | Supported |
| Readiness ⟶ BDA Adoption | .513 | *** | Supported |
| Innovation ⟶ BDA Adoption | .240 | *** | Supported |
| Innovation⟶Readiness⟶BDA Adoption | .085 | *** | Supported |

*Note: *** significant at $p < 0.001$*

## DISCUSSION

Big data analytics constantly continues to revolutionize and make big changes in health care industry. In fact, the onset of global pandemic has accelerated the digital transformation in health care, specifically deploying big data analytics in order to decrease treatment cost, prediction of pandemic outbreaks, avoid preventable diseases, reduction of lead time in serving the patients, and improve the overall quality of service and patient's life. However, there still exists a flip side both in literature and practice i.e., how to generate the business value from big data analytics. On one hand, the literature lacks the empirical studies studying the impact of different factors on adoption of big data analytics; on the other hand, practitioners till date are struggling to successfully implement the change program for adoption of data analytics. The findings from our study suggest that innovation leadership significantly impacts big data analytics adoption. Also, organization readiness partially mediates the relationship between innovation leadership and big data analytics adoption. This further implies that future scholars can explore the impact of other variables like financial feasibility (Lamba & Singh, 2018), organization culture (Joshi & Biswas, 2018), technological structure (Ghaleb et al., 2021), firm size (Agrawal, 2015), human resources and their skills (Schull and Maslan, 2018) etc., on adoption of technologies like big data analytics.

## THEORETICAL IMPLICATIONS

One of the most prominent changes in the healthcare is the advent of digital revolution. Specifically big data analytics for healthcare has been the central focus of attention for academicians and practitioners (Bag et al., 2021). However, relatively lesser studies have explored the application of innovation leadership for adoption of big data analytics (Bag et al., 2021). Developing on this gap, our study aimed at exploring the relationship between innovation leadership and big data analytics adoption with mediation of organization readiness.

Adding in the current literature, we grounded our concept on the well-established organization innovation processing theory, that states that for organizations to survive the turmoil of outer business environment are required to develop and orchestrate digital transformations within their organizations. This will help them in gathering right information at right time, thereby allowing them to respond in timely fashion.

By analysing survey data from 298 hospital administrators, this study empirically explored the direct and indirect relationship between three constructs, namely innovation leadership, organization readiness and big data analytics adoption. Very few studies have jointly covered all three aspects. The paper has a notable contribution to the current literature, so that researchers can better understand the role of executives in adoption of BDA. The study provides a theoretical base of mediating the role of organization readiness for project performance for BDA implementation which has not been discussed much in past literature.

## PRACTICAL IMPLICATIONS

The results of our study have several interesting insights for managers in health care industry. The findings of the study suggests that the context of modern working organizations is characterized by technological advancement. In respect of health care organizations, those who aspire to achieve effectiveness and efficiency in serving the patients, maintaining cost, and optimally utilize the resources, are required to innovate in terms of technology like big data analytics.

However, one cannot deny the fact that implementation of new technology is not an easy task, and therefore, demands certain strong antecedents prior to adoption. Our study identifies innovative leadership as one such enabler to adoption of big data analytics within health care organizations. Executives should aim at developing the leadership qualities that promotes creative ideas, create a climate of reciprocal trust, and develop the risk-taking capabilities within individuals. This in turn would aid in successful execution and realizing the maximum business value out of the newly adopted technology.

Besides, understanding how organization readiness affects the willingness to change may increase the chances for successful adoption and implementation of innovative technology. Managers, specifically top management plays a significant role in engendering the culture of change. Therefore, prior to adoption, top executives must ensure that employees understand the usefulness of new innovation, and positively perceive the ease of use thereby having intention to use that in turn is reflected in their behaviour to adoption. Subsequently, productive and pragmatic association between employees and new technology may serve as a formative indicator of organization success.

## REFERENCES

Agarwal, R., & Prasad, J. (1998). A conceptual and operational definition of personal innovativeness in the domain of information technology. *Information Systems Research*, *9*(2), 204–215. doi:10.1287/isre.9.2.204

Agrawal, K. (2015). Investigating the determinants of Big Data Analytics (BDA) adoption in Asian emerging economies. *AMCIS*.

Ajmal, S., Farooq, M. Z., Sajid, N., & Awan, S. (2012). Role of leadership in change management process. *Abasyn University Journal of Social Sciences*, *5*(2), 111–124.

Bag, S., Pretorius, J. H. C., Gupta, S., & Dwivedi, Y. K. (2021). Role of institutional pressures and resources in the adoption of big data analytics powered artificial intelligence, sustainable manufacturing practices and circular economy capabilities. *Technological Forecasting and Social Change*, *163*, 120420. doi:10.1016/j.techfore.2020.120420

Burkhardt, M. E., & Brass, D. J. (1990). Changing patterns or patterns of change: The effects of a change in technology on social network structure and power. *Administrative Science Quarterly*, *35*(1), 104–127. doi:10.2307/2393552

Carmeli, A., Gelbard, R., & Gefen, D. (2010). The importance of innovation leadership in cultivating strategic fit and enhancing firm performance. *The Leadership Quarterly*, *21*(3), 339–349. doi:10.1016/j.leaqua.2010.03.001

Cyganek, B., Graña, M., Krawczyk, B., Kasprzak, A., Porwik, P., Walkowiak, K., & Woźniak, M. (2016). A survey of big data issues in electronic health record analysis. *Applied Artificial Intelligence*, *30*(6), 497–520. doi:10.1080/08839514.2016.1193714

Dunham. R.B., Grube, J.A., Gardner, D.G., Cummings, L.L. & Pierce, J.L. (1989). The development of an attitude toward change instrument. In *Proceedings of the Academy of Management Annual Meeting*, Washington, DC

Ghaleb, E. A., Dominic, P. D. D., Fati, S. M., Muneer, A., & Ali, R. F. (2021). The Assessment of Big Data Adoption Readiness with a Technology–Organization–Environment Framework: A Perspective towards Healthcare Employees. *Sustainability*, *13*(15), 8379. doi:10.3390u13158379

Gigliotti, R., Vardaman, J., Marshall, D. R., & Gonzalez, K. (2019). The role of perceived organizational support in individual change readiness. *Journal of Change Management*, *19*(2), 86–100. doi:10.1080/14697017.2018.1459784

Hair, J. F., Ortinau, D. J., & Harrison, D. E. (2010). *Essentials of marketing research,* (Vol. 2). McGraw-Hill/Irwin.

Horth, D., & Buchner, D. (2014). Innovation leadership: How to use innovation to lead effectively, work collaboratively and drive results. Center for Creative Leadership, 18, 4221.

Joshi, M., & Biswas, P. (2018). An Empirical Investigation of Impact of Organizational Factors on Big Data Adoption. In *Proceedings of First International Conference on Smart System, Innovations and Computing,* (pp. 809-824). Springer, Singapore. 10.1007/978-981-10-5828-8_77

Kirrane, M., Lennon, M., O'Connor, C., & Fu, N. (2017). Linking perceived management support with employees' readiness for change: The mediating role of psychological capital. *Journal of Change Management*, *17*(1), 47–66. doi:10.1080/14697017.2016.1214615

Lamba, K., & Singh, S. P. (2018). Modeling big data enablers for operations and supply chain management. *International Journal of Logistics Management*, *29*(2), 629–658. doi:10.1108/IJLM-07-2017-0183

Leban, W., & Zulauf, C. (2004). Linking emotional intelligence abilities and transformational leadership styles. *Leadership and Organization Development Journal*, *27*(7), 554–564. doi:10.1108/01437730410561440

Lee, C. S., Lee, W., & Kim, J. (2007). Effects of Transformational Leadership and Self-leadership on Innovative Behaviors: Mediating roles of empowerment. *International area review, 10*(2), 163-176.

Lin, H. F., & Lee, G. G. (2005). Impact of organizational learning and knowledge management factors on e-business adoption. *Management Decision*, *43*(2), 171–188. doi:10.1108/00251740510581902

Lippert, S. K., & Davis, M. (2006). A conceptual model integrating trust into planned change activities to enhance technology adoption behavior. *Journal of Information Science*, *32*(5), 434–448. doi:10.1177/0165551506066042

Lyons, J. B., Swindler, S. D., & Offner, A. (2009). The impact of leadership on change readiness in the US military. *Journal of Change Management*, *9*(4), 459–475. doi:10.1080/14697010903360665

Mehta, N., & Pandit, A. (2018). Concurrence of big data analytics and healthcare: A systematic review. *International Journal of Medical Informatics*, *114*, 57–65. doi:10.1016/j.ijmedinf.2018.03.013 PMID:29673604

Neves, P., & Eisenberger, R. (2014). Perceived organizational support and risk taking. *Journal of Managerial Psychology*, *29*(2), 187–205. doi:10.1108/JMP-07-2011-0021

Nordin, N. (2011). The influence of emotional intelligence, leadership behaviour and organizational commitment on organizational readiness for change in higher learning institution. *Procedia: Social and Behavioral Sciences*, *29*, 129–138. doi:10.1016/j.sbspro.2011.11.217

Paley, N. (2017). *Leadership strategies in the age of big data, algorithms, and analytics*. Productivity Press. doi:10.1201/9781315164977

Raguseo, E., & Vitari, C. (2018). Investments in big data analytics and firm performance: An empirical investigation of direct and mediating effects. *International Journal of Production Research, 56*(15), 5206–5221. doi:10.1080/00207543.2018.1427900

Rogers, E. M. (1995). Lessons for guidelines from the diffusion of innovations. *The Joint Commission Journal on Quality Improvement, 21*(7), 324–328. doi:10.1016/S1070-3241(16)30155-9 PMID:7581733

Wang, Y., & Hajli, N. (2017). Exploring the path to big data analytics success in healthcare. *Journal of Business Research, 70*, 287–299. doi:10.1016/j.jbusres.2016.08.002

Wang, Y. M., Wang, Y. S., & Yang, Y. F. (2010). Understanding the determinants of RFID adoption in the manufacturing industry. *Technological Forecasting and Social Change, 77*(5), 803–815. doi:10.1016/j.techfore.2010.03.006

Yoon, S. N., Lee, D., & Schniederjans, M. (2016). Effects of innovation leadership and supply chain innovation on supply chain efficiency: Focusing on hospital size. *Technological Forecasting and Social Change, 113*, 412–421. doi:10.1016/j.techfore.2016.07.015

Zakir, J., Seymour, T., & Berg, K. (2015). Big Data Analytics. *Issues in Information Systems, 16*(2).

## ADDITIONAL READING

Schüll, A., & Maslan, N. (2018). On the Adoption of Big Data Analytics: Interdependencies of Contextual Factors. In ICEIS 1, pp. 425-431.\

Toufaily, E., Zalan, T., & Dhaou, S. B. (2021). A framework of blockchain technology adoption: An investigation of challenges and expected value. *Information & Management, 58*(3), 103444. doi:10.1016/j.im.2021.103444

# Chapter 14
# Women's Leadership and Workplace Culture

**Ifra Fayaz Zaroo**
https://orcid.org/0000-0001-7617-0063
*Central University of Kashmir, India*

**Abdul Gani**
*Central University of Kashmir, India*

## ABSTRACT

*From business boardrooms to senate chambers, universities to the courts, philanthropic groups to religious institutes, men are far more likely than women to be leaders. Society has determined that only men make good leaders, and this notion has denied easy access for women seeking leadership roles as they do not fit in the norm. Women with leadership aspirations continue to struggle for leadership positions in all spheres of governance in both the public and private sector however, the journey is never easy. Such bias against women is detrimental to the survival of all kinds of organisations in the growing digital era. For this reason, the chapter will specifically focus on women leadership and the challenges they face due to masculine workplace culture. It will also highlight the necessity of hiring women as leaders in the growing digital world. Recommendations will be stated that can assist the organisations in redesigning their workplace culture to support the initiative of providing opportunities to women and take up leadership positions for the future survival of organisations.*

## INTRODUCTION

Digitalization is about more than just technology and business concepts. Aside from technological challenges, there are other impediments along its path, the most significant of which is leadership and workplace culture. Workplace culture is equally important in successfully moving a company into the digital transformation; therefore, the success of a digital transformation is dependent on a thorough knowledge of the complexities of culture. To lead the change in the business environment of digitalization, a distinct leadership style than the popular leadership styles of yesterday is required, such transformational leader-

DOI: 10.4018/978-1-6684-5864-8.ch014

ship qualities have been found to be feminine. Workplace culture dominated by men, require women to "manage their own leadership choices (e.g., collaboration) within a world of hierarchical and top-down organisations and structures" (Kezar 2014, p. 126), despite women's significant achievements over the previous 50 years, males outnumber women in positions of power, particularly at the top. A shortage of competent women in leadership posts contributes to a gender disparity not only in one, but in many areas of the workplace. Some gender bias is extremely subliminal, but overt and illegal job bias against women remains a problem. Other than that, companies may continue to express a strong gender preference for some jobs without hesitance, but the leadership divide isn't just a corporate problem; women are more likely to assume top roles in the nonprofit sphere, though they still remain underrepresented.

Leaders enjoy tremendous respect and luxury; leadership in one sector opens doors to other options, thereby multiplying the rewards of leadership. Most companies top leaders are also the highly paid, and managers and directors often make more than non-leadership staff. Women are significantly less likely to be considered as rulers than men. In 2015, just 5% of the companies in the standard & Poor's 500 index had female CEOs (Catalyst, 2015a). Leaders carry tremendous power, so when women are excluded from positions of authority, they are denied all of the privileges and every opportunity to make a positive change. In almost every case, male leaders outweigh female leaders.

In terms of educational credentials, the pipeline for female leaders has grown dramatically during the previous half-century. Apart from professional degrees, women now hold the majority of university degrees at all levels. Significant changes in women's educational achievement and labor-force involvement have provided millions of women with the expertise and abilities needed to become leaders, filling jobs formerly designated for men and giving organisations a bigger and more varied pool of aspiring leaders. In other words, educated and determined women are abundant, many of these women are skilled professionals with extended length of service in the workforce, despite the fact that women are still relatively less likely than males to be in the workplace. Additionally, anti-female leadership attitudes and regulations may be found throughout history, most notably in all major world religion (Christ, 2014).

Despite the fact that the idea of leadership has been integrated with traditionally masculine attributes such as aggressive behavior, decision making, engaging in conflicts, physical power, and so on. Leadership is not inherently or blatantly masculine, both men and women strive to continuously improve the skills necessary for advancement to key leadership positions. According to research, workplace culture and women leadership are inextricably related since leadership is defined by decisiveness, intelligence, and honesty rather than masculinity. The chapter discusses women's leadership in particular, and workplace culture and leadership in general, and analyzes their relationship to digitalization. It also identifies gender inequalities in leadership and suggests recommendations to achieve gender parity in leadership.

## Background

Studies (e.g., Ayman & Korabik 2010; O'Neiil et al. 2008) have found that organizational cultures (and even staffing arrangement) are gendered, which means that preconceptions about leaders and the major drivers to strong and successful leadership are often male-normed. Very often, diversity training, targets and women's development initiatives do not result in the transformative transformation that businesses seek. This is because existing organisational culture, which is frequently unconscious, is stifling any efforts to achieve better gender parity. If a firm intends to modify its customary behavior, it must first identify the beliefs and assumptions that support such conduct in its workplace culture, then they can modify their work habits to support a new approach of doing things. As a renowned scholar of organisational culture, Schein's (2010) contributions to the literature have highlighted the term's interdisciplinary character and use, encompassing business, sociology, leadership, and other subjects. According to Schein, an organization's culture is shaped by historical events, religion, and group decisions, all of which contribute to a form of organisational identity. Furthermore, Schein provided a useful distinction between: (1) the visible organisational structures and processes; (2) the strategies, targets, and philosophies or proclaimed justifications; and (3) the unconscious or taken-for-granted beliefs, perceptions, thoughts, and feelings that ultimately shape a person's value systems and behavior.

Researchers have found a number of environmental, interpersonal, and internal variables that can stymie women's advancement into leadership, with many of those issues being tied to workplace culture as outlined by Ely and Rhode (2010) in the Handbook of Leadership Theory and Practice chapter headed "Defining the Challenges," women aspiring to leadership confront a slew of behavioral and attitudinal impediments.

A credit Suisse study (2012) discovered that corporations with at least one women in their boardroom had a greater return than corporations with no women on their board. A women-friendly workplace is often a reflection of a healthy corporate culture that cares about all employees, irrespective of gender, race, religion, or other characteristics. Corporate leaders who realize that diversity is critical to the success and that behavior ultimately determines culture are more likely to actively develop and enhance a culture of equality. Firms continue to pay reward, recognize performance, develop incentive and determine promotion using criteria that represent an all-male corporate leadership culture (Helgesen & Johnson, 2010, p. 58). Such cultural framework and expectations shape people's attitudes, behaviors and experiences in an organisation when it comes to leadership assessment. The existing organisational executive culture has severe vulnerabilities and has long neglected the numerous endemic impediments that adversely affect women seeking management and leadership roles (King, 2020). As a result, firms must look within and review their own workplace culture to ensure that all employees are on a fair playing field.

## LEADERSHIP

Leadership can be defined as a process in which the primary goal is to encourage members of a group to attain a common purpose (Northouse, 2018). This stresses the importance of leadership if goals need to be met (Yukl, 2006). As a result, it is conceivable to assert that leadership is neither a characteristic nor a specific trait, but rather an interplay that can be viewed as an instrumental value (Bass, 2009). This indicates that leadership can be defined as a two-way interaction between the leader and the followers (Northouse, 2018). Gender refers to the societal characteristics of men and women, which include conventions, relationships and roles. According to studies, people's conceptions of gender differ from one community to the next and change over time. Leadership and gender have a substantial relationship that should be addressed in order to enable smooth processes of an organisation. Leadership refers to realistic and practical abilities that include an individual's capacity to direct people toward a common goal. Essentially, leadership entails inspiring, leading, and interacting with colleagues to ensure that the task at hand is completed correctly. People who occupy formal positions of leadership in complex organisations in industry, government, education, politics, the arts, science and professions are referred to as "leaders" (Grant, Jan, 1977). Furthermore, leadership is defined as a behavior, a trait, and an act that involves personality, talents, and information-processing aspects (Northouse, 2013). Furthermore, several key activities of leaders can be defined, such as goal setting and goal formulation for teams and people, organisation, and decision making (Malik, 2014). Again, the concept of the leader's actions as well as the related roles vary substantially. According to Malik (2014), people can only be successful if they have "appropriate and good management" that enables them to "convert their qualities and skills into performance and success" (p. 14). At the same time, successful leaders are related with particular soft talents that "allow him to communicate well with his coworkers or teammates". This includes communication skills that aid in the formulation of organisational objectives, motivation and the ability to encourage others, reliability, the ability to provide constructive criticism, accountability for one's activities, flexibility, and the potential to decentralize work (Tang, 2019). "Women attempting to establish themselves as leaders must contend with popular perceptions of vulnerability, self-mastery, and a very male confidence. Not only must would-be female leaders contend with prolonged images of male dominance, but the only proficient literature available to women attempting to master what is required of contemporary leadership is largely comprised of information obtained by male lawmakers, assumed experts in leadership theories, and male admins." Curry (2000), p. ix.

## Trait Theory

In the early twentieth century, trait theory was an essential method to understand leadership. Trait theory seeks to explain distinguishing factors in leader effectiveness by identifying a collection of personal attributes." Potential leaders were thought to be determined through analyzing and assessing personality features" (Goff, 2003, p. 3).

These characteristics may be developed and inherited in an individual's personality. Stogdills (1948) defined five leadership trait categories based on a review of 124 studies: (a) capacity, (b) responsibility, (c) achievement, (d) status, and (e) involvement. Similar to the great-men idea, trait theory was one-way from leader to follower, with the focus on the role of the leader (Stodgill, 1948). Stodgill's discoveries (1948). The findings of Stodgill's (1948) investigations were critical in refuting trait theory:

"Leadership is not a matter of passive status, or mere possession of some mix of features." It appears to be a close relationship among group members in which the leader gains status through active engagement and display of his capability for carrying out cooperative responsibilities to accomplishment." (p. 66).

## Transformational Leadership

Transformational leadership encourages individuals to achieve company goals by addressing high-level self-actualization demands. Transformational leadership has four characteristics, according to Avolio (1999): (1) idealized influence; (2) intellectual stimulation; (3) inspiring drive; and (4) individual consideration. Idealized influence incorporates charismatic behavior and is related to the degree to which female leaders are trusted and appreciated. Intellectual stimulation encourages followers to think critically and creatively.

Inspirational motivation challenges their followers while emphasizing teamwork. Individual consideration illustrates the amount to which followers' potential is formed by meeting their needs and giving opportunities for learning (Bass et al., 2003). Some researchers refer to "internal change agents" in the role of the leader as a critical aspect that plays a crucial role in the development of new styles in management innovation in organisations. Furthermore, Birkinshaw et al. (2008) demonstrate that leadership is not only associated with managerial innovation, but also plays an important role in human activity.

## WORKPLACE CULTURE

Despite the fact that it is an ubiquitous term, many people are curious about 'what is workplace culture?' Workplace culture integrates an organization's core values and philosophies. It's the environment you've created for your employees, as well as the entirety of your company's traditions, relationships, ideas, values, and practices. A sound workplace culture focuses on the well-being of people while aligning organizational policies and behaviors of employees with the organization's goals. The set of principles, expectations, and norms that drive and inform the conduct of all team members is referred to as workplace culture. Consider it to be the set of characteristics that define your organisation. A great workplace culture displays good features that lead to enhanced performance, whereas a malfunctioning company culture elicits characteristics that can stymie even the most successful organisations.

### Characteristics of a Healthy Culture

Equality:

Everyone in an enterprise has worth, and addressing everyone fairly promotes employee morale. Bias and favoritism in the workplace can foster animosity and suspicion among coworkers, resulting in a hostile work environment. It is critical that you create an egalitarian workplace in which people are only judged based on their job.

Freedom of Expression:

Employee happiness and satisfaction are enhanced by workplace freedom of expression. It makes everyone feel cherished and respected. Leaders and managers can promote free speech by offering everyone an opportunity to share their thoughts and soliciting their feedback on organisational concerns.

Recognition:

Healthy workplace cultures value their employees' contributions. When an employee does well, it is critical to recognize them in order to build morale and push them to develop their skills. Avoid disparaging those who perform poorly. Instead, motivate them to do better the next time.

Employee-Friendly policies:

Employee policies that are friendly to employees tend to draw more talent and boost efficiency. Rules and regulations that affirm the staff's ideas and values are critical. Expecting staff to stay till the late on holidays or during significant religious occasions, for example, can create a sad and unhealthy workplace. If the policies are to stay effective and helpful to the organisation, discipline is still required.

### Women Leadership

Women in leadership positions are a frequently mentioned and relevant topic in our culture today. Although progress is gradual on a global scale, there is a trend toward active inclusion of women in leadership positions (Northouse, 2018). The term "glass ceiling" denotes to "the unseen, yet insurmountable barrier that prevents women from ascending to the top of the corporate ladder, irrespective of their accomplishments or abilities". To be more specific, it is one of the most compelling analogies for examining gender inequality in the workplace. According to the study, while women are currently able to enter administrative hierarchies through the front door, they will eventually encounter an unseen barrier that would prevent them from progressing further up. The "glass ceiling" is a metaphor for evaluating gender differences in the workplace between men and women. This condition is referred regarded as a "ceiling" because there is a restriction preventing upward advancement, and "glass" (transparent) since the restriction is not immediately evident and is usually an unwritten and informal guideline. This invisible barrier persists, despite the fact that there are no clear and direct barriers preventing minorities from advancing in their careers - there are no advertorials that specifically state "no minority groups appointed at this organisation," nor are there any formal regulations that state "minorities are not eligible" - but it does exist underneath the surface. The "glass ceiling" differs from statutory hurdles to promotion, such as educational or work experience requirements. This unseen barrier is most obvious in poor countries; in those enterprises, the effect is particularly "visible." However, women leadership remains rare in the commercial world, owing in large part to other impediments - subtle or visible - that women encounter (Eagly & Carli, 2007). There are examples of highly efficient and outstanding female leaders all around the world. Mary Barra, the chairperson and chief executive officer (CEO) of General Motors since 2014, is one example. She is the first female CEO of one of the world's largest automakers. Prominent instances are Virginia Rometty, the chairman, president, and CEO of IBM until April 2020, and Corie Barry, the CEO of the American retailer Best Buy (Welt, 2020; Best Buy, 2020). Nearly half of the U.S. workforce is female, and women earn more than 60% of master's degrees in the country, despite their participation in higher management roles being a mere fraction of this (Northouse, 2018; U.S. National Center for Education Statistics, 2016; Eagly & Carli, 2007). Women are joining men in increasing their participation in professions. However, insufficient representation of women in the majority of leadership responsibilities in decision-making positions were the most contentious subject throughout the last ten years. There was a major concern regarding women's underrepresentation in almost all decision - making positions every country. Furthermore, additional barriers and problems exist for women, such as the glass ceiling, an unseen barrier that inhibits women from climbing the job ladder, or the existing pay disparity between men and women (United Nations, 2020a; Van Emmerik, Wendt & Euwema, 201). Eagly and Carli (2007) identified three types of impediments that impede women's advancement to top management positions: the so-called concrete wall, the labyrinth, and the aforementioned glass ceiling. The literary term for this perplexing predicament is "glass ceiling." Glass ceiling refers to an unnoticed higher limit in every organisation, regardless of size. It is difficult or impossible for women to be in the upper echelons it is called "glass" because. It is not usually a visible barrier, and a woman may be unaware of its existence. She will continue to exist until she "hits" the barrier. In other words, there is no apparent practice of bias against women, even if certain actions, regulations, or mindsets that establish this barrier without the purpose to discriminate may exist. The glass ceiling idea refers to unseen hurdles to women's career growth. The set of impediments that hinder women from advancing to top-level professions has produced an unseen glass ceiling that women find difficult to shatter. The scenario is referred to as a "ceiling" since further advancement is restricted, and "glass" (transparent) because the constraints are not directly visible. It is the most potent influencing factor in the growth of men and women on the career ladder.

Because the gender of the team leader influences how people lead, there is a difference in the usual style of leadership of men and women (Gartzia & Van Engen, 2012). This is mostly due to men's and women's "different personalities since they developed different behavioral methods for reproduction in ages past," according to psychologists (Eagly & Carli, 2007). As a result, it is now critical to demonstrate the attributes of women leadership. Women leadership is viewed as cooperative, regenerative, empathic, and creative (Esser, Kahrens, Mouzughi, and Eomois, 2018). This is further confirmed by the fact that while becoming a mother, women must meet cultural standards (Esser, Kahrens, Mouzughi & Eomois, 2018).

Emotional intelligence is sometimes defined as the "capacity to understand sentiments and apply this understanding to life's activities" (Northouse, 2018). As a result, this is an important aspect for leadership effectiveness because it boosts the leader's potential to fix complicated challenges. According to research, women outperform men in this area (Mandell & Pherwani, 2003). Furthermore, women are more focused with connections, which is backed by the woman's capability to empathize (Sandberg, 2013). In his research, Schermerhorn (1999) claimed that women in leadership positions act more democratically than men and are more mindful with the feelings of their followers. Women, in comparison to "their male counterparts foster team cohesion, cooperative learning, and participative communication" (Post, 2015). This is particularly useful when teams are diverse, large, and geographically distributed (Post, 2015). As a result, foreign teams can operate more effectively when led by a woman. Furthermore, women are more capable than men in dealing with tragedies (Borgerson, 2018). The key reason for this is that women leaders have "emotional strength," which aids in effectively approaching and overcoming emergencies (Borgerson, 2018).

In contrast to women leadership, men prefer to lead in a far more task-oriented and dictatorial manner. Their leadership style can be described as more authoritative. Male leadership is frequently portrayed in the literature as aggressive, courageous, and assertive, especially when compared to female cooperative leadership (Born, Ranehill, & Sandberg, 2018; Kim & Shin, 2017; Eagly & Johannesen-Schmidt, 2001). Men embrace traditional authority and place a premium on structured organisational systems. Women leaders are clearly at a disadvantage because the original concept of leadership "is linked with men," even if both leadership styles can be effective depending on the context and situation (Steffens, Viladot, & Scheifele, 2019; Northouse, 2018; Eagly & Carli, 2007). The gender disparity in leadership that has been demonstrated is a global phenomena. As "the Mad Men period is still alive and well," nearly every country in the globe has a significant underrepresentation of female leaders (Moore & Diese, 2018; Szymanska & Rubin, 2018).

At this moment, it is worth noting that women have challenges that male leaders do not, because there is a "glaring contradiction between the expectations that people have of women and how they want a leader to behave" (Esser et al., 2018: 138; Koburtay et al., 2019). This is supported by empirical evidence, which is referred to as the role congruity theory (Eagly & Karau, 2002). Women are also subjected to other major challenges, such as discrimination, sexual harassment, and subtle sexism (Sandberg, 2013).

## LEADERSHIP AND WORKPLACE CULTURE

Leadership and organisational culture are in continuous interaction, and knowing the nature of their relationship is critical to understanding their combined influence on organisational phenomena (Bass & Avolio, 1993). This is a branch of culture study that explores the interacting influence of organisational culture and leadership, and empirically tests the moderator function of culture or leadership in how the two dimensions relate to key organisational outcomes. The majority of empirical research that look at how leaders and organisational cultures interact to effect organisational outcomes look at leadership as a hypothetical antecedent of organisational culture. The vast majority of these research obtained cross-sectional data, excluding out assumptions concerning causal links. There are numerous studies in this field that study the mediating role of organisational culture in the relationship between leadership and specific organisational outcomes such as efficiency, innovation, and dedication. Numerous studies have found that organisational culture acts as a moderator in the relationship between leadership styles and specific organisational outcomes. Both leadership and organisational culture are viewed as antecedent variables of organisational results in this line of research, while leadership impact on outcomes is at least partly funneled through subordinates' opinions of their organization's culture. The research on the mediating effect of culture has investigated and provided evidence for the joint effect of numerous organisational culture dimensions and leadership styles on organisational performance, innovation, employee commitment, and organisational identification, whereas research on the interactive effect of leadership and workplace culture has examined the combined effects of leadership and culture on outcomes testing for one culture dimension at a time. This is a critical topic since the coexistence of seemingly conflicting organisational principles and beliefs, such as cooperation and individual growth, has been deliberately highlighted for good organizational functioning (Xenikou & Furnham, 2013).

When it comes to appropriate leadership, globalization has presented a new difficulty (Northouse, 2016). In order to "create effective global corporations," the best and most suitable leaders must be chosen for subsidiaries all over the world (Northouse, 2016). To attain great leadership effectiveness, those leaders must fit within the culture of their particular organisations. However, only a tiny percentage of foreign managers are mindful that culture has a significant impact on their work (Meyer, 2014b). After mentioning the distinctiveness of female leadership, the relationship between women in positions of leadership and their respective cultures has to be examined further. Because the Gender Equality Index provides insights into women's job opportunities, this idea will be addressed in greater depth, emphasizing certain excellent countries. To summarize, women leadership is an important topic in today's economic environment. It is critical that organisations consider this phenomena in order to remain competitive in the long run. Gender equality and diversity are important drivers of profitability. Organizations in both developed and developing countries must be cognizant of women leadership and workplace bias against women. Changing mindsets and governmental rules are unavoidable and unquestionably required in order to further assist women in rising the career ladder.

When these two themes were combined, the research revealed that culture and leadership are inextricably linked. Despite the fact that we live in a worldwide world, great leadership isn't the same for every culture and region (ChamorroPremuzic & Sanger, 2016). As a result, leaders must be aware of cultural variations in order to boost their effectiveness and professionalism (Meyer, 2014b). The ability to adjust is essential in this situation (Northouse, 2016; Meyer, 2014b).

## Leadership, Workplace Culture and Digitalization

Many businesses are investing in new technology and undergoing digital business transition in order to stay ahead of the competition and appeal to a growing digital audience. According to studies, more than 80% of firms increasingly hold their IT departments liable for delivering a connected customer service. While choosing the proper technology is vital, it is also critical to match your corporate culture and leadership with the new direction and ensuring your people are capable of long-term support for your new digital approach. One of the most important aspects for developing outstanding workplace culture is effective leadership. Leadership has a significant impact on workplace culture. Leaders can reinforce organisational principles by providing opportunity for their employees to learn and expand through goal setting, opportunities, and acknowledgment.

Leadership and workplace culture are good allies because they impact and affect everything we do in our organisations. They are inextricably linked and should never be downplayed or ignored. Leadership establishes the tone for what is permitted, accepted, and becomes the norm in companies. These norms gradually become intertwined of company culture, guiding, shaping, and influencing future orientations, decisions, and, most crucially, behaviors. Most businesses are undergoing digital transformation, but the process may be severe and excruciating. Leaders must overcome numerous problems that are more about culture and traditions than technology. Digitalization and technical advancements, together with a shifting political and demographic landscape, have ushered a new era of disruption. Any global corporate leader's goal is to devise strategies to address the problems of digitalization, technical advancements and shifting political and demographic environments.

The key to success is a diverse and neutral work environment, as well as leadership chances for qualified and skilled applicants. Companies that foster a culture of transparency, accountability, equality and experimentation are more likely to obtain full business benefits within predicted timescales. Similarly, a continuous improved culture promotes timely benefit realization. When these ideals are woven into your organization's basis, any change adopted becomes a vehicle for development, and any other technology implementation will similarly enable business goals. Despite the fact that organisations claim to be gender-neutral, women's leadership shows only minimal evidence of development. According to Appelbaum, Audet and Miller (2013), women have fewer opportunities to occupy desirable leadership positions than men. The accomplishments of female leaders in recent years demonstrate that women have the ability to make substantial progressive decisions that shape both national and international advancement (Pew Research Center, 2015). Despite having exceptional leadership qualities, women hold few roles in government and industry. According to Appelbaum, Audet and Miller (2013), attitude fosters the belief that some individuals are good leaders than others in society. Self-confidence, attitude and the professional environment have also contributed to the low proportion of women in leadership positions. Moreover, for women, the workplace environment has an indirect association with both self-confidence and attitude. For example, feminine leaders working in toxic circumstances typified by unhealthy competitiveness, dynamic demands, and misaligned expectations promote rejection and self-domineering cultures that stymie efforts to improve leadership equality. The status quo, which perceives women as incapable, shows minor changes. An examination of gender norms demonstrates that the status of women in society encourages stasis in both developmental and social changes in terms of leadership. Women are portrayed as a feeble gender with an inferiority complex in the social and cultural context. Furthermore, social norms portray males as more prominent in leadership than women. Such assumption is false because both men and women exhibit leadership abilities when supplied with the required infrastructure, funds and other resources. Researchers have discovered that women tend to endorse a robust transformational leadership style that encourages through mental stimulation, charisma and individualized consideration (Bass & Riggio, 2006, as cited in Matsa & Miller, 2013).

Through social contacts, leaders can teach workplace culture. They can demonstrate to employees what behavior is acceptable and promoted by their own actions. The following are seven ways in which leadership influences workplace culture. Leadership:

- Core values are defined and taught.
- Encourages a desire to study
- Encourages a culture of acknowledgment
- Promotes a shared vision
- Culture is altered.
- Enhances job satisfaction
- Accountability is ensured.

Historically females were barred from assuming leadership roles in all spheres due to gender, as a result, the belief that males were better qualified than females for leadership positions was rarely questioned. However, in this rapidly changing digital era, a company's development is heavily reliant on diversity inclusiveness and leader's capacity to keep an organisation afloat. The digital disruption and pandemic have altered practically every business's operations. The possibilities are limitless, but only for businesses that grasp how much and how quickly they must adapt. This is a challenging task for many businesses. However, there are bigger advantages for those that are willing to shift and master the disruption. Organizations are responsible for developing effective tactics for successful leadership. The ability of leaders to encourage employees through rewards and other techniques is critical to an organization's growth.

Women are appointed to management positions at a much lower rate than men, halting diversity, increasing hostile environment and biased business culture making it practically difficult for businesses to compete and impossible for businesses to set the groundwork for long-term success. Following the outbreak of the covid-19 pandemic, businesses recognized the importance of diversity and women and began to hire experts irrespective of gender. However, the involvement of women still needs a shift in workplace culture and pressure to achieve the optimal results of encouraging potential leaders rather than gendered bias. They must engage in the profound cultural effort required to establish an environment in which all women feel appreciated. Women in leadership should be treated the same as men in leadership, which necessitates an equivalent degree of work divided across two pillars:

- To develop and establish a workplace culture that encourages women leadership from the start in businesses, so that women's capability can be maximized at all levels.
- Raise men's understanding of their blind spots when it comes to women leadership, enabling them to embrace women leadership and perceive it as a complementing idea to male leadership rather than replacing it.

Women are more prone than men to experience victimization that damage their professional standing, such as being stopped and having their judgment called into question. Their accomplishments and failings are frequently scrutinized, and they are more likely to experience actions and statements that reduce them to racist stereotypes.

Digital Transformation, which comprises corporate transition, organizational growth, corporate cultural shift, and organizational restructuring, is the only way to achieve operational efficiencies in the digital age. Few business executives, however, properly get how a company's culture evolves — and, more significantly, how it does not change — during a digital transformation. According to Hofstede et al. (2010) study on cultures around the world, patriarchal institutions have influenced (and continue to influence) issues of access and equity in many sectors of life, including workplace culture and its influence on climate (i.e., the environment as experienced by workers). It is far easier to improve old technology or even incorporate new technology. Creating an atmosphere and culture suitable to digitalization, on the other hand, is an entirely different scenario. The most crucial aspect of digitalization is the backing of the leadership team (C suite) (Kotter, 1996; Raut, 2017). When major businesses embark on so-called digitalization programs, it is commonly assumed that the most difficult problem will be integrating new technology with current systems. However, this is not always the case. Dealing with organisational culture is frequently a symptom of a larger issue. While some companies' DNA is more open to change, others are far more resistant. One of the most difficult problems of digitalization is striking a balance between culture and technology. Leaders must embrace a new leadership style to accomplish this and effectively lead staff through these significant changes. The e-leader is a new type of leader who is at the forefront of digitalization and technological innovation in their organisations. Women leaders are optimistic about progress, with realistic, clear and confident views on what can be accomplished they can play a critical role in achieving beneficial results from investments in new technology as digital enablers.

Leaders must establish a happy, connected, and cohesive and productive work atmosphere that doesn't leave anyone behind while driving the digital revolution forward. Employees should have a strong feeling of togetherness and belonging under the new company culture. Conventional social skills, such as the capacity to actively listen to and comprehend the feelings and points of view of others, are more vital than ever. In a fast changing environment, delivering and receiving clear feedback is critical for ongoing improvement. Furthermore, a concept such as feedforward can be valuable in gathering actionable ideas for the future. E-leaders must combine these abilities with the ability to use a range of virtual communication tools. They are increasingly requiring IT abilities to effectively identify and manage the utilization of diverse technologies. Only leaders who practice lifelong learning will be able to cultivate and master the requisite digital and social abilities. A leadership coach can help with this critical transition.

## SOLUTIONS AND RECOMMENDATIONS

Success in today's disruptive business world will necessitate determination and leadership, with an emphasis on long-term rather than short-term profits. As we struggle with the increasing problems of technology disruptions, the necessity for rich and diverse thinking at all areas of an enterprise becomes even more critical. Organisations must spend heavily in all aspects of diversity, equality, and inclusion to create change. This begins with strong initiatives to assure that women of varied identity are fully represented, but diversity of numbers alone isn't enough. Businesses must also foster a culture that fully embraces the importance of diversity in which women and other employees feel comfortable sharing their ideas, opinions, and insights. Women's enablement programs are a good way to bring more women into the business sector not only this but having women leaders understand how difficult it is to battle for participation and progression and would work to make it simpler for the next generation. Businesses must realize the significance of changes and acknowledge the value of recruiting specialists to manage these changes, regardless of gender.

To attain gender equality, we require women who are willing and capable of taking on leadership roles. We need more males who are eager and capable of taking on more familial tasks so that more women can pursue challenging careers. Employers must accept a more flexible work environment that allows both genders to move in and out of the workforce as they combine professions, families and personal aspirations. In essence, we must all actively seek to make inclusiveness and diversity a daily reality. The gender leadership gap will not expand significantly until the culture, policy and practices of the institutions where women study and work undergo significant changes. Accountability motivates action, there should be public measures to ensure that employers follow the right thing. This is a problem that has be solved to move past stereotyped views of leadership. Gender equality is a step forward for everyone, allowing women to achieve their ambitions regardless of their gender.

While there are no easy remedies for these issues, businesses may and should undertake steps to address them. First, they must implement more measures to guarantee that promotions are fair and equal. Companies are presently taking measure to avoid bias in recruitment and the same rigor should be applied to the performance assessment process. Extending this training would almost certainly result in improved promotions for women and other employees from underrepresented groups.

Second, businesses must keep a more detailed record of inclusion, hiring and promotion outcomes. Companies would also benefit from analyzing hiring and promotions to identify whether women are recruited and promoted at identical rates as men.

Businesses must increase their accountability and transparency efforts to expedite development for all women on all frontiers. Despite stating that gender diversity are among their top business concerns, just two-thirds of businesses hold senior leaders responsible for diversity growth.

Finally, businesses should clearly convey what is expected of their employees as well as what it means to have an inclusive environment. While incorporating this concept into organisational principles is a good start, organisations might benefit from identifying the precise behaviors and acts that encourage inclusiveness.

## FUTURE RESEARCH AND CONCLUSION

The study of organisations as cultures with value beliefs, behavioral norms, and practices in how they handle their members and make the most of the challenges posed by the external environment has contributed significantly to understanding the intricacies of organizational behavior, including leadership and organizational performance. Founders and their teams have a significant role in shaping their firm's culture since they are frequently defined by strong convictions about the decisions they must make in order for their organisation to successfully adapt to and prosper in its environment. Founders and other leaders have several techniques at their disposal to convey, develop, and reinforce their beliefs and fundamental assumptions, including as role modelling, mentoring, and the distribution of rewards and status. The coexistence and activation of seemingly disparate cultural elements within organisational settings has long been recognized as a critical component for organisational efficiency. Leaders have the ability to reconcile seemingly conflicting demands placed on organisations, such as a focus on task or connections, by deploying a variety of culture embedding mechanisms.

Leadership inequalities between men and women have a substantial impact on how a company operates. Despite substantial similarities in the performance of given jobs, society considers males as better leaders than women in a variety of ways. Essentially, both men and women are capable of implementing change as well as leading subordinates in an organisation to reach the specified mission and targets. Moreover, existing gender differences have a negligible contribution to leadership and cannot be used to assess a people's ability to provide required outcomes in a company.

Future research should look into the various mechanisms that leaders might use to manage their organization's culture. In addition to research on culture management tools, it is critical to examine the incongruence (dissimilarity) view in culture management. Researchers can expand on the research to discover the actual initiatives made to enhance leadership equality. Research can also be conducted at ground level to find women leaders who have been supported and promoted by organisations, making their journey easier for them. Furthermore, a research comparing successful female leaders to successful male leaders can be done to present explanations and additional data to advocate gender and leadership equality.

## REFERENCES

Appelbaum, S. Audet, L &Miller, J. (2013). Gender and leadership? Leadership and gender? A journey through the landscape of theories. *Leadership and Organization Development Journal, 24*(1), 43-51.

Avolio, B. J. (1999). *Full leadership development: Building the vital forces in organizations*. Sage.

Ayman, R., & Korabik, K. (2010). Leadership: Why gender and culture matter. *The American Psychologist, 65*(3), 157–170. doi:10.1037/a0018806 PMID:20350015

Bass, B. M. (2009). *The Bass Handbook of Leadership,* (4th ed.). Free Press.

Bass, B. M., & Avolio, B. J. (1993). Transformational leadership and organizational culture. *Public Administration Quarterly, 17*, 112–121.

Bass, B. M., Jung, D. I., Avolio, B. J., & Berson, Y. (2003). Predicting unit performance by assessing transformational and transactional leadership. *The Journal of Applied Psychology, 88*(2), 207–218. doi:10.1037/0021-9010.88.2.207 PMID:12731705

Bass, B. M., & Riggio, R. E. (2006). *Transformational leadership*. Psychology Pres. doi:10.4324/9781410617095

Birkinshaw, J., Hamel, G., & Mol, M. J. (2008). Management innovation. *Academy of Management Review, 33*(4), 825–845. doi:10.5465/amr.2008.34421969

Borgerson, J. L. (2018). *Caring and Power in Female Leadership. A Philosophical Approach*. Cambridge Scholars Publishing.

Born, A., Ranehill, E., & Sandberg, A. (2018). A man's world? – The impact of a male dominated environment on female leadership. *Working Papers in Economics*, 744.

Catalyst. (2015a). *Women CEOs of the S&P 500.* www.catalyst.org/knowledge/ women-ceos-sp-500.

Chamorro-Premuzic, T., & Sanger, M. 2016. What Leadership Looks Like in Different Cultures. *Harvard Business Review.* https://hbr.org/2016/05/what-leadership-lookslike-in-different-cultures.

Christ, C. P. (2014). Do we still need the Journal of Feminist Studies in Religion? *Journal of Feminist Studies in Religion, 30*(2), 139–141. doi:10.2979/jfemistudreli.30.2.139

Credit Suisse Research Institute. (2012). *Gender diversity and corporate performance.* infocus.credit-suisse.com/data/_product_documents/_articles/360157/cs_women_in_leading_positions_FINAL.PDF

Curry, B. K. (2000). *Women in power: Pathways to leadership in Education*. Teachers College Press.

Eagly, A. H., & Carli, L. L. (2007). *Through the Labyrinth. The Truth About How Women Become Leaders*. Harvard Business School Press.

Eagly, A. H., & Johannesen-Schmidt, M. C. (2001). The Leadership Styles of Women and Men. *The Journal of Social Issues, 57*(4), 781–797. doi:10.1111/0022-4537.00241

Eagly, A. H., & Karau, S. J. (2002). Role Congruity Theory of Prejudice Toward Female Leaders. *Psychological Review, 109*(3), 573–598. doi:10.1037/0033-295X.109.3.573 PMID:12088246

Ely, R. J., & Rhode, D. L. (2010). Women and leadership: Defining the challenges. In N. Nohria & R. Khurana (Eds.), *Handbook of Leadership Theory and Practice,* (pp. 377–410). Harvard Business Publishing.

Esser, A., Kahrens, M., Mouzughi, Y., & Eomois, E. (2018). A female leadership competency framework from the perspective of male leaders. *Gender in Management, 33*(2), 138–166. doi:10.1108/GM-06-2017-0077

Gartzia, L., & Van Engen, M. L. (2012). Are (male) leaders "feminine" enough? Gendered traits of identity as mediators of sex differences in leadership styles. *Gender in Management, 27*(5), 296–314. doi:10.1108/17542411211252624

Goff, D. G. (2003). *What do we know about good community college leaders: A study in leadership trait theory and behavioral leadership theory.* https://www.eric.ed.gov/contentdelivery/servlet/ERICServlet?accno=ED47645600000aacb361&acdnat=1352660180_58274f188a39a834f048266e1a3a3d8a

Helgesen, S. (2017). Gender, communication, and the leadership gap. *Gender, communication, and the leadership gap*, 3-11.

Helgesen, S., & Johnson, J. (2010). *The female vision: Women's real power at work.* Berrett-Koehler Publishers.

Hofstede, G., Hofstede, G. J., & Minkov, M. (2010). *Cultures and Organizations—Software of the Mind: Intercultural Cooperation and Its Importance for Survival.* McGraw-Hill.

Kim, S., & Shin, M. (2017). The effectiveness of transformational leadership on empowerment. The roles of gender and gender dyads. *Cross Cultural & Strategic Management, 24*(2), 271–287. doi:10.1108/CCSM-03-2016-0075

King, M. (2020). Leaders, Stop denying the gender inequity in your organization. *Harvard Business Review.*

Koburtay, T., Syed, J., & Haloub, R. (2019). Congruity between the female gender role and the leader role: A literature review. *European Business Review, 31*(6), 831–848. doi:10.1108/EBR-05-2018-0095

Kotter, J. A. (1996). *Leading change.* Harvard Business Review Press.

Malik, F. (2014). *Managing, Performing, Living: Effective Management for a New World.* Campus Verlag.

Mandell, B., & Pherwani, S. (2003). Relationship Between Emotional Intelligence and Transformational Leadership Style: A Gender Comparison. *Journal of Business and Psychology, 17*(3), 387–404. doi:10.1023/A:1022816409059

Matsa, D. A., & Miller, A. R. (2013). A female style in corporate leadership? Evidence from quotas. *American Economic Journal. Applied Economics, 5*(3), 136–169. doi:10.1257/app.5.3.136

Meyer, E. (2014b). *The Culture Map: Breaking Through The Invisible Boundaries Of Global Business,* (1st ed.). PublicAffairs.

Moore, S., & Diese, A. (2018). Women in Leadership. In F. L. Denmark & M. A. Paludi (Eds.), *Women and Leadership.* Springer. doi:10.1007/978-3-319-72182-8_8

Northouse, P. G. (2016). *Leadership: Theory and Practice,* (7th ed.). Sage.

Northouse, P. G. (2018). *Leadership: Theory and Practice,* (8th ed.). Sage.

O'Neil, D. A., Hopkins, M. M., & Bilimoria, D. (2008). Women's careers at the start of the 21st century: Patterns and paradoxes. *Journal of Business Ethics, 80*(4), 727–743. doi:10.100710551-007-9465-6

Post, C. (2015). When is female leadership an advantage? Coordination requirements, team cohesion, and team interaction norms. *Journal of Organizational Behavior, 36*(8), 1153–1175. doi:10.1002/job.2031

Raut, S. (2017). Why Culture change is essential for digital transformation. *Digitalist Magazine*. http://www.digitalistmag.com/future-of-work/2017/01/09/culture-change-is-essential-for-digitaltransformation-04824251

Sandberg, S. (2013). Lean. In *Women, Work and the Will to Lead.* Alfred A. Knopf.

Schein, E. H. (2010). *Organizational Culture and Leadership* (4th ed.). Jossey-Bass.

Schermerhorn, J. R. (1999). *Management,* (6th ed.). John Wiley & Sons.

Steffens, M. C., Viladot, M. A., & Scheifele, C. (2019). Male Majority, Female Majority, or Gender Diversity in Organizations: How Do Proportions Affect Gender Stereotyping and Women Leaders' Well-Being? *Frontiers in Psychology, 10*, 1037. doi:10.3389/fpsyg.2019.01037 PMID:31143147

Stogdill, R. M. (1948). Personal factors associated with leadership: A survey of the literature. *The Journal of Psychology, 25*(1), 35–71. doi:10.1080/00223980.1948.9917362 PMID:18901913

Szymanska, I. I., & Rubin, B. A. (2018). Gender and relationship differences in the perceptions of male and female leadership. *Gender in Management, 33*(4), 254–281. doi:10.1108/GM-06-2016-0127

Tang, K. N. (2019). *Leadership and Change Management*. Springer. doi:10.1007/978-981-13-8902-3

United Nations. (2020a). Gender Equality. https://www.un.org/en/sections/issuesdepth/gender-equality/

U.S. National Center for Education Statistics. (2016). Degrees conferred by race and sex. USNCES. https://nces.ed.gov/fastfacts/display.asp?id=72

Van Emmerik, H., Wendt, H., & Euwema, M. C. (2010). Gender ratio, societal culture, and male and female leadership. *Journal of Occupational and Organizational Psychology, 83*(4), 895–914. doi:10.1348/096317909X478548

Xenikou, A., & Furnham, A. (2013). *Group dynamics and organizational culture: Effective work groups and organizations*. Palgrave. doi:10.1007/978-1-137-26546-3

Yukl, G. A. (2006). *Leadership in Organizations,* (6th ed.). Pearson.

# Compilation of References


Abbu, H. R., & Gopalakrishna, P. (2021). Synergistic effects of market orientation implementation and internalization on firm performance: Direct marketing service provider industry. *Journal of Business Research, 125*, 851–863. doi:10.1016/j.jbusres.2019.06.004

Aberšek, B., & Flogie, A. (2017). Evolution of competences for new era or education 4.0. In *XXV Conference of Czech Educational Research Association (CERA/ČAPV) "Impact of Technologies in the Sphere of Education and Educational Research."* Czech.

Agarwal, S. D., Barthel, M. L., Rost, C., Borning, A., Bennett, W. L., and Johnson, C. N. (2014). Grassroots organizing in the digital age: considering values and technology in Tea Party and Occupy Wall Street. *Inform. Commun. Soc. 17*, 326–341. doi:. 873068 doi:10.1080/1369118X.2013

Agarwal, R., & Prasad, J. (1998). A conceptual and operational definition of personal innovativeness in the domain of information technology. *Information Systems Research, 9*(2), 204–215. doi:10.1287/isre.9.2.204

Agostini, L., Nosella, A., & Venturini, K. (2019). Toward increasing affective commitment in SME strategic networks. *Business Process Management Journal, 25*(7), 1822–1840. doi:10.1108/BPMJ-02-2018-0035

Agrawal, K. (2015). Investigating the determinants of Big Data Analytics (BDA) adoption in Asian emerging economies. *AMCIS*.

Ajmal, S., Farooq, M. Z., Sajid, N., & Awan, S. (2012). Role of leadership in change management process. *Abasyn University Journal of Social Sciences, 5*(2), 111–124.

Akdere, M., & Schmidt, S. W. (2008). Employee Perceptions of Quality Management Effects of Employee Orientation Training. *Paper presented at the Academy of Human Resource Development International Research Conference in the Americas,* Panama City. https://eric.ed.gov/?id=ED501643

Al A'ali, E., & Al-Sarraf, A. R. (2016). Ethical Consumerism: Contextual Issues Of Ethical Decision-making Processes: An Exploratory Study. In Ethical and Social Perspectives on Global Business interaction in Emerging Markets, (pp.133-149). IGI Global

Al A'Ali, E. (2020). The Role of Auditing Firms in Promoting Ethical Consumerism. In *Ethical Consumerism and Comparative Studies Across Different Cultures,* (pp. 39–52). IGI GLOBAL. doi:10.4018/978-1-7998-0272-3.ch004

Al Kahtani, N. S., Nawab, A. K., & Allam, Z. (2016). Unfair HRM practices in the telecom sector in Saudi Arabia. An empirical investigation of selected public and private sector companies. *International Journal of Applied Business and Economic Research, 14*(10), 6377–6396.

Al-Ayed, S. I. (2019). The impact of strategic human resource management on organizational resilience: An empirical study on hospitals. *Business: Theory and Practice, 20*, 179–186. doi:10.3846/btp.2019.17

Alcatel-Lucent. (2022). Digital Age Communications. Alcatel-Lucent. https://www.al-enterprise.com/en/solutions/digital-age-communications

Al-Emran, M., Mezhuyev, V., & Kamaludin, A. (2018). PLS-SEM in information systems research: A comprehensive methodological reference. *4th international conference on advanced intelligent systems and informatics.*

Alghafri, A. A. (2015). Literature Review on: 'The Advantages and Disadvantages of Implementing E-HRM for an Organisation, E-Learning as an Example.'. *American Journal of Economics*, *5*(2), 51–55. doi:10.5923/c.economics.201501.02

Ali, M., Zhang, L., Shah, S. J., Khan, S., & Shah, A. M. (2020). Impact of humble leadership on project success: The mediating role of psychological empowerment and innovative work behavior. *Leadership and Organization Development Journal*, *41*(3), 349–367. doi:10.1108/LODJ-05-2019-0230

Al-Kahtani, N. S., & Allam, Z. (2013). Supportive and defensive communication climate among subordinate staff of Salman bin Abdulaziz University: An empirical assessment. *Life Science Journal*, *10*(4), 502–509.

Al-Khatib, A. W., & Al-ghanem, E. M. (2021). Radical innovation, incremental innovation, and competitive advantage, the moderating role of technological intensity: Evidence from the manufacturing sector in Jordan. *European Business Review*, *34*(3), 344–369. doi:10.1108/EBR-02-2021-0041

Allam, Z. (2017). Employee Disengagement: A Fatal Consequence to Organization and its Ameliorative Measures. *International Review of Management and Marketing*, *7*(2), 49–52.

Allam, Z. (2018). Students' perception of quality in higher education: An empirical investigation. *Management Science Letters*, *8*(5), 437–444. doi:10.5267/j.msl.2018.4.002

Allam, Z. (2019). Exploring ambient discriminatory HRM practices: An insight from Kingdom Telecom Company. *The Journal of Social Sciences Research*, *5*(3), 646–654. doi:10.32861/jssr.53.646.654

Allam, Z. (2020). Demystifying the aspect of quality in higher education: Insights from Saudi Arabia. *SAGE Open*, *10*(1), 2158244019899057. doi:10.1177/2158244019899057

Allam, Z., & Malik, A. (2020). Exploring the Predictors of Student Satisfaction: A Case of Undergraduate Business School in King-dom of Saudi Arabia. *Universal Journal of Educational Research*, *8*(11B), 5760–5767. doi:10.13189/ujer.2020.082210

Allen, N. J., & Meyer, J. P. (1990). The measurement and antecedents of affective, continuance and normative commitment to the organization. *Journal of Occupational Psychology*, *63*(1), 1–18. doi:10.1111/j.2044-8325.1990.tb00506.x

Allen, N. J., & Meyer, J. P. (1996). Affective, Continuance, and Normative Commitment to the Organization: An Examination of Construct Validity. *Journal of Vocational Behavior*, *49*(3), 252–276. doi:10.1006/jvbe.1996.0043 PMID:8980084

Alqurashi, E. (2016). Self-Efficacy In Online Learning Environments: A Literature Review. [CIER]. *Contemporary Issues in Education Research*, *9*(1), 45–52. doi:10.19030/cier.v9i1.9549

Amin, W., Akram, U., Shahzad, F., & Amir, M. (2018). Impact of transformation leadership on affective employee's commitment. *European Online Journal of Natural and Social Sciences: Proceedings, 7*(1(s)), pp-48.

Anand, A., Walsh, I., & Moffett, S. (2019). Does humility facilitate knowledge sharing? Investigating the role of humble knowledge inquiry and response. *Journal of Knowledge Management*, *23*(6), 1218–1244. doi:10.1108/JKM-06-2018-0353

Anderson, J. C., & Gerbing, D. W. (1988). Structural equation modeling in practice: A review and recommended two-step approach. *Psychological Bulletin*, *103*(3), 411–423. doi:10.1037/0033-2909.103.3.411

Andersson, P., Movin, S., Mähring, M., Teigland, R., & Wennberg, K. (2018). *Managing digital transformation.* SSE Institute for Research, Stockholm School of Economics.

Andiyana, M. A., Maya, R., & Hidayat, W. (2018). Ability analysis thinking creative creative student mathematics students in material building construction. *Journal of Innovative Mathematics Learning/Jurnal Pembelajaran Matematika Inovatif, 1*(3), 239.

Annakis, J., Lobo, A. and Pillay, S. (2011) 'Exploring Monitoring, Work Environment and Flexibility as Predictors of Job Satisfaction within Australian Call Centers.' *International Journal of Business and Management, 6*(8), pp. 75-93, Research Gate. doi:10.5539/ijbm.v6n8p75

Appelbaum, S. Audet, L &Miller, J. (2013). Gender and leadership? Leadership and gender? A journey through the landscape of theories. *Leadership and Organization Development Journal, 24*(1), 43-51.

Appleton, S. L., Melaku, A. Y., Reynolds, C. A., Gill, T. K., De Batlle, J., & Adams, J. R. (2022). Multidimensional sleep health is associated with mental well-being in Australian adults. *Journal of Sleep Research, 31*(2), e13477. doi:10.1111/jsr.13477 PMID:34622511

Arafsha, F., Masudul Alam, K., & El Saddik, A. (2012). EmoJacket: consumer centric wearable affective jacket to enhance emotional immersion. In *Proceedings of the 2012 International Conference on Innovations in Information Technology (IIT)*, 350–355. 10.1109/INNOVATIONS.2012.6207766

Argandona, A. (2015). Humility in management. *Journal of Business Ethics, 132*(1), 63–71. doi:10.100710551-014-2311-8

Arora, C. R. P. (2019). Predicting Job Expectations of Millennials: A Generation with Soaring Work Projections. *SKIPS 1*(1).

Arora, P. (2020). *Understanding and Analyzing the Determinants of Millennials' Workplace Expectations: A Study on Management Aspirants With Special Focus on Gujarat State.* [Doctoral Dissertation] GLS University. http://hdl.handle.net/10603/308037

Arora, P., & Kshatriya, K. P. (2017). Millennials: The new generation with high employment expectations. *International Journal (Toronto, Ont.), 5*(8), 101–109.

Arora, P., & Kshatriya, K. P. (2018). Redefining Millennials: Understanding characteristics and Perceptions of Generation Y. *International Research Journal of Human Resources and Social Sciences, 5*(03), 181–199.

Atasoy, R., & Güçlü, N. (2020). Evaluation of numeracy skills of adults according to the results of PIAAC 2015 in Turkey. *World Journal of Education, 10*(2), 1–123. doi:10.5430/wje.v10n2p27

Aurelia, S., & Momin, M. M. (2020). Global reverberation and prediction for HRM amid and after COVID-19: A technological viewpoint. *Materials Today: Proceedings.* doi:10.1016/j.matpr.2020.11.544

Avey, J. B., Luthans, F., & Jensen, S. M. (2009). Psychological Capital: A Positive Resource For Combating Employee Stress And Turnover. *Human Resource Management, 48*(5), 677–693. doi:10.1002/hrm.20294

Avey, J. B., Luthans, F., Smith, R. M., & Palmer, N. F. (2010). Impact of positive psychological capital on employee well-being over time. *Journal of Occupational Health Psychology, 15*(1), 17–28. doi:10.1037/a0016998 PMID:20063956

Avgoustaki, A., & Bessa, I. (2019). Examining the link between flexible working arrangement bundles and employee work effort. *Human Resource Management, 58*(4), 431–449. doi:10.1002/hrm.21969

Avolio, B. J., Sosik, J. J., Kahai, S. S., & Baker, B. (2014). E-leadership: re-examining transformations in leadership source and transmission. Leader. Q. 25, 105–131. doi:10.1016/j.leaqua.2013.11.003

Avolio, B. J. (1999). *Full leadership development: Building the vital forces in organizations*. Sage.

Avolio, B. J., Kahai, S., & Dodge, G. E. (2000). E-leadership: Implications for theory, research, and practice. *The Leadership Quarterly*, *11*(4), 615–668. doi:10.1016/S1048-9843(00)00062-X

Ayman, R., & Korabik, K. (2010). Leadership: Why gender and culture matter. *The American Psychologist*, *65*(3), 157–170. doi:10.1037/a0018806 PMID:20350015

Bagozzi, R. P., Yi, Y., & Phillips, L. W. (1991). Assessing construct validity in organizational research. *Administrative Science Quarterly*, *36*(3), 421–458. doi:10.2307/2393203

Bag, S., Pretorius, J. H. C., Gupta, S., & Dwivedi, Y. K. (2021). Role of institutional pressures and resources in the adoption of big data analytics powered artificial intelligence, sustainable manufacturing practices and circular economy capabilities. *Technological Forecasting and Social Change*, *163*, 120420. doi:10.1016/j.techfore.2020.120420

Bakardjieva, M., Felt, M., & Dumitrica, D. (2018). The mediatization of leadership: Grassroots digital facilitators as organic intellectuals, sociometric stars and caretakers*. *Information Communication and Society*, *21*, 899–914. doi:10.1080/1369118X.2018.1434556

Baker, W. E., & Sinkula, J. M. (2007). Does market orientation facilitate balanced innovation programs? An organizational learning perspective. *Journal of Product Innovation Management*, *24*(4), 316–334. doi:10.1111/j.1540-5885.2007.00254.x

Bal, V., Campbell, M., Steed, J., & Meddings, K. (2008). The role of power in effective leadership. *Center for Creative Leadership*. www. ccl. org

Balthazard, P. A., Waldman, D. A., and Warren, J. E. (2009). Predictors of the emergence of transformational leadership in virtual decision teams. *Leader. Q. 20*, 651–663. doi:. 06.008 doi:10.1016/j.leaqua.2009

Balyer, A., & Öz, Ö. (2018). Academicians Views on Digital Transformation in Education. *International Online Journal of Education & Teaching*, *5*(4), 809–830.

Bambale, A. J. A., Mohd Shamsudin, F., & Subramaniam, C. (2011). Stimulating organizational citizenship behavior (OCB) research for theory development: Exploration of leadership paradigms. [IJARBSS]. *International Journal of Academic Research in Business & Social Sciences*, *1*, 48–69.

Bannon, S., Ford, K., & Meltzer, L. (2011). Understanding millennials in the workplace. *The CPA Journal*, *81*(11), 61.

Barasa, E., Mbau, R., & Gilson, L. (2018). What Is Resilience and How Can It Be Nurtured? A Systematic Review of Empirical Literature on Organizational Resilience. *International Journal of Health Policy and Management*, *7*(6), 491–503. doi:10.15171/ijhpm.2018.06 PMID:29935126

Barba-Aragón, M. I., & Jiménez-Jiménez, D. (2020). HRM and radical innovation: A dual approach with exploration as a mediator. *European Management Journal*, *38*(5), 791–803. doi:10.1016/j.emj.2020.03.007

Bardoel, E. A., Pettit, T. M., Cieri, H. D., & Mcmillan, L. (2014). Employee resilience: An emerging challenge for HRM. *Asia Pacific Journal of Human Resources*, *52*(3), 279–297. doi:10.1111/1744-7941.12033

Barker, J., & Gossman, P. (2013). The learning impact of a virtual learning environment: Students' views. *Teacher Education Advancement*, *5*(2), 19–38.

Barley, S. R. (2015). Why the internet makes buying a car less loathsome: How technologies change role relations. *Academy of Management Discoveries*, *1*(1), 5–35. doi:10.5465/amd.2013.0016

Bartol, K. M., & Liu, W. (2002). Information technology and human resources management: Harnessing the power and potential of netcentricity. *Research in Personnel and Human Resources Management*, *21*, 215–242. doi:10.1016/S0742-7301(02)21005-1

Bartolomé, A., Castañeda, L., & Adell, J. (2018). Personalisation in educational technology: The absence of underlying pedagogies. *International Journal of Educational Technology in Higher Education*, *15*(14), 1–17. doi:10.118641239-018-0095-0

Bass, B. M., and Avolio, B. J. (1993). Transformational leadership and organizational culture. *Public Admin. Q. 17*, 112–121.

Bass, B. M. (1981). *Stogdill's Handbook of Leadership: A Survey of Theory and Research. Revised and Expanded Edition* (2nd ed.). Free Press.

Bass, B. M. (1985). *Leadership and Performance Beyond Expectations* (1st ed.). Free Press.

Bass, B. M. (1990). From transactional to transformational leadership: Learning to share the vision. *Organizational Dynamics*, *18*(3), 19–31. doi:10.1016/0090-2616(90)90061-S

Bass, B. M. (2009). *The Bass Handbook of Leadership,* (4th ed.). Free Press.

Bass, B. M., & Avolio, B. J. (1993). Transformational leadership and organizational culture. *Public Administration Quarterly*, *17*, 112–121.

Bass, B. M., Jung, D. I., Avolio, B. J., & Berson, Y. (2003). Predicting unit performance by assessing transformational and transactional leadership. *The Journal of Applied Psychology*, *88*(2), 207–218. doi:10.1037/0021-9010.88.2.207 PMID:12731705

Bass, B. M., & Riggio, R. E. (2006). *Transformational leadership*. Psychology Pres. doi:10.4324/9781410617095

Beard, J. R., Officer, A., Araujo de Carvalho, I., Sadana, R., Pot, A.-M., Michel, J.-P., Lloyd-Sherlock, P., Epping-Jordan, J., Peeters, G., Mahanani, W.-R., Thiyagarajan, J. A., & Chatterji, S. (2017). The World report on ageing and health: A policy framework for healthy ageing. *Lancet*, *387*(10033), 2145–2154. doi:10.1016/S0140-6736(15)00516-4 PMID:26520231

Beckers, A. M., & Bsat, M. Z. (2002). A dss classification model for research in human resource information systems. *Information Systems Management*, *19*(3), 1–10. doi:10.1201/1078/43201.19.3.20020601/37169.6

Bekkhus, R., & Hallikainen, P. (2017). A new dualistic Cio toolbox: towards ambidexterity in the digital business transformation. In *Proceedings of the 17th Conferência da Associação Portuguesa de Sistemas de Informação, CAPSI'* (Guimarães), 23–41.

Bencsik, A., Horváth-Csikós, G., & Juhász, T. (2016). Y and Z Generations at Workplaces. *J. Compet.*, *8*, 90–106.

Benešová, A., & Tupa, J. (2017). Requirements for Education and Qualification of People in Industry 4.0. *Procedia Manufacturing*, *11*, 2195–2202. doi:10.1016/j.promfg.2017.07.366

Bennett, W. L., & Segerberg, A. (2013). *The Logic of Connective Action: Digital Media and the Personalization of Contentious Politics*. Cambridge University Press. doi:10.1017/CBO9781139198752

Bennis, W. G. (1989). Managing the dream: Leadership in the 21st century. *Journal of Organizational Change Management*, *2*(1), 6–10. doi:10.1108/09534818910134040

Bergiel, J. B., Bergiel, E. B., & Balsmeier, P. W. (2008). Nature of virtual teams: A summary of their advantages and disadvantages. *Management Research News*, *31*(2), 99–110. doi:10.1108/01409170810846821

Berman, S., & Korsten, P. (2014). Leading in the connected era. *Strategy and Leadership*, *42*(1), 37–46. doi:10.1108/SL-10-2013-0078

Berson, Y., & Avolio, B. J. (2004). Transformational leadership and the dissemination of organizational goals: A case study of a telecommunication firm. *The Leadership Quarterly*, *15*(5), 625–646. doi:10.1016/j.leaqua.2004.07.003

Beycioglu, K. (Ed.). (2014). *Multidimensional perspectives on principal leadership effectiveness*. IGI Global.

Bhamra, R., Dani, S., & Burnard, K. (2011). Resilience: The concept, a literature review and future directions. *International Journal of Production Research*, *49*(18), 5375–5393. doi:10.1080/00207543.2011.563826

Bharadwaj, A., El-Sawy, O. A., Pavlou, P. A., & Venkatraman, N. (2013). Digital business strategy: Toward a next generation of insights. *Management Information Systems Quarterly*, *37*(2), 471–482. doi:10.25300/MISQ/2013/37:2.3

Bhatnagar, D., Singh, S., Yadav, S., Kumar, A., & Kaur, I. (2017). Experimental and theoretical investigation of relative optical band gaps in graphene generations. *Materials Research Express*, *4*(1), 015101. doi:10.1088/2053-1591/4/1/015101

Bidee, J., Vantilborgh, T., Pepermans, R., Huybrechts, G., Willems, J., Jegers, M., & Hofmans, J. (2012). Autonomous motivation stimulates volunteers' work effort: A self-determination theory approach to volunteerism. *Voluntas*, *24*(1), 32–47. doi:10.100711266-012-9269-x

Birkinshaw, J., Hamel, G., & Mol, M. J. (2008). Management innovation. *Academy of Management Review*, *33*(4), 825–845. doi:10.5465/amr.2008.34421969

Bissola, R., & Imperatori, B. (2014). The unexpected side of relational e-HRM. *Employee Relations*, *36*(4), 376–397. doi:10.1108/ER-07-2013-0078

Bjorn, P., & Ngwenyama, O. (2009). Virtual team collaboration: Building shared meaning, resolving breakdowns and creating translucence. *Information Systems Journal*, *19*(3), 227–253. doi:10.1111/j.1365-2575.2007.00281.x

Boateng, S. L., & Narteh, B. (2016). Online relationship marketing and affective customer commitment–The mediating role of trust. *Journal of Financial Services Marketing*, *21*(2), 127–140. doi:10.1057/fsm.2016.5

Bobek, A., & Wickham, J. (2015) *Working Conditions in Ireland Project; Employment in the Irish Financial Services Sector: A preliminary Background Report*. https://www.tasc.ie/assets/files/pdf/20150929160149.pdf

Bodrov, V. A. (2012). *Psychological stress. Development and overcoming*. Per Se.

Boe, O., & Torgersen, G. E. (2018). Norwegian "digital border defense" and competence for the unforeseen: A grounded theory approach. *Frontiers in Psychology*, *9*, 1–15. doi:10.3389/fpsyg.2018.00555 PMID:29725314

Bogacheva, T. Yu. (2010) Health in the system of life values of a modern specialist. Ranepa. Moscow.

Boje, D. M., Rosile, G. A., Durant, R. A., & Luhman, J. T. (2004). Enron spectacles: A critical dramaturgical analysis. *Organization Studies*, *25*(5), 751–774. doi:10.1177/0170840604042413

Bolden, R., & O'Regan, N. (2016). Digital disruption and the future of leadership: An interview with Rick Haythornthwaite, chairman of Centrica and MasterCard. *Journal of Management Inquiry*, *25*(4), 438–446. doi:10.1177/1056492616638173

Bondarouk, T., Parry, E., & Furtmueller, E. (2017). Electronic hrm: Four decades of research on adoption and consequences. *International Journal of Human Resource Management*, *28*(1), 98–131. doi:10.1080/09585192.2016.1245672

Bondarouk, T., & Ruël, H. (2009). Electronic Human Resource Management: Challenges in the digital era. *International Journal of Human Resource Management*, *20*(3), 505–514. doi:10.1080/09585190802707235

Bondarouk, T., & Ruël, H. (2013). The strategic value of e-HRM: Results from an exploratory study in a governmental organization. *International Journal of Human Resource Management*, *24*(2), 391–414. doi:10.1080/09585192.2012.675142

Bondarouk, T., Ruël, H., & Looise, J. K. (2004). E-HRM: Innovation or Irritation. An Explorative Empirical Study in Five Large Companies on Web-based HRM. *Management Review*, *15*(3), 364–380. doi:10.5771/0935-9915-2004-3-364

Bondar, S., Hsu, J. C., Pfouga, A., & Stjepandić, J. (2017). Agile digital transformation of system-of-systems architecture models using Zachman framework. *Journal of Industrial Information Integration*, *7*, 33–43. doi:10.1016/j.jii.2017.03.001

Bonekamp, L., & Sure, M. (2015). Consequences of industry 4.0 on human labour and work organisation. *Journal of Business and Media Psychology*, *6*(1), 33–40.

Borchgrevink, C. P., & Boster, F. J. (1997). Leader-member exchange development: A hospitality antecedent investigation. *International Journal of Hospitality Management*, *16*(3), 241–259. doi:10.1016/S0278-4319(97)00013-3

Borgerson, J. L. (2018). *Caring and Power in Female Leadership. A Philosophical Approach*. Cambridge Scholars Publishing.

Borle, P., Boerner, F., Susanne, Z., Mahlknecht, V., Hasselhorn, H. M., & Ebener, M. (2020). The social and health implications of digital work intensification. Associations between exposure to information and communication technologies, health and work ability in different socio-economic strata. *International Archives of Occupational and Environmental Health*. doi:10.100700420-020-01588-5 PMID:33084928

Borman, W. C., & Motowidlo, S. J. (1997). Task Performance and Contextual Performance: The Meaning for Personnel Selection Research. *Human Performance*, *10*(2), 99–109. doi:10.120715327043hup1002_3

Born, A., Ranehill, E., & Sandberg, A. (2018). A man's world? – The impact of a male dominated environment on female leadership. *Working Papers in Economics*, 744.

Boyatzis, R. E. (2006). Using tipping points of emotional intelligence and cognitive competencies to predict financial performance of leaders. *Psicothema 18*, 124–131. https://www.redalyc.org/articulo.oa?id= 72709519

Boyatzis, R. E., Thiel, K., Rochford, K., & Black, A. (2017). Emotional and social intelligence competencies of incident team commanders fighting wildfires. *The Journal of Applied Behavioral Science*, *53*(4), 498–516. doi:10.1177/0021886317731575

Brady, M. (2016). *Better Quality of Work Life is Worth a $7,600 Pay Cut for Millennials*. https://www.businesswire.com/news/home/20160407005736/en/Quality-Work-Life-Worth-7600-Pay-Cut

Brannan, M. J., Parsons, E., & Priola, V. (2015). Brands at Work: The Search for Meaning in Mundane Work. *Organization Studies*, *36*(1), 29–53. doi:10.1177/0170840614553382

Breij, S., Qvist, J. Y., Holman, D., Mäcken, J., Seitsamo, J., Huisman, M., & Deeg, D. J. H. (2019). Educational inequalities in health after work exit: The role of work characteristics. *BMC Public Health*, *19*(1), 1515. doi:10.118612889-019-7872-0 PMID:31718592

Broadbelt, G. (2016) *Leadership in the Digital Age*. Impact. https://www.impactinternational.com/blog/2016/02/leadership-digital-age

Brockbank, W. (1999). If hr were really strategically proactive: Present and future directions in hr's contribution to competitive advantage. *Human Resource Management*, *38*(4), 337–352. doi:10.1002/(SICI)1099-050X(199924)38:4<337::AID-HRM8>3.0.CO;2-5

Brockner, J., Grover, S., Reed, T. F., & Dewitt, R. L. (1992). Layoffs, Job Insecurity, And Survivors' Work Effort: Evidence Of An Inverted-U Relationship. *Academy of Management Journal*, *35*(2), 413–425. doi:10.2307/256380

Brown, M. E., Trevino, L. K., & Harrison, D. A. (2005). Ethical leadership: A social learning perspective for construct development and testing. *Organizational Behavior and Human Decision Processes*, *97*(2), 117–134. doi:10.1016/j.obhdp.2005.03.002

Brown, R. B. (1993). Meta-Competence: A Recipe for Reframing the Competence Debate. *Personnel Review*, *22*(6), 25–36. doi:10.1108/EUM0000000000814

Brown, S. P., & Leigh, T. W. (1996). A new look at psychological climate and its relationship to job involvement, effort, and performance. *The Journal of Applied Psychology*, *81*(4), 358–368. doi:10.1037/0021-9010.81.4.358 PMID:8751453

Brunner, M., Gonzalez-Castañé, G., & Ravesteijn, P. (2021). How Digital Leadership competences and IT Capabilities affect an organization's ability to digitally transform and adopt new technologies. *Journal of International Technology and Information Management*, *30*(4), 139–156.

Bruskin, S. N., Brezhneva, A. N., Dyakonova, L. P., Kitova, O. V., Savinova, V. M., Danko, T. P., & Sekerin, V. D. (2017). Business performance management models based on the digital corporation's paradigm. *European Research Studies Journal*, *20*(4), 264–274.

Brynjolfsson, E., & Mcafee, A. (2014). *The second age machine*. W.W Norton & Company.

Buch, R. (2015). Leader–member exchange as a moderator of the relationship between employee–organization exchange and affective commitment. *International Journal of Human Resource Management*, *26*(1), 59–79. doi:10.1080/09585192.2014.934897

Bughin, J., Hazan, E., Lund, S., Dahlstrom, P., Wiesinger, A., & Subramaniam, A. (2018). *Skill shift: Automation and the future of the workforce*. McKinsey Global Institute.

Bughin, J., Hazan, E., Lund, S., Dahlström, P., Wiesinger, A., & Subramaniam, A. (2018). *Skill Shift: Automation and the Future of the Workforce*. McKinsey Global Institute.

Bughin, J., & Van Zeebroeck, N. (2017). The Best Response to Digital Disruption. *MIT Sloan Management Review*, *58*(4), 80–86.

Burgard, S. A., & Lin, K. Y. (2013). Bad Jobs, Bad Health? How Work and Working Conditions Contribute to Health Disparities. *The American Behavioral Scientist*, *57*(8), 1105–1127. doi:10.1177/0002764213487347 PMID:24187340

Burgess. (2008). Managing the new workforce Generation Y (Millennials). *Red Fusion*.

Burkhardt, M. E., & Brass, D. J. (1990). Changing patterns or patterns of change: The effects of a change in technology on social network structure and power. *Administrative Science Quarterly*, *35*(1), 104–127. doi:10.2307/2393552

Burner, T. (2018). Why is educational change so difficult and how can we make it more effective? *Forskning og forandring, 1*(1), 122-134.

Burns, J. M. (1978). *Leadership*. Harper & Row.

Büschgens, T., Bausch, A., & Balkin, D. B. (2013). Organizing for radical innovation—A multi-level behavioral approach. *The Journal of High Technology Management Research*, *24*(2), 138–152. doi:10.1016/j.hitech.2013.09.004

Bush, T. (2021). Leading through COVID-19: Managing a crisis. *Educational Management Administration & Leadership*, *49*(3), 373–374. doi:10.1177/1741143221997267

Butcher, K., Power, M. J., & Orr, M. P. (2021). Museum Leadership for Engaging, Equitable Education: The Transformative Potential of Digitized Collections for Authentic Learning Experiences. *Curator (New York, N.Y.)*, *64*(2), 383–402. doi:10.1111/cura.12423

Bygstad, B., Aanby, H., & Iden, J. (2017). Leading digital transformation: the Scandinavian way. Lecture notes in Business Information Processing. In *Proceedings of the 8th Scandinavian Conference on Information Systems*, SCIS (Halden), 1–14.

Cabello-Medina, C., Carmona-Lavado, A., Pérez-Luño, A., & Cuevas-Rodríguez, G. (2011). Do best and worst innovation performance companies differ in terms of intellectual capital, knowledge and radicalness. *African Journal of Business Management*, *5*(28), 11450–11466. doi:10.5897/AJBM11.600

Caligiuri, P., De Cieri, H., Minbaeva, D., Verbeke, A., & Zimmermann, A. (2020). International HRM insights for navigating the COVID-19 pandemic: Implications for future research and practice. *Journal of International Business Studies*, *51*(5), 697–713. doi:10.105741267-020-00335-9 PMID:32836500

Campbell, B. A., Coff, R., & Kryscynski, D. (2012). Rethinking sustained competitive advantage from human capital. *Academy of Management Review*, *37*(3), 376–395. doi:10.5465/amr.2010.0276

Campbell, J. P., & Pritchard, R. D. (1976). Motivation theory in industrial and organizational psychology. In M. Dunette (Ed.), *Handbook of Industrial and oeganizational psychology,* (pp. 63–130). Rand-McNally.

Campione, W. (2015). Corporate Offerings: Why aren't Millennials Staying? *Journal of Applied Business & Economics*, *17*(4), 60–75.

Canedo, J. C., Graen, G., Grace, M., & Johnson, R. D. (2017). Navigating the new workplace: Technology, millennials, and accelerating HR innovation. *AIS Transactions on Human-Computer Interaction*, *9*(3), 243–260. doi:10.17705/1thci.00097

Cann, O. (2016). Five million jobs by 2020: The real challenge of the fourth industrial revolution. World Economic Forum. *International Organisation for Public Private Cooperation,* Geneva, Switzerland.

Carmeli, A., Gelbard, R., & Gefen, D. (2010). The importance of innovation leadership in cultivating strategic fit and enhancing firm performance. *The Leadership Quarterly*, *21*(3), 339–349. doi:10.1016/j.leaqua.2010.03.001

Carte, T. A., Chidambaram, L., & Becker, A. (2006). Emergent leadership in self-managed virtual teams. *Group Decision and Negotiation*, *15*(4), 323–343. doi:10.100710726-006-9045-7

Cascio, W. F., & Montealegre, R. (2016). How technology is changing work and organizations. *Annual Review of Organizational Psychology and Organizational Behavior*, *3*(1), 349–375. doi:10.1146/annurev-orgpsych-041015-062352

Casimir, G., Ng, Y. N. K., Wang, K. Y., & Ooi, G. (2014). The relationships amongst leader-member exchange, perceived organizational support, affective commitment, and in-role performance: A social-exchange perspective. *Leadership and Organization Development Journal*, *35*(5), 366–385. doi:10.1108/LODJ-04-2012-0054

Castells, M. (2012). *Networks of Outrage and Hope: Social Movements in the Internet Age*. Wiley-Blackwell.

Catalyst. (2015a). *Women CEOs of the S&P 500.* www.catalyst.org/knowledge/ women-ceos-sp-500.

Celik, D.A. and Oz, E.U. (2011). The Effects of Emotional Dissonance and Quality of Work Life Perceptions on Absenteeism and Turnover Intentions among Turkish Call Center Employees. *Procedia Social and Behavioral Science, 30*(1), pp. 2515– 2519, Research Gate. . doi:10.1016/j.sbspro.2011.10.491

Celma, D., Martinez-Garcia, E., & Raya, J. M. (2018). Socially responsible HR practices and their effects on employees' wellbeing: Empirical evidence from Catalonia, Spain. *European Research on Management and Business Economics*, *24*(2), 82–89. doi:10.1016/j.iedeen.2017.12.001

Chakraborty, A. R., & Mansor, N. N. (2013). Adoption of Human Resource Information System: A Theoretical Analysis. *Procedia: Social and Behavioral Sciences*, *75*, 473–478. doi:10.1016/j.sbspro.2013.04.051

Chamorro-Premuzic, T., & Sanger, M. 2016. What Leadership Looks Like in Different Cultures. *Harvard Business Review*. https://hbr.org/2016/05/what-leadership-lookslike-in-different-cultures.

Chang, E., & Hancock, K. (2003). Role stress and role ambiguity in new nursing graduates in Australia. *Nursing & Health Sciences*, *5*(2), 155–163. doi:10.1046/j.1442-2018.2003.00147.x PMID:12709171

Chang, W., Franke, G. R., Butler, T. D., Musgrove, C. F., & Ellinger, A. E. (2014). Differential mediating effects of radical and incremental innovation on market orientation-performance relationship: A meta-analysis. *Journal of Marketing Theory and Practice*, *22*(3), 235–250. doi:10.2753/MTP1069-6679220301

Chanias, S., & Hess, T. (2016). Understanding digital transformation strategy formation: Insights from Europe's automotive industry. *PACIS 2016 Proceedings*, Chiayi, Taiwan, 296. https://aisel.aisnet.org/pacis2016/296

Cheng, M. (2019) *8 Characteristics of Millennials That Support Sustainable Development Goals (SDGs)* https://www.forbes.com/sites/margueritacheng/2019/06/19/8-characteristics-of-millennials-that-support-sustainable-development-goals-sdgs/?sh=66e01a7029b7

Chen, L., Liu, S., Wang, Y., & Hu, X. (2021). Humble leader behavior and team creativity: The team learning perspective. *Journal of Managerial Psychology*, *36*(3), 272–284. doi:10.1108/JMP-09-2019-0536

Chen, X., & Wei, S. (2020). The impact of social media use for communication and social exchange relationship on employee performance. *Journal of Knowledge Management*, *24*(6), 1289–1314. doi:10.1108/JKM-04-2019-0167

Cho, J., Schilpzand, P., Huang, L., & Paterson, T. (2021a). How and when humble leadership facilitates employee job performance: The roles of feeling trusted and job autonomy. *Journal of Leadership & Organizational Studies*, *28*(2), 169–184. doi:10.1177/1548051820979634

Cho, V., Roll, L. C., Wu, C. H., & Tang, V. (2021b). Changing Digital Age in the Wake of COVID-19: How Does Humility Impact on Virtual Leaderless Teams? [JGIM]. *Journal of Global Information Management*, *30*(4), 1–23. doi:10.4018/JGIM.290831

Christ, C. P. (2014). Do we still need the Journal of Feminist Studies in Religion? *Journal of Feminist Studies in Religion*, *30*(2), 139–141. doi:10.2979/jfemistudreli.30.2.139

Cisco (2010). The Cisco Connected World Report. *Cisco Systems*.

Coad, A., Holm, J. R., Krafft, J., & Quatraro, F. (2018). Firm age and performance. *Journal of Evolutionary Economics*, *28*(1), 1–11. doi:10.100700191-017-0532-6

Cogliser, C. C., & Schriesheim, C. A. (2000). Exploring work unit context and leader–member exchange: A multi-level perspective. *Journal of Organizational Behavior*, *21*(5), 487–511. doi:10.1002/1099-1379(200008)21:5<487::AID-JOB57>3.0.CO;2-P

Cole, G., Smith, R., & Lucas, L. (2002). The debut of Generation Y in the American workforce. *Journal of Business Administration Online*, *1*(2), 1–10.

Conger, J. A., & Kanungo, R. N. (1988). The Empowerment Process: Integrating Theory and Practice. *Academy of Management Review*, *13*(3), 471–482. doi:10.2307/258093

Cooper, B., Wang, J., Bartram, T., & Cooke, F. L. (2018). Well-being-oriented human resource management practices and employee performance in the Chinese banking sector: The role of social climate and resilience. *Human Resource Management*, *58*(1), 85–97. doi:10.1002/hrm.21934

Cooper, C. D., & Kurland, N. B. (2002). Telecommuting, professional isolation, and employee development in public and private organizations. *Journal of Organizational Behavior: The International Journal of Industrial. Occupational and Organizational Psychology and Behavior*, *23*(4), 511–532. doi:10.1002/job.145

Cooper, D. R., & Schindler, P. S. (2008). *Business Research Methods,* (10th ed.). McGraw Hill.

Cortellazzo, L. Bruni, E. & Zampieri, R. (2019). The Role of Leadership in a Digitalized world: A Review. *Frontiers in psychology, 10,* 1938. doi:10.3389/fpsyg.2019.1938

Cortellazzo, L., Bruni, E., & Zampieri, R. (2019, August). The Role of Leadership in a Digitalized World: A Review. *Frontiers in Psychology*, *10*, 1–21. doi:10.3389/fpsyg.2019.01938 PMID:31507494

Coutu, D. L. (2000). Too old to learn? *Harvard Business Review*, *78*, 37–42. https://hbr.org/2000/11/too-old-to-learn PMID:11184976

Coutu, D. L. (2002). How resilience works. *Harvard Business Review*, *80*, 46–55. PMID:12024758

Cozijnsen, A. J., Vrakking, W. J., & van IJzerloo, M. (2000). Success and failure of 50 innovation projects in Dutch companies. *European Journal of Innovation Management*, *3*(3), 150–159. doi:10.1108/14601060010322301

Credit Suisse Research Institute. (2012). *Gender diversity and corporate performance.* infocus.credit-suisse.com/data/_product_documents/_articles/360157/cs_women_in_leading_positions_FINAL.PDF

Creto, S. C., & Creto, S. T. (2019) Modern Management; concepts and skills (global edition). UK. Pearson Education limited.

Crossan, M. M., & Apaydin, M. (2010). A multi-dimensional framework of organizational innovation: A systematic review of the literature. *Journal of Management Studies*, *47*(6), 1154–1191. doi:10.1111/j.1467-6486.2009.00880.x

Curry, B. K. (2000). *Women in power: Pathways to leadership in Education.* Teachers College Press.

Cyganek, B., Graña, M., Krawczyk, B., Kasprzak, A., Porwik, P., Walkowiak, K., & Woźniak, M. (2016). A survey of big data issues in electronic health record analysis. *Applied Artificial Intelligence*, *30*(6), 497–520. doi:10.1080/08839514.2016.1193714

Dadaczynski, K., Paulus, P., & Horstmann, D. (2020). The predictive value of individual and work-related resources for the health and work satisfaction of German school principals. *Health Education Journal*, *79*(2), 225–236. doi:10.1177/0017896919867118

Dagenais-Desmarais, V., Leclerc, J.-S., & Londei-Shortall, J. (2018). The relationship between employee motivation and psychological health at work: A chicken-and-egg situation? *Work and Stress*, *32*(2), 147–167. doi:10.1080/02678373.2017.1317880

Dahl, R. A. (1957). The concept of power. *Behavioral Science*, *2*(3), 201–215. doi:10.1002/bs.3830020303

Dansereau, F. Jr, Graen, G., & Haga, W. J. (1975). A vertical dyad linkage approach to leadership within formal organizations: A longitudinal investigation of the role making process. *Organizational Behavior and Human Performance*, *13*(1), 46–78. doi:10.1016/0030-5073(75)90005-7

Dartey-Baah, K., & Addo, S. A. (2018). Psychological identification with job: A leadership-OCB mediator. *The International Journal of Organizational Analysis*, *27*(3), 548–565. doi:10.1108/IJOA-10-2017-1262

Davenport, T. H., & Harris, J. G. (2007). *Competing on Analytics: The New Science of Winning*. HBS Review Press.

David, Y., & Baden, C. (2018). Reframing community boundaries: The erosive power of new media spaces in authoritarian societies. *Information Communication and Society*. doi:10.1080/1369118X.2018.1486869

Day, C., & Leithwood, K. (Eds.). (2007). *Successful School Leadership in Times of Change*. Springer-Kluwer. doi:10.1007/1-4020-5516-1

De Cooman, R., De Gieter, S., Pepermans, R., Jegers, M., & Van Acker, F. (2009). Development and validation of the work effort scale. *European Journal of Psychological Assessment*, *25*(4), 266–273. doi:10.1027/1015-5759.25.4.266

de Villiers, C., Kuruppu, S., & Dissanayake, D. (2020). A new role for business – Promoting the United Nations' Sustainable Development Goals through the internet-of-things and blockchain technology. *Journal of Business Research*.

De-la-Calle-Durán, M. C., & Rodríguez-Sánchez, J. L. (2021). Employee Engagement and Wellbeing in Times of COVID-19: A Proposal of the 5Cs Model. *International Journal of Environmental Research and Public Health*, *18*(10), 5470. doi:10.3390/ijerph18105470 PMID:34065338

Deloitte (2016). *The 2016 Deloitte Millennial Survey winning over the next generation of leaders*. Deloitte Touche Tohmatsu Limited, United Kingdom.

Denison, D. R., Hooijberg, R., & Quinn, R. E. (1995). Paradox and performance: Toward a theory of behavioral complexity in managerial leadership. *Organization Science*, *6*(5), 524–540. doi:10.1287/orsc.6.5.524

Desanctis, G. (1986). Human Resource Information Systems: A Current Assessment. *Management Information Systems Quarterly*, *10*(1), 15. doi:10.2307/248875

DeSanctis, G., & Poole, M. S. (1994). Capturing the complexity in advanced technology use: Adaptive structuration theory. *Organization Science*, *5*(2), 121–147. doi:10.1287/orsc.5.2.121

Desmet, D., Duncan, E., Scanlan, J., & Singer, M. (2015). *Six building blocks for creating a high performing digital enterprise*. McKinsey & Company.

Dexter, S. (2011). School technology leadership: Artifacts in systems of practice. *Journal of School Leadership*, *21*(2), 166–189. doi:10.1177/105268461102100202

Dey, T., Kumar, A., & Kumar, Y. L. N. (2014). A New Look at the Antecedents and Consequences of Organizational Commitment: A Conceptual Study. *International Journal of Humanities and Social Science*, *4*(1).

Diamante, T., & London, M. (2002). Expansive leadership in the age of digital technology. *Journal of Management Development*, *21*(6), 404–416. doi:10.1108/02621710210430597

Diaz-Saenz, H. R. (2011). In A. Bryman, D. Collinson, K. Grint, B. Jackson, & M. Uhl-Bien (Eds.), *"Transformational leadership," in The Sage Handbook of Leadership,* (pp. 299–310). Sage Publications Ltd.

Dimitrios, N. K., Sakas, D. P., & Vlachos, D. S. (2013). The Role of Information Systems in Creating Strategic Leadership Model. *Procedia: Social and Behavioral Sciences*, *73*, 285–293. doi:10.1016/j.sbspro.2013.02.054

Dimitrov, A. (2018). The digital age leadership: a transhumanistic perspective. In *Symposium: "Envisioning Future Leadership: Utopia, Dystopia, or More of the Same?",* University of Phoenix. 10.1002/jls.21603

Dimock, (2019). *Defining generations: Where Millennials end and Generation Z begins*. Pew Research Centre. https://www.pewresearch.org/fact-tank/2019/01/17/where-millennials-end-and-generation-z-begins/

Domínguez-Escrig, E., Broch, F. F. M., Alcamí, R. L., & Gómez, R. C. (2021). Leaders who empower: A gateway to radical innovation. *Journal of Management & Organization*, *27*(5), 930–947. doi:10.1017/jmo.2019.73

Domínguez-Escrig, E., Broch, F. F. M., Gómez, R. C., & Alcamí, R. L. (2016). How does altruistic leader behavior foster radical innovation? The mediating effect of organizational learning capability. *Leadership and Organization Development Journal*, *37*(8), 1056–1082. doi:10.1108/LODJ-03-2015-0050

Domínguez-Escrig, E., Broch, F. F. M., Lapiedra, R., & Chiva, R. (2018). Promoting radical innovation through end-user computing satisfaction. *Industrial Management & Data Systems*, *118*(8), 1629–1646. doi:10.1108/IMDS-06-2017-0256

Donkin, R. (2010). *The history of work*. Palgrave Macmillan. doi:10.1057/9780230282179

Draganidis, F., & Mentzas, G. (2006). Competency Based Management: A Review of Systems and Approaches. *Journal of Information Management and Computer Security*, *14*(1), 51–64. doi:10.1108/09685220610648373

Drake, T. L., & Roe, W. H. (2005). *The principalship* (6th ed.). Merrill/Prentice Hall.

Dubois, D. (1993). *Competency-Based Performance Improvement: A Strategy for Organizational Change*. Harvard Press.

Duchek, S. (2019). Organizational resilience: A capability-based conceptualization. *Business Research*, *13*(1), 215–246. doi:10.100740685-019-0085-7

Ducheneaut, N., & Moore, R. J. (2005). More than just 'XP': Learning social skills in massively multiplayer online games. *Interactive Technology and Smart Education*, *2*(2), 89–100. doi:10.1108/17415650580000035

Dunham. R.B., Grube, J.A., Gardner, D.G., Cummings, L.L. & Pierce, J.L. (1989). The development of an attitude toward change instrument. In *Proceedings of the Academy of Management Annual Meeting*, Washington, DC

Dunkle, D., & Gurbaxani, V. (2019). Gearing up for Successful Digital Transformation. *MIS Quarterly Executive*, *18*(3), 209–220. doi:10.17705/2msqe.00017

Dunwill, E. (2016). *4 changes that will shape the classroom of the future: Making education fully technological*. https://elearningindustry.com/4-changes-will-shape-classroom-of-the-future-making-education-fully-technological

Eagly, A. H., & Carli, L. L. (2007). *Through the Labyrinth. The Truth About How Women Become Leaders*. Harvard Business School Press.

Eagly, A. H., & Johannesen-Schmidt, M. C. (2001). The Leadership Styles of Women and Men. *The Journal of Social Issues*, *57*(4), 781–797. doi:10.1111/0022-4537.00241

Eagly, A. H., & Karau, S. J. (2002). Role Congruity Theory of Prejudice Toward Female Leaders. *Psychological Review*, *109*(3), 573–598. doi:10.1037/0033-295X.109.3.573 PMID:12088246

Ebert, R. J., & Griffin, R. W. (2019) Business essential. New York, NY. Pearson.

Ederer, F. P. (2004). Feedback and Motivation in Dynamic Tournaments. SSRN *Electronic Journal*. doi:10.2139/ssrn.691384

Ekechukwu, J., & Lammers, T. (2019). *Digital Technology to Enhance Project Leadership Practice: The Case of Civil Construction*. Digital Transformation in Business and Society.

Ellickson, M. C., & Logsdon, K. (2002). Determinants of job satisfaction of municipal government employees. *Public Personnel Management*, *31*(3), 343–358. doi:10.1177/009102600203100307

Ely, R. J., & Rhode, D. L. (2010). Women and leadership: Defining the challenges. In N. Nohria & R. Khurana (Eds.), *Handbook of Leadership Theory and Practice,* (pp. 377–410). Harvard Business Publishing.

Ensley, M. D., Hmieleski, K. M., & Pearce, C. L. (2006). The importance of vertical and shared leadership within new venture top management teams: implications for the performance of startups. *Leader. Q. 17*, 217–231. doi:10.1016/j.leaqua.2006.02.002

Erim, T. (2018). *Expanding the Conceptual Boundaries of Work Effort*. Springer Fachmedien Wiesbaden.

Erkutlu, H. V., & Chafra, J. (2006). Relationship between leadership power bases and job stress of subordinates: Example from boutique hotels. *Management Research News*, *29*(5), 285–297. doi:10.1108/01409170610674419

Esser, A., Kahrens, M., Mouzughi, Y., & Eomois, E. (2018). A female leadership competency framework from the perspective of male leaders. *Gender in Management*, *33*(2), 138–166. doi:10.1108/GM-06-2017-0077

European Commission (2017). Attitudes Towards the Impact of Digitisation and Automation on Daily Life. 1–171.

Eyal, H. (2016). Digital fit as a leg-up for Nongovernmental Organizations' media and political success. *Political Communication*, *33*(1), 118–135. doi:10.1080/10584609.2015.1011294

Fedorenko, E.Yu. (2009) Health as a result of education. *National education*, *4*, 257-261

Fenech, R., Baguant, P., & Ivanov, D. (2019). The Changing Role of Human Resource Management in an Era of Digital Transformation. *Journal of Management Information and Decision Sciences*, *22*(2), 166–175.

Fiedler, F. R. E. D. (2015). Contingency theory of leadership: Fred Fiedler. In J. B. Miner (Ed.), *Organizational behavior 1: Essential theories of motivation and leadership, (pp. 232-255)*. Routledge.

Fındıklı, M. A., & Bayarçelik, E. (2015). Exploring the Outcomes of Electronic Human Resource Management (E-HRM)? *Procedia: Social and Behavioral Sciences*, *207*, 424–431. doi:10.1016/j.sbspro.2015.10.112

Fireman, S. M. (1999). *A model of telecommuting withdrawal: Employee perceptions predicting the reduction or stopping of telework*. [Doctoral Dissertation] University of Washington.

Fisher, D. M., & Waller, L. R. (2013). The 21st century principal: A study of technology leadership and technology integration in Texas K-12 schools. *The Global E Learning Journal*, *2*(4), 1-44.

Fisher, C. D., Locke, E. A., & Henne, D. L. (1992). The new look in job satisfaction theory and research. In *Job satisfaction: Advances in research and applications*, (pp. 165–194). The Free Press.

Fisk, P. (2017). *Education 4.0 … the future of learning will be dramatically different, in school and throughout life*. https://www.thegeniusworks.com. https://www.forbes.com/sites/barbarakurshan/2019/11/12/profiles-in-innovation-leading-at-the-edge-of-education/?sh=520401ad6109

Fitzgerald, M., Kruschwitz, N., Bonnet, D., & Welch, M. (2013). Embracing digital technology: A new strategic imperative | Capgemini consulting worldwide. *MIT Sloan Management Review*, *55*(1), 1–13.

Foerster, C., & Duchek, S. (2018). Leaders' resilience – A systematic literature review and future research agenda. In *Proceedings of the 78th Annual Meeting of the Academy of Management, AOM 2018*, Chicago, IL. 10.5465/AMBPP.2018.212

Fogarty, P., Frantz, S., Hirschfeld, J., Keating, S., Lafont, E., Lufkin, B., Mishael, R., Ponnavolu, V., Savage, M., & Turits, M. (2020, October 23). *Coronavirus: How the world of work may change forever*. Bbc.com. BBC. https://www.bbc.com/worklife/article/20201023-coronavirus-how-will-the-pandemic-change-the-way-we-work

Fornell, C., & Larcker, D. F. (1981). Evaluating structural equation models with unobservable variables and measurement error. *JMR, Journal of Marketing Research*, *18*(1), 39–50. doi:10.1177/002224378101800104

Frank, A. G., Mendes, G. H. S., Ayala, N. F., & Ghezzi, A. (2019). Servitization and Industry 4.0 convergence in the digital transformation of product firms: A business model innovation perspective. *Technological Forecasting and Social Change*, *141*, 341–351. doi:10.1016/j.techfore.2019.01.014

Frank, E., & Brandstätter, V. (2002). Approach versus avoidance: Different types of commitment in intimate relationships. *Journal of Personality and Social Psychology*, *82*(2), 208–221. doi:10.1037/0022-3514.82.2.208 PMID:11831411

Frankenberger, K., Mayer, H., Reiter, A. & Schmidt, M. (2020). *The Digital Transformer's Dilemma: How to Energize Your Core Business While Building Disruptive Products and Services*. New Jersey. John Wiley & Sons.

Fredrickson, B. L. (2001). The role of positive emotions in positive psychology: The broaden-and-build theory of positive emotions. *The American Psychologist*, *56*(3), 218–226. doi:10.1037/0003-066X.56.3.218 PMID:11315248

Freixanet, J., & Rialp, J. (2022). Disentangling the relationship between internationalization, incremental and radical innovation, and firm performance. *Global Strategy Journal*, *12*(1), 57–81. doi:10.1002/gsj.1412

French, J. R., Raven, B., & Cartwright, D. (2016). The bases of social power. In J.M., Shafritz, J. S., Ott, & Y. S., Jang (Eds.) Classics of Organization Theory, pp. 311-320. Cengage Learning.

Frey, B. B. (Ed.). (2018). *The SAGE encyclopedia of educational research, measurement, and evaluation*. Sage Publications. doi:10.4135/9781506326139

Fullan, M. (2001). *Leading in a culture of change*. Jossey-Bass.

Fuqua, H. E., Payne, K. E., & Cangemi, J. P. (2000). Leadership and the effective use of power. *National Forum of Educational Administration and Supervision Journal, 17*, 1-6.

Gabriel, M., & Pessl, E. (2016). Industry 4.0 and sustainability impacts: Critical discussion of sustainability aspects with a special focus on future of work and ecological consequences. Annals of the Faculty of Engineering Hunedoara. *International Journal of Engineering*, *14*(2), 131–136.

Gainey, T. W., Kelley, D. E., & Hill, J. A. (1999). Telecommuting's impact on corporate culture and individual workers: Examining the effect of employee isolation. *S.A.M. Advanced Management Journal*, *64*(4), 4.

Galliker, S., Nyffenegger, D., Semmer, N. K., & Elfering, A. (2020). Women and men in leadership positions: Health and work-related attitudes and their associations with work-related stressors, private stressors, and privacy-work conflict. *Z. Arb. Wiss*, *75*(1), 29–45. doi:10.100741449-020-00203-0

Garcia, G.A., Gonzalez-Miranda, D.R., Gallo, O. & Roman-Calderon, J.P. (2019) Employee Involvement and Job Satisfaction: A Tale of the Millennial Generation. *Employee Relations: The International Journal, 41*(3), pp. 374-388. Emerald Insight. . doi:10.1108/ER-04-2018-0100

Garcia, J. (2016) Passing the Torch: What Motivates Millennials? *Resources Magazine*, pp. 26-27, http://eds.b.ebscohost.com/eds/pdfviewer/pdfviewer?vid=5&sid=adadf2dc-c848- 4ce8-bcbd-2319ec31e273@pdc-v-sessmgr03 .

García-Villaverde, P. M., Elche, D., Martinez-Perez, A., & Ruiz-Ortega, M. J. (2017). Determinants of radical innovation in clustered firms of the hospitality and tourism industry. *International Journal of Hospitality Management*, *61*, 45–58. doi:10.1016/j.ijhm.2016.11.002

Gardner, W. L., Lowe, K. B., Moss, T. W., Mahoney, K. T., & Cogliser, C. C. (2010). Scholarly leadership of the study of leadership: A review of The leadership quarterly's second decade, 2000–2009. *The Leadership Quarterly*, *21*(6), 922–958. doi:10.1016/j.leaqua.2010.10.003

Garfield, E. (1979). In E. Garfield (Ed.), *"Citation indexing: its theory and application in science, technology, and humanities," in Mapping the Structure of Science,* (pp. 98–147). Wiley.

Garfield, E. (2004). Historiographic mapping of knowledge domains literature. *Journal of Information Science*, *30*(2), 119–145. doi:10.1177/0165551504042802

Garg, P., & Paul, H. (2012). Elevating organizational consequences through employee resilience. *In conference proceeding of National Conference on Emerging Challenges for Sustainable Business held at IIT Roorkee during June, 1*(2), 811-828

Garthe, N., & Hasselhorn, H. M. (2021). Leaving and staying with the employer— Changes in work, health, and work ability among older workers. *International Archives of Occupational and Environmental Health, 94*(1), 85–93. doi:10.100700420-020-01563-0 PMID:32893311

Gartner (2021). C-Suite: Redesigning Work for a Hybrid Future. *Gartner.*

Gartzia, L., & Van Engen, M. L. (2012). Are (male) leaders "feminine" enough? Gendered traits of identity as mediators of sex differences in leadership styles. *Gender in Management, 27*(5), 296–314. doi:10.1108/17542411211252624

Garvin, D. A. (2013). How Google Sold its Engineers on Management. *Harvard Business Review*. https://hbr.org/2013/12/how-google-sold-its-engineers-on-management

Gatignon, H., Tushman, M. L., Smith, W., & Anderson, P. (2002). A structural approach to assessing innovation: Construct development of innovation locus, type, and characteristics. *Management Science, 48*(9), 1103–1122. doi:10.1287/mnsc.48.9.1103.174

Gebelein, S. H. (2001). Leadership Competency. Leadership. *Excellence, 18*(3), 10.

Geoffrion, A. M. (2002). Progress in operations management. *Production and Operations Management, 11*(1), 92–100. doi:10.1111/j.1937-5956.2002.tb00186.x

Gerbaudo, P. (2017). Social media teams as digital vanguards: The question of leadership in the management of key Facebook and Twitter accounts of Occupy Wall Street, Indignados and UK Uncut. *Information Communication and Society, 20*(2), 185–202. doi:10.1080/1369118X.2016.1161817

Gerhana, M., Mardiyana, M., & Pramudya, I., (2017). The Effectiveness of Project Based Learning in Trigonometry. *Journal of Physics: Conference Series, 895*, 012-027.

Gerstner, C. R., & Day, D. V. (1997). Meta-analytic review of leader-member exchange theory: Correlates and construct issues. *The Journal of Applied Psychology, 82*(6), 827–844. doi:10.1037/0021-9010.82.6.827

Gerth, A. B., & Peppard, J. (2016). The dynamics of CIO derailment: How CIOs come undone and how to avoid it. *Business Horizons, 59*(1), 61–70. doi:10.1016/j.bushor.2015.09.001

Ghaleb, E. A., Dominic, P. D. D., Fati, S. M., Muneer, A., & Ali, R. F. (2021). The Assessment of Big Data Adoption Readiness with a Technology–Organization–Environment Framework: A Perspective towards Healthcare Employees. *Sustainability, 13*(15), 8379. doi:10.3390u13158379

Gheni, A. Y., Jusoh, Y. Y., Jabar, M. A., Ali, N. M., Abdullah, R. H., & Abdullah, S., (2016). The virtual teams: E-leaders challenges. In *Proceedings of the IEEE Conference on E-Learning, e-Management and e-Services*, Melaka, 38–42.

Ghorbani, N., Pourhosein, R., Armita, G.S. (2018) Self-compassion, mental health and work ethics: mediating role of self-compassion in the correlation between work stress and mental health. *Middle East Journal of Family Medicine*, 16(1), 113-121

Gigliotti, R., Vardaman, J., Marshall, D. R., & Gonzalez, K. (2019). The role of perceived organizational support in individual change readiness. *Journal of Change Management, 19*(2), 86–100. doi:10.1080/14697017.2018.1459784

Gilchrist, A. (2016). Industry 4.0: The industrial internet of things. *Apress.* doi:10.1007/978-1-4842-2047-4

Gill, M., & Vanboskirk, S. (2016). The Digital Maturity Model 4.0. Cambridge, Massachusetts.

Glazer, S., Mahoney, A., & Randall, Y. (2019). Employee development's role in organizational commitment: A preliminary investigation comparing generation X and millennial employees. *Industrial and Commercial Training*, *51*(1), 1–12. doi:10.1108/ICT-07-2018-0061

Goethals, G. R., Sorenson, G., & MacGreger Burns, J. (2002). Leadership in the Digital Ag. Wilson III, Ernest J. " Scholarship and 17 Practice in the Transactions to Knowledge Society. *Items*, *2002*(Spring/Summer), 1–44.

Goff, D. G. (2003). *What do we know about good community college leaders: A study in leadership trait theory and behavioral leadership theory.* https://www.eric.ed.gov/contentdelivery/servlet/ERICServlet?accno=ED47645600000aacb361&acdnat=1352660180_58274f188a39a834f048266e1a3a3d8a

Goldie, J. G. S. (2016). Connectivism: A knowledge learning theory for the digital age? *Medical Teacher*, *38*(10), 1064–1069. doi:10.3109/0142159X.2016.1173661 PMID:27128290

Goleman, D., & Senge, P. (2014). The Triple Focus: A New Approach to Education. More than Sound Productions. Florence.

Goleman, D. (2000). Leadership that gets results. *Harvard Business Review*, *78*, 78–90. https://hbr.org/2000/03/leadership-that-gets-results

Golembiewski, R. T. (2001). *Handbook of Organizational Behavior*. Marcel Dekker.

Gordon, E. (2007). Mapping digital networks from cyberspace to Google. *Information Communication and Society*, *10*, 885–901. doi:10.1080/13691180701751080

Graen, G. B., & Scandura, T. A. (1987). Toward a psychology of dyadic organizing. *Research in Organizational Behavior*, *9*, 175–208.

Graen, G. B., & Uhl-Bien, M. (1995). Relationship-based approach to leadership: Development of leader-member exchange (LMX) theory of leadership over 25 years: Applying a multi-level multi-domain perspective. *The Leadership Quarterly*, *6*(2), 219–247. doi:10.1016/1048-9843(95)90036-5

Grafström, M., & Falkman, L. L. (2017). Everyday narratives: CEO rhetoric on Twitter. *Journal of Organizational Change Management*, *30*(3), 312–322. doi:10.1108/JOCM-10-2016-0197

Green, F. (2004). Why Has Work Effort Become More Intense? *Industrial Relations*, *43*(4), 709–741. doi:10.1111/j.0019-8676.2004.00359.x

Green, F., & McIntosh, S. (2001). The intensification of work in Europe. *Labour Economics*, *8*(2), 291–308. doi:10.1016/S0927-5371(01)00027-6

Griffin, R. W. & Moorhead, G. (2014) *Organizational Behavior*. Boston, MA, Cengage learning

Griffin, M., Neal, A., & Neale, M. (2000). The Contribution of Task Performance and Contextual Performance to Effectiveness: Investigating the Role of Situational Constraints. *Applied Psychology*, *49*(3), 517–533. doi:10.1111/1464-0597.00029

Griffin, M., & Rafferty, A. E. (2006). Perceptions of organizational change: A stress and coping perspective. *The Journal of Applied Psychology*, *91*(5), 1154–1162. doi:10.1037/0021-9010.91.5.1154 PMID:16953776

Grisoni, L., & Beeby, M. (2007). Leadership, gender and sense-making. *Gender, Work and Organization*, *14*(3), 191–209. doi:10.1111/j.1468-0432.2007.00339.x

Grissom, J. A., & Harrington, J. R. (2010). Investing in administrator efficacy: An examination of professional development as a tool for enhancing principal effectiveness. *American Journal of Education*, *116*(4), 583–612. doi:10.1086/653631

Gruen, T. W., Summers, J. O., & Acito, F. (2000). Relationship marketing activities, commitment, and membership behaviors in professional associations. *Journal of Marketing, 64*(3), 34–49. doi:10.1509/jmkg.64.3.34.18030

Gudergan, G., Mugge, P., Kwiatkowski, A., Abbu, H., Hoeborn, G., & Conrad, R. (2021). Digital Leadership - Which leadership dimensions contribute to digital transformation success? *IEEE International Conference on Engineering, Technology and Innovation (ICE/ITMC)*, 1-8. 10.1109/ICE/ITMC52061.2021.9570231

Guest, D. E. (2017). Human resource management and employee well-being: Towards a new analytic framework. *Human Resource Management Journal, 27*(1), 22–38. doi:10.1111/1748-8583.12139

Gupta, S., & Pathak, G. S. (2018). Virtual team experiences in an emerging economy: A qualitative study. *Journal of Organizational Change Management, 31*(4), 778–794. doi:10.1108/JOCM-04-2017-0108

Gurr, D., & Drysdale, L. (2020). Leadership for challenging times. *International Studies in Educational Administration, 48*(1), 24–30.

Haddud, A., & McAllen, D. (2018). Digital workplace management: exploring aspects related to culture, innovation, and leadership. In *Proceedings of the Portland International Conference on Management of Engineering and Technology, PICMET 2018*, Honolulu: HI, 1–6. 10.23919/PICMET.2018.8481807

Hair, J. F., Black, W. C., Babin, B. J., Anderson, R. E., & Tatham, R. (2006). *Multivariate data analysis,* (6th ed.). Prentice Hall.

Hair, J. F., Ortinau, D. J., & Harrison, D. E. (2010). *Essentials of marketing research,* (Vol. 2). McGraw-Hill/Irwin.

Håkansson, C., Gard, G., & Lindegård, A. (2020). Perceived work stress, overcommitment, balance in everyday life, individual factors, self-rated health and work ability among women and men in the public sector in Sweden – a longitudinal study. *Archives of Public Health, 78*(1), 132. doi:10.118613690-020-00512-0 PMID:33317600

Hambley, L. A., O'Neill, T. A., & Kline, T. J. B. (2007). Virtual team leadership: The effects of leadership style and communication medium on team interaction styles and outcomes. *Organizational Behavior and Human Decision Processes, 103*(1), 1–20. doi:10.1016/j.obhdp.2006.09.004

Hancock, B., Schaninger, B., & Weddle, B. (2021). Culture in the hybrid workplace. *Mckinsey.* https://www.mckinsey.com/business-functions/people-and-organizational-performance/our-insights/culture-in-the-hybrid-workplace

Hansen, J., & Leuty, M. (2012). Work Values Across Generations. *Journal of Career Assessment, 20*(1), 34–52. doi:10.1177/1069072711417163

Hargreaves, A., & Fullan, M. (2020). Professional capital after the pandemic: Revisiting and revising classic understandings of teachers' Work. *Journal of Professional Capital and Community, 5*(3/4), 327–336. doi:10.1108/JPCC-06-2020-0039

Harkins, A. M. (2008). Leap frog principles and practices: Core components of Education 3.0 and 4.0. *Futures Research Quarterly, 8*, 1-15. https://www.hurriyet.com.tr/gundem/bakan-selcuktan-pns-cagi-uyarisi-40969660

Harris, J. G., & Mehrotra, V. (2014). Getting value from your data scientists. *MIT Sloan Manage. Rev. 56*, 15–18. https://sloanreview.mit.edu/ article/getting-value-from-your-data-scientists/

Harvard Business Review Analytic Services. (2017). Operationalizing Digital Transformation: New Insights Into Making Digital Work. 1–12. https://hbr.org/sponsored/2017/05/operationalizing-digitaltransformation-new-insights-into-making-digital-transformation-work

Harvard Health Letter. (2020) *Are you healthy enough to age in place?* Harvard.

Health Psychology. (2006). *Textbook for universities*, G. S. Nikiforov (ed.). St. Petersburg, Russia. p. 607

Hearsum, S. (2015). How to develop digital leadership capability. *Strategic HR Review*, *14*(5), 208. doi:10.1108/SHR-08-2015-0059

Heinz, U., Baga, T., Gebert, D., & Kearney, E. (2006). Leadership and cooperation as success factors in innovative R&D projects on electronic platforms. *Team Perform. Manage. Int. J.*, *12*(3/4), 66–76. doi:10.1108/13527590610674077

Helgesen, S. (2017). Gender, communication, and the leadership gap. *Gender, communication, and the leadership gap*, 3-11.

Helgesen, S., & Johnson, J. (2010). *The female vision: Women's real power at work*. Berrett-Koehler Publishers.

Henderikx, M., & Stoffers, J. (2022). An Exploratory Literature Study into Digital Transformation and Leadership: Tiward Future-Proof Middle Managers. *Sustainability*, *14*(2), 687. https://DOI.org/10.3390/su14020687. doi:10.3390u14020687

Hendrickson, A. R. (2003). Human resource information Systems: Backbone technology of contemporary human resources. *Journal of Labor Research*, *24*(3), 381–394. doi:10.100712122-003-1002-5

Henttonen, K., Pussinen, P., & Koivumäki, T. (2012). Managerial perspective on open source collaboration and networked innovation. *Journal of Technology Management & Innovation*, *7*(3), 135–147. doi:10.4067/S0718-27242012000300012

Hess, T., Matt, C., Benlian, A., & Wiesbock, F. (2018). Options for formulating a Digital Transformation Strategy. *MIS Quarterly Executive*, *15*(2), 123–139.

Hickey, A., Henning, M., & Sirois, L. (2022). Lessons Learned During Large-Scale Implementation Project Focused on Workplace Lactation Practices and Policies. *American Journal of Health Promotion*, *36*(3), 477–486. doi:10.1177/08901171211055692 PMID:34806416

Hitt, D., & Tucker, P. D. (2016). Systematic review of key leader practices found to influence student achievement: A unified framework. *Review of Educational Research*, *86*(2), 531–569. doi:10.3102/0034654315614911

Hobfoll, S. E. (2001). The Influence of Culture, Community, and the Nested-Self in the Stress Process: Advancing Conservation of Resources Theory. *Applied Psychology*, *50*(3), 337–421. doi:10.1111/1464-0597.00062

Hobfoll, S. E., Chen, S., & Westman, M. (2015). The Commerce and Crossover of Resources: Resource Conservation in the Service of Resilience. *Stress and Health*, *31*(2), 95–105. doi:10.1002mi.2574 PMID:25873421

Hoch, J. E., & Kozlowski, S. W. J. (2014). Leading virtual teams: Hierarchical leadership, structural supports, and shared team leadership. *The Journal of Applied Psychology*, *99*(3), 390–403. doi:10.1037/a0030264 PMID:23205494

Hoegl, M., & Muethel, M. (2016). Enabling shared leadership in virtual project teams: A practitioners' guide. *Project Management Journal*, *47*(1), 7–12. doi:10.1002/pmj.21564

Hofstede, G., Hofstede, G. J., & Minkov, M. (2010). *Cultures and Organizations—Software of the Mind: Intercultural Cooperation and Its Importance for Survival*. McGraw-Hill.

Horner-Long, P., & Schoenberg, R. (2002). Does e-business require different leadership characteristics? An empirical investigation. *European Management Journal*, *20*(6), 611–619. doi:10.1016/S0263-2373(02)00112-3

Horth, D., & Buchner, D. (2014). Innovation leadership: How to use innovation to lead effectively, work collaboratively and drive results. Center for Creative Leadership, 18, 4221.

http://www.who.int

Huber, G. P. (1990). A theory of the effects of Advanced Information Technologies on organizational design, intelligence, and decision making. *Academy of Management Review*, *15*(1), 47–71. doi:10.2307/258105

Hughes, T. (2004). *Human-Built World: How to Think About Technology and Culture*. Chicago University Press. doi:10.7208/chicago/9780226120669.001.0001

Hu, J., Erdogan, B., Jiang, K., Bauer, T. N., & Liu, S. (2018). Leader humility and team creativity: The role of team information sharing, psychological safety, and power distance. *The Journal of Applied Psychology*, *103*(3), 313–323. doi:10.1037/apl0000277 PMID:29094959

Huselid, M. A. (1995). The Impact Of Human Resource Management Practices On Turnover, Productivity, And Corporate Financial Performance. *Academy of Management Journal*, *38*(3), 635–672. doi:10.2307/256741

Huselid, M. A., & Delaney, J. T. (1996). The Impact Of Human Resource Management Practices On Perceptions Of Organizational Performance. *Academy of Management Journal*, *39*(4), 949–969. doi:10.2307/256718

Huselid, M. A., Jackson, S. E., & Schuler, R. S. (1997). Technical and strategic human resources management effectiveness as determinants of firm performance. *Academy of Management Journal*, *40*(1), 171–188. doi:10.2307/257025

Ichniowski, C., Kochan, T. A., Levine, D. I., Olson, C., & Strauss, G. (1996). What Works at Work: Overview and Assessment. *The American Workplace*, 1–37. doi:10.1017/CBO9780511620027.002

IMD. (2022, September 27). *Top 21 Digital Transformation Strategies (part 1)*. IMD business school for management and leadership courses. https://www.imd.org/imd-reflections/digital-programs-reflections/digital-transformation-strategies/

Imran, F., Shahzad, K., Butt, A., & Kantola, J. (2020). Leadership Competences for Digital Transformation: Evidence from Multiple Cases. *Proceedings of the AHFE 2020 Virtual Conferences on Human Factors, Business Management and Society, and Human Factors in Management and Leadership*, July 16-20, USA, 81-87.

Ishak, R., & Mansor, M. (2020). The Relationship between Knowledge Management and Organizational Learning with Academic Staff Readiness for Education 4.*0. Eurasian Journal of Educational Research*, *20*(85), 169–184. doi:10.14689/ejer.2020.85.8

Islam, I. (2018). Automation and the future of employment: Implications for India. *SA Journal of Human Resource Management*, *5*(2), 234–243.

Ismail, M. H., Khater, M., & Zaki, M. (2017). *Digital Business Transformation and Strategy: What Do We Know So Far?* Cambridge Service Alliance.

Iverson, R. D., & Buttigieg, D. M. (1999). Affective, normative and continuance commitment: Can the 'right kind' of commitment be managed? *Journal of Management Studies*, *36*(3), 307–333. doi:10.1111/1467-6486.00138

Jackson, D. (2009). Profiling Industry-Relevant Management Graduate Competences: The Need for a Fresh Approach. *International Journal of Management Education*, *8*(1), 85–98. doi:10.3794/ijme.81.281

Jakubik, M., & Berazhny, I. (2017). Rethinking Leadership and It's Practices in the Digital Era. In Suzana Laporšek; Sedmak Suzana & Doris Gomezelj Omerzel (eds.), *Managing the Global Economy. Proceedings of the Management International Conference*, Monastier di Treviso, Italy, 471–483.

Jalilvand, M. R., & Vosta, L. N. (2015). Examining the relationship between managerial power and affective organizational commitment: An empirical study in the sport sector of Iran. *Sport, Business and Management*, *5*(4), 344–364. doi:10.1108/SBM-04-2011-0041

Jamal, M. (1999). Job stress and employee well-being: A cross-cultural empirical study. *Stress Medicine*, *15*(3), 153–158. doi:10.1002/(SICI)1099-1700(199907)15:3<153::AID-SMI809>3.0.CO;2-0

James, L. A., & James, L. R. (1989). Integrating work environment perceptions: Explorations into the measurement of meaning. *The Journal of Applied Psychology, 74*(5), 739–751. doi:10.1037/0021-9010.74.5.739

Jawadi, N., Daassi, M., Favier, M., & Kalika, M. (2013). Relationship building in virtual teams: A leadership behavioral complexity perspective. *Human Systems Management, 32*(3), 199–211. doi:10.3233/HSM-130791

Jha, N., Sareen, P., & Potnuru, R. K. G. (2018). Employee engagement for millennials: Considering technology as an enabler. *Development and Learning in Organizations.*

Jim, H. (2021). The Future of Leadership. *Reimagine Leadership.* https://www.reimagine-leadership.org/the-future-of-leadership-get-digital-or-get-out

Johnson, J. L., & Wiechelt, S. A. (2004). Introduction to the Special Issue on Resilience. *Substance Use & Misuse, 39*(5), 657–670. doi:10.1081/JA-120034010 PMID:15202803

Johnson, J. R. (1998). Embracing change: A leadership model for the learning organisation. *International Journal of Training and Development, 2*(2), 141–150. doi:10.1111/1468-2419.00042

Johnson, S. K., Bettenhausen, K., & Gibbons, E. (2009). Realities of working in virtual teams: Affective and attitudinal outcomes of using computer-mediated communication. *Small Group Research, 40*(6), 623–649. doi:10.1177/1046496409346448

Jones, B., Harris, M. E., & Santana, M. (2008). Mastering developing new leadership for transformative change. *Journal of Academy of Business and Economics, 8*(2), 66–74.

Jones, L. W. (2021). COVID-19 and Employee Mental Health: What Employers Can Do. *Employee Relations Law Journal, 47*(1).

Jones, M. (2017). E-leadership case study and the impact of (un)faithful appropriation of technology. In *Proceedings of the 5th International Conference on Management Leadership and Governance, ICMLG 2017,* Johannesburg, 191–199.

Joshanloo, M., & Jovanović, V. (2021). Subjective health in relation to hedonic and eudaimonic wellbeing: Evidence from the Gallup World Poll. *Journal of Health Psychology, 26*(3), 438–448. doi:10.1177/1359105318820104 PMID:30582374

Joshi, M., & Biswas, P. (2018). An Empirical Investigation of Impact of Organizational Factors on Big Data Adoption. In *Proceedings of First International Conference on Smart System, Innovations and Computing,* (pp. 809-824). Springer, Singapore. 10.1007/978-981-10-5828-8_77

Juhro, S. M., & Aulia, A. F. (2019). New sources of growth: The role of frugal innovation and transformational leadership. *Bulletin of Monetary Economics and Banking, 22*(3), 383–402. doi:10.21098/bemp.v22i3.1195

Juhro, S. M., Aulia, A. F., Hadiwaluyo, D., Aliandrina, D., & Lavika, E. (2020). The Role of Catalytic Collaboration in Leveraging Transformational Leadership Competences to Generate Sustainable Innovation. *International Journal of Organizational Leadership, 9*(1), 48–66.

Kadakia, C. (2017). *The Millennial Myth: Transforming Misunderstanding into Workplace Breakthroughs.* Berrett-Koehler Publishers.

Kahai, S. S., Sosik, J. J., & Avolio, B. J. (2013). Effects of transformational leadership and media on collaboration and performance in virtual teams. In *Leadership in Virtual Groups: Looking Back and Charting Paths Forward. Symposium Conducted at the Meetings of the Academy of Management,* N. S. Hill and N. M. Lorinkova, Eds, Orlando, FL.

Kahai, S. S., & Avolio, B. J. (2006). Leadership style, anonymity, and the discussion of an ethical issue in an electronic context. *International Journal of e-Collaboration, 2*(2), 1–26. doi:10.4018/jec.2006040101

Kane, G. C. P. D., Phillips, A. N., Kiron, D., & Buckley, N. (2015). Strategy, not technology, drives digital transformation, 1-25. Deloitte University Press.

Kane, G. C., Palmer, D., Phillips, A. N., Kiron, D., & Buckley, N. (2015). Strategy, not technology, drives digital transformation. *MIT Sloan Management Review and Deloitte University Press, 14*, 1–25.

Kane, G. C., Phillips, A. N., Copulsky, J., & Andrus, G. (2019). How Digital Leadership Is(n't) Different. *MIT Sloan Management Review, 60*(3), 34–39.

Kanfer, R. (1990). Motivation theory and Industrial/Organizational psychology. In M. D. Dunette and L. Hough (Eds.), Handbook of industrial and organizational psychology, Volume 1: Theory in industrial and organizational psychology, (pp.77-170). Palo Alto, CA. Consulting Psychologists Press.

Kara, N., & Sevim, N. (2013). Adaptive learning systems: Beyond teaching machines. *Contemporary Educational Technology, 4*(2), 108–120. doi:10.30935/cedtech/6095

Kelemen, T. K., Matthews, S. H., Matthews, M. J., & Henry, S. E. (2022). Humble leadership: A review and synthesis of leader expressed humility. *Journal of Organizational Behavior*. doi:10.1002/job.2608

Kerr, S., & Jermier, J. M. (1978). Substitutes for leadership: Their meaning and measurement. *Organizational Behavior and Human Performance, 22*(3), 375–403. doi:10.1016/0030-5073(78)90023-5

Kidwell, R. E., & Sprague, R. (2009). Electronic surveillance in the global workplace: Laws, ethics, research, and practice. *New Technology, Work and Employment, 24*(2), 194–208. doi:10.1111/j.1468-005X.2009.00228.x

Killgore, W. D., Cloonan, S. A., Taylor, E. C., & Dailey, N. S. (2020). Loneliness: A signature mental health concern in the era of COVID-19. *Psychiatry Research, 290*, 113117. doi:10.1016/j.psychres.2020.113117 PMID:32480121

Kim, K., & Park, H. (2018). The Effects of Technostress On Information Technology Acceptance. *Journal of Theoretical and Applied Information Technology, 96*(24), 1817-3195

Kim, S. G., & Kim, J. (2014). Integration strategy, transformational leadership and organozational commitment in Korea's corporate split-offs. *Procedia: Social and Behavioral Sciences, 109*, 1353–1364. doi:10.1016/j.sbspro.2013.12.637

Kim, S., & Shin, M. (2017). The effectiveness of transformational leadership on empowerment. The roles of gender and gender dyads. *Cross Cultural & Strategic Management, 24*(2), 271–287. doi:10.1108/CCSM-03-2016-0075

King, A. S. (1990). *Evolution of Leadership Theory*. http.//journals.sagepub.com/doi/pdf/10.1177/0256090919900205

King, M. (2020). Leaders, Stop denying the gender inequity in your organization. *Harvard Business Review*.

Kingo, A. G. (2022). Secrets of a Successful Hybrid Work Model. *Toptal*. https://www.toptal.com/insights/future-of-work/hybrid-work-model#:~:text=The%20hybrid%20work%20model%20has,in% 2Doffice%20and%20remote%20working

King, R. C., & Sethi, V. (1997). The moderating effect of organizational commitment on burnout in information systems professionals. *European Journal of Information Systems, 6*(2), 86–96. doi:10.1057/palgrave.ejis.3000259

Kinicki, A., & Williams, B. K. (2020). *Management* (9th ed.). McGraw-Hill Education.

Kirkland, R. (2014). Artificial Intelligence Meets the C-suite. McKinsey Quarterly. https://www.mckinsey.com/insights/strategy/artificial_ intelligence_meets_the_c-suite.

Kirkpatrick, S., & Locke, E. (1991). Leadership: Do traits matter? *The Academy of Management Perspectives, 5*, 48–60. doi:10.5465/ame.1991.4274679

Kirrane, M., Lennon, M., O'Connor, C., & Fu, N. (2017). Linking perceived management support with employees' readiness for change: The mediating role of psychological capital. *Journal of Change Management*, *17*(1), 47–66. doi:10.1080/14697017.2016.1214615

Klein, M. (2020). Leadership Characteristics in the Era of Digital Transformation. *Business and Management Studies International Journal*, *8*(1), 883–902. doi:10.15295/bmij.v8i1.1441

Kline, R. B. (2005). *Principles and Practice of Structural Equation Modeling*. The Guilford Press.

Koburtay, T., Syed, J., & Haloub, R. (2019). Congruity between the female gender role and the leader role: A literature review. *European Business Review*, *31*(6), 831–848. doi:10.1108/EBR-05-2018-0095

Kodama, M. (2007). Innovation through boundary management - A case study in reforms at Matsushita electric. *Technovation*, *27*, 15–29. doi:10.1016/j.technovation.2005.09.006

Kolb, A. Y., & Kolb, D. A. (2005). Learning styles and learning spaces: Enhancing experiential learning in higher education. *Academy of Management Learning & Education*, *4*(2), 193–212. doi:10.5465/amle.2005.17268566

Kong, H., Sun, N., & Yan, Q. (2016). New Generation, Psychological Empowerment: Can Empowerment Lead to Career Competencies and Career Satisfaction? *International Journal of Contemporary Hospitality Management*, *28*(11), 2553–2569. doi:10.1108/IJCHM-05-2014-0222

Kotera, Y., Van Laethem, M., & Ohshima, R. (2020). Cross-cultural comparison of mental health between Japanese and Dutch workers: Relationships with mental health shame, selfcompassion, work engagement and motivation'. *Cross Cultural & Strategic Management*, *27*(3), 511–530. doi:10.1108/CCSM-02-2020-0055

Kotter, J. A. (1996). *Leading change*. Harvard Business Review Press.

Kovach, K. A., & Cathcart, C. E. Jr. (1999). Human resource information systems (HRIS): Providing business with rapid data access, information exchange and strategic advantage. *Public Personnel Management*, *28*(2), 275–282. doi:10.1177/009102609902800208

Krisberg, K. (2020). Global framework works to improve youth mental health, well-being. *The Nation's Health*, (August), 15.

Kulkarni, N., & Bharadwaj, B. (2021). *Future of Work – The Arrival of the Hybrid Digital workplace*. Zinnov.

Kuntz, J. R., Malinen, S., & Näswall, K. (2017). Employee resilience: Directions for resilience development. *Consulting Psychology Journal*, *69*(3), 223–242. doi:10.1037/cpb0000097

Kurland, H., Peretz, H., & Hertz-Lazarowitz, R. (2010). Leadership style and organizational learning: The mediate effect of school vision. *Journal of Educational Administration*, *48*(1), 7–30. doi:10.1108/09578231011015395

LaBerge, L., O'Toole, C., Schneider, J., & Smaje, K. (2020, October 5). *McKinsey Digital and Strategy & Corporate Finance Practices*. McKinsey & Company. https://www.mckinsey.com/business-functions/strategy-and-corporate-finance/our-insights/how-covid-19-has-pushed-companies-over-the-technology-tipping-point-and-transformed-business-forever

Lahui-Ako, B. (2001). The instructional leadership behaviour of Papua New Guinea high school principals. A provincial case study. *Journal of Educational Administration*, *39*(3), 233–265. doi:10.1108/09578230110392875

Lamba, K., & Singh, S. P. (2018). Modeling big data enablers for operations and supply chain management. *International Journal of Logistics Management*, *29*(2), 629–658. doi:10.1108/IJLM-07-2017-0183

Lane, K. A., Esser, J., Holte, B., & McCusker, M. A. (2010). A study of nurse faculty job satisfaction in community colleges in Florida. *Teaching and Learning in Nursing*, *5*(1), 16–26. doi:10.1016/j.teln.2009.05.001

Langkamer, K. L., & Ervin, K. S. (2008). Psychological Climate, Organizational Commitment and Morale: Implications for Army Captains' Career Intent. *Military Psychology*, *20*(4), 219–236. doi:10.1080/08995600802345113

Larjovuori, R.-L., Bordi, L., & Heikkila-Tammi, K. (2018). in *Proceeding of the 22nd International Academic Mindtrek*. 10.1145/3275116.3275122

Larouche, R., Garriguet, D., Gunnell, E. K., Goldfield, G. S., & Tremblay, M. S. (2016). Outdoor time, physical activity, sedentary time, and health indicators at ages 7 to 14: 2012/2013 Canadian Health Measures Survey. Statistics Canada, Catalogue no. 82-003-X *Health Reports*, *27*(9), 3–13. PMID:27655167

Le Deist, F. D., & Winterton, J. (2005). What is Competence? *Human Resource Development International*, *8*(1), 27–46. doi:10.1080/1367886042000338227

Leahy, S. M., Holland, C., & Ward, F. (2019). The digital frontier: Envisioning future technologies impact on the classroom. *Futures*, *113*, 102422.

Leban, W., & Zulauf, C. (2004). Linking emotional intelligence abilities and transformational leadership styles. *Leadership and Organization Development Journal*, *27*(7), 554–564. doi:10.1108/01437730410561440

Ledermann, T., & Kenny, D. A. (2017). Analyzing dyadic data with multilevel modeling versus structural equation modeling: A tale of two methods. *Journal of Family Psychology*, *31*(4), 442–452. doi:10.1037/fam0000290 PMID:28165269

Lee, C. S., Lee, W., & Kim, J. (2007). Effects of Transformational Leadership and Self-leadership on Innovative Behaviors: Mediating roles of empowerment. *International area review*, *10*(2), 163-176.

Lee, D. (2021). Hybrid work: Revolution or evolution? *Cisco Systems*. https://newsroom.cisco.com/c/r/newsroom/en/us/a/y2021/m10/hybrid-work-revolution-or-evolution-.html

Lee, F. L. F., & Man Chan, J. (2016). Digital media activities and mode of participation in a protest campaign: A study of the Umbrella Movement. *Information Communication and Society*, *19*(1), 4–22. doi:10.1080/1369118X.2015.1093530

Lee, M. R. (2009). E-ethical leadership for virtual project teams. *International Journal of Project Management*, *27*(5), 456–463. doi:10.1016/j.ijproman.2008.05.012

Lei, S., Peng, L., & Guo, Y. (2021). Investigating the effect of leader humility on subordinates' service creativity: A moderated dual path model. *Current Psychology (New Brunswick, N.J.)*, 1–13. doi:10.100712144-021-01887-1

Leithwood, K. (2012). *The Ontario Leadership Framework 2012 with a discussion of the research foundations*. Institute for Educational Leadership and the Ontario Ministry of Education.

Leithwood, K. (2019). Characteristics of effective leadership networks: A replication and extension. *School Leadership & Management*, *39*(2), 175–197. doi:10.1080/13632434.2018.1470503

Leithwood, K., Harris, A., & Hopkins, D. (2020). Seven strong claims about successful school leadership revisited. *School Leadership & Management*, *40*(1), 1–18. doi:10.1080/13632434.2019.1596077

Leithwood, K., & Louis, K. S. (2012). *Linking leadership to learning*. Jossey-Bass.

Leithwood, K., Sun, J., & Schumacker, R. (2019). How school leadership influences student learning: A test of "The four paths model". *Educational Administration Quarterly*, *56*(4), 570–599. doi:10.1177/0013161X19878772

Lengnick-Hall, C. A., Beck, T. E., & Lengnick-Hall, M. L. (2011). Developing a capacity for organizational resilience through strategic human resource management. *Human Resource Management Review*, *21*(3), 243–255. doi:10.1016/j.hrmr.2010.07.001

Levin, B., & Riffel, J. A. (2019). *Schools and the changing world: Struggling toward the future*. Routledge. doi:10.4324/9780203046562

Libert, B., Beck, M., & Wind, Y. (2016). 7 Questions to ask before your next digital transformation. *Harvard Business Review*.

Lin, H. F., & Lee, G. G. (2005). Impact of organizational learning and knowledge management factors on e-business adoption. *Management Decision*, *43*(2), 171–188. doi:10.1108/00251740510581902

Lippert, S. K., & Davis, M. (2006). A conceptual model integrating trust into planned change activities to enhance technology adoption behavior. *Journal of Information Science*, *32*(5), 434–448. doi:10.1177/0165551506066042

Lippert, S. K., & Swiercz, P. M. (2005). Human resource information systems (HRIS) and technology trust. *Journal of Information Science*, *31*(5), 340–353. doi:10.1177/0165551505055399

Lisk, T. C., Kaplancali, U. T., & Riggio, R. E. (2012). Leadership in multiplayer online gaming environments. *Simulation & Gaming*, *43*(1), 133–149. doi:10.1177/1046878110391975

Liu, D., Baumeister, R. F., Yang, C. C., & Hu, B. (2019). Digital communication media use and psychological well-being: A meta-analysis. *Journal of Computer-Mediated Communication*, *24*(5), 259–273. doi:10.1093/jcmc/zmz013

Liu, W., Mao, J., & Chen, X. (2017). Leader humility and team innovation: Investigating the substituting role of task interdependence and the mediating role of team voice climate. *Frontiers in Psychology*, *8*, 1115. doi:10.3389/fpsyg.2017.01115 PMID:28713316

Locke, E. A., Frederick, E., Lee, C., & Bobko, P. (1984). Effect of self-efficacy, goals, and task strategies on task performance. *The Journal of Applied Psychology*, *69*(2), 241–251. doi:10.1037/0021-9010.69.2.241

Longstaff, P. H., & Yang, S. U. (2008). Communication management and trust: Their role in building resilience to "surprises" such as natural disasters, pandemic flu, and terrorism. *Ecology and Society*, *13*(1). doi:10.5751/ES-02232-130103

Lopes, M. C., Fialho, F. A., Cunha, C. J., & Niveiros, S. I. (2013). Business games for leadership development: A systematic review. *Simulation & Gaming*, *44*(4), 523–543. doi:10.1177/1046878112471509

Lord, R., De Varder, C., & Alliger, G. (1986). A meta-analysis of the relation between personality traits and leadership perceptions: An application of validity generalization procedures. *The Journal of Applied Psychology*, *71*(3), 402–410. doi:10.1037/0021-9010.71.3.402

Lorenz, M., Rüßmann, M., Strack, R., Lueth, K. L., & Bolle, M. (2015). *Man and Machine in Industry 4.0. How Will Technology Transform the Industrial Workforce Through 2025?* The Boston Consulting Group.

Lowry, T. (1996). *Alternative work arrangements: The effects of distance and media use on the supervisor-subordinate relationship.* [Doctoral Dissertation] Rice University.

Lu, L., Shen, C., and Williams, D. (2014). Friending your way up the ladder: connecting massive multiplayer online game behaviors with offline leadership. *Comput. Hum. Behav. 35*, 54–60. doi:.02.013 doi:10.1016/j.chb.2014

Lumapps (2022). What is a Digital Workplace? Definition and Examples. https://www.lumapps.com/digital-workplace/

Luthans, F. (2002). The need for and meaning of positive organizational behavior. *Journal of Organizational Behavior*, *23*(6), 695–706. doi:10.1002/job.165

Luthans, F., Vogelgesang, G. R., & Lester, P. B. (2006). Developing the Psychological Capital of Resiliency. *Human Resource Development Review*, *5*(1), 25–44. doi:10.1177/1534484305285335

Luthans, F., & Youssef, C. (2007). Positive Organizational Behavior in the Workplace: The Impact of Hope, Optimism, and Resilience. *Journal of Management*, *33*(5), 774–800. doi:10.1177/0149206307305562

Lynn Pulley, M., & Sessa, V. I. (2001). E-leadership: Tackling complex challenges. *Industrial and Commercial Training*, *33*(6), 225–230. doi:10.1108/00197850110405379

Lyons, S. and Kuron, L. (2014). Generational Differences in the Workplace: A Review of the Evidence and Directions for Future Research. *Journal of Organizational Behavior, 35*(1), pp. 139-157, JSTOR Journals. . doi:10.1002/job.1913

Lyons, J. B., Swindler, S. D., & Offner, A. (2009). The impact of leadership on change readiness in the US military. *Journal of Change Management*, *9*(4), 459–475. doi:10.1080/14697010903360665

Machado, L. J., & Chung, C. J. (2015). Integrating Technology: The Principals' Role and Effect. *International Education Studies*, *8*(5), 43–53. doi:10.5539/ies.v8n5p43

Mack, T. C. (2015). Leadership in the Future. In Sowcik et al. (Eds.) Leadership 2050. Challenges, Key Contexts, and Emerging Trends.

Mak, B. L., & Sockel, H. (2001). A confirmatory factor analysis of IS employee motivation and retention. *Information & management, 38*(5), 265-276.

Maldonado, T., Carden, L., Brace, C., & Myers, M. (2021). Fostering Innovation Through Humble Leadership and Humble Organizational Culture. *The Journal of Business Strategy*, *38*(2), 73–94. doi:10.54155/jbs.38.2.73-94

Malhotra, A., Majchrzak, A., & Rosen, B. (2007). Leading virtual teams. *The Academy of Management Perspectives*, *21*(1), 60–70. doi:10.5465/amp.2007.24286164

Malik, F. (2014). *Managing, Performing, Living: Effective Management for a New World.* Campus Verlag.

Mallén, F. F., & Domínguez-Escrig, E. (2021). When leaders forgive: Encouraging radical innovation in more altruistic organizations. *Baltic Journal of Management*, *16*(5), 712–728. doi:10.1108/BJM-02-2021-0068

Mallén, F., Domínguez-Escrig, E., Lapiedra, R., & Chiva, R. (2019). Does leader humility matter? Effects on altruism and innovation. *Management Decision*, *58*(5), 967–981. doi:10.1108/MD-11-2018-1180

Mandell, B., & Pherwani, S. (2003). Relationship Between Emotional Intelligence and Transformational Leadership Style: A Gender Comparison. *Journal of Business and Psychology*, *17*(3), 387–404. doi:10.1023/A:1022816409059

Manz, C. C., & Sims, H. P. Jr. (1987). Leading workers to lead themselves: The external leadership of self-managing work teams. *Administrative Science Quarterly*, *32*(1), 106–129. doi:10.2307/2392745

Mao, J., Chiu, C. Y., Owens, B. P., Brown, J. A., & Liao, J. (2019). Growing followers: Exploring the effects of leader humility on follower self-expansion, self-efficacy, and performance. *Journal of Management Studies*, *56*(2), 343–371. doi:10.1111/joms.12395

Marique, G., Stinglhamber, F., Desmette, D., Caesens, G., & De Zanet, F. (2012). Organizational identification and commitment: The impact of POS and prestige. Universite catholique de Louvain.

Marler, J. H. (2009). Making human resources strategic by going to the net: Reality or myth? *International Journal of Human Resource Management*, *20*(3), 515–527. doi:10.1080/09585190802707276

Marston, C. (2019). Tips for keeping Millennial Employees: Understanding Myths about Millennials. https://www.thebalancecareers.com/tips-forretaining-millennial-employees-1918679.

Martin, G., Reddington, M., & Alexander, H. (2008). *Technology, outsourcing and transforming Hr*. Elsevier. doi:10.4324/9780080560984

Marvel, M. R., & Lumpkin, G. T. (2007). Technology entrepreneurs' human capital and its effects on innovation radicalness. *Entrepreneurship Theory and Practice*, *31*(6), 807–828. doi:10.1111/j.1540-6520.2007.00209.x

Masten, A. S. (2001). Ordinary magic: Resilience processes in development. *The American Psychologist*, *56*(3), 227–238. doi:10.1037/0003-066X.56.3.227 PMID:11315249

Matsa, D. A., & Miller, A. R. (2013). A female style in corporate leadership? Evidence from quotas. *American Economic Journal. Applied Economics*, *5*(3), 136–169. doi:10.1257/app.5.3.136

Matt, C., Hess, T., & Benlian, A. (2015). Digital transformation strategies. *Business & Information Systems Engineering*, *57*(5), 339–343. doi:10.100712599-015-0401-5

Mazurchenko, A., & Maršíková, K. (2019). Digitally-Powered Human Resource Management: Skills and Roles in the Digital Era. *Acta Informatica Pragensia*, *8*(2), 72–87. doi:10.18267/j.aip.125

McAfee, A., & Brynjolfsson, E. (2008). Investing in the IT that makes a competitive difference. *Harvard Business Rev. 86*, 98–107. https://hbr.org/2008/07/investing-in-the-it-that-makes-a-competitive difference

McClean, E., & Collins, C. J. (2011). High-commitment HR practices, employee effort, and firm performance: Investigating the effects of HR practices across employee groups within professional services firms. *Human Resource Management*, *50*(3), 341–363. doi:10.1002/hrm.20429

McClelland, D. (1973). Testing for competence rather than for intelligence. *The American Psychologist*, *28*(1), 1–14. doi:10.1037/h0034092 PMID:4684069

McConnell, J. (2018). How Digital Leaders Inspire Engagement. *MIT Sloan Management Review*.

McDermott, C. M., & O'Connor, G. C. (2002). Managing radical innovation: An overview of emergent strategy issues. *Journal of Product Innovation Management*, *19*(6), 424–438. doi:10.1111/1540-5885.1960424

McElhinney, E., Kidd, L., & Francine, M. C. (2018). Health literacy practices in social virtual worlds and the influence on health behavior. *Global Health Promotion*, *25*(4), 34–47. doi:10.1177/1757975918793334

McKinsey. (2009). How companies are benefiting from Web 2.0: McKinsey Global Survey Results. *The McKinsey Quarterly*.

Megahed, N. (2018). A Critical Review of the Literature and Practice of Competency Modelling. *KnowledgeE Social Sciences*, KnE Publishing, 104–126.

Megahed, N. (2015). Capturing Competences and Behavioral Indicators of Diplomats for a Multiple-Jobs Competency Model. *Journal of Human Resources Management and Labor Studies*, *3*(1), 54–78. doi:10.15640/jhrmls.v3n1a4

Megahed, N., Heijden, B. V., Shaker, M., & Wahba, K. (2012). A Framework for Developing a Multiple-Jobs Competency Model for Diplomats. *International Journal of Business and Social Science*, *3*, 42–55.

Mehta, N., & Pandit, A. (2018). Concurrence of big data analytics and healthcare: A systematic review. *International Journal of Medical Informatics*, *114*, 57–65. doi:10.1016/j.ijmedinf.2018.03.013 PMID:29673604

Meng, H., Luo, Y., Huang, L., Wen, J., Ma, J., & Xi, J. (2017). On the relationships of resilience with organizational commitment and burnout: A social exchange perspective. *International Journal of Human Resource Management*, *30*(15), 2231–2250. doi:10.1080/09585192.2017.1381136

Meredith, L. S., Sherbourne, C. D., Gaillot, S. J., Hansell, L., Ritschard, H. V., Parker, A. M., & Wrenn, G. (2011). Promoting psychological resilience in the US military. *Rand Health Quarterly*, *1*(2). PMID:28083176

Meyer, E. (2014b). *The Culture Map: Breaking Through The Invisible Boundaries Of Global Business,* (1st ed.). PublicAffairs.

Meyer, J. P., Klein, H. J., & Becker, T. E. (Eds.). (2009). *Commitment in Organizations: Accumulated Wisdom and New Diretions,* (1st ed.). Routledge. doi:10.4324/9780203883122

Milojevic, I. (2005). *Educational futures: Dominant and contesting visions*. Routledge. doi:10.4324/9780203413982

Moore, S., & Diese, A. (2018). Women in Leadership. In F. L. Denmark & M. A. Paludi (Eds.), *Women and Leadership*. Springer. doi:10.1007/978-3-319-72182-8_8

Moreno, J. P., Gera, P., Colangelo, M., Proverbio, M., Skan, J., Busch, W., & Caroll, G. (2015). *The Everyday Bank a New Vision for the Digital Age*. Accenture.

Morgareidge, D., Cai, H., & Jia, J. (2014). Performance-driven design with the support of digital tools: Applying discrete event simulation and space syntax on the design of the emergency department. *Frontiers of Architectural Research*, *3*(3), 250–264. doi:10.1016/j.foar.2014.04.006

Morris, A., & Staggenborg, S. (2004). In D. A. Snow, S. A. Soule, & H. Kriesi (Eds.), *"Leadership in social movements," in The Blackwell Companion to Social Movements,* (pp. 171–196). John Wiley & Sons.

Mouhamadou Sow & Solomon Aborbie. (2018) Impact of Leadership on Digital Transformation. In Macrothink Institute, Business and Economic Research, 8(3), (pp.139-148).

Mukherjee, A. N., Bhattacharyya, S., & Bera, R. (2014). Role of Information Technology in Human Resource Management of SME: A Study on the use of Applicant Tracking System. *IBMRD's. Journal of Management Research*, *3*(1).

Müller, J. M., Kiel, D., & Voigt, K. I. (2018). What Drives the Implementation of Industry 4.0? The Role of Opportunities and Challenges in the Context of Sustainability. *Sustainability*, *10*(1), 247. doi:10.3390u10010247

Munoz-Cristobal, J. A., Jorrin-Abellan, I. M., Asensio-Perez, J. I., Martinez-Mones, A., Prieto, L. P., & Dimitriadis, Y. (2014). Supporting teacher orchestration in ubiquitous learning environments: A study in primary education. *IEEE Transactions on Learning Technologies*, *8*(1), 83–97. doi:10.1109/TLT.2014.2370634

Nabi, M. N., Liu, Z., & Hasan, N. (2022). Investigating the effects of leaders' stewardship behavior on radical innovation: a mediating role of knowledge management dynamic capability and moderating role of environmental uncertainty. Management Research Review.

Naim, M. F., & Lenka, U. (2018). Development and retention of Generation Y employees: A conceptual framework. *Employee Relations*, *40*(2), 433–455. doi:10.1108/ER-09-2016-0172

Nakagawa, K., & Yellowlees, P. (2020). Inter-generational Effects of Technology: Why Millennial Physicians May Be Less at Risk for Burnout Than Baby Boomers. *Current Psychiatry Reports*, *22*(9), 45. doi:10.100711920-020-01171-2 PMID:32661817

Nasır, S. (2015). *Customer Relationship Management Strategies in the Digital Era*. Business Science Reference. doi:10.4018/978-1-4666-8231-3

Näswall, K., Kuntz, J., Hodliffe, M., & Malinen, S. (2015). *Employee resilience scale (EmpRes) measurement properties*. Resilient Organizations Research Programme.

Neves, P., & Eisenberger, R. (2014). Perceived organizational support and risk taking. *Journal of Managerial Psychology, 29*(2), 187–205. doi:10.1108/JMP-07-2011-0021

Newman, S. A., & Ford, R. C. (2021). Five steps to leading your team in the virtual COVID-19 workplace. *Organizational Dynamics, 50*(1), 100802. doi:10.1016/j.orgdyn.2020.100802

Nijssen, E. J., & Ordanini, A. (2020). How important is alignment of social media use and R&D–Marketing cooperation for innovation success*? Journal of Business Research, 116*, 1–12. doi:10.1016/j.jbusres.2020.04.056

Nivlouei, F. B. (2014). Electronic Human Resource Management System: The Main Element in Capacitating Globalization Paradigm. *International Journal of Business and Social Science, 5*(2), 147–159.

Nohria, N., & Berkley, J. D. (1994). In C. Heckscher & A. Donnellon (Eds.), *"The virtual organization: bureaucracy, technology, and the implosion of control," in The Post-Bureaucratic Organization: New Perspectives on Organizational Change,* (pp. 108–128). Sage Publications Ltd.

Nonaka, I., & Takeuchi, H. (2011). The wise leader. *Harvard Business Review, 89*(5), 58–67. PMID:21548419

Nordin, N. (2011). The influence of emotional intelligence, leadership behaviour and organizational commitment on organizational readiness for change in higher learning institution. *Procedia: Social and Behavioral Sciences, 29*, 129–138. doi:10.1016/j.sbspro.2011.11.217

Northouse, P. G. (2016). *Leadership: Theory and Practice,* (7th ed.). Sage.

Nunnally, J. C. (1978). *Psychometric Theory*. McGraw-Hill.

O'Boyle, E. H. Jr, Banks, G. C., & Gonzalez-Mule, E. (2017). The Chrysalis effect: How ugly initial results metamorphosize into beautiful articles. *Journal of Management, 43*(2), 376–399. doi:10.1177/0149206314527133

O'Neil, D. A., Hopkins, M. M., & Bilimoria, D. (2008). Women's careers at the start of the 21st century: Patterns and paradoxes. *Journal of Business Ethics, 80*(4), 727–743. doi:10.100710551-007-9465-6

Obschonka, M., Fisch, C., & Boyd, R. (2017). Using digital footprints in entrepreneurship research: A Twitter-based personality analysis of superstar entrepreneurs and managers. *J. Business Venturing Insights, 8*, 13–23. doi:10.1016/j.jbvi.2017.05.005

OECD/Eurostat. (2018). Oslo manual 2018: Guidelines for collecting, reporting and using data on innovation. The measurement of scientific, technological and innovation activities. 4th ed. Paris/Eurostat, Luxembourg. OECD Publishing.

Organ, D. W. (1997). Organizational Citizenship Behavior: It's Construct Clean-Up Time. *Human Performance, 10*(2), 85–97. doi:10.120715327043hup1002_2

Orlikowski, W. J. (1992). The duality of technology: Rethinking the concept of technology in organizations. *Organization Science, 34*(3), 398–427. doi:10.1287/orsc.3.3.398

Ou, A. Y., Tsui, A. S., Kinicki, A. J., Waldman, D. A., Xiao, Z., & Song, L. J. (2014). Humble chief executive officers' connections to top management team integration and middle managers' responses. *Administrative Science Quarterly, 59*(1), 34–72. doi:10.1177/0001839213520131

Owens, B. P., & Hekman, D. R. (2012). Modeling how to grow: An inductive examination of humble leader behaviors, contingencies, and outcomes. *Academy of Management Journal, 55*(4), 787–818. doi:10.5465/amj.2010.0441

Owens, B. P., Johnson, M. D., & Mitchell, T. R. (2013). Expressed humility in organizations: Implications for performance, teams, and leadership. *Organization Science, 24*(5), 1517–1538. doi:10.1287/orsc.1120.0795

Pacheco, G. and Webber, D. (2016). Job Satisfaction: How Crucial is Participative Decision Making? *Personnel Review, 45*(1), pp. 183-200. Emerald Insight. . doi:10.1108/PR-04-2014-0088

Paley, N. (2017). *Leadership strategies in the age of big data, algorithms, and analytics.* Productivity Press. doi:10.1201/9781315164977

Panayotopoulou, L., Vakola, M., & Galanaki, E. (2007). E-HR adoption and the role of HRM: Evidence from Greece. *Personnel Review, 36*(2), 277–294. doi:10.1108/00483480710726145

Parsons, T. (1968). *The Structure of Social Action.* Free Press.

Parviainen, P., Tihinen, M., Kääriäinen, J., & Teppola, S. (2017). Tackling the digitalization challenge: How to benefit from digitalization in practice. *International Journal of Information Systems and Project Management, 5*(1), 63–77. doi:10.12821/ijispm050104

Patton, M. Q. (2002). *Qualitative Research & Evaluation Methods.* California, USA. Sage publication

Pavlou, P. A., & El Sawy, O. A. (2010). The "third hand": IT-enabled competitive advantage in turbulence through improvisational capabilities. *Information Systems Research, 21*(3), 443–471. doi:10.1287/isre.1100.0280

Pearce, C. L. (2004). The future of leadership: Combining vertical and shared leadership to transform knowledge work. *The Academy of Management Executive, 18*(1), 47–57. doi:10.5465/ame.2004.12690298

Pearce, C. L., Manz, C. C., & Sims, H. P. Jr. (2009). Where do we go from here? Is shared leadership the key to team success? *Organizational Dynamics, 38*(3), 234–238. doi:10.1016/j.orgdyn.2009.04.008

Pelikan, J. M., Ganahl, K., & Roethlin, F. (2018). Health literacy as a determinant, mediator and/or moderator of health: Empirical models using the European Health Literacy Survey dataset. *Global Health Promotion, 25*(4), 57–66. doi:10.1177/1757975918788300 PMID:30427258

Penney, J. (2017). Social media and citizen participation in "official" and "unofficial" electoral promotion: a structural analysis of the 2016 Bernie Sanders digital campaign. *J. Commun. 67,* 402–423. doi:. 12300 doi:10.1111/jcom

Pentland, A., & Choudhury, T. (2000). Face recognition for smart environments. *Computer, 33*(2), 50–55. doi:10.1109/2.820039

Peteraf, M. A., Di Stefano, G., & Verona, G. (2013). The elephant in the room of dynamic capabilities: Bringing two diverging conversations together. *Strategic Management Journal, 34*(12), 1389–1410. doi:10.1002mj.2078

Petrucci, T., & Rivera, M. (2018). Leading Growth through the Digital Leader. In *Symposium: "Envisioning Future Leadership: Utopia, Dystopia, or More of the Same?",* Phoenix, AZ. 10.1002/jls.21595

Pfeffer, J., Anderson, P., Arthur, M. B., Baruch, J. J., Bowen, D. E., & Bessant, J. (2002). Competitive Advantage Through People (J. Henry & D. Mayle, Eds.). In Managing Innovation and Change, (2nd ed.), pp. 61-73). London, MK. SAGE Publications.

Philip, J., Najmi, H., Orudzheva, L., & Struckell, E. (2017). Work life overlap in the millennial generation: The role of ubiquitous technology. *Journal of Strategic Innovation and Sustainability, 12*(1), 80–98.

Phoenix, A. Z., Druskat, V. U., & Wheeler, J. V. (2003). Managing from the boundary: The effective leadership of self-managing work teams. *Academy of Management Journal, 46*(4), 435–457. doi:10.2307/30040637

Pierce, J. (2019). *Minimizing Employee Turnover in a Changing Workforce.* Forbes. https://www.forbes.com/sites/forbeshumanresourcescouncil/2019/09/05/minimizing-employee-turnover-in-a-changing-workforce/?sh=54b470c73884

Pierro, A., Raven, B. H., Amato, C., & Bélanger, J. J. (2013). Bases of social power, leadership styles, and organizational commitment. *International Journal of Psychology*, *48*(6), 1122–1134. doi:10.1080/00207594.2012.733398 PMID:23072507

Pitts, J. S., Milstein, B., & Saha, S. (2022, July). The Role of Business in Supporting Vital Conditions Necessary for the Well-Being of People, Places, and Racial Justice. *American Journal of Health Promotion*, *36*(6), 1050–1060. doi:10.1177/08901171221092576c PMID:35699324

Plowman, D. A., Solansky, S., Beck, T. E., Baker, L. K., Kulkarni, M., & Travis, D. V. (2007). The role of leadership in emergent, self-organization. *The Leadership Quarterly*, *18*(4), 341–356. doi:10.1016/j.leaqua.2007.04.004

Podsakoff, P. M., MacKenzie, S. B., Paine, J. B., & Bachrach, D. G. (2000). Organizational Citizenship Behaviors: A Critical Review of the Theoretical and Empirical Literature and Suggestions for Future Research. *Journal of Management*, *26*(3), 513–563. doi:10.1177/014920630002600307

Pooworawan, Y. (2015). *Challenges of New Frontier in Learning: Education 4.0*. Document by Innovative Learning Center, Chulalongkorn University.

Popenici, S., & Kerr, S. (2017). Exploring the impact of artificial intelligence on teaching and learning in higher education. *Research and Practice in Technology Enhanced Learning*, *12*(22), 1–13. doi:10.118641039-017-0062-8 PMID:30595727

Porter, L. W., Steers, R. M., Mowday, R. T., & Boulian, P. V. (1974). Organizational commitment, job satisfaction, and turnover among psychiatric technicians. *The Journal of Applied Psychology*, *59*(5), 603–609. doi:10.1037/h0037335

Post, C. (2015). When is female leadership an advantage? Coordination requirements, team cohesion, and team interaction norms. *Journal of Organizational Behavior*, *36*(8), 1153–1175. doi:10.1002/job.2031

Prentice, W. C. H. (2004). Understanding leadership. *Harvard Business Review*, *82*(1), 102–109. PMID:14723181

Pressman, S. D., Gallagher, M. W., & Lopez, S. J. (2013). Is the Emotion-Health Connection a "First-World Problem"? *Psychological Science*, *24*(4), 544–549. doi:10.1177/0956797612457382 PMID:23443305

Priatmoko, S. (2018). Memperkuat eksistensi pendidikan islam di era 4.0 [Strengthening the existence of islamic education in 4.0 era]. *Jurnal Studi Pendidikan Islam*, *1*(2), 1–19. doi:10.52166/talim.v1i2.948

Prince, K. A. (2017). Industrie 4.0 and Leadership. In *Proceedings of the 17th International Conference on Electronic Business, ICEB 2017,* Dubai, 132–139.

Printy, S. M., Marks, H. M., & Bowers, A. (2009). Integrated leadership: How principals and teachers share instructional influence. *Journal of School Leadership*, *19*, 504–532. doi:10.1177/105268460901900501

Puncreobutr, V. (2016). Education 4. 0: New challenge of learning. *St. Theresa. Journal of the Humanities and Social Sciences*, *2*(2), 92–97.

Purvanova, R. K., & Bono, J. E. (2009). Transformational leadership in context: Face-to-face and virtual teams. *The Leadership Quarterly*, *20*(3), 343–357. doi:10.1016/j.leaqua.2009.03.004

Rafaeli, A., Ravid, S., & Cheshin, A. (2009). Sensemaking in virtual teams: The impact of emotions and support tools on team mental models and team performance. *International Review of Industrial and Organizational Psychology*, *24*, 151–182. doi:10.1002/9780470745267.ch5

Raguseo, E., & Vitari, C. (2018). Investments in big data analytics and firm performance: An empirical investigation of direct and mediating effects. *International Journal of Production Research*, *56*(15), 5206–5221. doi:10.1080/00207543.2018.1427900

Rahim, M. A., & Afza, M. (1993). Leader power, commitment, satisfaction, compliance, and propensity to leave a job among US accountants. *The Journal of Social Psychology*, *133*(5), 611–625. doi:10.1080/00224545.1993.9713916

Rahman, T. (2021). Surviving and thriving in the hybrid workplace. *People Matters Digital Magazine.* https://www.peoplematters.in/article/hr-technology/surviving-and-thriving-in-the-hybrid-workplace-31601

Raina, (2016). *What's different about the Indian Millennial?* Strategic HR.Gurgaon. New Delhi

Raines, C. (2002). Managing millennials. *Connecting Generations: The Sourcebook, 16.*

Raut, S. (2017). Why Culture change is essential for digital transformation. *Digitalist Magazine*. http://www.digitalistmag.com/future-of-work/2017/01/09/culture-change-is-essential-for-digitaltransformation-04824251

Redwood, S., Holmstrom, M., & Vetter, A. (2016). Transitioning to the future of work and the workplace embracing digital culture, tools and approaches. *Deloitte.* https://www2.deloitte.com/content/dam/Deloitte/us/Documents/human-capital/us-human-capital-transitioning-to-the-future-of-work.pdf

Rego, A., Owens, B., Leal, S., Melo, A. I., Cunha, M. P., Gonçalves, L., & Ribeiro, P. (2017). How leader humility helps teams to be humbler, psychologically stronger, and more effective: A moderated mediation model. *The Leadership Quarterly*, *28*(5), 639–658. doi:10.1016/j.leaqua.2017.02.002

Reis, J., Amorim, M., Melão, N., & Matos, P. (2018). Digital Transformation: A Literature Review and Guidelines for Future Research. *Proceedings of the World Conference on Information Systems and Technologies*, 411–421. 10.1007/978-3-319-77703-0_41

Richardson, J. W., & Sterrett, W. L. (2018). District technology leadership then and now: A comparative study of district technology leadership from 2001 to 2014. *Educational Administration Quarterly*, *54*(4), 589–616. doi:10.1177/0013161X18769046

Richert, A., Plumanns, L., Gross, K., Schuster, K., & Jeschke, S. (2015). Learning 4.0: Virtual immersive engineering education. *Digital Universities: International Best Practices and Applications*, *2*, 51–66.

Rindner, L., Nordeman, L., Strömme, G., Svenningsson, I., Premberg, A., Hange, D., Gunnarsson, R., & Rembeck, G. (2020). Prognostic factors for future mental, physical and urogenital health and work ability in women, 45–55 years: A six-year prospective longitudinal cohort study. *BMC Women's Health*, *20*(1), 171. doi:10.118612905-020-01015-4 PMID:32787825

Robin, B. R., McNeil, S. G., Cook, D. A., Agarwal, K. L., & Singhal, G. R. (2011). Preparing for the changing role of instructional technologies in medical education. *Academic Medicine*, *86*(4), 435–439. doi:10.1097/ACM.0b013e31820dbee4 PMID:21346506

Robinson, G. W. (1998). New Teacher Induction: A Study of Selected New Teacher Induction Models and Common Practices.

Robison, J. (2019). Why Millennials Are Job Hopping. https://www.gallup.com/workplace/267743/why-millennials-job-hopping.aspx%20OCTOBER%2028,%202019%20JENNIFER%20ROBISON

Roblyer, M., & Doering, A. (2014). *Integrating educational technology into teaching.* Pearson.

Rodríguez-Carvajal, R., de Rivas, S., Herrero, M., Moreno-Jiménez, B., & Van Dierendonck, D. (2014). Leading people positively: Cross-cultural validation of the Servant Leadership Survey (SLS). *The Spanish Journal of Psychology*, *17*, 17. doi:10.1017jp.2014.73 PMID:26055345

Rogers, E. M. (1995). Lessons for guidelines from the diffusion of innovations. *The Joint Commission Journal on Quality Improvement*, *21*(7), 324–328. doi:10.1016/S1070-3241(16)30155-9 PMID:7581733

Roman, A. V., Van Wart, M., Wang, X., Liu, C., Kim, S., & McCarthy, A. (2018). *Defining e-leadership as competence in ICT-mediated communications: An exploratory assessment*. Public Admin. Rev. doi:10.1111/puar.12980

Ronald, B. (2014). Comprehensive leadership review-literature, theories and research. *Advances in Management*, *7*(5), 52.

Rosenbloom, R. S. (2000). Leadership, capabilities, and technological change: The transformation of NCR in the electronic era. *Strategic Management Journal*, *21*(10-11), 1083–1103. doi:10.1002/1097-0266(200010/11)21:10/11<1083::AID-SMJ127>3.0.CO;2-4

Ross, J. W., Sebastian, I. M., & Beath, C. M. (2017). How to Develop a Great Digital Strategy? *MIT Sloan Management Review*, *58*(2), 7–9.

Rothwell, A., & Arnold, J. (2005). How hr professionals rate 'continuing professional development'. *Human Resource Management Journal*, *15*(3), 18–32. doi:10.1111/j.1748-8583.2005.tb00151.x

Rousseau, D. M., Sitkin, S. B., Burt, R. S., & Camerer, C. (1998). Not so different after all: A cross-discipline view of trust. *Academy of Management Review*, *23*(3), 393–404. doi:10.5465/amr.1998.926617

Roy, S., & Edan, Y. (2018). Investigating joint-action in short-cycle repetitive handover tasks: The role of giver versus receiver and its implications for human–robot collaborative system design. *International Journal of Social Robotics*.

Ruscigno, M. (2018) Health Benefits of Shared Meals. Environmental Nutrition, 41(11).

Rutter, H., Cavill, N., Bauman, A., & Bull, F. (2019). Systems approaches to global and national physical activity plans. *Bulletin of the World Health Organization*, *97*(2), 162–165. doi:10.2471/BLT.18.220533 PMID:30728623

Saha, N., Gregar, A., & Sáha, P. (2017). Organizational agility and hrm strategy: Do they really enhance firms' competitiveness? *International Journal of Organizational Leadership*, *6*(3), 323–334. doi:10.33844/ijol.2017.60454

Sailer, M., Hense, J., Mandl, H., & Klevers, M. (2013). Psychological Perspectives on Motivation through Gamification. *Interaction Design and Architecture(s). Journal*, *19*, 28–37.

Sainger, G. (2018). Leadership in Digital Age: A Study on the Role of Leader in this Era of Digital Transformation. *International Journal of Leadership*, *6*(1), 1–6.

Salicru, S. (2015). The Global Leadership Psychological Contract Model – Actionable to Shape the Future to 2050. In Sowcik et al. (Eds.) 2015. Leadership 2050. Challenges, Key Contexts, and Emerging Trends, 159-173. Emerald Publishing.

Salmon, G. (2019). May the fourth be with you: Creating Education 4.0. *Journal of Learning for Development-JL4D, 6*(2).

Salvetti, F., & Bertagni, B. (2020). Leadership 5.0: An Agile Mindset for a Digital Future. *International Journal of Advanced Corporate Learning*, *13*(2), 57–66. doi:10.3991/ijac.v13i2.17033

Sam, B. (2021). *Digital Leadership in a New Era: The constantly increasing importance of cultivating workplace culture*. Beyond Business Buzzwords.

Sandberg, S. (2013). Lean. In *Women, Work and the Will to Lead*. Alfred A. Knopf.

Sareen, P., & Subramanian, K. V. (2012). E-HRM: A Strategic Review. *International Journal of Human Resource Studies*, *2*(3), 119. doi:10.5296/ijhrs.v2i3.2100

Scarlett, H. (2019) Neuroscience for Organizational Change: An Evidence-based Practical Guide to Managing Change, (2nd ed.). Kogan Page Ltd, London. p. 274

Schein, E. H. (1999). Sense and nonsense about culture and climate. Massachusetts Institutes of Technology.

Schein, E. H. (2010). *Organizational Culture and Leadership* (4th ed.). Jossey-Bass.

Schermerhorn, J. R. (1999). *Management,* (6th ed.). John Wiley & Sons.

Schiuma, G., Schettini, E., Santarsiero, F., & Carlucci, D. (2022). The transformative leadership compass: Six Competences for digital transformation entrepreneurship. *International Journal of Entrepreneurial Behaviour & Research, 28*(5), 1273–1291. doi:10.1108/IJEBR-01-2021-0087

Schneider, R. (2013). Research Data Literacy, *Commun. Comput. Inf. Sci, vol. 397. CCIS*, (October), 134–140.

Schwarzmüller, T., Brosi, P., Duman, D., & Welpe, I. M. (2018). How does the digital transformation affect organizations? Key themes of change in work design and leadership. *Management Review, 29*(2), 114–138. doi:10.5771/0935-9915-2018-2-114

Semizdralova, O.A. (2010) Psychological health of the teacher and ways to preserve it. *National education, 1*, 130-135

SETA [SİYASET, EKONOMİ VE TOPLUM ARAŞTIRMALARI VAKFI]. (2019). *Öğretim Lideri, vs. Okul Müdürü.* İstanbul. SETA Yayınları.

Shachaf, P., & Hara, N. (2007). Behavioral complexity theory of media selection: A proposed theory for global virtual teams. *Journal of Information Science, 33*(1), 63–75. doi:10.1177/0165551506068145

Shafiq, M., & Mujawar, S. B. S. (2021). Influence Of Digitalization On Leadership: The Case Of Sandvik In Sweden [Thesis]. University of Gavle.

Shahroom, A., & Hussin, N. (2018). Industrial revolution 4.0 and education. *International Journal of Academic Research in Business and Social Sciences, 8*(9), 314–319.

Shantz, A., & Booth, J. E. (2014). Service Employees and Self-verification: The Roles of Occupational Stigma Consciousness and Core Self-evaluations. *Human Relations, 67*(12), 1439–1465. doi:10.1177/0018726713519280

Sharma, J., & Dhar, R. L. (2016). Factors influencing job performance of nursing staff: Mediating role of affective commitment. *Personnel Review, 45*(1), 161–182. doi:10.1108/PR-01-2014-0007

Shaw, S., & Fairhurst, D. (2008). Engaging a new generation of graduates. *Education + Training, 50*(5), 366–378. doi:10.1108/00400910810889057

Sheridan, T. B. (2008). Risk, Human Error, and System Resilience: Fundamental Ideas. *Human Factors, 50*(3), 418–426. doi:10.1518/001872008X250773 PMID:18689048

Sheth, J. N., & Parvatlyar, A. (1995). Relationship marketing in consumer markets: Antecedents and consequences. *Journal of the Academy of Marketing Science, 23*(4), 255–271. doi:10.1177/009207039502300405

Shields, C. M. (2020). *Transformative leadership*. Oxford Research Encyclopedia of Education. doi:10.1093/acrefore/9780190264093.013.632

Shin, J., Taylor, M. S., & Seo, M.-G. (2012). Resources for Change: The Relationships of Organizational Inducements and Psychological Resilience to Employees' Attitudes and Behaviors toward Organizational Change. *Academy of Management Journal, 55*(3), 727–748. doi:10.5465/amj.2010.0325

Shoss, M. K., Jiang, L., & Probst, T. M. (2018). Bending without breaking: A two-study examination of employee resilience in the face of job insecurity. *Journal of Occupational Health Psychology, 23*(1), 112–126. doi:10.1037/ocp0000060 PMID:27786505

Sinclair, R. R., Britt, T. W., Shen, W., Grossman, M. R., & Klieger, D. M. (2016). How Much Do We Really Know About Employee Resilience? *Industrial and Organizational Psychology: Perspectives on Science and Practice*, *9*(2), 378–404. doi:10.1017/iop.2015.107

Sitrin, M. (2006). *Horizontalism: Voices of popular politics*. Cambridge University Press.

Slater, S. F., Mohr, J. J., & Sengupta, S. (2014). Radical product innovation capability: Literature review, synthesis, and illustrative research propositions. *Journal of Product Innovation Management*, *31*(3), 552–566. doi:10.1111/jpim.12113

Solis, B. (2017, December). The Digital Change Agent's Manifesto, 1–29. https://marketing.prophet.com/acton/media/33865/he-digital-change-agents-manifesto--altimeter

Somerville, M. M. (2013). Digital Age Discoverability: A Collaborative Organizational Approach. *Serials Review*, *39*(4), 234–239. doi:10.1080/00987913.2013.10766404

Sony, M., & Naik, S. (2020). Industry 4.0 integration with socio-technical systems theory: A systematic review and proposed theoretical model. *Technology in Society*, *61*, 101248. doi:10.1016/j.techsoc.2020.101248

Sorescu, A. B., Chandy, R. K., & Prabhu, J. C. (2003). Sources and financial consequences of radical innovation: Insights from pharmaceuticals. *Journal of Marketing*, *67*(4), 82–102. doi:10.1509/jmkg.67.4.82.18687

Sosik, J. J., Avolio, B. J., & Kahai, S. S. (1997). Effects of leadership style and anonymity on group potency and effectiveness in a group decision support system environment. *The Journal of Applied Psychology*, *82*(1), 89–103. doi:10.1037/0021-9010.82.1.89

Sosik, J. J., Kahai, S. S., & Avolio, B. J. (1998). Transformational leadership and dimensions of creativity: Motivating idea generation in computer-mediated groups. *Creativity Research Journal*, *11*(2), 111–121. doi:10.120715326934crj1102_3

Sousa, M. J., & Rocha, Á. (2018). Skills for disruptive digital business. *Journal of Business Research*, *94*, 257–263. doi:10.1016/j.jbusres.2017.12.051

Sow, M., & Aborbie, S. (2018). Impact of Leadership on Digital Transformation, Macrothink Institute. *Business and Economic Review*, *8*(3), 138–148.

Spencer, E. M., & Spencer, S. M. (1993). *Competence at Work*. John Wiley & Sons, Inc.

Spencer, L. M., & Spencer, S. M. (1993). *Competence at Work: Models for Superior Performance*. John Wiley and Sons Inc.

Spicer, A. (2020). Organizational culture and COVID-19. *Journal of Management Studies*, *57*(8), 1737–1740. doi:10.1111/joms.12625

Srinivasan, G. (2022). The future of work: A Hybrid Model. *The Economic Times*. https://economictimes.indiatimes.com/news/company/corporate-trends/the-future-of-work-a-hybrid-model/articleshow/89561612.cms?from=mdr

Stahl, A. (2019). *5 Keys to Retaining Millennial Employees, the 'Job-Hopper' Generation*. https://www.forbes.com/sites/ashleystahl/2019/09/17/5-keys-to-retaining-millennial-employees-the-job-hopper-generation/?sh=6701baf63bdd

Steffens, M. C., Viladot, M. A., & Scheifele, C. (2019). Male Majority, Female Majority, or Gender Diversity in Organizations: How Do Proportions Affect Gender Stereotyping and Women Leaders' Well-Being? *Frontiers in Psychology*, *10*, 1037. doi:10.3389/fpsyg.2019.01037 PMID:31143147

Stephens, K. K., & Rains, S. A. (2011). Information and Communication Technology sequences and message repetition in interpersonal interaction. *Communication Research*, *38*(1), 101–122. doi:10.1177/0093650210362679

St-Hilairea, F., Gilbertb, M.-H., & Brunb, J.-P. (2019). What if subordinates took care of managers' mental health at work? *International Journal of Human Resource Management*, *30*(2), 337–359. doi:10.1080/09585192.2016.1276090

Stogdill, R. (1974). *Handbook of Leadership*. Free Press.

Stogdill, R. M. (1948). Personal factors associated with leadership: A survey of the literature. *The Journal of Psychology*, *25*(1), 35–71. doi:10.1080/00223980.1948.9917362 PMID:18901913

Stolze, A., Sailer, K., & Gillig, H. (2018). Entrepreneurial mindset as a driver for digital transformation - A novel educational approach form university-industry interactions. In *Proceedings of the 13th European Conference on Innovation & Entrepreneurship, ECIE 2018*, Aveiro, 806–813.

Story, V. M., Daniels, K., Zolkiewski, J., & Dainty, A. R. (2014). The barriers and consequences of radical innovations: Introduction to the issue. *Industrial Marketing Management*, *43*(8), 1271–1277. doi:10.1016/j.indmarman.2014.09.001

Stout, J. K., & Posner, J. L. (1984). Stress, Role Ambiguity, and Role Conflict. *Psychological Reports*, *55*(3), 747–753. doi:10.2466/pr0.1984.55.3.747 PMID:6522540

Strauss, A., & Corbin, J. (1998). *Basics of Qualitative Research*. Sage Publications Ltd.

Strohmeier, S. (2007). Research in e-hrm: Review and implications. *Human Resource Management Review*, *17*(1), 19–37. doi:10.1016/j.hrmr.2006.11.002

Suarez, F. F., & Oliva, R. (2005). Environmental change and organizational transformation. *Industrial and Corporate Change*, *14*(6), 1017–1041. doi:10.1093/icc/dth078

Sullivan, G. M., & Artino, A. R. Jr. (2013). Analyzing and interpreting data from Likert-type scales. *Journal of Graduate Medical Education*, *5*(4), 541–542. doi:10.4300/JGME-5-4-18 PMID:24454995

Sullivan, S. D., Lungeanu, A., Dechurch, L. A., & Contractor, N. S. (2015). Space, time, and the development of shared leadership networks in multiteam systems. *Network Science*, *3*(1), 124–155. doi:10.1017/nws.2015.7

Szymanska, I. I., & Rubin, B. A. (2018). Gender and relationship differences in the perceptions of male and female leadership. *Gender in Management*, *33*(4), 254–281. doi:10.1108/GM-06-2016-0127

Tabrizi, B., Lam, E., Girard, K., & Irvin, V. (2019). Digital transformation is not about technology. *Harvard Business Review*, *13*, 1–6.

Tang, K. N. (2019). *Leadership and Change Management*. Springer. doi:10.1007/978-981-13-8902-3

Tan, J. P. L., Choo, S. S., Kang, T., & Liem, G. A. D. (2017). Educating for twenty-first century competencies and future ready learners: Research perspectives from Singapore. *Asia Pacific Journal of Education*, *37*(4), 425–436.

Tannenbaum, R., & Schmidt, W. (1973). How to choose a leadership pattern. *Harvard Business Review*, *51*, 162–180.

Tan, S. C. (2010). School technology leadership: Lessons from empirical research. In C. H. Steel, M. J. Keppell, P. Gerbic, & S. Housego (Eds.), *Curriculum, technology & transformation for an unknown future. Proceedings Ascilite Sydney 2010,* (pp. 896–906).

Teimouri, H., Izadpanah, N., Akbariani, S., Jenab, K., Khoury, S., & Moslehpour, S. (2015). The effect of managerial power on employees' affective commitment: Case study. *Journal of Management*, *3*(2), 21–30.

Teo, T. S., Lim, G. S., & Fedric, S. A. (2007). The adoption and diffusion of human resources information systems in Singapore. *Asia Pacific Journal of Human Resources*, *45*(1), 44–62. doi:10.1177/1038411107075402

Thannimalai, R., & Raman, A. (2018). The Influence of Principals Technology Leadership and Professional Development on Teachers' Technology Integration in Secondary Schools. *Malaysian Journal of Learning and Instruction*, *15*(1), 201–226. doi:10.32890/mjli2018.15.1

The Economist Intelligence Unit. (2015).Organizational Resilience: Building an Enduring Enterprise. *The British Standards Institution.* https://www.bsigroup.com/en-GB/our-services/Organizational-Resilience/Organizational-Resilience-research-EIU/

Toepfl, F. (2018). From connective to collective action: Internet elections as a digital tool to centralize and formalize protest in Russia. *Information Communication and Society*, *21*(4), 531–547. doi:10.1080/1369118X.2017.1290127

Tosi, D., & Jackson, S. F. (1999). Influencing Others yo Act in Harold D. Stolovitech and Erica, J.Keeps (eds) Handbook of Human Performance and Technology.San Francisco: International Society fir performance improvement

Towler, A. (2020). *The Job Characteristics Model: What it is and Why it Matter More Than Ever.* https://www.ckju.net/en/dossier/job-characteristicsmodel-what-it-is-and-why-it-matters-more-ever

Troshani, I., Jerram, C., & Gerrard, M. (2010). Exploring the organizational adoption of human resources information systems (HRIS) in the Australian public sector. *Proceedings of the 21st Australasian Conference on Information Systems (ACIS2010)*, Brisbane, Australia.

Tsai, M., (2017). *Attracting and Retaining Millennial Workers in the Modern Business Era.*

Tsai, W. H. S., & Men, L. R. (2017). Social CEOs: The effects of CEOs' communication styles and parasocial interaction on social networking sites. *New Media & Society*, *19*(11), 1848–1867. doi:10.1177/1461444816643922

Turing, A. M. (1950). Computing Machinery and Intelligence. *Mind*, *49*(236), 433–460. doi:10.1093/mind/LIX.236.433

Tusaie, K., & Dyer, J. (2004). Resilience: A Historical Review of the Construct. *Holistic Nursing Practice*, *18*(1), 3–10. doi:10.1097/00004650-200401000-00002 PMID:14765686

U.S. National Center for Education Statistics. (2016). Degrees conferred by race and sex. USNCES. https://nces.ed.gov/fastfacts/display.asp?id=72

Ulrich, D. (1998). A New Mandate for Human Resources. *Harvard Businee Review, 01.*

Ulrich, D., Storey, J., & Wright, P. M. (2019). *Strategic human resource management: A research overview*. Routledge.

United Nations. (2020a). Gender Equality. https://www.un.org/en/sections/issuesdepth/gender-equality/

Urban, B., & Wood, E. (2015). The Importance of Opportunity Recognition Behavior and Motivators of Employees When Engaged In Corporate Entrepreneurship. *Journal of Business Economics and Management*, *16*(5), 980–994. doi:10.3846/16111699.2013.799087

Van Dam, A., Noordzij, G., & Born, M. P. (2020). Linking the Fit Between Achievement Goal Orientation and Learning Opportunities With Employee Well-Being and Absenteeism. *Journal of Personnel Psychology*, *19*(4), 184–196. doi:10.1027/1866-5888/a000260

Van der Westhuizen, D., Pacheco, G., & Webber, D. (2012). Culture, Participative Decision Making and Job Satisfaction. *International Journal of Human Resource Management*, *23*(13), 2661–2679. doi:10.1080/09585192.2011.625967

Van Dierendonck, D., & Nuijten, I. (2011). The servant leadership survey: Development and validation of a multidimensional measure. *Journal of Business and Psychology*, *26*(3), 249–267. doi:10.100710869-010-9194-1 PMID:21949466

Van Emmerik, H., Wendt, H., & Euwema, M. C. (2010). Gender ratio, societal culture, and male and female leadership. *Journal of Occupational and Organizational Psychology*, *83*(4), 895–914. doi:10.1348/096317909X478548

Van Outvorst, F., Visker, C., & De Waal, B. (2017). Digital leadership: the consequences of organizing and working in a digital society. In *Proceedings of the 5th International Conference On Management, Leadership & Governance, ICMLG 2017,* Johannesburg, 43–471.

Van Wart, M., Roman, A., Wang, X. H., & Liu, C. (2017). Integrating ICT adoption issues into (e-)leadership theory. *Telematics and Informatics*, *34*(5), 527–537. doi:10.1016/j.tele.2016.11.003

Vial, G. (2019). Understanding digital transformation: A review and a research agenda. *The Journal of Strategic Information Systems*, *28*(2), 118–144. doi:10.1016/j.jsis.2019.01.003

Vidal, M. E. S., & Valle, R. S. (2007). Antecedents of repatriates; job satisfaction and its influence on turnover intentions: Evidence from Spanish repatriated managers. *Journal of Business Research*, *60*(12), 1272–1281. doi:10.1016/j.jbusres.2007.05.004

Vidgen, R., Shaw, S., & Grant, D. B. (2017). Management challenges in creating value from business analytics. *European Journal of Operational Research*, *261*(2), 626–639. doi:10.1016/j.ejor.2017.02.023

Wang, C. H., Liu, G. H. W., Lee, N. C. A., & Chen, K. J. (2018). On online engagement: Does the leadership style matter? In *Proceedings of the 18th International Conference on Electronic Business, ICEB*, Guilin, 430–438.

Wang, L., Owens, B. P., Li, J. J., & Shi, L. (2018). Exploring the affective impact, boundary conditions, and antecedents of leader humility. *The Journal of Applied Psychology*, *103*(9), 1019–1038. doi:10.1037/apl0000314 PMID:29781636

Wang, Y. M., Wang, Y. S., & Yang, Y. F. (2010). Understanding the determinants of RFID adoption in the manufacturing industry. *Technological Forecasting and Social Change*, *77*(5), 803–815. doi:10.1016/j.techfore.2010.03.006

Wang, Y., & Hajli, N. (2017). Exploring the path to big data analytics success in healthcare. *Journal of Business Research*, *70*, 287–299. doi:10.1016/j.jbusres.2016.08.002

Warner, K. S. R., & Wäger, M. (2019). Building dynamic capabilities for digital transformation: An ongoing process of strategic renewal. *Long Range Planning*, *52*(3), 326–349. doi:10.1016/j.lrp.2018.12.001

Warnick, A. (2019) WHO: Better nutrition standards needed to improve global health. *The Nation's Health, 19.*

Webster, N. (1977). *The Merriam-Webster dictionary*. Pocket Books.

Weeks, K. P., Weeks, M., & Long, N. (2017). Generational perceptions at work: In-group favoritism and out-group stereotypes. *Equality, Diversity and Inclusion*, *36*(1), 33–53. doi:10.1108/EDI-07-2016-0062

Weiner, J., Balijepally, V., & Tanniru, M. (2015). Integrating strategic and operational decision making using data-driven dashboards: The case of St. Joseph mercy Oakland hospital. *Journal of Healthcare Management*, *60*, 319–330. doi:10.1097/00115514-201509000-00005

Wikimedia Foundation. (2022, October 7). *Information and Communications Technology*. Wikipedia. https://en.wikipedia.org/wiki/Information_and_communications_technology https://en.wikipedia.org/wiki/Digital_transformation

Williams, N., & Vorley, T. (2014). Economic resilience and entrepreneurship: Lessons from the Sheffield City Region. *Entrepreneurship and Regional Development*, *26*(3-4), 257–281. doi:10.1080/08985626.2014.894129

Wilson, E. J., Goethals, G. R., Sorenson, G., & Burns, J. M. (2004). Leadership in the digital age. Encyclopedia of leadership, 4, 858-861.

World Economic Forum. (in collaboration with Accenture) (2018). Digital Transformation Initiative - Unlocking $100 Trillion for Business and Society from Digital Transformation (Executive Summary), 1–71. https://reports.weforum.org/digital-transformation/wp-content/blogs. dir/94/mp/files/pages/files/dti-executive-summary-20180510.pdf

Wright, P. M., & McMahan, G. C. (1992). Theoretical perspectives for Strategic human resource management. *Journal of Management, 18*(2), 295–320. doi:10.1177/014920639201800205

Wu, C.-H., & Parker, S. K. (2016). The Role of Leader Support in Facilitating Proactive Work Behavior. *Journal of Management, 43*(4), 1025–1049. doi:10.1177/0149206314544745

Xenikou, A., & Furnham, A. (2013). *Group dynamics and organizational culture: Effective work groups and organizations*. Palgrave. doi:10.1007/978-1-137-26546-3

Xie, J. L., & Johns, G. (2000). Interactive effects of absence culture salience and group cohesiveness: A multi-level and cross-level analysis of work absenteeism in the Chinese context. *Journal of Occupational and Organizational Psychology, 73*(1), 31–52. doi:10.1348/096317900166868

Yoon, S. N., Lee, D., & Schniederjans, M. (2016). Effects of innovation leadership and supply chain innovation on supply chain efficiency: Focusing on hospital size. *Technological Forecasting and Social Change, 113*, 412–421. doi:10.1016/j.techfore.2016.07.015

Youn, S., Stepich, D., & Cox, D. (2006). Building a Competency-Based Curriculum Architecture to Educate 21st Century Business Practitioners. *Journal of Education for Business, 81*(6), 307–311. doi:10.3200/JOEB.81.6.307-314

Yu, C., & Frenkel, S. J. (2012). Explaining task performance and creativity from perceived organizational support theory: Which mechanisms are more important? *Journal of Organizational Behavior, 34*(8), 1165–1181. doi:10.1002/job.1844

Yukl, G. A. (2006). *Leadership in Organizations,* (6th ed.). Pearson.

Zaharee, M., Lipkie, T., Mehlman, S., & Neylon, S. (2018). Recruitment and Retention of Early-Career Technical Talent. *Research Technology Management, 61*(5), 51–61. doi:10.1080/08956308.2018.1495966

Zakir, J., Seymour, T., & Berg, K. (2015). Big Data Analytics. *Issues in Information Systems, 16*(2).

Zaleznik, A. (1977). Managers and leaders: Are they different. *Houston Police Department Leadership Journal, 17*(4), 47–63.

Zhang, T. and Li, B. (2020). Job Crafting and Turnover Intention: The Mediating Role of Work Engagement and Job Satisfaction. *Social Behavior and Personality: An international journal, 48*(2), pp. 1-9. Psychology and Behavioral Sciences Collection. . doi:10.2224/sbp.8759

Zheng, P., Wang, H., Sang, Z., & Zhongm, R. Y. (2018). Smart manufacturing systems for industry 4.0: Conceptual framework, scenarios and future perspective. *Frontiers of Mechanical Engineering, 13*(2), 137–150.

Zhou, F., & Wu, Y. J. (2018). How humble leadership fosters employee innovation behavior: A two-way perspective on the leader-employee interaction. *Leadership and Organization Development Journal, 39*(3), 375–387. doi:10.1108/LODJ-07-2017-0181

Zhou, X., Wu, Z., Liang, D., Jia, R., Wang, M., Chen, C., & Lu, G. (2021). Nurses' voice behaviour: The influence of humble leadership, affective commitment and job embeddedness in China. *Journal of Nursing Management, 29*(6), 1603–1612. doi:10.1111/jonm.13306 PMID:33706409

Zhou, Y., Liu, G., Chang, X., & Wang, L. (2020). The impact of HRM digitalization on firm performance: Investigating three-way interactions. *Asia Pacific Journal of Human Resources, 59*(1), 20–43. doi:10.1111/1744-7941.12258

Zhu, Y., Zhang, S., & Shen, Y. (2019). Humble leadership and employee resilience: Exploring the mediating mechanism of work-related promotion focus and perceived insider identity. *Frontiers in Psychology*, *10*, 673. doi:10.3389/fpsyg.2019.00673 PMID:31001166

Zinchenko, Yu. P. (2011). Methodological foundations of security psychology. *National Psychological Journal*, (2), 11–14.

Zupic, I., & Cater, T. (2015). Bibliometric methods in management and organization. *Organizational Research Methods*, *18*, 429–447. doi:10.1177/1094428114562629

# About the Contributors

**Ebtihaj Al A'Ali** is an associate professor. She worked for University of Bahrain. She holds a Ph.D. In Industrial psychology and industrial sociology from University of Lancaster in U.k. Her research interests are mainly women in management, Organizational Behavior, Organizational theory, Business Ethics, management change and Islamic philosophy. She published many articles in different journals. She as well co-edited two books published by IGI

**Meryem Masmoudi** is Assistant Professor of Management at the University of Bahrain, College of Business Administration. She holds a PhD in Management from University of Tunis (2013). She has been involved in teaching and research in the areas of management, organizational change and development and management science. Meryem has published research papers in top international refereed journals (ANOR, JORS, ITOR, INFOR). She is a member of the International Society on Multiple Criteria Decision Making and the Tunisian Decision Aid Society.

***

**Nidhi Arora** is a technophile and a fervent scholar with deep expertise in information technology. She has been a dedicated enthusiast in exploring fundamentals of high-end technologies and has written many research papers in National and International journals.

**Poonam Arora** has rich and vivid experience of over 15 years in the field of quantitative and research analysis. She has been awarded with "Best Researcher Award" in 2019 for her contribution to research in management. Her areas of expertise include Research Methodology, Quantitative Techniques and Human Resource Management. She is a research enthusiast and an active researcher who is associated as a reviewer in various esteemed national and international peer reviewed journals.

**Ramazan Atasoy**. He received his MA in Girne American University and Ph.D. in educational sciences from Gazi University. He currently works as an assistant professor at Harran University. His research interests include leadership, quality of education, education policy, PIAAC adult competency, literacy skills, numeracy skills and problem solving skills in technology rich environments.

**Asma Ayari** is a Ph.D. Holder in Management from IAE University de Lille _ France Assistant Professor at the University of Bahrain teaching management, organizational behavior, and HRM MSc and MBA Thesis supervisor and reviewer.

**Reyhan Baykara** graduated from Bogazici University in 2013; she received her first master's degree in Organizational Psychology from Istanbul Bilgi University and her second master's degree in Global Communication and Diversity from the University of Luxembourg in 2022. Her research interests include digitalization, resilience, organizational management, digital marketing and communication in global context.

**Emilio Domínguez** is an assistant lecturer in the Department of Business Administration and Marketing at Universitat Jaume I (Castellón). He currently teaches subjects related to human resources management, organizational change and business administration. As far as training is concerned, he has a PhD in Economics and Business (UJI), a Master's degree in Marketing and Market Research (UJI-UV) and a degree in Advertising and Public Relations (UJI). He also belongs to the Universitat Jaume I research group "IDEA - Organizational Transformation and Human Development". His lines of research focus mainly on innovation in companies, the behaviour of leaders and organisational learning.

**Abdul Gani** is Professor & Head, Department of Management Studies, Central University of Kashmir M.Com, PGDE, MADE, Ph. D Recepient of Fulbright fellowship, Shastri Indo-Canadian fellowship, Indo-French Fellowship UKOB Business School International Award Member of various academic and professional bodies

**Deniz Kantur** received her PhD in Business Administration in 2010 from Boğaziçi Universty. Her research interests are corporate entrepreneurship, social entrepreneurship, organizational resilience, ambidexterity, corporate reputation and employer branding. She has published her research in several recognized international and national journals. She teaches courses in entrepreneurship, corporate entrepreneurship, human resource management, organizational behavior and other related fields in undergraduate and graduate studies. Kantur has been working in the Business Administration Department of Istanbul Bilgi University since 2012. Between 2012 and 2018, she served as the Director of Human Resources Management Graduate Programs and between 2018 - 2021 she has been the Dean of Graduate Programs Institute.

**Aakanskha Kataria** is an assistant professor.

**Anitha Kumari** is currently a Doctoral Fellow at the School of Management, Hindustan Institute of Technology and Science, where she is doing her teaching and research. Her Bachelor's degree was in Computer Applications, while she obtained a Master's in Business Administration with a specialisation in finance and systems. She is interested in business, management, operations, information technology, data analysis, accounts, and finance. Her current research focus is on new technologies, information systems, and digital banking services. She has conference presentations and published journal articles to her credit. She has five years of teaching experience in finance and systems.

**Fermín Mallén-Broch** is an Associate Professor at the Department of Business Administration and Marketing at Universitat Jaume I (Castellón). Currently, he teaches subjects related to people management, information systems and vocational training for teachers. Doctor in Business Management (Universitat Jaume I), Master in Market Research and Information Systems (UNED) and Master in Work Psychology, Human Resources and Organizations (UJI). In addition, he holds a degree in Business Administration and Management (extraordinary prize) from the UJI and a Bachelor of Science and Statistical Techniques (prize for academic performance) from the University of Valencia. He currently belongs to a research group at Universtitat Jaume I called "People and Organizations Development", whose lines of research are, among others, the direction and development of human resources, organizational learning, leadership and innovation. Having participated in several research projects, he has published in journals such as Journal of Business Ethics, Review of Managerial Science or Industrial Management & Data Systems. Since 2016 he is exclusively dedicated to university teaching, but has been an associate professor for 14 years. During this time, his professional activity outside the university has been linked mainly to Market Research and, in the educational field, to Vocational Training.

**Nada Megahed** is an academic with over 22 years of accumulated experience in research and consultancy fields. She is currently Assistant Professor of Management in the College of Business Administration at the University of Bahrain. Earlier, she held the position of Advisor for Capacity Building and HR Development at the Ministry of Foreign Affairs in Bahrain (during which she implemented the first-of-a-kind competency-based HR reform strategy in a GCC public entity). Being a member of the American Association of International Researchers, she excelled in implementing various research projects with leading organizations worldwide, such as; National Science Foundation (USA), British Council (UK), International Research Policy Institute (USA), and UN Development Program (Egypt). She also taught numerous courses, for undergraduate and graduate level, in a multitude of universities including Maastricht University in the Netherlands, American University in Cairo, and Middlesex University in UK.

**Fleming Sampson** is an HR professional and currently works at HCLTech, India. He has done his Bachelors in Visual Communication and Masters in Business Administration with a specialisation in Human Resources. He has 12+ years of experience. He has been involved in talent development, organisational development, employee engagement, and diversity and inclusion.

**Ifra Zaroo** is a Research Scholar at Central University of Kashmir Department of Management Studies.

# Index

## G



## H



## I



## J



## K



## L



## N



## O



## P



## R

## S



## T



## W

www.ingramcontent.com/pod-product-compliance
Lightning Source LLC
LaVergne TN
LVHW080526300926
849162LV00007B/1546